Facts
about Germany

Facts
about Germany

Societäts-Verlag

Picture sources

t = top, b = bottom, r = right, l = left

ACON: 331 b l; action press: 156 b; Adam Opel AG: 57, 229; AEG: 227, 412; AID/
Henke: 263 b r; Airbus Industrie: front cover t l; AKG, Berlin: 7 t l, 7 b r, 447, 449;
Architekton/Dieter Leistner: 122, 243, 454; Architekturphoto/Friedrich Busam: 431
t r, 458; Architekturphoto/Ralph Richter: 222; Karl-Günter Balzer: 383; BASF AG:
114, 267; Bayerische Verwaltung der Staatlichen Schlösser, Gärten und Seen: 472
b; Bayerisches Staatsministerium für Wirtschaft, Verkehr und Technologie: 401 t l,
401 b r; Bilderberg/Rainer Drexel: 468; bb/Michael Engler: 329; bb/Thomas
Ernsting: 428; bb/Peter Ginter: 266, 367; bb/Wolfgang Kunz: 284; bb/Wolfgang
Volz: front cover t r, 424; BONGARTS/Rüdiger Fessel: back cover t r; Bildarchiv
Preußischer Kulturbesitz, Berlin: 7 t r, 11, 12, 18, 21; Bremer Lagerhaus-Gesell-
schaft: 215 t r; Bundesbildstelle Bonn: front cover b r, 7 b l, 13, 26, 28, 33-49, 51 t,
71, 130, 131 t l, 131 b l, 133-146, 156 t, 165, 169 t l, 169 b r, 183 t l, 183 t r, 185,
187, 197, 199, 203, 215 t l, 230, 232, 234, 253, 298, 335, 364, 387, 462, 467;
Bundesministerium für Arbeit und Soziales: 237, 331 t r, 339, 347, 351; Bundesministerium für Verteidigung: 260; Bundesministerium für wirtschaftliche Zusam-
menarbeit: 207, 211; CMA: 309; Concorde/Peter W. Engelmeier: 477; DAAD: 212;
Daimler-Benz Aerospace Airbus GmbH: 98, 215 b l; Deutsche Bahn AG: 314;
Deutsche Börse AG: 215 b r; Deutsche Messe AG: 292; Deutsche Telekom AG: 322,
323; Deutscher Bundestag, Bonn: 147; Deutscher Volkshochschulverband: 420;
Deutsches Institut für Filmkunde: 479; DFJW: 359 t l; DLR: 401 b l, 425, 429; dpa:
51 b, 155, 157, 483; FAG Foto M. Skaryd: 319; Forschungszentrum Jülich: 257;
Forschungszentrum Karlsruhe: 174; Fraunhofer-Gesellschaft: 401 t r; Rainer
Gaertner: 456/457; Friedrich Gier: 113, 443; Hanowerb: 463; Jörg Henning: 317;
H.F.&P.: 369; IBM Deutschland GmbH: 268; Dr. Arno Kappler: 81, 91, 244, 275,
287; R. Kiedrowski/Foto N. Koshofer: back cover b l; Foto Gundel Kilian: 403, 431
b l, 473; KNA-Bild: 384; Bildagentur Helga Lade: back cover b r, 61 t l, 61 t r, 75 t
l, 75 b l, 83, 84/85, 86, 88/89, 99, 101, 102, 104, 105, 111, 116, 119, 120/121,
127, 131 b r, 151, 181, 183 b l, 209, 263 b l, 271, 274, 283, 299, 303, 314/315,
318, 328, 331 t l, 331 b r, 343, 359 t r, 359 b r, 405, 408, 417, 431 t l, 444, 461,
469, 472 t; Wolfgang Lechthaler: 61 b l, 65 t r, 131 t r; Mainbild: 169 t r, 242, 334,
378 t; Rainer Martini/LOOK: 375; Bildagentur Mauritius: 55, 169 b l; Max-Planck-
Gesellschaft: 225, 226, 431 b r; Bernd C. Möller/FOCUS: 293; Mollenhauer/
BAVARIA: front cover b l; Horst Müller: 374, 376; NATO Photos: 183 b r; Isolde
Ohlbaum: 437, 439; Bildarchiv OKAPIA: back cover t l, 65 b l, 96, 103, 231, 250,
251, 278, 281, 286, 305, 326/327, 357, 361, 378 b, 455; Rheinisches Bildarchiv
Köln/Museum Ludwig Köln: 450/451; s.e.t. photo productions: 470; Wolfgang
Saucke: 438; Schlossfestspiele Heidelberg: 481; Georg Schreiber: 474; Siemens AG:
213, 258, 272, 297, 426; Klaus-D. Sonntag: 310; Gerhard Steidl: 435; STIEF
PICTURES, Frankfurt: 93, 94, 107, 108, 110, 124, 125, 263 t l, 263 t r, 276, 285,
311, 355, 362, 381, 392; Stiftung Warentest: 247; Süddeutscher Verlag: 25;
Thüringer Landesfremdenverkehrsverband: 129; TRANSDIA/Kulartz: 61 b r; TRANS-
DIA/Mosler: 153; ULLSTEIN: 80, 90; VISUM/Thomas Pflaum: 117; VISUM/ Dirk
Reinartz: 436; ZDF 359 b l, 397, 399

Maps: Westermann Schulbuchverlag GmbH, Brunswick: 62, 76/77;
Bertelsmann Lexikon Verlag GmbH, Gütersloh: 14/15, 29

Front cover, top left: Lufthansa Airbus A340-200; top right: The Brandenburg Gate
in Berlin against the backdrop of the wrapped Reichstag; bottom left: The Frankfurt
am Main skyline; bottom right: Professor Reinhard Selten, winner of the 1994 Nobel
Prize for Economics; back cover, top left: Lighthouse in North Friesland/Schleswig-
Holstein; top right: The victorious German eight at the 1993 World Championship;
bottom right: Welding a machine component; bottom right: Dresden's Zwinger: Salon
and Wallpavillon

Editors: Dr. Arno Kappler, Adriane Grevel M.A.
Cover and layout: Peter Lenz
Translator: Kathleen Müller-Rostin, Bonn
Copy deadline: April 1995
© Societäts-Verlag, Frankfurt am Main
All rights reserved
Typesetting: Peter Lenz, Wiesbaden –
Societäts-Druck, Frankfurt am Main
Graphics: ICON, Bonn
Reproductions: Gehringer, Kaiserslautern
Printing: Westermann, Brunswick
Printed in Germany, 1995
Printed on chlorine-free bleached paper
ISBN 3-7973-0592-3

Contents

History

German history up to 1945

Up to the last century it was a widely held belief that German history began in the year A.D. 9. That was when Arminius, a prince of a Germanic tribe called the Cherusci, vanquished three Roman legions in the Teutoburg Forest (southeast of modern-day Bielefeld). Arminius, about whom not much else is known, was regarded as the first German national hero and a huge memorial to him was built near Detmold in the years 1838-1875.

Nowadays a less simplistic view is taken. The fusing of a German nation was a process which took hundreds of years. The word "deutsch" (German) probably began to be used in the 8th century and initially defined only the language spoken in the eastern part of the Franconian realm. This empire, which reached the zenith of its power under Charlemagne, incorporated peoples speaking Germanic and Romance dialects. After Charlemagne's death (814) it soon fell apart. In the course of various inheritance divisions, a western and an eastern realm developed, whose political boundary approximately coincided with the boundary between German and French speakers. Only gradually did a feeling of cohesion develop among the inhabitants of the eastern realm. Then the term "deutsch" was transferred from the language to its speakers and ultimately to the region they lived in, "Deutschland".

The German western frontier was fixed relatively early and remained fairly stable. But the eastern frontier moved to and fro for hundreds of years. Around 900 it ran approximately along the Elbe and Saale rivers. In subsequent centuries German settlement extended far to the east. This expansion stopped only in the middle of the 14th century. The ethnic boundary then made between Germans und Slavs remained until World War II.

■ ■ ■ **High Middle Ages.** The transition from the East Franconian to the German "Reich" is usually dated from 911, when, after the Carolingian dynasty had died out, the Franconian duke Conrad I was elected king. He is regarded as the first German king. (The official title was "Frankish King", later "Roman King"; from the 11th century the name of the realm was "Roman Empire", from the 13th century "Holy Roman Empir", and in the 15th century the words "of the German Nation" were added.) It was an electoral monarchy, that is to say, the high nobility chose the king. In addition, "dynastic right" also applied and so the new king had to be a blood relation of his predecessor. This principle was broken several times. There were also a number of double elections. The medieval empire had no capital city; the king ruled roving about from place to place. There were no imperial taxes; the king drew his sustenance mainly from "imperial estates" he administered in trust. His authority was not always recognized by the powerful tribal dukes unless he was militarily powerful and a skilful forger of alliances. Conrad's successor, the Saxon duke Henry I (919-936), was the first to succeed in this, and to an even greater extent his son, Otto (936-973). Otto made himself the real ruler of the realm. His great power found obvious expression when he was crowned Emperor in 962 in Rome.

From then on the German king could claim the title "Emperor". The emperorship was conceived as universal and gave its incumbent control over the entire Occident. However, this notion never became full political reality. In order to be crowned emperor by the Pope the king had to make his way to Rome. With that began the Italian policy of the German kings. For 300 years they were able to retain control of upper and central Italy but because of this were diverted from important tasks in Germany. And so Otto's successors inevitably suffered big setbacks. However, under the succeeding Salian dynasty a new upswing occurred. With Henry III (1039-1056) the German kingship and emperorship reached the zenith of its power, maintaining above all a supremacy over the Papacy. Henry IV (1056-1106) was not able to hold this position. In a quarrel with Pope Gregory VII over whether bishops and other influential church officials should be appointed by the Pope or by the temporal ruler he was superficially successful. But Gregory retaliated by excommunicating Henry, who thereupon surrendered his authority over the church by doing penance to the Pope at Canossa (1077), an irretrievable loss of power by the emperorship. From then on Emperor and Pope were equal-ranking powers.

In 1138 the century of rule by the Staufer or Hohenstaufen dynasty began. Frederick I Barbarossa (1152-

1190), in wars with the Pope, the upper Italian cities and his main German rival, the Saxon duke Henry the Lion, led the empire into a new golden age. But under him began a territorial fragmentation which ultimately weakened the central power. This decline continued under Barbarossa's successors, Henry VI (1190-1197) and Frederick II (1212-1250) despite the great power vested in the emperorship. The religious and temporal princes became semi-sovereign territorial rulers. The end of Hohenstaufen rule (1268) also meant the end of the Emperor's universal rule in the Occident as well. Internal disintegrative forces prevented Germany from becoming a national state, a process just beginning then in other western European countries. Here lies one of the reasons why the Germans became a "belated nation".

■ ■ ■ **Late Middle Ages to modern times.** Rudolf I (1273-1291) was the first Habsburg to take the throne. Now the material foundation of the emperorship was no longer the lost imperial estates but the "house estates" of the dynasties, and house power politics became every emperor's main preoccupation.

The "Golden Bull" (imperial constitution) issued by Charles IV in 1356 regulated the election of the German king by seven electors privileged with special rights. These sovereign electors and the towns, because of their economic power, gradually gained influence while that of the small counts, lords and knights declined. The towns' power further increased when they linked up in leagues. The most important of these, the Hanseatic League, became the leading Baltic power in the 14th century.

From 1438 the crown – although the empire nominally was an electoral monarchy – practically became the property of the Habsburg dynasty which had become the strongest territorial power. In the 15th century demands for imperial reform increased. Maximilian I (1493 to 1519), the first to accept the imperial title without a papal coronation, tried to implement such a reform but without much success. The institutions newly created or reshaped by him – Reichstag (Imperial Diet), Reichskreise (Imperial Counties), Reichskammergericht (Imperial Court) – lasted until the end of the Reich (1806), but were not able to halt its continuing fragmentation. Consequently, a dualism of "Emperor and Reich" developed: the head of the Reich was offset by the estates of the

Emperor Charles IV and the seven electors (armorial, ca. 1370)

Reich – electors, princes and towns. The power of the emperors was curtailed and increasingly eroded by "capitulations", which they negotiated at their election with the electors. The princes, especially the powerful among them, greatly expanded their rights at the expense of imperial power. But the Reich continued to hold together, the glory of the imperial idea remained alive, and the small and medium-sized territories were protected in the Reich system from attack by powerful neighbours.

The towns became centres of economic power, profiting above all from growing trade. In the burgeoning textile and mining industries, forms of economic activity grew which went beyond the guilds system of the craftsmen and, like long-distance trading, were beginning to take on early capitalistic traits. At the same time an intellectual change was taking place, marked by the Renaissance and Humanism. The newly risen critical spirit turned above all on church abuses.

■ ■ ■ **Age of religious schism.** The smouldering dissatisfaction with the church broke out, mainly through the actions of Martin Luther from 1517, in the Reformation, which quickly spread. Its consequences went far beyond the religious sphere. Social unrest abounded. In 1522/23 the Reich knights rose up and in 1525 the Peasants' Revolt broke out, the first larger revolutionary movement in German history to strive for both political and social change. Both uprisings failed or were bloodily quelled.

Peasants in revolt (woodcut by Hans Burgkmair, 1525)

The territorial princes profited most from the Reformation. After the changing fortunes of war they were given the right to dictate their subjects' religion by the 1555 Peace of Augsburg. This accorded the Protestants equal rights with those of the Catholics. The religious division of Germany was thus sealed.

On the imperial throne at the time of the Reformation was Charles V (1519-1956), heir to the biggest realm since the time of Charlemagne. His international political interests were too demanding for him to be able to assert himself within Germany. After his abdication the empire was split up. The German territorial states and the western European national states together now formed the new European system of states.

At the time of the Peace of Augsburg, four fifths of Germany were Protestant but the struggle between the faiths had not ended. In the following decades the Catholic Church was able to recapture many areas (Counter-Reformation). The differences between the faiths sharpened, religious parties – the Protestant Union (1608) and the Catholic League (1609) – were formed. A local conflict in Bohemia then triggered the Thirty Years' War which widened into a European conflict over religious and political differences. Between 1618 and 1648 much of Germany was devastated and depopulated. The 1648 Peace of Westphalia brought the cession of territories to France and Sweden and confirmed the withdrawal of

Switzerland and the Netherlands from the Reich. The estates of the Reich were accorded all major sovereign rights in religious and temporal matters and the right to enter alliances with foreign partners.

■ ■ ■ **Age of absolutism.** The almost sovereign principalities took over the absolutist form of government modelled on the French. Absolutism gave the ruler limitless power while at the same time allowing tight administrations to be built up, an organized fiscal policy to be introduced and new armies to be mobilized. Many princes

Frederick II, the Great (1712-1786)

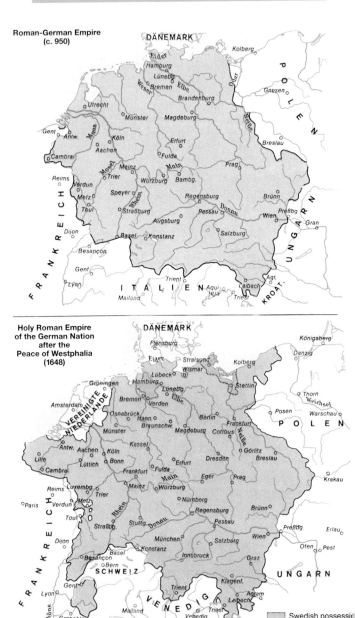

Roman-German Empire (c. 950)

DÄNEMARK
Kolberg
Eider
Hamburg
Lüneburg
Bremen
Weser
Elbe
Brandenburg
Oder
Utrecht
Münster
Magdeburg
Neisse
Gnesen
P O L E N
Gent
Antw.
Maas
Köln
Aachen
Erfurt
Fulda
Breslau
Cambrai
Mosel
Meinz
Trier
Würzburg
Bambg.
Main
Prag
Reims
Verdun
Speyer
Rhein
Regensburg
Donau
Brünn
Metz
Toul
Straßburg
Passau
Wien
Preßbg.
Gran
Dijon
Augsburg
Salzburg
U N G A R N
Besançon
Basel
Konstanz
F R A N K R E I C H
Genf
Lyon
Trient
I T A L I E N
Aqui-leja
Laibach
Agr.
Triest
KROAT.
Mailand

Holy Roman Empire of the German Nation after the Peace of Westphalia (1648)

DÄNEMARK
Königsberg
Flensburg
Danzig
Eider
Stralsund
Wismar
Kolberg
Gröningen
Hamburg
Lübeck
Stettin
Amsterdam
Bremen
Verden
Lüneburg
Elbe
Thorn
Weichsel
VEREINIGTE
NIEDERLANDE
Osnabrück
Hann.
Berlin
Frankfurt
Posen
Warschau
Münster
Braunschw.
Magdeburg
Cottbus
Neisse
P O L E N
Antw.
Aachen
Köln
Kassel
Lüttich
Bonn
Fulda
Erfurt
Dresden
Görlitz
Breslau
Lille
Frankfurt
Main
Eger
Prag
Cambrai
Krakau
Reims
Luxembg.
Trier
Mainz
Würzburg
Nürnberg
Paris
Verdun
Metz
Rhein
Regensburg
Donau
Brünn
Toul
Stuttg.
Passau
Straßbg.
München
Wien
Preßbg.
Erlau
Dijon
Basel
Konstanz
Innsbruck
Salzburg
Graz
Ofen
Pest
Besançon
Bern
F R A N K R E I C H
SCHWEIZ
Klagenf.
U N G A R N
Lyon
Genf
Trient
V E N E D I G
Agram
Laibach
Rhône
Grenoble
Mailand
Venedig
Triest

Swedish possession

German Empire 1871 – 1918

DÄNEMARK
Ribe · Kopenhagen
Memel · Memel
Königsberg
Flensburg
Danzig
Rostock · Kolberg
Hamburg · Lübeck
Stettin
Gröningen · Lüneburg
Thorn
Bialystok
Bremen · Elbe
Posen · Weichsel · Warschau
Amsterd. · Hannover
Küstrin
Utrecht · Braunschwg. · Magdeburg
Berlin · Frankfurt
Kalisch
NIEDERLANDE · Münster
Leipzig
Maas · Düsseld. · Kassel · Erfurt
Görlitz
Breslau
R U S S L A N D
Brüssel · Köln
Dresden
Aachen
Krakau
Lütt. · Rhein · Frankfurt
Eger · Prag
Kattowitz
BELGIEN · Main
LUX. · Mainz · Würzburg
Nürnberg
Luxembg. · Saarbrücken
Verdun · 1871 · Regensbg. · Donau
Ö S T E R R E I C H –
Toul · Straßburg · Stuttgart
Brünn
FRANKREICH · Passau
München · Salzburg
Wien
Konstanz
U N G A R N
Basel
Besançon · Bern · Innsbruck
Graz
S C H W E I Z
Klagenfurt

Boundary of the German Confederation (1815–1866)

Germany within the borders of 1937

DÄNEMARK
Ribe · Kopenhagen
Memel · Memel
LITAUEN
Königsberg
Flensburg
Kiel
Danzig
DANZIG
Kolberg
Lübeck · Rostock
Stettin
Weichsel
Thorn
Gröningen · Hamburg · Schwerin
Neubrandenburg
Lüneburg
Amsterdam · Weser · Bremen · Elbe
Berlin · Küstrin
Posen
Warschau
Utrecht · Hannover
Potsd. · Frankfurt
Oder
NIEDERLANDE · Braunschweig · Magdeburg
P O L E N
Münster
Halle · Cottbus
Maas · Düsseldorf · Kassel · Leipzig · Dresden
Brüssel · Rhein · Aach.? · Köln
Erfurt · Görlitz
Breslau
Lüttich · Bonn
Kattowitz
BELGIEN · Frankfurt
Karlsbad · Prag
Krakau
Wiesbaden · Main
LUX. · Mainz · Würzburg
Eger · T S C H E C H O S L O W A K E I
Luxembg. · Mosel
Saarbrücken
Verdun · Nürnberg · Donau
Toul · Straßburg · Stuttgart
Brünn
FRANKREICH
Regensburg
München · Passau
Wien
Konstanz
Salzbg.
Basel
Ö S T E R R E I C H
Besançon · Bern · Innsbruck
S C H W E I Z

1:15 000 000   0   100   200   300   400   500

aspired to making their residences cultural focal points. Some of them, representatives of "enlightened absolutism", encouraged learning and philosophy, albeit within the confines of their power interests. The policy of state control of all economic life also allowed the absolutistically ruled states to gain in economic strength. Thus lands such as Bavaria, Brandenburg (the later Prussia), Saxony and Hanover were able to develop into power centres in their own right. Austria, which repelled the attacking Turks and acquired Hungary as well as parts of the formerly Turkish Balkan countries, rose to a large power. A rival to it developed in the 18th century in the form of Prussia which, under Frederick the Great (1740-1786), grew into a first-rank military power. Both states sought to assert their authority in Europe.

■ ■ ■   **Age of the French Revolution.** The nudge which brought the crumbling Reich crashing down came from the west. Revolution broke out in France in 1789. Under pressure from the middle classes, the feudal social order which had existed since the early Middle Ages was swept away; a separation of powers and human rights were to assure the liberty and equality of all. The attempt by Prussia and Austria to intervene by force in events in the neighbouring country failed ignominiously and triggered a counter-thrust by the revolutionary armies. Under the stormy advances of the forces of Napoleon, who had assumed the revolutionary heritage in France, the Reich finally collapsed. France took the left bank of the Rhine. To compensate the former owners of these areas for their losses, an enormous territorial reshuffling took place at the expense of the smaller and particularly the ecclesiastical principalities. Through the "Reichsdeputationshauptschluss" of 1803 some four million subjects changed rulers. The medium-sized states were the beneficiaries. In 1806 most of them grouped together under French protection in the Confederation of the Rhine (Rheinbund). In the same year Emperor Franz II laid down the crown and the Holy Roman Empire of the German Nation ceased to exist.

The French revolution did not spread into Germany. Although there, too, various individuals had over the years tried time and again to do away with the barriers between the aristocracy and the common people, and although leading thinkers welcomed the overthrow in the west as the start of a new era, one major reason why the spark could not catch easily was that, in contrast to centrally oriented France, the federalistic structure of the Reich hampered the spread of new ideas. Another big reason was that France, the motherland of the revolution, opposed the Germans as an enemy and an occupying power. Indeed, the struggle against Napoleon forged a new national movement which culminated in wars of liberation. But Germany did not remain unaffected by the forces of social change. First in the states of the Confederation of the Rhine and then in Prussia (in the latter connected with names like Stein, Hardenberg, Scharnhorst, W. von Humboldt) reforms were begun aimed at breaking down feudal barriers and creating a society of free, responsible citizens. The objectives were abolition of serfdom, freedom of trade, municipal self-administration, equality before the law and general conscription. But many reform moves were pulled up short. Participation by the populace in legislation was refused almost everywhere. Only hesitantly did some princes grant their states constitutions, especially in southern Germany.

■■■ **The German Confederation.** After the victory over Napoleon the Congress of Vienna (September 1814 to June 1815) redrew the map of Europe. The hopes of many Germans for a free, unitary nation-state were not fulfilled. The German Confederation (Deutscher Bund) which replaced the old Reich was a loose association of the individual sovereign states. Its sole organ was the Federal Diet (Bundestag) in Frankfurt, not an elected but a delegated diet. It was able to act only if the two great powers, Prussia and Austria, agreed. It saw its main task in the ensuing decades in suppressing all aspirations and efforts aimed at unity and freedom. Press and publishing were subject to rigid censorship, the universities were under close supervision, and political activity was virtually impossible.

Meanwhile a modern economic development which worked against these reactionary tendencies had begun. In 1834 the German Customs Union (Deutscher Zollverein) was founded, creating a unitary inland market. In 1835 the first German railway line went into operation. Industrialization began. With the factories there grew the new class of factory workers. At first they found better incomes, but the rapid growth of the population soon led to a labour surplus. And since there were no social welfare provisions, the mass of factory workers lived in great misery. Tensions exploded violently, for example in the 1844 uprising of the Silesian weavers, which was harshly put down by the Prussian military. Very hesitantly at first, a workers' movement began to form.

■ ■   **The 1848 revolution.** In contrast to the revolution of 1789, the French revolution of February 1848 found immediate response in Germany. In March there were uprisings in all states, and these forced many concessions from the stunned princes. In May the National Assembly (Nationalversammlung) convened in St. Paul's Church in Frankfurt. It elected Austrian Archduke Johann Imperial Administrator (Reichsverweser) and set up a Reich Ministry which, however, had no powers or authority. The tune was called in the National Assembly by the Liberal centre, which strove for a constitutional monarchy with limited suffrage. The splintering of the National Assembly from Conservatives to Radical Democrats, which already indicated the spectrum of parties to come, made it difficult to draw up a constitution.

But not even the Liberal centre could overcome the differences between the protagonists of "greater Germany" and "smaller Germany" concepts, that is, a German Reich with or without Austria. After hard bargaining a

The Frankfurt National Assembly of 1848/49

democratic constitution was drawn up which attempted to combine old and new ideas and required a government responsible to parliament. But when Austria insisted on bringing into the future Reich its entire realm, encompassing more than a dozen different peoples, the "smaller Germany" concept won the day and the National Assembly proffered Frederick William IV of Prussia the hereditary German imperial crown. The king turned it down, not wanting to owe imperial majesty to a revolution. In May 1849 popular uprisings in Saxony, the Palatinate and Baden which aimed at enforcing the constitution "from below" failed.

That was the seal on the failure of the whole revolution. Most of the achievements were rescinded, the constitutions of the individual states revised along reactionary lines. In 1850 the German Confederation was restored.

■■ ■ **The rise of Prussia.** The 1850s were years of great economic upswing. Germany became an industrial country. Although its production output still lagged far behind England's it was growing faster. Pacemakers were heavy industry and mechanical engineering. Prussia also became the predominant economic power of Germany. Industrial power strengthened the political self-confidence of the liberal middle class. The German Progress Party (Deutsche Fortschrittspartei), formed in 1861, became the strongest party in the Prussian Diet and denied the government the funds when it wanted to make reactionary changes to the structure of the army. The newly appointed Prime Minister (Ministerpräsident), Otto von Bismarck (1862), took up the challenge and for some years governed without the parliamentary approval of the budget which was required by the constitution. The Progress Party dared offer no further resistance than parliamentary opposition, however.

Bismarck was able to offset his precarious position on the domestic front by foreign policy successes. In the German-Danish war (1864) Prussia and Austria forced the Danes to cede the duchies of Schleswig and Holstein, which they initially administered jointly. But Bismarck had from the outset pursued the annexation of the two duchies and steered for open conflict with Austria. In the Austro-Prussian War (1866) Austria was defeated and had to leave the German stage. The German Confederation was dissolved and replaced by the North German Confederation (Norddeutscher Bund) of states north of the River Main, with Bismarck as Federal Chancellor (prime minister).

■ ■ ■ **The Bismarck Reich.** From then on Bismarck worked towards "smaller German" unity. He broke France's resistance in the Franco-German War of 1870/71, triggered by a diplomatic conflict over the succession to the Spanish throne. Defeated France had to cede Alsace-Lorraine and pay huge reparations. In the patriotic enthusiasm of the war, the southern German states joined up with the North German Confederation to form the German Empire (Deutsches Reich). At Versailles near Paris, King William I of Prussia was proclaimed German Emperor on 18 January 1871.

German unity had not come about by popular decision "from below" but by a treaty between princes "from above". Prussia's predominance was stifling. To many the new Reich seemed like a "greater Prussia". The Reichstag (Imperial Diet) was elected by universal and equal suffrage. Although it had no say in the formation of the cabinet, it could influence government by its participation in lawmaking and its budgetary power. Although the Reich Chancellor was accountable only to the Emperor and not to parliament, he did have to try to get majorities for his policies in the Reichstag.

Suffrage in the individual Länder (states) still varied. In eleven it was still class suffrage, dependent on tax paid; in four there was still the old division into estates. The south German states, with their longer parliamentary tradition, reformed their electoral laws after the turn of the century, and Baden, Württemberg and Bavaria made theirs the same as the Reich laws. Although Germany's emergence as a modern industrial country strengthened the influence of the economically successful middle class, the people who still called the tune in society were the aristocrats, above all in the army officer corps where they predominated.

Bismarck ruled as Reich Chancellor for 19 years. Through a consistent peace and alliance policy he tried to give the Reich a secure position in the new European balance of power. In contrast to this far-sighted foreign policy was his home policy. He had no feeling for the democratic tendencies of his time. To him, political op-

William I being proclaimed German Emperor
(painting by A. Werner)

position was "hostility to the Reich". Bitterly, but ultimately vainly, he fought the left wing of the liberal middle class, political Catholicism, and especially the organized labour movement which for 12 years (1878-1890)
was practically banned by a Socialists Act (Sozialistenge-
setz). Hence the vastly growing working class, despite
progressive social legislation, was alienated from the
state. Bismarck ultimately became a victim of his own
system when he was dismissed in 1890 by the young
Emperor William II.

William II wanted to rule himself but he lacked the
knowledge and staying power. More by speeches than by
actions he created the impression of a peace-threatening
dictator. Under him there took place a transition to
"Weltpolitik" (world policy), with Germany trying to
shorten the lead of the great imperialist powers and
thereby becoming more isolated. In his home policies
William soon took a reactionary course after his attempt
to win the working class over to a "social emperorship"
failed to bring the quick success he had hoped for. His

chancellors had to rely on changing coalitions of Conservatives and National Liberals. Social Democrats, although one of the strongest parties, obtaining millions of votes, continued to be excluded from any participation in government.

■ ■   **World War I**. The assassination of the heir to the Austrian throne on 28 June 1914 triggered the outbreak of World War I. The question as to who was to blame for this war remains in dispute. Certainly Germany and Austria on the one side, and France, Russia and Britain on the other, did not consciously seek it but they were prepared to risk it. From the start, all had definite war aims for which military action was at least not unwelcome. The Germans failed in their aim quickly to vanquish France. After the defeat of Germany in the Battle of the Marne, the fighting in the west soon froze into trench warfare, ultimately peaking in senseless material attrition with enormous losses on both sides. With the outbreak of war, the Emperor receded into the background. As it progressed, the weak Reich Chancellors had to submit more and more to the will of the army supreme command, whose nominal chief was Field Marshal Paul von Hindenburg but whose real head was General Erich Ludendorff. The entry into the war of the United States in 1917 brought the decision which had long been developing and which could no longer be changed by the revolution in Russia and the peace in the east. Although the country had bled dry, Ludendorff, completely misjudging the situation, continued until September 1918 to insist on "peace through victory" but then surprisingly demanded an immediate armistice. Military defeat also meant political collapse. Unresisting, the Emperor and the princes yielded their thrones in November 1918. Not a hand stirred to defend a monarchy which had lost all credibility. Germany became a republic.

■ ■   **The Weimar Republic.** Power fell to the Social Democrats. Their majority had long since abandoned the revolutionary notions of earlier years and saw their mission in securing an orderly transition from the old to the new form of state. Private ownership of industry and agriculture remained untouched. The mostly anti-republican civil servants and judges were taken over without exception. The imperial officer corps retained command of the armed forces. Attempts by radical leftists to drive the revolution in a socialist direction were quelled by the army. In the National Assembly elected in January 1919, which convened at Weimar and drew up a new Reich constitution, three unconditionally republican parties – the Social Democrats, the German Democratic Party and the Catholic Centre – had the majority. But through the 1920s the parliamentary parties and popular forces which were more or less hostile to a democratic state went from strength to strength. The Weimar Republic was a "republic without republicans", rabidly fought by its opponents and only half-heartedly defended by its supporters. Especially the postwar economic misery and the oppressive terms of the Treaty of Versailles which Germany had to sign in 1919 made the people deeply skeptical of the republic. Growing domestic instability was the result.

In 1923 the confusion of the postwar era reached its peak (inflation, Ruhr occupation by France, Hitler's coup, communist overthrow attempts). This was followed by economic recovery and with it some political pacification. The foreign policy of Gustav Stresemann regained political equality for defeated Germany through the Locarno Pact (1925) and accession to the League of Nations (1926). The arts and sciences experienced a brief, intensive flowering in the "golden 20s". After the death of the first Reich President, the Social Democrat Friedrich Ebert, former Field Marshal Paul von Hindenburg was elected head of state in 1925 as the candidate of the right. Although he abided strictly by the constitution, he never developed a personal commitment to the republican state.

The ultimate collapse of the Weimar Republic began with the world economic crisis in 1929. Left-wing and right-wing radicalism exploited unemployment and the general recession. No more majorities capable of government could be found in the Reichstag, the cabinet being dependent on the support of the Reich President. From 1930, the up to then insignificant National Socialist movement of Adolf Hitler, which fused extreme anti-democratic tendencies and a raging anti-Semitism with pseudo-revolutionary propaganda, grew from strength to strength and by 1932 had become the most powerful party. On 30 January 1933, Hitler became Reich Chancellor. Apart from members of his own party his cabinet

included politicians of the right and non-partisan specialist ministers, so that it was hoped that sole rule by the National Socialists could be prevented.

■ ■ ■ **The National Socialist dictatorship.** Hitler soon
rid himself of his allies. An "Enabling Act", approved by
all the middle-class parties, gave him practically limitless
power. He banned all parties but his own. The trade
unions were smashed, basic rights virtually removed and
press freedom abolished. The regime exercised ruthless
terror and violence against anyone who stood in its way.
Thousands disappeared without trial in hastily constructed concentration camps. Parliamentary institutions at all
levels were abolished or made powerless. When Hindenburg died in 1934, Hitler assumed the roles of president
and chancellor. By this he gained control as commander-
in-chief of the armed forces, which up to then had still
had a certain inner life of their own.

In the few years of the turbulent Weimar Republic the
majority of Germans had not acquired any deep-rooted
affinity to democracy. More than anything else, years of
political turmoil, violence between the various camps –
including bloody street battles – and the mass unemployment engendered by the world economic crisis had shat-
tered confidence in government. Hitler, on the other
hand, succeeded with job-creation and armament production programmes in reinvigorating the economy and
quickly reducing unemployment. He was helped by the
fact that the world depression came to an end.

The fact that initially Hitler was also able to achieve his
foreign policy aims virtually without resistance further
strengthened his postion. In 1935 the Saar region, until
then administered by the League of Nations, returned to
Germany and in the same year the Reich regained its defence sovereignty. In 1936 German troops moved into the
up to then demilitarized Rhineland. In 1938 Austria was
joined to the Reich and the Western powers allowed Hitler to annex the Sudetenland. All this made it easier for
him to achieve his further aims, even though there were
people from all walks of life who courageously resisted
the dictator.

Immediately after taking power, the regime began to
carry out its anti-Semitic programme. Step by step the
Jews were stripped of all human and civic rights. Those
who could tried to escape the persecution by fleeing

abroad. The persecution of political opponents and the suppression of free speech also drove thousands out of the country. Many of the best German writers, artists and scientists fled the country.

■ ■ ■ **World War II and its consequences.** Hitler was not to be satisfied. From the outset he prepared for a war he was willing to wage to subjugate Europe. He demonstrated this as early as March 1939 when he had his troops march into Czechoslovakia. With his attack on Poland on 1 September 1939, he unleashed World War II, which lasted five and a half years, devastated much of Europe and killed 55 million people.

The German armies first defeated Poland, Denmark, Norway, Holland, Belgium, Luxembourg, France, Yugoslavia and Greece. In the Soviet Union they advanced to a position just short of Moscow and in North Africa they threatened the Suez Canal. Harsh occupation regimes were set up in the conquered countries. They were fought by resistance movements. In 1942 the regime began the "Final Solution of the Jewish Question": All the Jews the regime could lay its hands on were taken to concentration camps and murdered. The total number of victims is estimated at six million. The year in which this incon-

The ramp of the Auschwitz concentration camp, Poland

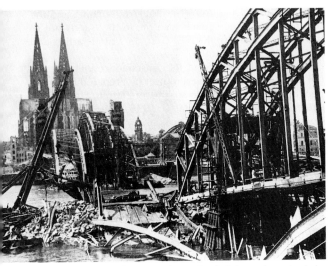

1945: View over Cologne's Hohenzollernbrücke to the cathedral

ceivable crime began marked the turning point in the war. From then on Germany and her allies suffered setbacks in all theatres.

The terror of the regime and the military setbacks strengthened resistance against Hitler in all classes of society. A coup attempt on 20 July 1944, carried out mainly by officers, failed. Hitler survived a bomb planted in his headquarters and took terrible revenge. More than 4,000 people from all walks of life who had been involved in the resistance were executed in the following months. Outstanding figures of the resistance, whose names stand for all the victims, were General Ludwig Beck, Colonel Graf Stauffenberg, the former lord mayor of Leipzig Carl Goerdeler, and the Social Democrat Julius Leber.

The war continued, Hitler prosecuting it under enormous losses, until the entire Reich area was occupied by enemies. Then, on 30 April 1945, he killed himself. Eight days later the successor he had willed by testament, Grand Admiral Karl Dönitz, carried out the unconditional capitulation.

From 1945 to the present

■ ■ ■ **Reorientation after 1945.** Following the unconditional surrender of the German forces on 8/9 May 1945, the last government of the German Reich, headed by Grand Admiral Karl Dönitz, remained in power for another two weeks. Its members were then arrested and, together with other National Socialist leaders, tried by the International Military Tribunal in Nuremberg for crimes against peace and humanity.

On 5 June the victorious powers – the United States, the United Kingdom, the Soviet Union and France – assumed supreme authority in the territory of the Reich. Their basic objective, according to the London Protocol (12 September 1944) and follow-up agreements, was to exercise total control over Germany. They divided the country into three occupation zones, and Berlin, the capital, into three sectors. There was an Allied Control Council composed of the three commanders-in-chief.

Once and for all Germany was to be prevented from again aspiring to world domination as she had done in 1914 and 1939. The Allies wanted to curb the "Teutonic appetite for conquest", destroy Prussia as a stronghold of militarism, punish the Germans for genocide and war crimes, and reeducate them in the democratic spirit.

At the conference of Yalta (Crimea) held in February 1945, France was coopted as the fourth controlling power and allocated its own occupation zone. In Yalta the only Allied intention which remained valid was that of terminating Germany's existence as an independent state but keeping the country intact. Stalin especially was keen to preserve Germany's economic unity. He demanded such huge reparations for the Soviet Union's terrible sacrifices as a result of Germany's invasion that they could not possibly have been made by one occupation zone alone. Moscow wanted 20 billion dollars and control over 80 % of all of Germany's factories.

In contrast to the original plans, the British and Americans, too, wanted to preserve a viable rump Germany, not out of greed for reparations but because, as from about the autumn of 1944, U.S. President Roosevelt was aiming to establish a stable Central Europe as part of a system of global equilibrium. Germany's economic stability was indispensable to this plan. He had therefore quickly discarded the notorious Morgenthau Plan (September 1944), which would have reduced Germany to an agricultural country and would have divided it into a north German and a south German state.

Soon the only common aim remaining to the victorious powers was that of disarming and demilitarizing Germany. The original idea of partitioning the country quickly became no more than "lip service to a dying idea" (Charles Bohlen) when the Western powers watched with dismay as Stalin, immediately upon liberating, that is to say conquering, Poland and Southeastern Europe, launched a massive operation to sovietize those regions.

On 12 May 1945 Churchill cabled President Truman that an "iron curtain" had descended in front of the Soviet troops and that no one knew what was going on behind it. But the Western powers carefully weighed up the possible consequences of letting Stalin have a say in reparations on the Rhine and the Ruhr.

The result was that at the Potsdam Conference (17 July to 2 August 1945), the original aim of which was to create a new European order, agreements were reached which consolidated rather than eased the tensions. The four powers agreed on the matter of denazification, demilitarization, economic decentralization and the reedu-

The Potsdam Conference of 1945: Attlee, Truman and Stalin

Germany after World War II

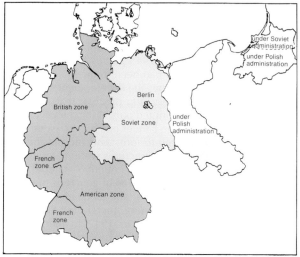

——— Germany within the borders of 1937

Western zones and Western sectors of Berlin
(Federal Republic of Germany from 1949)

Soviet zone and Eastern sector of Berlin
(German Democratic Republic from 1949)

German eastern territories under Polish or Soviet administration

cation of the Germans along democratic lines. The Western powers also gave their fateful consent to the expul-
sion of Germans from Poland, Hungary and Czechoslovakia. The West had insisted that the transfer be carried
out in a "humane" fashion, but in the following years
some 6.75 million Germans were brutally deported. They
were made to suffer for Germany's war crimes, but also
for the shift in Poland's western boundary as a result of
the Soviet Union's occupation of Königsberg and eastern
Poland. Practically the only point on which East and
West agreed was that the four occupation zones should
be preserved as economic and political units. At first,
each power was to draw its reparations from its own
zone. As was to be seen later, however, this set a precedent in that not only the reparations arrangement but
also the attachment of the four zones to different political
and economic systems made Germany the country
where the Cold War manifested itself most of all. This
came about in stages.

Meanwhile the task of establishing German political parties and administrative authorities had begun in the individual occupation zones. This happened very quickly in the Soviet zone under rigid control, with the result that even before the end of 1945 parties and several central administrative bodies had been formed.

In the three Western zones the development of a political system was a bottom-to-top process, that is to say, political parties were permitted only at local level at first, then at state level after the Länder had been created. Only later were they allowed to form associations at zonal level. Zonal administrative structures were materializing very slowly, and as the destroyed country's material want could only be overcome by means of generous planning across state and zonal borders, and as quadripartite administration was not functioning, the United States and the United Kingdom decided in 1947 to merge their zones economically into what was known as the bizone.

The conflicting systems of government in East and West and the different approach to reparations in the individual occupation zones were an obstacle to the introduction of uniform financial, taxation, raw materials and production policy throughout Germany and led to considerable regional disparities. France was not interested in a common economic administration (bizone/trizone) at first. Stalin wanted to have a say in the management of the Ruhr but at the same time sealed his own zone off to the others. He would not have any Western interference with the appointment of pro-communist officials in the Soviet-occupied zone. The Western powers were powerless to prevent such arbitrary Soviet measures as the compulsory merger of the German Communist Party (KPD) and the Social Democratic Party (SPD) to form the Socialist Unity Party (SED) in April 1946.

In view of the intensifying conversion of the Soviet occupation zone into a communist dictatorship – as early as 1948 it was no longer possible to speak of a system based on freedom there – the British and Americans began to work hard to promote the development of their own zones. If uniform administration of postwar Germany was no longer possible, the Western occupying powers were concerned to at least alleviate misery and need in the Western zones and pave the way for the creation of a democratic state structure based on freedom. Thus the beginning of the Cold War and the division of Germany were almost simultaneous events.

■■■ **An enemy becomes a partner.** With his famous speech in Stuttgart on 6 September 1946, U.S. Secretary of State Byrnes had indicated the changed approach. Stalin's occupation of Poland and the redrawing of that country's borders were described as merely temporary measures. As Byrnes saw it, the military role of the Western Allies in western Germany changed from one of occupation and control to that of protecting powers. And he said that a "soft" reparations policy was intended to deter the Germans from any nationalist thoughts of revenge and encourage their cooperation.

Finally, on the initiative of the United Kingdom and the United States, a trizone was established as a unified Western economic area, after initial French resistance. The threat of another Soviet advance westwards following the coup d'état in Prague on 25 February 1948 induced the French to fall into line. Byrnes' views were reflected first in the Brussels Pact of 17 March 1948 and ultimately in the North Atlantic Treaty of 4 April 1949.

For such an organization to work western Germany had to have a coherent political and economic system. Thus at the Six-Power Conference in London (23 February to 3 March and 20 April to 1 June 1948), which was attended for the first time by the Benelux countries, France, the United Kingdom and the United States agreed that the Western occupation zones should have a common political structure.

At the 82nd meeting of the Control Council on 20 March 1948, the Soviet representative, Marshal Sokolovski, asked for information on the London Conference. When his Western colleagues answered evasively Sokolovski walked out, never to return.

While the Western powers were still finalizing their recommendations for a constituent assembly to be convened by the western German minister-presidents (the heads of government of the states), Stalin used the introduction of the Deutsche Mark (DM) in the west (currency reform of 20 June 1948) as a pretext for imposing a blockade on Berlin (West) with the aim of annexing it to the Soviet-occupied zone. During the night of 23 June 1948 all land routes between the Western zones and Berlin (West) were closed. Supplies of energy and food from the

Eastern sector of Berlin and the Soviet zone stopped. On 3 August 1948 Stalin demanded that Berlin (East) be recognized as the capital of the German Democratic Republic (GDR), which on 7 October 1949 was given a government of its own. But U.S. President Harry Truman refused to budge, having declared on 20 July that the Western Allies could not forgo Berlin (West) ("no Munich of 1948") nor the creation of a west German state. Until 12 May 1949 Berlin (West) was kept supplied by an Allied airlift. This visible solidarity with Berlin (West) as a Western outpost, together with America's demonstration of strength, evoked a spirit of cooperation in western Germany, with the result that former enemies became partners.

■ ■ ■ **The founding of the Federal Republic of Germany.** Western Germany had already begun receiving American foreign aid in 1946 (under the GARIOA Programme), but it was George C. Marshall's programme to combat "hunger, poverty, despair and chaos" (the Marshall Plan) that provided the crucial boost for western Germany's economic recovery (1.4 billion dollars between 1948 and 1952). While in the Soviet-occupied zone the process of transferring industry to public ownership continued, the "social market economy" system (Alfred Müller-Armack, 1947) continued to gain ground in the west after the currency reform. The new economic order was intended to prevent, on the one hand, the "stagnation of capitalism" (Walter Eucken) and, on the other, a centrally planned economy which would be a hindrance to creativity and initiative. This concept was supplemented by the rule-of-law and social-state principles embodied in the Basic Law and by the country's federal structure. The constitution was deliberately termed the "Basic Law" in order to emphasize its provisional character. The idea was that a definitive constitution should only be adopted after Germany's reunification. Upon its ceremonial promulgation by the Parliamentary Council in Bonn, the Basic Law entered into force on 23 May 1949.

The Basic Law naturally included many of the intentions of the Western occupying powers, who, with the Frankfurt Documents presented on 1 July 1948, authorized the western German minister-presidents to draw up a constitution. But that document also reflects much of Germany's experience with the Weimar Republic and the unjust National Socialist state. The constitutional con-

In 1948/49 an airlift lasting 462 days supplied Berlin (West)

vention held at Herrenchiemsee (10-23 August 1948) and the Parliamentary Council which met in Bonn on 1 September 1948 (65 delegates of the state parliaments) incorporated in the Basic Law (adopted on 8 May 1949) provisions requiring future governments, parties and other political groupings to protect the democratic system. Ever since, all attempts to do away with the free, democratic basic order, or to replace it with a right-wing or left-wing dictatorship, have been treated as criminal offences and the organizations concerned can be banned. The Federal Constitutional Court, the guardian of the constitution, is the authority which decides whether a party is legal or not.

Whereas the authors of the Weimar constitution, naively believing in the uprightness of parliament, had, through its article 76, made it possible for enemies of the constitution to destroy what in those days was the most liberal constitution in the world, article 79 of the Basic Law prohibits any change in the commitment of all public authority to the protection of human rights (article 1). Any attempt to do away with the country's democratic, social and federal order is likewise prohibited (article 20 (4)).

These requirements were an immediate reaction to what had happened under the National Socialist dictatorship, at whose hands most of the "politicians of the Federal Republic's first hour" had suffered, those men and women who were now rebuilding Germany on the democratic traditions of 1848 and 1919 and in the spirit of the "revolt of the conscience" of 20 July 1944. All of them personified in the eyes of the world the "other Germany" and won the respect of the occupying powers. They included the first Federal President Theodor Heuss (FDP), the first Federal Chancellor Konrad Adenauer (CDU) and Economics Minister Ludwig Erhard (CDU), the "locomotive" of the "economic miracle", but also the outstanding leaders of the SPD opposition such as Kurt Schumacher and Erich Ollenhauer, as well as the cosmopolitan Carlo Schmid. It was they who gave the new party system in western Germany its unmistakable character. Gradually, German involvement and political influence increased (Occupation Statute, Petersberg Protocol, membership of GATT, accession to the European Coal and Steel Community). In July 1951 the United Kingdom, France and the United States declared that Germany was no longer a war enemy. The Soviet Union did the same on 25 January 1955.

■ ■ ■ **Security through integration with the West and European reconciliation.** To Federal Chancellor Konrad Adenauer, who until 1963 had largely held the reins of foreign and domestic policy himself ("Chancellor democ-

The Paris Treaties 1954: Mendès-France, Adenauer, Eden, Dulles

1957: The signing of the Treaties of Rome

racy"), Germany's reunification in peace and freedom was the foremost political objective. To achieve this it was necessary for western Germany to be integrated into the Atlantic Alliance. Accordingly, the restoration of the Federal Republic's sovereignty on 5 May 1955 coincided with its accession to NATO. This alliance was to be the main protective shield, the proposed European Defence Community having proved abortive due to French resistance. At the same time the European Communities (Treaties of Rome, 1957) were developed into an anticommunist bastion.

Adenauer's distrust of Moscow was so deep-rooted that in 1952 he, together with the other Western powers, rejected Stalin's offer of reuniting Germany as a neutral country as far as the Oder-Neisse line. The dictator's offer appeared to him too unclear for him to place the upcoming integration of the Federal Republic into the West at risk. His suspicion seemed only too justified when, on 17 June 1953, the people's uprising in the GDR in protest against their lack of freedom and against the unbearable productivity norms imposed by the regime was savagely put down by Soviet tanks. It was, however, also evident that without Moscow little progress could be made on the German question. Thus for sober political reasons it was expedient to establish diplomatic relations with the So-

U.S. President Kennedy in Berlin (West) on 26 June 1963

viet Union as the largest power in Europe. This was accomplished during Adenauer's visit to Moscow in September 1955, on which occasion he also secured the release of the last 10,000 German prisoners of war and about 20,000 civilians.

The crushing of the popular revolt in Hungary by Soviet troops in November 1956, as well as the "Sputnik shock" (4 October 1957), signalled a considerable growth of Soviet power, which manifested itself in the establishment of a socialist system in the GDR, but above all in the Berlin ultimatum issued by Stalin's successor, Nikita Khrushchev, who demanded that the Western Allies leave Berlin (West) within six months.

Their adamant refusal caused Khrushchev to try a softer approach on Berlin. His visit to the United States in 1959 did indeed considerably improve the atmosphere ("spirit of Camp David"), and the American President, Dwight D. Eisenhower, to the great concern of the Bonn government, felt that the Soviet transgressions of international agreements regarding Berlin were not so serious as to warrant a military conflict outside Germany.

Bonn's disquiet with regard to Berlin's security increased when John F. Kennedy became President of the United States. This represented a change of generation in the American leadership which considerably reduced Adenauer's influence on U.S. policy towards Europe.

True, Kennedy guaranteed with his three "essentials" (25 July 1961) free access to Berlin, the presence of the Western powers in the city, and its overall security, but when the Berlin Wall was built on 13 August 1961 the Allied reaction went little beyond diplomatic protests and symbolic threats. Once again Moscow was able to safeguard its protectorate. Barricades, death strips and repression prevented the people from "voting with their feet" against the GDR regime. Prior to the building of the Wall, almost three million people had left the GDR. In July 1961 alone, more than 30,000 had fled.

The Wall had staked out the claims of the superpowers. Although the German question had not been resolved it at least seemed regulated. Even after the Cuba crisis in 1962 the two superpowers continued to seek a better understanding – they had to on account of the nuclear stalemate.

Bonn therefore had no option but to look in other directions, and the temporary estrangement with Washington was in fact outwardly compensated for by the "summer of French friendship". With the Elysée Treaty which they signed in January 1963, Chancellor Adenauer and President de Gaulle laid special emphasis on Franco-German friendship. In order to stress the new quality of this relationship de Gaulle, during his triumphant state

Chancellor Adenauer greeting President de Gaulle in Bonn
on 5 July 1963

visit to Bonn a few months previously, had spoken of the "great German nation". In his view the Second World War had to be seen more in terms of tragedy than of guilt.

As the Federal Republic became increasingly integrated into the Western community the atmosphere also began to improve in the relationship with Eastern Europe. In December 1963 NATO, at a ministerial meeting in Athens, had signalled this change with its new strategy of flexible response in place of that of massive retaliation.

In an attempt to soften the rigid East-West relationship, the Federal Republic tried to improve contacts at least with the Soviet Union's satellite countries. Without officially abandoning the Hallstein Doctrine, that is to say Bonn's policy of severing relations with any country which recognized the GDR, Adenauer's successors, Ludwig Erhard and Kurt Georg Kiesinger, based their policy on the harsh realities prevailing in Central Europe. They were prompted to do so not least by the new approach adopted by the SPD opposition, which promoted Egon Bahr's formula of "change through rapprochement" (15 July 1963).

The establishment of German trade missions in Bucharest and Budapest was a promising start. In the West increasing efforts were being made to merge the European Coal and Steel Community (ECSC), the European Atomic Energy Community (EURATOM) and the European Economic Community (EEC) into one European Community (EC, 8 April 1965). The establishment of diplomatic relations with Israel despite pan-Arab protests was a major step in the Federal Republic's policy of rapprochement. At the beginning of 1967 Bonn established diplomatic relations with Romania, and in June of that year the Federal Republic and Czechoslovakia opened trade missions in their respective capitals.

The Harmel Report of December 1967 at least prepared the way for further steps towards detente by laying down the Western Alliance's twofold aim of maintaining its military strength whilst at the same time being ready to talk to the Eastern bloc. In that year Bonn and Belgrade resumed diplomatic relations, which had been broken off by the Federal Republic on account of Yugoslavia's recognition of the GDR. And from Poland came proposals for a non-aggression pact.

Adenauer with Israel's Prime Minister Ben Gurion (1960)

In addition to the policy of reconciliation with Germany's European neighbours and her integration into the Western community, Adenauer, too, had attached special importance to restitution for the Jews. Six million Jews had been systematically exterminated by the National Socialists. It was not least the close personal relationship between the Federal Republic's first Chancellor and Israel's Prime Minister Ben Gurion which fostered the process of reconciliation between Jews and Germans. One outstanding event at that time was their meeting in New York's Waldorf Astoria Hotel on 14 March 1960. Addressing parliament in 1961, Adenauer stressed that the Federal Republic could only prove that the Germans had broken completely with their National Socialist past by making material restitution as well.

As early as 1952 the first agreement had been signed in Luxembourg. It provided for assistance for the integration of Jewish refugees in Israel. Of the total sum of about DM 90 billion provided for restitution purposes, roughly one third went to Israel and Jewish organizations, and especially to the Jewish Claims Conference, a hardship fund which helped Jews all over the world who had been persecuted by the National Socialists. However, diplomatic relations between the two countries were not established until 1965.

■ ■ ■ **German-German dialogue in spite of the GDR's self-detachment.** In spite of the GDR's continuing efforts to cut itself off completely from the West (e.g. by requiring passports and visas for persons in transit between the Federal Republic and Berlin (West)) and in spite of the Warsaw Pact's crushing of attempted reforms in Czechoslovakia (Prague Spring) in 1968, the "Brezhnev Doctrine" of the indivisibility of the socialist bloc did not have any serious repercussions on the process of détente. In April 1969 Bonn said it was ready to enter into agreements with the GDR below the level of international recognition.

Obviously, German-German agreements of this kind could hardly be achieved without some kind of prior understanding with Moscow. When the Soviet Union proposed a non-aggression pact, the "Ostpolitk" (new eastern policy) adopted by the Social-Liberal coalition that had assumed power in Bonn on 21 October 1969 quickly began to take on substance.

A few months previously (5 March 1969) Gustav Heinemann, who even in Adenauer's day had been a strong advocate of East-West rapprochement, had been elected Federal President. Willy Brandt, who had played an active part in the resistance against the Hitler dictatorship, was now head of a federal government which directed its energies to the construction of a peaceful order throughout Europe. The international constellation was favourable. Moscow and Washington were negotiating on the limitation of strategic arms (SALT), and NATO proposed negotiations on mutual balanced force reductions (MBFR). On 28 November 1969 the Federal Republic became a party to the Treaty on the Non-proliferation of Nuclear Weapons (NPT). Following the turbulence experienced by its predecessor, the grand coalition government (Vietnam conflict, emergency legislation, Auschwitz trials, Extra-Parliamentary Opposition and student revolts), the new cabinet, by embarking on its "Ostpolitik", placed itself under considerable pressure to produce results.

While talks on a non-aggression agreement were being conducted in Moscow and Warsaw, Bonn and Berlin (East), too, explored the possibilities of improving relations. On 19 March 1970 the heads of government of both German states, Willy Brandt and Willi Stoph, met for the first time in Erfurt. This was followed by another meeting on 21 May 1970 in Kassel. On 12 August 1970 a treaty on the renunciation of force and recognition of the status quo was signed in Moscow. Both sides proclaimed that they had no territorial claims against "anyone". In a "letter on German unity" presented to the Soviet Government in Moscow, the Federal Republic stated that the treaty did not contradict its aim of working towards a state of peace in Europe "in which the German people will regain their unity in free self-determination".

On 7 December of that year the Treaty of Warsaw was signed which reaffirmed the inviolability of the existing border (the Oder-Neisse line). Warsaw and Bonn, too, gave an assurance that they had no territorial claims against one another and declared their intention of improving mutual cooperation. In an "information" document on humanitarian measures, Warsaw agreed to the transfer of ethnic Germans from Poland and the reunion of separated families by the Red Cross.

In order to pave the way for the ratification of those treaties, France, the United Kingdom, the United States and the Soviet Union signed the Quadripartite Agreement on Berlin which stated that the Western sectors of Berlin were not a constituent part of the Federal Republic but that Bonn was entitled to represent them. In addition, the "ties" between the Western sectors of Berlin and the Federal Republic were to be improved and relations between Berlin (East)/GDR and Berlin (West) developed (signing of the Transit Agreement on 17 December). Germany's efforts to foster peace and détente received worldwide recognition which culminated in the award of the Nobel Peace Prize to Willy Brandt (1971).

However, the CDU/CSU, who were in the opposition for the first time, considered the results of the negotiations too meagre. Yet their constructive vote of no confidence against Brandt came to grief (247 for, 249 against) and the German Bundestag (parliament) ratified the treaties with the Soviet Union and Poland on 17 May 1972. Most CDU/CSU members of parliament abstained. The Bundestag, in an "interpretative resolution", declared that the treaties did not conflict with the aim of restoring German unity by peaceful means.

The series of treaties with Eastern Europe was rounded off by a Treaty on the Basis of Relations (Basic Treaty) between the two German states which had been preceded by talks and negotiations since June 1972. After Willy Brandt's reelection as Chancellor on 14 December 1972, the way was clear for the signing of the Treaty in December of the same year. Both sides undertook not to threaten or use force against one another and to respect each other's independence. The inviolability of the border between the two German states was also endorsed. Furthermore, the two sides expressed their willingness to resolve humanitarian problems in a practical manner. It was agreed that, owing to the special nature of their relationship, they would establish "representations" in their respective capitals instead of the usual embassies.

At the signing ceremony the Federal Government again handed over a letter emphasizing its intention to pursue German unity. The government of the state of Bavaria asked the Federal Constitutional Court to confirm that the treaty did not run contrary to this objective. This the Court did, also noting that the German Reich continued to exist in international law and was partially identical with the Federal Republic. The Court ruled that the GDR could not be regarded as a foreign country, only as domestic territory.

In 1973 the Treaty of Prague between Czechoslovakia and the Federal Republic was signed. It declared the Munich Agreement of 1938 to be null and void "in accordance with this Treaty". The two sides also agreed that their borders were inviolable and that they would not use force against one another.

Whilst negotiations were going on in Vienna on mutual and balanced force reductions (MBFR), the Soviet Union and the United States completed an agreement designed to prevent a nuclear war, and 35 countries attended a Conference on Security and Cooperation in Europe (CSCE) in Helsinki, little change came about in the relationship between the GDR and the Federal Republic. On the one hand, Berlin (East) benefited both materially and financially from the follow-up agreements to the Basic Treaty, but on the other the GDR regime meticulously kept its ideological distance.

Nonetheless, Helmut Schmidt, too, strived to continue the policy of developing a balanced relationship. On 16 May 1974 he had succeeded Willy Brandt, who had resigned from the chancellorship when one of his aides,

Günther Guillaume, was unmasked as a GDR spy. The "swing" arrangement, a facility which allowed the GDR to overdraw by as much as DM 850 million on its credit from the Federal Republic, was extended until 1981.

The GDR continued to profit handsomely from the various transit agreements which were financed by the West, without budging on the political issues. The Final Act of the CSCE (Helsinki, 1975), which called for greater freedom of movement in transboundary traffic and more respect for human and civil rights, proved to be a disappointment, not only to the people in the GDR. There was no end to the chicanery at the GDR's borders. People were arbitrarily turned back, as were visitors to the Leipzig Fair. Western journalists who criticized the GDR were forced to leave the country.

The GDR regime suffered a further loss of prestige around the world when it deprived Wolf Biermann, a well-known singer-songwriter, of his citizenship. In spite of all this, the Federal Republic decided for the sake of the people in the GDR to continue its efforts to improve relations. Thus in 1978 an agreement was reached to build an autobahn from Berlin to Hamburg and to repair the transit waterways to Berlin (West), the greater proportion of the cost being borne by the Federal Republic. The Federal Government also continued to buy the release of political prisoners from the GDR. Bonn ultimately paid over DM 3.5 billion to obtain the release of 33,755 people and to have 250,000 families reunited.

■ ■ ■ **Missiles versus détente.** Whereas the process of European integration continued steadily in the West, the transition from the 70s, the decade of détente, to the 80s was marked by fresh conflicts in Eastern Europe. The Soviet invasion of Afghanistan and the imposition of martial law in Poland, as well as the emplacement of new intermediate-range missiles (SS-20) in the Soviet Union, worsened the climate of East-West relations.

NATO reacted to this serious upset of the balance of security by deciding that it, too, would introduce new missiles as from 1983. But at the same time it proposed arms control negotiations to the Soviet Union. This was the "two-track" decision. In protest at the invasion of Afghanistan, the United States, the United Kingdom, Canada, Norway and the Federal Republic refused to take part in the Moscow Summer Olympics (1980).

The Americans tried a new initiative, the "zero" solution, by which the Soviets would remove their intermediate-range missiles whilst NATO would promise not to deploy its Pershing II and the new cruise missiles.

Chancellor Schmidt insisted on the missile modernization alternative so as not to leave any gaps in the Western security shield, but at the same time tried to keep the damage to the German-German relationship within limits. Schmidt visited the GDR, but without getting any substantial concessions from Honecker. The regime's hardening ideological stance was not least a reaction to the growing protest movements in neighbouring Poland, where more and more people were demanding economic reform, freedom and disarmament.

But the missile question was not only problematical in the East. In Bonn the FDP decided to change its tack on economic policy and began to drift out of the coalition. Grass-roots SPD followers, largely because of pressure from the peace movement and some union factions, withdrew their support for Schmidt for adhering to the NATO two-track decision. As a result, Helmut Kohl replaced him as Chancellor at the head of a CDU/CSU/FDP coalition on 1 October 1982. The new Chancellor continued Bonn's security policy and close cooperation with Paris and Washington with a view to uniting Europe within a stable and secure framework. In spite of massive peace demonstrations, Helmut Kohl's government maintained its position: In November 1983 the German Bundestag agreed to the deployment of the new missiles. The credibility of the Western Alliance was thus strengthened and a crisis within NATO averted.

A new dialogue on disarmament between the superpowers began as early as the mid-80s. It was soon possible for the missiles which had just been deployed in the Federal Republic to be removed once again. Disarmament then became a reality for the first time: "Maintain peace with fewer weapons." (Federal Chancellor Kohl)

■ ■ ■ **From the decline of the GDR to German unity.** The German Democratic Republic, which had been founded on 7 October 1949, was a product of the Soviet Union. It was from the outset a communist dictatorship built on the foundations of the rule of the Socialist Unity Party (SED). But the command economy, secret police, the all-powerful SED and strict censorship increasingly alienated the people and the regime. In spite of this, very cheap housing, health care and social services gave this self-contained system a certain amount of flexibility which enabled the people to eke out an existence in many different ways. The GDR's great success in international sports was a sort of compensation, just as the "workers" gained satisfaction from the fact that they soon had the highest rate of industrial production and the highest standard of living in the Eastern bloc, despite having to make huge reparations to the Soviet Union. The people's reaction to state control and tutelage was to withdraw into their private sphere.

In spite of all the propaganda about annual production targets having been more than achieved, and behind the facade of anti-imperialist hatred spread in the schools, factories and the armed forces, it became increasingly clear that GDR's original intention of overtaking the Federal Republic economically would remain a dream. Depleted resources and industry's vicious destruction of the environment, coupled with dwindling productivity as a result of central planning, forced the SED regime to go easy on its promises. It had to raise increasingly large loans in the West. Improvisation became the order of the day with regard to consumer goods. The quality of life and infrastructure (housing, transport, environmental protection) thus deteriorated. There was a Big-Brother spy network which kept watch on everybody, and the system's indoctrination and strained appeals for solidarity made the claim about the leadership role of "the working class and their Marxist-Leninist party" (article 1 of the GDR constitution) sound like hollow rhetoric, especially to the young generation. The people began to demand above all a say in running their own lives, more individual freedom and more and better consumer goods.

As the atmosphere of diplomatic relations deteriorated as a result of the quarrel over the deployment of intermediate-range missiles, the proposed Strategic Defence Initiative (SDI), a space-based defensive umbrella proposed by the Americans, and the GDR's continued aggravation of the West (for instance, by building a second wall at the Brandenburg Gate and impeding traffic in the air corridor to Berlin), the people of the GDR themselves put pressure on their own leadership. Some had entered the Federal

Republic's permanent representation in Berlin (East) and refused to leave until they had been given a definite assurance that they could move to the West.

In order to make life easier for the Germans in the east, the Federal Government arranged several large bank credits for the GDR. Moscow's fear that this would soften the socialist system was allayed by Erich Honecker, who wrote in "Neues Deutschland", the regime's mouthpiece, in 1984: "Merging socialism and capitalism is just as impossible as merging fire and water." But this self-assurance on the surface could hardly conceal the fact that the reform movements in Eastern Europe had thrown the whole socialist bloc onto the defensive.

From the beginning of 1985 more and more people sought admission to the Federal Republic's permanent representation in Berlin (East) and the German Embassy in Prague. Soon the new General Secretary of the Soviet Communist Party, Mikhail Gorbachev, who had succeed-ed Konstantin Chernenko (who had died in March), be-came the main standard bearer for the people of the GDR, who were longing to gain their freedom. In 1986, Gorbachev declared that his main political objective was to eliminate nuclear weapons by the end of the century. His meetings with U.S. President Ronald Reagan in Ge-neva and Reykjavik, the Conference on Confidence- and Security-building Measures and Disarmament in Europe (CDE) held in Stockholm, as well as the preparations for negotiations on the reduction of conventional forces in Europe, showed that the East was ready for dialogue. This new approach was conducive to agreements between the two German states on cultural, educational and scientif-ic cooperation. A skeleton agreement providing for coop-eration in the field of environmental protection was also signed. That same year Saarlouis and Eisenhüttenstadt made a twinning arrangement, the first of its kind be-tween cities in eastern and western Germany.

But the SED regime did not want to be infected by Gor-bachev's "perestroika" and "glasnost". They didn't want the process of democratic reform in the Soviet Union to spread to the GDR. Kurt Hager, a member of the Politbu-ro and the SED's principal ideologue, stubbornly argued that there was "no need to redecorate one's home just be-cause the neighbour is doing so".

The extent to which the GDR leaders ignored the expectations of their own people was shown by the protest demonstrations in Berlin (East) on 13 August, the anniversary of the building of the Wall. Chancellor Helmut Kohl spoke against the continuation of Germany's division when, during Honecker's working visit to Bonn (1987), he said: "We respect the present borders but we want to overcome the country's division by peaceful means through a process of mutual understanding. We have a joint responsibility for preserving the vital foundations of our nation."

A step towards safeguarding those vital foundations was the INF Treaty signed by Reagan and Gorbachev. Under that accord, all U.S. and Soviet missiles with a range of 500 to 5,000 km deployed in Europe had to be withdrawn and destroyed. The Federal Republic for its part pledged to destroy its 72 Pershing IA missiles.

The general climate of détente led to increasing demands for greater freedom and reform in the GDR. During demonstrations in Berlin (East) in early 1988, 120 supporters of the peace movement known as "Church from the Grass Roots" were arrested. Prayers were said for them in the Gethsemane Church. Over 2,000 people attended the service, and a fortnight later their number had swollen to 4,000. In Dresden the police broke up a demonstration for human rights, free speech and freedom of the press. In May Honecker used the occasion of a visit by the Soviet Defence Minister Yasov to warn about the danger of imperialism and to call for a stronger Warsaw Pact.

Although Chancellor Kohl, in his state of the nation address to the German Bundestag in December 1988, welcomed the lifting of some travel restrictions, he had to denounce the suppression of the reform movement in the GDR. To Erich Honecker, however, the new civil rights movements were merely examples of "extremist intemperance". In response to appeals to remove the Wall, he replied on 19 January 1989: "The wall protecting us from fascism will stay there until such time as the conditions which led to its erection are changed. It will still be in existence in 50, 100 years' time."

The stubborn rigidity of the GDR leaders at a time when Gorbachev saw a "common European home" taking shape and Helmut Kohl was speaking optimistically about "the disintegration of ossified structures in Europe" aroused even more discontent among the GDR population. At times the Federal Republic's permanent representation in Berlin (East) had to be closed because of the surge of people wanting to move west. In September 1989 Hungary opened its border, thus permitting thousands of people from the GDR to pass through to Austria and from there into the Federal Republic. This breach of Warsaw Pact discipline encouraged ever more people in the GDR to take to the streets in protest, including growing numbers outside the church. And when the GDR leaders, in October 1989, celebrated the 40th anniversary of the founding of the GDR with great pomp and ceremony, mass demonstrations were held, primarily in Leipzig. ("We are the people!")

Honecker finally realized that his only chance of preserving the essence of the SED regime was for him to resign. He was succeeded as SED secretary general and GDR head of state by Egon Krenz, but the latter's promise of "change" was drowned by the protests of the people, who did not trust him. Under the pressure of events the council of ministers and the SED Politburo resigned en bloc. The peaceful revolution seemed to paralyze the authorities. As a result, a mistaken announcement by Günter Schabowski, the SED party secretary in the district of Berlin, that travel restrictions were to be eased prompted thousands of people to cross the border on the evening of 9 November 1989. The authorities could only watch numbly. The Wall was open. Soon it was to be broken down and tiny pieces offered as souvenirs.

News of the breach in the Wall reached Chancellor Kohl whilst he was on a visit to Warsaw. He suspended his engagements for a day and hurried to Berlin where he addressed a crowd of 20,000 from the balcony of Schöneberg Town Hall. He asked them to remain calm in that joyous hour, and thanked Gorbachev and Germany's friends in the West for their support. He said the spirit of freedom had gripped the whole of Europe. Upon his return to Warsaw he signed a declaration in which Germany and Poland promised to intensify their cooperation in the cause of peace, security and stability in Europe.

The revolution in the GDR opened up the opportunity for the Germany's reunification after a wait of decades. But caution was required. Paris and London did not have German unity on the agenda. Gorbachev, during talks

The Wall is open: free access to Berlin (West)

with U.S. President Ronald Reagan off the coast of Malta (December 1989), warned against any attempt to force the German issue. And in the GDR itself the new government under Hans Modrow, though demanding rapid reform, also wanted the GDR to keep its statehood. Helmut Kohl therefore proposed a ten-point programme for achieving national unity. It envisaged a "contractual arrangement" based on a confederal system leading to fundamental political and economic change in the GDR. The Chancellor proposed that the direct negotiations with the GDR should take place within a pan-European setting under the aegis of the European Community and the CSCE. He avoided specifying a time frame for the negotiations so as not to spark any further comment abroad about Germany seeking superpower status. The road to unity still seemed long to both sides, especially when Gorbachev, addressing the Communist Party Central Committee, said as late as 9 December 1989 that Moscow would not leave the GDR "in the lurch", that it was Moscow's strategic ally in the Warsaw Pact and that one still had to start from the assumption of two German states, though there was no reason why they should not develop a relationship of peaceful cooperation.

Chancellor Kohl said the people in the GDR themselves should be the ones to decide on the speed and the substance of unification. But the government saw events rapidly slipping from its control. The people in the GDR distrusted their new government. They became increasingly attracted to the West and the process of destabilization increased rapidly. But still Gorbachev held back, particularly as Poland and Hungary were escaping Moscow's grasp, Ceausescu's overthrow in Romania was in the offing, and therefore the GDR's departure from the Warsaw Pact would upset the balance of power. From Western quarters, too, came exhortations to the Germans to "take account of the legitimate concerns of neighbouring countries" (U.S. Secretary of State James Baker speaking in Berlin) as they pursued national unity.

And finally, the unification process could only be continued after Bonn had given an assurance that there would be no shifting of the present borders, that, in the event of unification, NATO's "structures" would not be extended to the territory of the former GDR, and that Germany would reduce its armed forces to offset its strategic advantage. U.S. President Bush was in favour of German unification provided the Federal Republic remained a member of NATO.

In order that the GDR could be represented in the negotiations with a democratic mandate, free elections were held there on 18 March 1990, the first in 40 years. Lothar de Maizière became the head of a grand coalition made up of the CDU, DSU, DA, SPD and FDP. With him the Bonn government agreed on a timetable for monetary, economic and social union with effect from 1 July 1990, it having become palpably clear that the GDR had no economic basis on which to continue alone and that the majority of the people in the GDR wanted accession to the Federal Republic.

In August 1990 the Volkskammer (the GDR parliament) voted in favour of accession as soon as possible, and on 31 August of the same year GDR State Secretary Günter Krause and Wolfgang Schäuble, Federal Minister of the Interior, were able to sign the "Unification Treaty". Thus on 3 October 1990 the German Democratic Republic officially acceded to the Federal Republic in accordance with article 23 of the Basic Law.

The GDR states of Brandenburg, Mecklenburg-Western Pomerania, Saxony, Saxony-Anhalt and Thuringia became states (Länder) of the Federal Republic of Germany.

*Green light for German unification: Chancellor Kohl and Foreign
Minister Genscher talking to Mr Gorbachev in the Caucasus*

Berlin was made the capital and the Basic Law, after appropriate amendments, entered into force in the territory
of the former GDR as well.

The road to unity had been opened by Mikhail Gorbachev, who had given his approval after talks with Chancellor Kohl in Moscow and the Caucasian town of Stav-
ropol in July 1990. He did so on the condition that the

*Interior Minister Schäuble (West) and State Secretary Krause (East)
after signing the German Unification Treaty (1990)*

Federal Republic would forgo ABC weapons and reduce its forces to 370,000, and that NATO's military organization would not be extended to GDR territory so long as Soviet forces remained stationed there. The two leaders also agreed that the Soviet troops would be withdrawn from eastern Germany by the end of 1994, and that the Federal Republic would provide financial support for their repatriation. Gorbachev's agreement also meant that the so-called Two-plus-Four Treaty could be signed. Within that framework the Soviet Union, the United States, France and the United Kingdom, as well as the representatives of the two German states, confirmed the unification of Germany consisting of the territories of the former GDR, the Federal Republic and Berlin. Germany's external borders were recognized as definitive. Bonn and Warsaw concluded a separate treaty to take account of Poland's special security needs in the light of history. The two sides agreed to respect each other's territorial integrity and sovereignty.

The ratification of the Unification Treaty and the Two-plus-Four Treaty marked the termination of the rights and responsibilities of the four victorious powers "with respect to Berlin and Germany as a whole". Germany thus regained the complete sovereignty over her internal and external affairs which she had lost 45 years previously with the fall of the National Socialist dictatorship.

■■■ **Setting the stage for the future.** Following the restoration of German unity and the colossal political changes occurring in the wake of the collapse of the communist systems in the eastern part of Europe, the Federal Republic and its partners faced and continue to face completely new challenges.

– The recovery process in the new federal states must be accelerated and the internal unity of Germany completed.

– The European Union must be further developed and deepened.

– A global structure promoting peace and security must be established and maintained.

National, European and global responsibilities are inseparably interwoven. Recovery and consolidation in the new federal states cannot take place unless they are closely bound up with the process of European integration. Europe cannot retain its new structure without opening itself up to the reformist states in Central and Eastern Europe. Economically as well as politically the states of eastern Central Europe must be led step by step towards the collective European and Atlantic organizations. In this spirit, a Partnership and Cooperation Agreement was signed between the European Union and Russia in Corfu on 24 June 1994. The extensive aid provided by the Federal Government to Russia is in keeping both with its vital interest in the success of the democratic transformation process and with the newly-shared political values. Since the end of 1989, Germany's financial expenditure and existing obligations to the former Soviet Union and the present CIS states have totalled more than DM 90 billion (as of the end of 1994). The greater part of the German support for the political and economic reform process in the CIS states has consisted of the credit guarantees and sureties of the Hermes-Exportkreditversicherung (export credit insurance scheme) amounting to DM 47.1 billion. In addition, the Germans have come to the aid of people in Russia through spontaneous donation campaigns. Between 1990 and 1992 private donations were collected to the tune of DM 650 million.

On 31 August 1994, in the presence of Federal Chancellor Helmut Kohl and the Russian President Boris Yeltsin, Germany took leave of the last soldiers belonging to the Russian troops stationed on its soil. At the time of German unification almost 340,000 Soviet soldiers and about 210,000 civilian dependents had been living in eastern Germany. The funds furnished by the Federal Government to support the withdrawal of the Russian troops amounted to DM 14.6 billion; most of this money was used to build about 45,000 civilian dwellings for soldiers returning to Russia, Belarus and Ukraine.

The fact that Germany ranks third among contributors to the United Nations (8.9% of the budget) and pays 22.8% of the NATO budget and 28.5% of the WEU budget already emphasizes purely outwardly the willingness of the Federal Government, in continuation of its policy to date, to contribute to stability and the maintenance of peace within a bilateral and multilateral framework. A consequence of this is the German application for a permanent seat on the Security Council. At the request of the Secretary-General of the United Nations, a transport company of the Bundeswehr took part for the first time in a United Nations blue helmet operation in the summer of 1993 in "pacified areas" of Somalia. This operation was the subject of controversial political discussion in Germany. Then, in July 1994, the Federal Constitutional Court judged that German armed forces could participate in operations within the framework of NATO or WEU activities in support of the implementation of resolutions of the United Nations Security Council. In accordance with the judgment of this Court the same applies to the participation of German armed forces in United Nations peacekeeping troops.

■ ■ ■ **On the road to European Union.** The common internal market of the then twelve EC states was launched at the beginning of 1993. This market united 345 million Europeans to form the economic area with the greatest purchasing power on earth. With the exception of Switzerland, the states of the European Free Trade Association EFTA (Austria, Sweden, Norway, Finland, Iceland and Liechtenstein) and the European Community formed the European Economic Area. The first stage for achieving monetary union began in mid-1990; during this period capital transfers among EC states were liberalized and coordination of economic policy between the partners as well as cooperation between their central banks was intensified. Since the beginning of the second stage on 1 January 1994, the European Monetary Institute (EMI) has been preparing the establishment of a European Central Bank which will be headquartered in Frankfurt am Main. The decision on irrevocably entering the third stage – the final stage of monetary union – will be taken at the end of 1996 at the earliest. A high degree of monetary stability and budgetary discipline is a precondition for the planned creation of complete economic and monetary union. The Federal Government attached particular significance to the fact that in 1991 in Maastricht the Heads of State or of Government not only negotiated the Treaty on Economic and Monetary Union but furthermore agreed on European Union, which provides a superstructure for the further deepening of the European Community. The Treaty entered into force in November 1993. In the view of the Federal Government the deepening of the Union must go hand in hand with its enlargement – after the accession of former EFTA states,

Training with the latest equipment

in the long term also by bringing the states of Central, Eastern and Southeastern Europe closer to the European Union.

With this in mind, at the EU summit which took place in Essen in December 1994 and was attended by 21 Heads of State or of Government a concept was adopted for smoothing the path towards the European Union for the six Central and Eastern European reformist states which are linked to the EU by Europe Agreements (Poland, Hungary, the Czech Republic, Slovakia, Romania and Bulgaria). By mid-1995 an EU White Paper will be available listing the necessary adaptation measures to be taken by our Eastern neighbours. Over the next five years the Union will provide financial assistance to these countries totalling at least DM 10.6 billion. Preparations are already underway for the intergovernmental conference which is to take place in 1996 and after critical self-reflection is to decide which reforms must be made in the cooperation among the states of the EU. On 1 January 1995 the EU grew to 15 member states through the accession of Finland, Austria and Sweden. Since April 1995 the Schengen Agreement has been in force: There are no longer any checks on travellers at the borders between

Germany, the Benelux countries, France, Spain and Portugal, but there are, however, stricter passport and customs checks at the outer frontiers. Once the corresponding preparations have been carried out, further EU states
will also proceed in this manner.

■ ■ ■ **The economic unification of Germany.** The process of bringing western and eastern Germany into balance is being completed in the context of European unification and in parallel with a process of global political
and economic restructuring brought about by the collapse of the Eastern European system of states.

Conversion of the economy of the former GDR, structured as it was on planned economy lines, into a functioning system based on the principles of the social market economy was and remains a challenge which is
unique in history to date. It requires not only a massive
transfer of finances from western to eastern Germany –
public spending up to the end of 1994 reached a volume
of DM 640 billion, and by the end of 1995 this amount is
expected to increase to DM 840 billion – but also the restructuring of the entire management. Many factories in
the former GDR were in such poor condition that their
continued operation would have been irresponsible. A
key role was played in the restructuring of the economy
in the new federal states by the Treuhandanstalt (Trust
Agency). By the time it ceased operations at the end of
1994, the Trust Agency had privatized about 14,000 enterprises, yielding proceeds of approximately DM 65 billion, and had secured DM 207 billion in investment
pledges. In addition, it had obtained commitments to retain or create around 1.5 million jobs. The latter was an
especially significant result of the Agency's work because
the conversion of the economy has required particularly
painful intervention in terms of employment; many
jobs have been lost in the course of restoring competitiveness. For this reason, since unification the Federal
Government has expended considerable financial resources to further the creation of new jobs. As a consequence of the ongoing exceptional economic growth
in the new federal states, but also not least because of
the efforts which have been made in the area of active labour market policy, a turning point in the unemployment
rate has become noticeable since the beginning of
1995.

Automobile assembly in eastern Germany

By the end of 1994, three million dwellings had been renovated in the new federal states with financial resources provided by the Federal Government, and about 150,000 new ones had been built. Including the figure for 1994, the former Reichsbahn (the GDR railway), which was in a poor state of repair, had received approximately DM 25 billion for the renovation of its dilapidated equipment; after the merger with its western counterpart, the Bundesbahn (Federal Railway), another roughly DM 70 billion will be available up through the year 2002 in order to bring it up to western standards. In the area of Telekom, considerable financial resources are to be utilized to achieve a telephone connection rate of 95% of all households by 1997. In the past few years, small and medium-sized enterprises in particular have shown themselves to be a driving force behind recovery in the new states. To date, more than 460,000 persons there have become self-employed, 140,000 in the craft trades alone. A wide variety of financial incentives and consultancy support the investment activity in the new federal states. These include:

– the equity capital assistance programme financed by the Federal Government;

– the European Recovery Program (ERP) providing more than 240,000 promotion loans since 1990;

– the joint federal/state programme "Improving the Regional Economic Structures" financed by the Federation, the states and the European Union; and
– the programme of the Kreditanstalt für Wiederaufbau (Development Loan Corporation) for small and medium-sized enterprises.

Economic development as a whole in eastern Germany has been on the upswing for three years. In 1994 the gross domestic product there increased by 8.9%, and growth of between 8% and 10% is expected for 1995. The new federal states are thus the fastest-growing region in the European Union. In 1994 consumer prices there rose by only 1.8%; incomes and pensions will be gradually adjusted in line with those in western Germany and in mid-1995 will reach approximately 84% of the level in the west. Many branches of the eastern economy (the construction industry and the craft trades, for instance) are today increasingly characterized by self-sustained growth. In others, however, there are still problems which are due among other things to the lower level of productivity per employee in the new federal states. In 1994 productivity in the east nevertheless reached about 52% of the level in the west; the comparable figure in 1991 had been only 31%. Since the beginning of 1995 the new states have been included in the normal financial equalization system among the federal states. Until then, the "German Unity Fund" had ensured their financial capacity to act.

In order to compensate for the massive costs incurred as a result of recovery and restructuring in the new states, as well as to prevent the Federation's net new borrowing from assuming boundless proportions (debt service now consumes almost 20% of total federal resources), since 1 January 1995 a solidarity surcharge has been levied in Germany amounting to 7.5% of wage, income and corporation taxes. Persons with low incomes are exempted.

■ ■ ■ **Maintaining Germany's attractiveness as an industrial location.** The Federal Government has ushered in a phase of consolidation of public budgets with a strict savings policy. It is hoped that new borrowing can thus be reduced considerably in the next few years. According to IMF statistics, Germany's new borrowing is still lower than the average for Western countries, in spite of the historic challenge posed by German unity.

The trend which had already become apparent in 1994 continued in 1995, so that economic growth of 3% is expected for Germany as a whole. Preconditions for growth are the economic recovery underway in the European partner countries, which has caused a dramatic increase in the demand for German capital goods, as well as the sensible wage policy pursued by partners to collective agreements, due to which unit labour costs fell in 1994 in comparison to the previous year for the first time in the history of the Federal Republic. The competitiveness of German products on world markets has thus improved considerably. The intention of the Federal Government is for Germany to be and remain an attractive location not only for international firms. Tax incentives have been established under the Investment Promotion Act above all for small and medium-sized enterprises, insofar as their assessed value and business capital do not exceed certain thresholds. The maximum taxation rate for business income has been reduced to 47%. The corporation tax rate for the retained profit of stock corporations and limited liability companies has been reduced to 45%, and to 30% profit distributions.

■ ■ ■ **A period of political stability**. The overwhelming majority of Germans are actively in favor of national unification. Understandably, many Germans in east and west have different opinions on the contribution which the people in the old states are making to help those in the new. The alienation that had developed over a period of more than 40 years of isolation is now becoming less and less pronounced, especially since the general initial euphoria has given way to a sober assessment of what is feasible. People have realized that while it is comfortable to expect the standard of living in eastern and western Germany to be quickly brought into balance, this is in fact unrealistic. Today people look at the progress which has actually been made. On this basis it is possible to see a steady increase in the number of people who express their satisfaction with the process of recovery in the new federal states; they presently represent over 60% of the overall population. A difficult aspect of coming to terms with the period of rule by the SED has been and continues to be the handling of so-called government crime by the courts. How, for instance, should the guilt of those be assessed who bore political responsibility for giving the order for the shootings along the Wall and the barbed-wire fences? Another painful issue is the scrutiny of the vast quantities of files maintained by the GDR State Security Service (Stasi). Many people in eastern Germany want to know what kind of information the Stasi held on them, and many of them discover upon reading their files that they were spied on by individuals they had trusted.

In the course of 1994, the danger of an unstable political situation in Germany was repeatedly the subject of discussion in the foreign media. The results of the numerous elections which have taken place have proved the opposite to be the case. No right-wing extremist groups are represented in the Bundestag (Federal Parliament). The official final result of the Bundestag elections held on 16 October 1994 was as follows: Christian Democratic Union of Germany/Christian Social Union (CDU/CSU) 41.5%; Social Democratic Party of Germany (SPD) 36.4%; Free Democratic Party (FDP) 6.9%; Alliance 90/The Greens 7.3%; Party of Democratic Socialism (PDS) 4.4%. According to surveys carried out by opinion research institutes, the overwhelming majority of Germans place their trust in democracy.

People in Germany as well as abroad have been greatly disturbed in recent years by xenophobic acts of violence in Germany, which were often motivated by right-wing extremist ideas. Thanks to the wide variety of measures undertaken by the Federal Government, the federal states and almost all major groups in society it has, however, been possible to successfully counter such activities. All the elections held in 1994 and 1995 demonstrated that there is no political support for xenophobia and right-wing extremism in Germany. A matter of particular concern for the Federal Government at present is to prevent internal Turkish conflicts from being carried out on German territory.

8 May 1995 marked the 50th anniversary of the end of the Second World War. This event was commemorated in the awareness that the war caused terrible suffering to many innocent people and that a consistent policy of peace is what unifies Europe as it now stands, that Germany today is one of the most stable democracies in the world and a country which faces its responsibility to the international community of states.

Country and people

· The country · The people

The country

The Federal Republic of Germany is situated in the heart of Europe. It has nine neighbours: Denmark in the north, the Netherlands, Belgium, Luxembourg and France in the west, Switzerland and Austria in the south, and the Czech Republic as well as Poland in the east. This central location has been more pronounced since 3 October 1990 when Germany was reunited. The Federal Republic is more than ever a link between East and West, but also between Scandinavia and the Mediterranean. As an integral part of the European Union and NATO, Germany is a bridge to the countries of Central and Eastern Europe.

The Federal Republic of Germany covers an area of 357,000 sq km. The longest distance from north to south as the crow flies is 876 km, from west to east 640 km. Its extremities are List on the island of Sylt in the north, Deschka, Saxony, in the east, Oberstdorf, Bavaria, in the south, and Selfkant, North Rhine-Westphalia, in the west. The total length of the country's borders is 3,758 km. Germany has a population of about 80 million, the largest in Europe after Russia's, followed by Italy (population 58 million), the United Kingdom (57 million) and France (56 million). In size, however, Germany is smaller than France (544,000 sq km) and Spain (505,000 sq km).

■■■ **Geographical features.** Germany has various charming landscapes. Low and high mountain ranges intermingle with upland plains, terrace country, hilly regions and lakelands, as well as wide, open lowlands. From north to south Germany is divided into five regions with different topographical features: the North German Plain, the Central Upland Range, the terrace panorama of the southwest, the Alpine foothills in the south, and the Bavarian Alps.

In the north are dry, sandy lowlands with many lakes as well as heaths and moors. There is also the fertile land south of the Central Upland Range. These lowland penetrations include the Lower Rhenish Bight, the Westphalian Bight and the Saxon-Thuringian Bight. The marshes along the North Sea coast extend as far as the geest. Characteristic features of the Baltic Sea coastline are, in Schleswig-Holstein, the fjords, in Mecklenburg-Western

Pomerania the lakes and the counterbalancing coastline. The main islands in the North Sea are the East Frisian Islands such as Borkum or Norderney, the North Frisian Islands of Amrum, Föhr, Sylt and the Halligen, as well as Helgoland in the Helgoland Bight. Situated in the Baltic Sea are the islands of Rügen, Hiddensee and Fehmarn. Some parts of the Baltic coast have flat, sandy shores, others steep cliffs. Between the North and Baltic Seas lies the low-hill country called "Holsteinische Schweiz" (Holstein Switzerland).

The Central Upland Range divides north Germany from the south. The central Rhine valley and the Hessian depressions serve as the natural north-south traffic arteries. The Central Uplands include the Rhenish Slate Mountains (Hunsrück, Eifel, Taunus, Westerwald, Bergisches Land and Sauerland), the Hessian Mountains, and the Weser and Leine Mountains in western and central Ger-

Mountains, rivers, islands:

Zugspitze (northern Alps)	2962 m
Watzmann (northern Alps)	2713 m
Feldberg (Black Forest)	1493 m
Großer Arber (Bavarian Forest)	1456 m
Fichtelberg (Erzgebirge)	1215 m
Brocken (Harz)	1142 m
Rivers within Germany:	
Rhine	865 km
Elbe	700 km
Main	524 km
Weser	440 km
Spree	382 km
Shipping canals:	
Mittelland Canal	321 km
Dortmund-Ems Canal	269 km
Kiel Canal	99 km
Lakes and dams:	
Lake Constance (total area)	538.5 sq km
Lake Constance (German part)	305 sq km
Müritz	110.3 sq km
Schwammenauel	205 million cubic metres
Eder Dam (Lake Eder)	202 million cubic metres
Islands:	
Rügen	930 sq km
Usedom (German part)	373 sq km
Fehmarn	185 sq km
Sylt	99 sq km

many. Right in the centre of Germany are the Harz Mountains. In the eastern region are the Rhön Mountains, the Bavarian Forest, the Upper Palatinate Forest, the Fichtelgebirge, the Frankenwald, the Thuringian Forest and the mountains of the Erzgebirge.

The terrace landscape of the Central Uplands in the southwest embrace the upper Rhine valley with the adjacent mountain ranges of the Black Forest, the Odenwald and Spessart, the Palatinate Forest with the Haardt, and the Swabian-Franconian terrace country with the Alb.

In a narrow valley between Bingen and Bonn the river Rhine, the main north-south axis, slices through the Rhenish Slate Mountains, whose not very fertile highland areas (Hunsrück, Taunus, Eifel, Westerwald) are considerably less densely populated than the sheltered wine-growing areas on both sides of the Rhine which are very popular with tourists. The Alpine foothills embrace the Swabian-Bavarian highlands and lakes, the broad, gravel plains, the hilly landscape of Lower Bavaria, and the Danube valley. Characteristic features of this region are the moors, dome-shaped hill ranges and lakes (Chiemsee, Starnberger See) as well as small villages.

The German part of the Alps between Lake Constance and Berchtesgaden is limited to the Allgäu, the Bavarian Alps and the Berchtesgaden Alps. In this Alpine world lie picturesque lakes, such as the Königssee near Berchtesgaden, and popular tourist resorts such as Garmisch-Partenkirchen or Mittenwald.

■ ■ ■ **Climate.** Germany is situated in the temperate zone between the Atlantic Ocean and the eastern part of the European continent. Sharp changes in temperature are rare. There is precipitation all the year round. In winter the average temperature is between 1.5°C in the lowland areas and minus 6°C in the mountains. In the warmest month of the year, July, temperatures are between 18°C in low-lying regions and 20°C in the sheltered valleys of the south. Exceptions are the Upper Rhine Trough with its extremely mild climate, Upper Bavaria with its warm Alpine wind (Föhn) from the south, and the Harz Mountains, a climatic zone of its own with cold winds, cool summers and heavy snow in winter.

The people

Germany has a population of nearly 81 million (including 6.9 million foreigners) and is one of the most densely populated countries in Europe (226 people per sq km). Only Belgium and the Netherlands have a higher population density.

The population is distributed very unevenly. Greater Berlin, which has been growing rapidly since Germany's unification and has more than 3.5 million inhabitants, will probably have eight million by the end of the millennium. More than four million people (about 5,500 per sq km) live in the Rhine-Ruhr industrial agglomeration where towns and cities are so close together that there are no distinct boundaries between them.

Other concentrations are to be found in the Rhine-Main area around Frankfurt, Wiesbaden and Mainz, and the Rhine-Neckar region focusing on Mannheim and Ludwigshafen, the industrial area around Stuttgart, as well as the catchment areas of Bremen, Cologne, Dresden, Hamburg, Leipzig, Munich and Nuremberg/Fürth. These contrast with the thinly populated moorlands of the North German Plain, parts of the Eifel Mountains, the Bavarian Forest, the Upper Palatinate, the March of Brandenburg, and large parts of Mecklenburg-Western Pomerania.

The western part of Germany is much more densely populated than the five new states in the east, where only about a fifth of the population (16 million) live on roughly 30% of the national territory. Of the 19 cities with more than 300,000 inhabitants, three are in the eastern part of Germany.

Nearly a third of the population live in the 84 cities (of more than 100,000 inhabitants). They number about 26 million. But the great majority live in small towns and villages: nearly 7.5 million in municipalities with a population of less than 2,000, 47 million in towns with between 2,000 and 100,000 inhabitants.

The population in both the old and new federal states began to decline in the 70s because the birthrate was falling. In the west, however, there has been a slightly upward trend since 1990. With eleven births a year to ev-

Age structure of the population of Germany on 1 January 1994

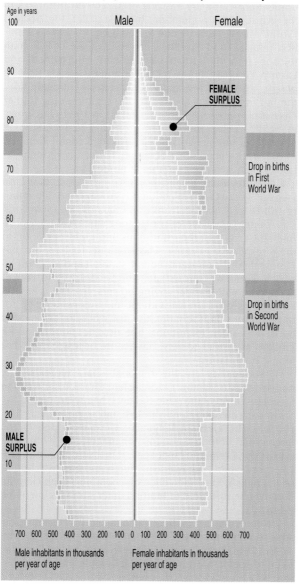

Age in years

Male   Female

FEMALE SURPLUS

Drop in births in First World War

Drop in births in Second World War

MALE SURPLUS

700 600 500 400 300 200 100 0 100 200 300 400 500 600 700

Male inhabitants in thousands per year of age

Female inhabitants in thousands per year of age

ery 1,000 inhabitants (in the Federal Republic prior to unification) Germany has one of the lowest birthrates in the world. The population increase after the Second World War was mainly due to immigration. Some 13 million refugees and expellees entered the present German territory from the former German eastern provinces and Eastern Europe. There was a continuous strong flow of people who fled from eastern to western Germany until the Berlin Wall was erected by the regime in the former German Democratic Republic (GDR) in 1961 which hermetically sealed the border. From the early 60s large numbers of foreign workers came to the Federal Republic of old whose expanding economy needed additional labour which was not available at home.

■ ■ ■ **Regional disparities.** Over the past thousand years or so the German nation has grown out of a number of tribes, such as the Franks and Saxons, Swabians and Bavarians. They have of course long since lost their original character, but their traditions and dialects live on in their respective regions. Those ethnic regions are not identical to the present federal states (Länder), most of which were only formed after the Second World War in agreement with the occupying powers. In most cases the boundaries were drawn without much consideration for old traditions. Furthermore, the flows of refugees and the massive postwar migrations, but also the mobility of the modern industrial society, have more or less blurred the ethnic boundaries.

What remains are the regional characteristics. The natives of Mecklenburg, for instance, are reserved, the Swabians thrifty, the Rhinelanders happy-go-lucky, the Saxons hardworking and shrewd, and so on.

■ ■ ■ **The German language**. German is one of the large group of Indo-Germanic languages, and within that one of the Germanic languages. It is thus related to Danish, Norwegian and Swedish, Dutch and Flemish, but also to English. The emergence of a common High German language is attributed to Martin Luther's translation of the Bible.

Germany has a wealth of dialects but it is usually possible to determine a person's native region. If, on the other hand, a Frisian or a Mecklenburger and a Bavarian were to speak in pure dialect they would have great difficulty understanding one another. Moreover, whilst the country was divided the two German states developed a different political vocabulary. New words were also coined which were not necessarily understood in the other part of the country. The common language was one of the links which held the divided nation together.

German is the native language of more than 100 million people. About one in every ten books published throughout the world has been written in German. As regards translations into foreign languages, German is third after English and French, while more works have been translated into German than into any other language.

■ ■ ■ **Integrated ethnic groups.** The Lusatian Sorbs are the descendants of Slavic tribes. They settled the territory east of the Elbe and Saale rivers in the 6th century in the course of the migration of peoples that occurred in the early centuries A.D. The first document in which they are mentioned dates from 631. In the 16th century, under the influence of the Reformation, a Sorbian written language evolved. During the flush of democratic aspira-

The largest cities

Population	City
3,465,700	Berlin
1,688,700	Hamburg
1,256,600	Munich
960,600	Cologne
668,900	Frankfurt a.M.
627,200	Essen
600,600	Dortmund
599,400	Stuttgart
578,100	Düsseldorf
554,200	Bremen
539,000	Duisburg
523,600	Hanover
500,100	Nuremberg
496,600	Leipzig
481,600	Dresden

tions in the 19th century, the Sorbs experienced a phase of national rebirth, yet at the time of the fascist dictatorship in our century, plans were made for their annihilation. Reunified Germany has committed itself to encouraging the Sorbian minority. In addition to the Institute for Sorbian Studies at the University of Leipzig, there are numerous schools, associations and other institutions devoted to the cultivation of the Sorbian language and culture.

The Frisians are the descendants of a Germanic tribe on the North Sea coast (between the Lower Rhine and the Ems River) and have preserved numerous traditions in addition to their own distinct language. A Danish minority lives in the Schleswig region of the state of Schleswig-Holstein, especially around the city of Flensburg.

■ ■ ■ **Foreign nationalities.** For years Chancellor Helmut Kohl has been saying that Germany is friendly towards foreigners. And quite rightly so, as the statistics prove. Of Germany's more than 80 million inhabitants 6.88 million are from abroad. They were all glad to come and stay in Germany. For decades there were no racial problems. The category of "guest workers", initially consisting of Italians, was extended to include Greeks and Spaniards, and then Portuguese, Yugoslavs and Turks. Occasional tensions within the community were far outweighed by the friendships made with neighbours and colleagues at work.

Integration within the European Union and the Western world, the dissolution of the Eastern bloc, and the immigration of people from Asian and African countries naturally meant a considerable increase in the number of foreigners of different colour in Germany.

The Turks, who number 1,918,000, have long been the largest foreign community, followed by people from the states which belonged to the former Yugoslavia, whose number, including war refugees, can only be roughly assessed at one million because of the many war refugees. Next are the Italians (563,000), Greeks (351,000), Poles (260,000), Austrians (186,000), Romanians (162,000) and Spaniards (133,000). Iranians, Portuguese, British, Americans and Dutch each number between 100,000 and 115,000, and the Bulgarians, Hungarians, and French each between 50,000 and 100,000. When

Demonstration condemning attacks on foreigners

speaking of foreigners we today think of people of non-European origin, the 95,000 Vietnamese, 82,000 Moroccans, 55,000 Lebanese, 46,000 Sri Lankans, 46,000 Afghans and 36,000 Indians. The 63,000 people from the former Soviet Union are more conspicuous in the eastern part of the country than in the west.

Nearly 50% of all foreigners have been living in Germany for ten years or more. Over two thirds of foreign children were born here. The Federal Republic has not only proved itself to be an open society by bringing in asylum-seekers and war refugees. It has always been a champion of free movement of labour within the European Community. Nearly two million German repatriates from the countries of the former East bloc, especially from the territory of the former Soviet Union, have come to the Federal Republic of Germany since 1987; in 1994 they numbered approximately 222,600. Germany's willingness to open her doors to foreigners who have been persecuted on political grounds compares favourably with that of other countries. The new article 16a of the Basic Law, like the previous article 16, still guarantees protection from political persecution in the form of an individual basic right. In 1992, for instance, Germany alone took in nearly 80% of all people seeking asylum in the whole of the European Community. In 1989 the number seeking asylum in Germany was 121,318; in 1991 the figure rose to 256,112, and then to 438,191 in 1992. At the same time the proportion of those who could be recognized as genuine victims of persecution fell to less than 5%. In 1993, up to the end of August, some 322,600 asylum-seekers entered Germany. Their number fell significantly when the new legislation on the right of asylum became effective on 1 July 1993: In 1994 only 127,210 people sought asylum.

Under the new legislation (which was carried by a two-thirds majority in parliament) the right of asylum has been focused on its true purpose (which is the normal state of affairs in other countries) of affording protection to those who actually have been persecuted on political grounds and really do need protection. As a result, foreigners who enter Germany from a safe third country may no longer invoke this basic right. Germany also reserves the right, notwithstanding the Geneva convention on refugees, to draw up a list of countries where, according to official sources of information, no one is subject to persecution so that there is, as a rule, no ground for asylum. Nonetheless, every person whose application for asylum has been rejected may appeal, if necessary right through to the Federal Constitutional Court.

■■ ■ **The country's debt to foreigners.** Germany owes a great deal to her foreign workers and businessmen. They have contributed largely to the country's economic growth and every year add some DM 100 billion to the country's gross national product. 40% of the workforce of some of Germany's world-famous companies, such as Siemens AG, are foreigners. Cooperation between German and foreign workmates is good and fosters mutual respect. Hence there are far fewer conflict situations at work than in neighbourhoods where sizeable ethnic communities have formed.

Attacks by Germans on foreigners prior to 1991 were recorded like all other crime statistics, including those by foreigners on Germans. It was only after the GDR became part of the Federal Republic that attacks on foreigners began to occur which focused not on the individual victim but on his identity as a "foreigner", irrespective of the person's actual nationality.

Various factors contributed to the increased violence. The growing number of foreigners who wrongly claimed to have been persecuted on political grounds in order to circumvent the immigration laws aroused much concern and anger among the population. Then there was the ostensibly nationalistic reflex action of many people in the former GDR to a Marxist-Leninist doctrine which had been imposed by the old regime and no longer had to be obeyed. And another obvious cause was the impression gained by some young people, in eastern Germany but also in the west, that they themselves were underprivileged in life and should take it out on foreigners (see also the chapter "Youth").

■■■ **Crime against foreigners.** In the autumn of 1991 foreigners and Germans alike were alarmed by the violence and firebomb attacks in Hoyerswerda, Saarlouis and other towns where it was all too easy for the perpetrators to commit their appalling crimes. To the dismay of the overwhelming majority of the population, their bad example was widely copied. Whereas in 1990, in the Federal Republic prior to unification, less than 200 attacks by right-wing extremists, not primarily against individuals, were registered, the number in 1991 was 1,483, and in the following year as many as 2,584 (1993: 1,737; 1994: 1,127). In this volatile atmosphere the membership of extremist parties of the right increased, which was first reflected in the Bremen and Schleswig-Holstein state elections where they were able to clear the 5% hurdle and enter parliament.

The tragic climax of the attacks on asylum-seekers, following the new wave of violence in Rostock, were the murders committed in Mölln in November 1992 and Solingen in May 1993. In those firebomb attacks eight Turkish women and children died. In both cases the offenders were young people. And in fact the majority who commit such crimes out of blind hatred are youngsters between the age of 12 and 20 acting alone.

Germany leaves no doubt that she condemns xenophobia, that she will resolutely prosecute and severely punish violent attacks, and that she will protect foreign residents and offer all those who stay permanently every chance to become integrated. The government has on many occasions declared its support for foreigners. The public have demonstrated their concern for the foreign members of the community in rallies and candlelight vigils (the one in Munich being the largest demonstration since the Second World War). The unions and the business community have organized many different activities to stress the solidarity of the workforce irrespective of nationality. Their action has counteracted a growing lack of confidence in German companies, products and services, especially in the United States.

■ ■ ■ **Promoting integration.** The federal and state governments will not be deterred by demonstrations of xenophobia from pursuing their long-term aims. They have in several instances made the laws less restrictive, thus making it easier for foreigners, and especially young people, who have lived in Germany for many years to become naturalized citizens. The Federal Government considers this to be the more consistent approach in comparison with the much-debated half-measures of allowing foreigners to vote in local government elections (a proposal which, by the way, was rejected by the Federal Constitutional Court in 1990) or a merging of the two fundamental principles of nationality, jus soli (place of birth) and jus sanguinis (lineage). And the law is very tolerant towards foreigners who wish merely to work in Germany but not to participate in the social and cultural life of the country by allowing them to practice their native customs and way of life.

The federal states

· Baden-Württemberg · The Free State of Bavaria · Berlin
· Brandenburg · The Free Hanseatic City of Bremen
· The Free and Hanseatic City of Hamburg · Hesse
· Mecklenburg-Western Pomerania · Lower Saxony
· North Rhine-Westphalia · Rhineland-Palatinate · Saarland
· The Free State of Saxony · Saxony-Anhalt
· Schleswig-Holstein · The Free State of Thuringia

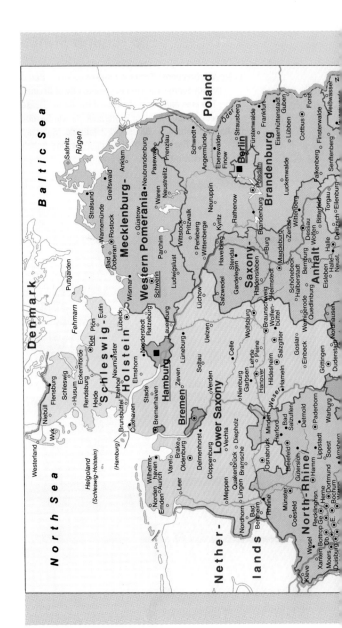

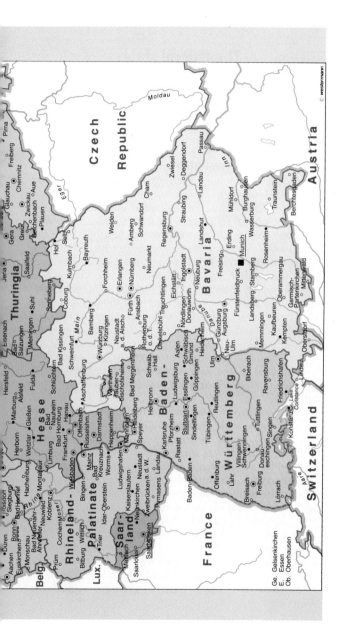

The federal states

The Federal Republic of Germany consists of 16 states known as "Länder": Baden-Württemberg (Stuttgart), Bavaria (Munich), Berlin, Brandenburg (Potsdam), Bremen, Hamburg, Hesse (Wiesbaden), Mecklenburg-Western Pomerania (Schwerin), Lower Saxony (Hanover), North Rhine-Westphalia (Düsseldorf), Rhineland-Palatinate (Mainz), Saarland (Saarbrücken), Saxony (Dresden), Saxony-Anhalt (Magdeburg), Schleswig-Holstein (Kiel) and Thuringia (Erfurt).

Germany has always been divided into states but the map has changed its shape over the centuries. The most important changes in the modern age resulted from the Napoleonic wars at the beginning of the 19th century, the Austro-Prussian War of 1866, and the First and Second World Wars. After the latter Germany was occupied and divided and the country's largest state, Prussia, dissolved. Most of the federal states as we know them today were established after 1945, but they have largely retained their ethnic traditions and characteristics and some of the old boundaries. Until Germany was reunited in 1990 the Federal Republic consisted of eleven states which had been created in the former Western occupation zones and had adopted democratic constitutions between 1946 and 1957.

In the Soviet-occupied zone, which later became the German Democratic Republic (GDR), five states were formed, partly along the traditional lines, but as early as 1952 this structure was smashed by the GDR regime and replaced by a centralized administration. Soon after the fall of the Wall on 9 November 1989 the people began to demand the restoration of those former states. Following the first free election in the former GDR on 18 March 1990, the parliament created five federal states.

Then, on 3 October 1990, the German Democratic Republic, and hence the states of Brandenburg, Mecklenburg-Western Pomerania, Saxony, Saxony-Anhalt and Thuringia, acceded to the Federal Republic of Germany. At the same time Berlin (East) was merged with Berlin (West).

State election 1992	
CDU	39.6 %
SPD	29.4 %
Republicans	10.9 %
Alliance 90 / The Greens	9.5 %
FDP/DVP	5.9 %

Population	10.2 million
Area	35,751 sq km
Capital	Stuttgart

Baden-Württemberg

■■ **Natural beauty, abundance of culture.** Baden-Württemberg has some of the country's most charming countryside. It embraces not only the Black Forest, a very popular recreational area in the Central Uplands, or Lake Constance, known locally as the "Swabian Sea", but also the green valleys of the Rhine and the Danube, the Neckar and the Tauber, the rugged Schwäbische Alb and the gentle Markgräflerland, all major holiday resorts. The different soil conditions are ideal for fruit, wine, asparagus and tobacco.

Not only blessed by nature, it is also an ideal crossroads for transport and communications which heightens its attractiveness to tourists and industry. The inventiveness and business sense of the people are proverbial, and their intellectual and artistic achievements fill many a chapter of German cultural and literary history, as testified by such names as the writers Friedrich Schiller (1759-1805) and Friedrich Hölderlin (1770-1843) or the philosophers Georg Wilhelm Friedrich Hegel (1770-1831) and Martin Heidegger (1889-1976). The central Neckar region with the state capital Stuttgart (population 599,400) is Baden-Württemberg's industrial and cultural centre. Mannheim's Kunsthalle and Reiss-Museum are outstanding landmarks. The minsters of Ulm and Freiburg are monuments to southern Germany's architectural pre-eminence. Heidelberg's castle and the old city centre attract visitors from all over the world. And the Black Forest's traditional cuckoo clocks are not confined to the Clock Museum in Furtwangen but taken to all corners of the globe by tourists.

■■ **Cars and microchips.** Baden-Württemberg is a highly industrialized region and thus, in economic terms,

Stuttgart's Neues Schloss and Jubiläumssäule

one of Germany's most powerful states. Precision engineering, which is concentrated in the Black Forest of
cuckoo-clock fame, and the automotive industry have
the longest tradition.

Traditional crafts and modern industry are the back-
bone of the economy. In and around Stuttgart are to be
found the headquarters of such world-famous firms as
Daimler-Benz, Bosch, IBM, SEL and the sports car manufacturer Porsche. Here, as everywhere else in Baden-
Württemberg, there is a highly organized network of
small and medium-sized firms who supply state-of-the-
art parts and equipment to the big companies.

Adjacent to the central Neckar industrial region are
Karlsruhe (279,000) with its oil refineries, Mannheim
(318,000) and Heidelberg (136,000), which make buses
and printing machinery respectively, but also Freiburg
(189,000) and Ulm (106,000) with their extensive service
industries. When Germany was reunited Baden-
Württemberg began to establish close ties, not only in the
economic sphere, with the new state of Saxony, which is
similar in structure.

The tower of Freiburg's Minster

■ ■ ■ **Science and research**. Among Baden-Württemberg's numerous academic and scientific institutions is the Nuclear Research Centre at Karlsruhe, the German Cancer Research Centre in Heidelberg, as well as several Max Planck Institutes and nine universities. Heidelberg University, founded in 1386, is the oldest in Germany, whereas Karlsruhe is home to Germany's oldest technical college. That city is also the seat of Germany's supreme courts, the Federal Court of Justice and the Federal Constitutional Court.

State election 1994	
CSU	52.8 %
SPD	30.1 %
Alliance 90 / The Greens	6.1 %

Population	11.8 million
Area	70,554 sq km
Capital	Munich

The Free State of Bavaria

■ ■ ■ **A white-and-blue tradition with a future.** Bavaria is by far the largest of Germany's states and has the longest political tradition, there having been a Bavarian tribal dukedom as early as the 6th century. Bavaria owes much of its reputation as a tourist's paradise to its cultural heritage and captivating landscapes. Germany's most popular holiday destination, this state offers the Alps, with the country's highest mountain the Zugspitze (2,962 m), the picturesque lakes in the hilly Alpine foreland, the Bavarian Forest with the first German national park, and the valleys of the Danube and Main and their tributaries, a region of beautiful scenery and towns through which passes the "Romantic Route". In former times Munich was the rural capital of Germany's largest farming area. After the Second World War it enjoyed calling itself "Germany's secret capital" and became the focal point of a rapidly growing industrial region (automobiles and aircraft, electrical engineering and electronics industry, insurance and publishing). And with its university and other institutions of higher education, the Max Planck Institute and its nuclear reactor, Bavaria's capital (population 1.25 million) is also a major academic and research centre. In 1992 Munich opened a new international airport named after the late Franz-Josef Strauss, Bavaria's long-serving minister-president.

■ ■ ■ **Industry and agriculture.** Nuremberg (500,100) lies at the intersection of Europe's future motorway network stretching from Naples to Stockholm and from Lisbon via Prague to Warsaw. Together with Fürth and Erlangen, Nuremberg forms an industrial agglomeration focusing on engineering and the electrical and toy industries (Siemens, Quelle, Grundig). Nuremberg's annual International Toy Fair is the most important of its kind.

Augsburg (264,000) is home to the engineering and textile industries. Regensburg (121,000) has a young electrical and an even younger automobile industry (BMW). Ingolstadt, too, is a car manufacturing centre (Audi). East Bavaria's glassworks (Zwiesel) and porcelain factories (Rosenthal, Hutschenreuther) carry on the region's famous crafts. Large parts of Bavaria, especially the Alps and the Alpine foothills, are still mainly farming areas. The region's Franconian wines are highly rated by connoisseurs. There are also hundreds of breweries producing Bavaria's famous beer, which flows in abundance at, for instance, Munich's Oktoberfest.

■ ■ ■ **Culture from all ages**. Regensburg has retained most of its medieval townscape. Nuremberg,

Stone bridge, Salzstadl and St. Peter's Cathedral, Regensburg

the city of Albrecht Dürer (1471-1528), has some of the finest examples of late medieval treasures in its churches and museums, whereas Augsburg has the purest Renaissance heritage. The churches in the Banz and Ettal monasteries, Vierzehnheiligen, and Steingaden's "Wieskirche", which appears in UNESCO's list of world cultural assets, as well as Würzburg, former residence of the prince-bishops, are outstanding examples of baroque and rococo architecture.

In Munich we find not only Germany's largest university but also the Deutsches Museum, the world's biggest exhibition of science and technology. The city also boasts numerous historic buildings, famous art galleries and theatres. The Herrenchiemsee, Linderhof and Neu-

The Olympic area, Munich

Construction Machinery Trade Fair (bauma), Munich

schwanstein castles, built by the "fairy-tale king" Ludwig II in the 19th century, are tourist magnets. So, too, are the towns of Rothenburg ob der Tauber, Nördlingen and Dinkelsbühl with their traditional half-timber houses. Music lovers, too, are well catered for in Bavaria, for instance at the annual Richard Wagner Festival in Bayreuth. Richard Wagner lived there from 1872 to 1883.

State election 1990	
CDU	40.4 %
SPD	30.4 %
PDS	9.3 %
FDP	7.1 %
Alternative List*	5.0 %
Alliance 90 / The Greens**	4.4 %

Population	3.5 million
Area	889 sq km
Capital	Berlin

Berlin

■ ■ ■ **A city with a turbulent past.** For decades Berlin was the symbol of Germany's division and a flashpoint in the Cold War between the victorious Western powers and the Soviet Union. In 1948 only the unforgettable airlift enabled the people of Berlin (West) to survive an 11-month Soviet blockade of the city. Aircraft of the U.S. Air Force, supported by the British and French Allies, kept the people of Berlin (West) supplied with vital necessities.

In the 50s the three Western sectors and Berlin (East) grew more and more apart. The city's partition seemed to be cemented forever when the GDR began to build that infamous wall on 13 August 1961. With his famous call "Ich bin ein Berliner" in front of Schöneberg Town Hall on 26 June 1993, U.S. President John F. Kennedy endorsed his support for the city and its people. Among Berlin's governing mayors are such famous names as Ernst Reuter, Willy Brandt and Richard von Weizsäcker. And on 12 June 1987 U.S. President Ronald Reagan, in a speech near the Brandenburg Gate, appealed to the Soviet Union to "tear down this wall". The wall was indeed opened – on 9 November 1989 – in the wake of the peaceful revolution in the GDR. That was the city's chance to make a new start.

■ ■ ■ **Germany's capital and a European cultural centre.** Prior to its spiritual and cultural decline under the National Socialist dictatorship, and prior to the destruction caused by the Second World War, Berlin was not only the hub of German industry but, in the "golden twenties", also one of Europe's cultural capitals. Berlin boasts three opera houses (Deutsche Oper, Deutsche

* The Alternative List stood in West Berlin only.
**The Alliance 90/The Greens stood in East Berlin only.

The Gendarme Market with the Schauspielhaus,

French Cathedral and Huguenot Museum

Staatsoper Unter den Linden, Komische Oper), several major orchestras and dozens of theatres, and it continues to be one of the world's greatest museum cities. The leading newspapers are "Berliner Morgenpost", "Berliner Zeitung" and "Der Tagesspiegel". The national newspaper "Die Welt" has its editorial headquarters in Berlin. The university in the eastern part of the city is named after the von Humboldt brothers, Wilhelm (1767-1835), the scholar and politician, and Alexander (1769-1859), a famous naturalist and traveller. In the western part are the Free University and the Technical University, both founded in 1948. Berlin also has many famous research establishments, such as the Hahn Meitner Institute of Nuclear Physics, the Heinrich Hertz Institute of Communications Technology, and the Prussian Cultural Heritage Foundation.

The future seat of the Federal Government continues to grow, and it is estimated that the metropolitan area's present population of roughly 3.5 million will almost double by the year 2000. Great efforts are being made to modernize the city's transport systems (roads, city and underground railways, ferries, airports) without destroying its many parks, woods and lakes.

Berlin is still one of Europe's largest industrial centres, focusing mainly on engineering, food and beverages,

View over the Victory Column and Tiergarten
towards the eastern part of Berlin

The Brandenburg Gate, symbol of German unity

pharmaceuticals, textiles and especially electrical goods. Two world-famous companies were established there in the 19th century: Siemens AG and AEG. With Berlin as their base they have successfully coped with the transition to the information age.

The reunited city faces tremendous challenges. The people in both parts of Berlin, having lived for decades under different political systems, are now growing accustomed to one another again and the economic disparity is being overcome. Hundreds of thousands of flats, especially in the eastern districts, are being brought up to standard. Unification has sparked an economic boom, but the measures needed to link the two parts together, to develop and modernize the future seat of government and to accommodate the rapidly growing population demand creativity, investment and enterprise. German and foreign investors have meanwhile acquired large plots of land at Potsdamer Platz, which had remained derelict since the Second World War. Planning for the new government quarter in the Spreebogen is well advanced.

State election 1994	
SPD	54.1 %
CDU	18.7 %
PDS	18.7 %

Population	2.5 million
Area	29,056 sq km
Capital	Potsdam

Brandenburg

■ ■ ■ **The legacy of Frederick II.** The state of Brandenburg encircles the German capital. Just outside Berlin lies
the state capital of Potsdam (140,000), venue of the Potsdam Conference where, in the summer of 1945, the leaders of the United States, the United Kingdom and the Soviet Union took decisions which greatly affected the future of conquered Germany. Potsdam had been deliberately chosen for the conference because of its close association with Prussian-German history, King Frederick II
(1712-1786) having made it his residence. Frederick's architectural masterpieces in Potsdam, especially those in
the beautiful park of Sanssouci, outlived Prussia's existence as a state. It was there that the enlightened mon-
arch held philosophical discussions with his friends, who
included Voltaire (1694-1778). And there he also received other famous guests such as Johann Sebastian
Bach (1685-1750). On 17 August 1991 the coffin of Frederick II, which had been hidden during the Second World
War and moved to the ancestral seat of the Hohenzollern
dynasty in Hechingen (Baden-Württemberg) in 1952, was
brought back to Sanssouci.

■ ■ ■ **Dutchmen and Huguenots.** For a long time thinly
populated Brandenburg remained economically underdeveloped. In order to rectify this situation its rulers
opened the borders to large numbers of foreigners in the
17th and 18th centuries.

Dutch immigrants as well as Protestants who had been
expelled from France and Bohemia brought their knowledge and skills and played a major part in the region's
advancement. We are still reminded of this by such
names as the "Dutch Quarter" and the "French Church"
in Potsdam.

The courtyard of the Cecilienhof, Potsdam

The countryside around Berlin was impressively de-scribed by Theodor Fontane (1819-1898), a descendant of French Huguenots, in his famous "Walks in the March of Brandenburg".

■ ■ ■ **Steel and rye.** Brandenburg is the largest of the new German states. Industry and service enterprises are among the most important branches of its economy. The industrial centres are around Eisenhüttenstadt (steel) and Cottbus, where lignite mines provide the raw materials for the chemical industry and energy. A significant percentage of the workforce is employed in mechanical engineering and in the automotive industry. Mercedes-Benz has a truck assembly works in Ludwigsfelde to the south of Berlin; it plans to invest DM 1 billion there. Frankfurt an der Oder is known for its electrical engineering and appliance construction industries.

35% of the total area of the state is forest (mainly fir). Major crops are rye, wheat, oilseed, potatoes and sugar beets and, in a belt around Berlin and in the Oderbruch near Frankfurt an der Oder, fruits and vegetables. Increasing numbers of tourists are attracted to Brandenburg's rugged but nonetheless charming landscape of forests and lakes.

Boat trips in the Spreewald are popular with tourists

The old (1508-1811) and new (since 1991) university town of Frankfurt an der Oder is acquiring a new significance as a distribution port for Eastern Europe now that visas are no longer required for travel between Germany and Poland. Since 1991 a German-Polish intergovernmental commission for regional and transborder cooperation has been promoting good-neighbourly contacts in the Euro-regions of "Viadrina" and "Spree-Neisse-Bobr".

Brandenburg sees good prospects of sharing in Berlin's economic boom. In April 1995 the two states of Brandenburg and Berlin resolved to merge to form one federal state around the year 2000; the capital will be Potsdam. In the spring of 1996 the inhabitants of both states will vote on the merger.

State election 1995	
SPD	33.4 %
CDU	32.6 %
Alliance 90 / The Greens	13.0 %
Work for Bremen	10.7 %

Population	684,000
Area	404 sq km
Capital	Bremen

The Free Hanseatic City of Bremen

■■■ **The two-city state.** Two cities, one state: Bremen and Bremerhaven are 65 km apart but nonetheless belong together. They constitute the smallest German state in terms of both area and population. Yet this Free Hanseatic City of Bremen is, next to Bavaria, the oldest body politic in Germany and, after San Marino, the second oldest city republic in the world.

Bremen is also many centuries older than Bremerhaven. Founded as a bishopric in 787, it quickly flourished, thanks to the privileges bestowed upon it as a market town. In the 11th century it was described as the "Rome of the North". In 1358 Bremen became a member of the Hanseatic League, which dominated trade in the North and Baltic Seas until well into the 16th century.

■■■ **Risk and win.** "Outside and in, risk and win", is the motto which tells of this city's growth and affluence. In 1827, when it seemed that the river Weser would be silted up, Mayor Smidt founded a new port at the mouth of the Weser and named it Bremerhaven, which, together with adjacent townships, grew into a city.

Bremerhaven handles mostly (about 60%) container traffic and since 1983 has had the largest container terminal in the world. Bremen almost has a monopoly of imports of tea and coffee, tobacco and cotton.

Bremen has made itself less dependent on maritime trade and shipbuilding by developing a highly productive aerospace industry. It has also resumed car production and is making its mark in the electronics sector and in the food and beverage industry. Bremerhaven is the focal point of German polar research. Also afloat there are the old barges and men-o'-war of the German Maritime Museum.

Maritime Museum and Columbus Quay, Bremerhaven

■ ■ ■ **Bremen's "parlour".** On the market place stands the Gothic cathedral of St. Peter and the magnificent Renaissance town hall with its very hospitable wine cellar. In front of it is Roland's column (1404), symbol of the city's freedom and a local landmark, like the nearby "town musicians", a statue of the animals in a Grimm's fairy tale. From the market square the visitor enters the Böttcherstrasse, a narrow street of shops and museums built on the initiative of the merchant Ludwig Roselius in 1924-1931. It is a brick monument to Bremen's civic spirit. Every year, on the second Friday in February, Bremen's maritime community holds its traditional "Schaffermahlzeit" in the Rathaus. Distinguished public figures are invited.

State election 1993	
SPD	40.4 %
CDU	25.1 %
GAL	13.5 %
STATT	5.6 %

Population	1.7 million
Area	755 sq km
Capital	Hamburg

The Free and Hanseatic City of Hamburg

■ ■ ■ **Germany's gateway to the world.** Hamburg is Germany's principal seaport and largest overseas trade and transshipment centre as exemplified by the fact that some 130 Japanese and more than 20 Chinese trading companies are represented there. The port's industrial area encompasses shipyards, refineries and processing plants for raw materials from abroad. In addition to these port-related activities, the aerospace, electronics, precision engineering, optical and chemical industries play an increasingly important role in this city-state.

Hamburg began to flourish as a commercial town in 1189, when it was granted customs and commercial rights. One of the first members of the Hanseatic League, it soon became the main transshipment port between the North Sea and the Baltic Sea. In 1460, and then finally in 1510, Hamburg was raised to the status of an imperial city – an autonomous status it has retained to this day. However, the devastating fire of 1842 and the Second World War spared but few of this commercial centre's medieval buildings.

■ ■ ■ **A green industrial city.** Hamburg is Germany's second largest industrial centre and the hub of an economic area with a population of 2.8 million. Nonetheless, the spacious parks (e.g. "Planten un Blomen") and gardens, woodlands, moors and heaths have retained its character as one of Germany's "greenest cities". As a result of Germany's unification, the port of Hamburg, with its ramified links with the waterway network, has regained its old hinterland. This enhances the city-state's prospects of becoming the hub of trade, services and communications between east and west as in former times. Hamburg is also the banking and service centre for northern Germany. The fact that it is the world's principal consular city after New York underscores its international status. The Congress Centre, venue for many international exhibitions, is one of the most modern conference centres in Europe.

Hamburg's role as a media city is uncontested. It is home to Germany's largest periodicals, the German Press Agency (dpa), and various television and radio networks and studios.

■ ■ ■ **Civic pride and passion for art.** Hamburg has always been an attractive cultural city as well. It was here that Germany's first permanent opera house was established in 1678, where George Frideric Handel (1685-1759) staged his first opera ("Almira"). One of the city's famous sons was the composer Johannes Brahms (1833-1897). In 1767 the Deutsches Nationaltheater was founded. It was linked with the name of Lessing and achieved fame chiefly on account of its performances of Shakespeare. At that time Friedrich Gottlieb Klopstock (1724-1803) and Matthias Claudius (1740-1815) were Hamburg's "literary institutions".

In the present century Rolf Liebermann, director of Hamburg's opera house, and Gustaf Gründgens, the actor, gave to opera and the theatre respectively a strong

Assembling the Airbus A321 in Hamburg

Cargo being transshipped in containers

international flavour with their avant-garde productions. Unforgotten is the Hamburg-born actor Hans Albers (1891-1960), especially for his film role as Baron "Münchhausen". Today the city is also host to musical productions, such as Andrew Lloyd Webber's "Phantom of the Opera", for which a new theatre ("Neue Flora") was specially built. Public generosity stemming from civic pride, and a far-sighted buying policy, have given Hamburg's Kunsthalle, Museum für Kunst und Gewerbe, and Völkerkundemuseum, to name only three, outstanding collections.

State election 1995	
CDU	39.2 %
SPD	38.0 %
Alliance 90 / The Greens	11.2 %
FDP	7.5 %

Population	5.9 million
Area	21,114 sq km
Capital	Wiesbaden

Hesse

■ ■ ■ **The Rhine-Main crossroads.** The central location of
Hesse in the Federal Republic of Germany prior to the
country's unification was a boon to its biggest city Frankfurt am Main (668,900), Germany's main financial centre, and to its industrial fairs. This city is a huge autobahn
intersection and railway junction, and it has the vast (17
sq km) Rhine-Main Airport which is the largest cargo and
second largest passenger airport in Europe. Frankfurt on
the river Main is the seat of many major German and foreign banks as well as the seat of the European Monetary
Institute. It is also the headquarters of the Bundesbank,
which guards the stability of the Deutsche Mark.

■ ■ ■ **Industry and beaux arts.** The Rhine-Main region
is, with Berlin, Germany's second largest industrial centre after the Rhine-Ruhr district. It is home to such firms
as Hoechst, Opel and Degussa. Other major industries
(machinery, locomotives and wagons, automobiles) have
established themselves in the northern part of the state
around Kassel. This city has an excellent reputation
among art lovers owing to its excellent collections of
Dutch paintings and its "documenta", the largest exhibition of contemporary art in the world. Southern Hesse is
home to the leather industry (Offenbach). This region's
centre is Darmstadt with its famous Technical University.
From 1899 the Mathildenhöhe (Art Nouveau museum in
the Ernst Ludwig Haus) developed into the city's artists'
colony.

Frankfurt am Main, the birthplace of Johann Wolfgang
von Goethe (1749-1832), is also a city of art, theatre and
publishing. The river Main's "museum embankment" is
constantly growing. Also new in the city centre are the
"Schirn" art gallery (1986) and the Museum of Modern

Art (1991). The International Book Fair, at which the Peace Prize of the German Book Trade is awarded annually, is the largest of its kind in the world.

Amidst charming landscapes are the university towns of Marburg and Giessen, as well as Wetzlar, famous for its optical instruments. The Bergstrasse and the Rhinegau are among Germany's best fruit and wine-growing areas. In eastern Hesse is the bishopric of Fulda, a baroque town of considerable historical importance. The state capital Wiesbaden (268,000) is not only an administrative centre but also an elegant spa with a much-frequented casino.

■■■ **Republican tradition.** Hesse has existed in its present form only since 1945. In previous centuries it had

The Mathildenhöhe and Wedding Tower, Darmstadt

A landscape in the Taunus, looking towards Walsdorf

nearly always been split up into small principalities. It became a focal point in the 16th century, when Landgrave Philipp the Magnanimous became one of the political leaders of the Reformation. Frankfurt was for a long time a free imperial city and the place where German emperors were crowned. The city's St. Paul's Church has become a national monument. It was there in 1848 and 1849 that the National Assembly convened, the first democratic German parliament. It failed, however, because of the power wielded by Germany's ruling princes.

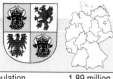

State election 1994		Population	1.89 million
CDU	37.7 %	Area	23,559 sq km
SPD	29.5 %	Capital	Schwerin
PDS	22.7 %		

Mecklenburg-Western Pomerania

■ ■ ■ **Land of a thousand lakes.** Perhaps no other German state is as rural, no other has such a varied coastline, and no other is as thinly populated as Mecklenburg-Western Pomerania. Its greatest treasure is its untouched nature and "thousand lakes".

Its striking brick architecture bears the unmistakable characteristics of the Hanseatic trade centres Stralsund and Wismar, and of the old university towns of Greifswald (founded in 1456) and Rostock. Rostock, an old Hanseatic town, is today the state's largest city (240,000). However, it is Schwerin (130,000) which became the state capital after Germany's unification.

Schwerin's Stadtschloss is now the seat of the state parliament

■ ■ ■ **Nature and art.** Mecklenburg-Western Pomerania is a gently undulating region with hundreds of lakes, a patchwork of fields, woods and livestock enclosures. Mecklenburg's largest lake is the Müritz (117 sq km), which has an extensive nature reserve along its eastern shore. Throughout the region there are some 260 protected areas. There are countless testimonies to its rich cultural history and many of them, such as Schwerin's castle with its 300 towers, are being renovated.

A big attraction are the chalk cliffs of Rügen, Germany's largest island (926 sq km). Caspar David Friedrich (1774-1840), the painter from Greifswald, captured the seascapes with romantic exuberance. The writer Fritz Reuter (1810-1874) vividly described the area and its people in his low German idiom. The sculptor and writer Ernst Barlach (1870-1938) spent his productive period in Güstrow. And Uwe Johnson (1934-1984) erected with his

The container section of the port of Rostock

The chalk cliffs of Rügen, a wonder of nature

novels a literary monument to his native region and its people.

■ ■ ■ **Tourism, the industry of tomorrow.** Agriculture has traditionally been an important branch of the economy. Another permanent source of employment is the fisheries industry, which is currently being rapidly modernized and adapted to changing consumer demand. The coastal area is a location of Germany's shipbuilding industry and its ancillary suppliers, which now, after privatization, have good prospects for the future. But the most promising industry is tourism. In 1992 Mecklenburg-Western Pomerania had about ten million visitors. Rambling and biking are extremely popular. The region is striving to develop its tourist infrastructure, but planners want to make sure that this constantly growing industry does not become a burden on the environment.

State election 1994	
SPD	44.3 %
CDU	36.4 %
Alliance 90 / The Greens	7.4%

Population	7.6 million
Area	47,351 sq km
Capital	Hanover

Lower Saxony

■ ■ ■ **A variegated landscape.** The second largest state in Germany (47,351 sq km) can be subdivided into three main regions: the Harz, the Weserbergland (Weser Highlands) and the North German Lowlands around the Lüneburg Heath. A world to themselves are the moors of the Emsland, the marshland behind the North Sea dikes, and the East Frisian islands in the shallow coastal waters.

The major north-south and west-east autobahn and railway arteries intersect in Lower Saxony, and here, too, the Elbe Canal links up the Rhine, Elbe and Oder, the principal waterways of Western and Eastern Europe.

■ ■ ■ **Mining tradition and Volkswagen.** Nearly two thirds of this region is given over to farming. There is a wide-ranging food industry which produces such famous delicacies as bacon from the Oldenburg area or honey from the Lüneburg Heath. It also has a long mining tradition, especially in the Harz. Even in medieval times the imperial town of Goslar owed its wealth to silver mining. In 1775 a school for miners and foundry workers was established in Clausthal which developed into a world-famous mining college. Lüneburg gained prominence because of local salt deposits, and the potash industry is a major branch of Lower Saxony's economy. Salzgitter is the centre of Europe's third largest iron-ore deposit. Significant quantities of local oil and gas are also extracted, providing about 5% of the country's requirements. Brunswick is home to the Federal Institute of Physics and Metrology, the national authority for the testing, standardization and licensing of materials. It also determines the exact Central European Time (CET) per radio signal. Emden has Germany's third largest port on the North Sea.

Famous companies produce container vessels and automobiles there.

But one town in Lower Saxony epitomizes car manufacturing in Germany: Wolfsburg, home of the famous Volkswagen. Volkswagen AG is the biggest company in the region and the Volkswagen Foundation the largest non-governmental foundation for the promotion of science and scholarship in Germany.

■ ■ ■ **Hanover and the industrial fair, Göttingen and its university.** Half a million of this state's 7.6 million inhabitants live in the capital, Hanover. It is the venue for the world-famous industrial fair and the "CeBIT" exhibition of communications technology. Every year they show the present generation the world of tomorrow. Hanover is now looking forward to hosting the World Exhibition in the year 2000.

The university town of Göttingen has played an outstanding role in the country's political and scientific history. In 1837 a group of professors, the "Göttingen Seven", protested against the sovereign's decision to annul

The Lüneburg Heath, an attractive recreational area

The Hanover Fair is the largest industrial fair in the world

the constitution. For this they were dismissed, but most of these liberal spirits met again in 1848 as deputies to the National Assembly in Frankfurt. Another famous name associated with Göttingen is that of the mathematician and astronomer Carl Friedrich Gauss (1771-1859).

In the 20th century Göttingen has been a source of major developments in the field of nuclear physics. Of all those who taught or studied in Göttingen one need only mention the Nobel Prize winners Max Born (1882-1970) and Werner Heisenberg (1901-1976).

State election 1995	
SPD	46.0 %
CDU	37.7 %
Alliance 90 / The Greens	10.0 %

Population	17.7 million
Area	34,070 sq km
Capital	Düsseldorf

North Rhine-Westphalia

■ ■ ■ **A powerhouse in the heart of Europe.** The present state of North Rhine-Westphalia was formed in 1946, when the British, who occupied the region after the war, merged the greater part of the former Prussian Rhine province and the province of Westphalia with the state of Lippe-Detmold. North Rhine-Westphalia covers an area of approximately 34,000 sq km and is thus as large as Belgium and Luxembourg together. Not only is it the most populated state in the Federal Republic (over 17 million), it is also Europe's largest conurbation. About half of this region's population live in cities with more than 500,000 inhabitants. The Ruhr district is an a huge web of towns and cities with a total population of about 7.5 million, and it is Europe's largest industrial region. With its 31 giant power stations the Ruhr is Germany's main source of energy.

■ ■ ■ **Tradition and innovation.** In a massive effort on the part of industry, the state and the Federal Government over many years, North Rhine-Westphalia has succeeded in restructuring its economy, which has traditionally been based on coal and steel, to meet world market demand. Hundreds of thousands of new jobs have been created through the settlement of innovative industries, with the result that today it is the future-oriented branches alongside such internationally famous companies as Klöckner-Humboldt-Deutz AG, the world's largest engine manufacturer, that dominate the scene. Proof of the state's economic vitality is the fact that, apart from heavy industry, there are 450,000 small and medium-sized firms, many of them with state-of-the-art technology, for instance those making cloth in Krefeld or cutlery in Solingen. A traditional yet expanding branch of the ser-

vice sector is that of insurance, while Dortmund is the location of Germany's largest breweries. The northern parts
concentrate on farming and animal husbandry, while the
Münsterland is famous for horse breeding and riding. The
most visible sign of North Rhine-Westphalia's dynamic
economy is the dense network of autobahns, railways
and waterways. It incorporates Europe's traffic arteries
and links together the region's principal cities of Cologne, Essen, Dortmund, Düsseldorf, Duisburg, Bochum,
Wuppertal, Bielefeld, Leverkusen and Aachen. Duisburg
has the largest inland port in the world.

■ ■ ■ **Leisure, culture and higher education.** This coal
mining region is undergoing a transformation. Former

Bonn's baroque city hall

The gothic cathedral is Cologne's landmark

landscapes of smoking chimney stacks and conveyor belts are being turned into green areas and the open-cast mining areas on the Rhine recultivated. The Sauerland and the Bergisches Land are popular recreational areas, particularly for people in the Rhine and Ruhr district. North Rhine-Westphalia has 44 spas. Cologne, now the state's largest city (960,600) and a major centre since Roman times, is famous for its romanesque churches and gothic cathedral, but also for its museums (Wallraf-Richartz-Museum / Museum Ludwig, Roman-Germanic Museum, and many more). Düsseldorf (578,100), the state capital, is one of the country's main financial centres. It has made its name as a cultural city through its outstanding collections of paintings, its Deutsche Oper am Rhein (Düsseldorf/Duisburg), and its famous Schauspielhaus. Münster in Westphalia, with a most attractive city centre, has a major university. South of Cologne lies Bonn, until 1949 a medium-sized university town, but from that year until the country's unification capital of the Federal Republic of Germany. Although the seat of the Federal Government, too, is to be switched to Berlin, Bonn will continue to play an important role as an administrative and scientific centre.

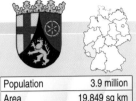

State election 1991	
SPD	44.8 %
CDU	38.7 %
FDP	6.9 %
Alliance 90 / The Greens	6.5 %

Population	3.9 million
Area	19,849 sq km
Capital	Mainz

Rhineland-Palatinate

■ ■ ■ **More than sagas and vineyards.** Rhineland-Palatinate was formed in 1946 from parts of Bavarian, Hessian and Prussian territory which previously had never belonged together. In the meantime they have become closely knit and Rhineland-Palatinate has acquired its own identity. Initially one of the poorer regions, it is today the state with the largest export quota and headquarters of Europe's biggest chemical corporation, BASF in Ludwigshafen, and Europe's most extensive TV and radio network, ZDF (Channel Two), based in Mainz. Every year seven million visitors to Rhineland-Palatinate seek recreation or curative treatment in such spas as Bad Neuenahr, Bad Ems or Bad Bertrich. Many of the region's mineral waters gush from springs in the volcanic rocks of the Central Uplands. The vineyards on the Rhine, the Ahr and the Mosel yield two thirds of the country's wine. Extensive forests are a major source of employment.

■ ■ ■ **Yesterday and today.** The Rhineland was settled by Celts, Romans, Burgundians and Franks. In Speyer, Worms and Mainz, all on the Rhine, are to be found the great imperial cathedrals of the Middle Ages. The elector of Mainz was arch chancellor of the "Holy Roman Empire of the German Nation". Worms has Germany's oldest synagogue (construction of which began in 1034 in the romanesque style). It was in Worms, too, at the imperial diet of 1521, that the reformer Martin Luther refused to recant his theses. Three hundred years later, in Koblenz, the liberal paper "Rheinischer Merkur" opposed Napoleonic rule and censorship of the press, and Hambach Castle was the scene of the first democratic-republican assembly in Germany (1832). The world-famous Gutenberg Museum in Mainz displays the treasures of Johannes

Gutenberg (1400-1468), the inventor of book-printing using movable characters. His epoch-making achievement was the breakthrough for Luther's Reformation. Trier is the birthplace of another kind of revolutionary, Karl Marx (1818-1883), the philosopher and critic of the "Political Economy".

■ ■ ■ **The Rhine, the state's main artery.** The 290 km section of the river Rhine passing through or bordering Rhineland-Palatinate is the state's main economic artery. On it lie the three main cities: Ludwigshafen (158,000),

Merl on the Mosel River with the former church tower

*BASF in Ludwigshafen is the largest
chemical industry complex in Europe*

the chemical centre, Mainz (175,000), the state capital,
and Koblenz (107,000), the service centre at the conflu-
ence of the Rhine and the Mosel. With a population of
just under 100,000 are Kaiserslautern, where Emperor
Frederick I (Barbarossa) built a castle in 1152, and Trier,
the 2,000-year-old city on the Mosel. One of Germany's
most beautiful landscapes is the stretch of the Rhine valley between Bingen and Bonn. With its many castles it is
steeped in legend and its praises have been sung by
countless poets, painters and musicians. The Rhine's tributaries, too, the Mosel, Nahe, Lahn and Ahr, have a
charm of their own. At the foot of the Palatinate Forest
runs the "German Wine Route". The unusual light above
this lovely hilly area was captured by the painter Max
Slevogt (1868-1932). Many of his pictures are to be found
in Ludwigshöhe Palace near Edenkoben. Some are also to
be found, together with works by Hans Purrmann (1880-
1966), who was ostracized by the National Socialist regime, in the Federal Chancellery in Bonn.

State election 1994	
SPD	49.4 %
CDU	38.6 %
Alliance 90 / The Greens	5.5 %

Population	1.1 million
Area	2,570 sq km
Capital	Saarbrücken

Saarland

■ ■ ■ **Good-neighbourly relations.** The political evolution of this by far the smallest of Germany's states (apart from the city-states) mirrors the vicissitudes of German history in the 20th century.

This coal and steel region was detached from the German Reich in 1920 and placed under the administration of the League of Nations. In 1935 the population voted with a large majority in favour of its return to Germany. The same happened after the Second World War. The Saar was again severed from Germany, and again it was returned after a referendum, this time as a state of the Federal Republic of Germany. France's agreement to this referendum is a landmark in the process of Franco-German reconciliation. The reintegration of the Saarland on 1 January 1957 was effected in accordance with article 23 of the Basic Law (constitution) – an unprecedented step which was to serve as a model for German unification in 1990.

■ ■ ■ **City, state and river.** This state takes its name from the Saar River, a tributary of the Mosel. The Saar Canal between Dillingen and Konz on the Mosel makes it a major waterway for large vessels. The Saar meanders charmingly through the forested Hunsrück range of the Central Uplands. Its lower reaches are a wine-growing area. The state capital, Saarbrücken (192,000), is a trade fair and congress centre. It is a symbiosis of the French and German way of life. The Saarlanders have a partiality for culinary delights and wine. A native of the city, the director Max Ophüls (1902-1957), made film history with such charming comedies as "Liebelei". The Saarland's higher education institutions, among them the university, the art college and the music academy, are concentrated in the city and many students come from neighbouring France.

The name of the state's second largest city, Saarlouis, reminds us that here, about 300 years ago, the French King Louis XIV built a fortress to defend his conquests in western Germany. This city is today a location for industry (automobiles, steel, food and electronics).

■ ■ ■ **One of Europe's core regions.** Like science and scholarship, industry, too, has long since crossed national boundaries. The Saarland in Germany, Lorraine in France, and Luxembourg are developing ever closer ties, so that the abbreviation "Saar-Lor-Lux" now stands for one of Europe's core regions. Traditional branches of industry of supraregional importance are glass and ceramics. The distinctive features of goods produced by large

The Ludwigskirche, Saarbrücken

Colliers about to descend into the coal mine

companies such as Villeroy & Boch are high quality as
well as richness of form and colour. True, the Saarland
has been somewhat affected by the coal and steel crisis,
but a restructuring programme and innovations have already prepared the ground for the establishment of modern industries. Today most Saarlanders are employed in
the capital goods and services sector. The region also
hopes to derive fresh impetus from the European internal
market that came into effect in January 1993, especially
in the mechanical engineering, metal-processing and
chemical industries.

State election 1994	
CDU	58.1 %
SPD	16.6 %
PDS	16.4 %

Population	4.6 million
Area	18,341 sq km
Capital	Dresden

The Free State of Saxony

■ ■ ■ **"Little Paris" and "Florence on the Elbe".** Saxony is the most densely populated and most industrialized of the new German states. Saxony is a state with a long industrial tradition. Saxon enterprises were consistently in the vanguard during the industrialization of Germany in the 19th and 20th centuries. More than one fifth of the region's 4.6 million inhabitants live in Leipzig (496,600) and Dresden (481,600). Leipzig, famous for its international industrial fair and referred to by Goethe as "little Paris", was one of the main centres of peaceful resistance to the SED regime in the GDR. The "Monday demonstrations" in the city culminated on 9 October 1989 in the chant: "We are the people!" And Dresden, that "pearl of baroque architecture" which was reduced almost to ashes in the inferno of the 1945 bombings, has been made capital of the restored "Free State of Saxony". Dresden is currently developing into one of the most important locations of the microelectronics industry.

The Meissen porcelain factory has been producing its famous merchandise continuously since 1710. The year before, Johann Friedrich Böttger (1682-1719) had produced his formula for this "white gold". Also world-famous are the wood carvings and pillow lace from the Erzgebirge.

Chemnitz, with its technical university and research institutes, focuses on mechanical engineering and, of late, microelectronics. Zwickau is a car manufacturing centre, though instead of the legendary Trabant ("Trabi") Volkswagen's "Polo" is now produced there. Leipzig, once Germany's most important commercial centre and hub of the publishing world, will carry on its tradition as a trade fair city with the Leipzig fair.

Dresden, popularly known as "Florence on the Elbe", hopes to be able to live up to its reputation as one of Germany's cultural centres. It is still a leading city in the world of music, with the Opera House, built in the Italian Renaissance style by Gottfried Semper in 1870-78 and restored to its former glory, the Staatskapelle, and the famous choir, the Kreuzchor. It is an El Dorado of the visual arts with its extensive collections of precious stones, pearls and works of art in the Grünes Gewölbe and its paintings by European masters in the Gemäldegalerie Alte Meister.

The Elbe Sandstone Mountains in the "Switzerland of Saxony" are a popular holiday region, but not only on account of the ideal climbing conditions they have to offer. Great efforts are being made to expand the tourist trade. An "Erzgebirge Silver Route" is being developed which will lead visitors to 150 places of interest in Saxony.

A painter demonstrating her skill in the Meissen porcelain factory

Kronentor, Salon und Wallpavillon in Dresden's Zwinger

The Neues Gewandhaus, Leipzig

■ ■ ■ **Creative energy and enterprising spirit.** Saxony features in many chapters of German cultural history. The works of Johann Sebastian Bach (born in Eisenach in 1685) are traditionally performed by the St. Thomas Choir in Leipzig where he was cantor from 1723 until his death in 1750. Gottfried Wilhelm Leibniz (1646-1716), philosopher, mathematician and diplomat, discovered the binary number system and – independently of Newton – infinitesimal calculus. Gotthold Ephraim Lessing (1729-1781) extolled the virtues of humanity and tolerance in his drama "Nathan the Wise". Other sons of Saxony are the composers Robert Schumann (1810-1856) and Richard Wagner (1813-1883).

Even when eastern Germany had a centrally planned economy the Saxons retained their artistic and business sense. Now their characteristic enterprise is beginning to reassert itself. Of the new federal states, this one is considered to have the best economic prospects.

State election 1994	
CDU	34.4 %
SPD	34.0 %
PDS	19.9 %
Alliance 90 / The Greens	5.1 %

Population	2.82 million
Area	20,607 sq km
Capital	Magdeburg

Saxony-Anhalt

■ ■ ■ **Classical central Germany.** Saxony-Anhalt is the classical embodiment of central Germany on the rivers Elbe and Saale, covering the area between the Harz Mountains, with the Brocken (1,142 m), the Blocksberg of Goethe's "Faust", and the Fläming, a ridge of hills in the east between the Auwiesen in the north and the vineyards along the Saale and Unstrut. Halberstadt's gothic cathedral and the manuscript of the "Merseburg Charms", which is over a thousand years old, bear witness to a historical continuity from the days of Charlemagne. In many towns the past has lived on.

The state is only thinly populated, particularly in the northern parts, Altmark and Magdeburger Börde, whose loess soil is ideal for farming (wheat, sugar beets and vegetables). There is an extensive food industry (sugar factories). Nearly one in five of the state's nearly three million inhabitants lives in Halle (299,000), Magdeburg (272,000) and Dessau (101,000). Halle, Bitterfeld, Leuna, Wolfen and Merseburg, hitherto centres of the chemical and lignite mining industries, are in a phase of radical change as a result of the misguided policies of the former German Democratic Republic. Extensive investment in new installations to reverse environmental pollution and create a new infrastructure give this centre of the chemical industry good prospects for the future. Such investment will have to be maintained for many years – as in all of the new German states. Capital goods production industries, especially the branches of steel and light-metal construction, rail vehicle construction and mechanical engineering, also figure prominently in the state's industrial structure. The opening of the first Max Planck Institute in eastern Germany, in Halle in 1992, was another step to boost the region's economy.

■ ■ ■ **Testimony to a great past.** The decision in 1990 to make Magdeburg, which has a technical university and a school of medicine and is a centre of heavy engineering, capital of Saxony-Anhalt settled the traditional rivalry with Halle, at least in this respect. Both cities have a distinctive medieval past. The cathedral of Magdeburg, seat of emperors and bishops, is one of the largest in Germany. The old salt town of Halle, birthplace of the composer George Frideric Handel (1685-1759), is dominated by the cathedral, the Marktkirche and the Red Tower. The German-American painter Lyonel Feininger (1871-1956) captured the city's landmarks with his fascinating modernistic style. His works and those of his contemporaries can be seen in Moritzburg's Staatliche Galerie. But one of the major centres of 20th-century art was

Industry with a future: a chemical plant in Wittenberg

Merseburg's skyline with the cathedral and palace

Dessau, thanks mainly to its Bauhaus school of architecture.

Tangermünde, with its brick architecture, is regarded as the "Rothenburg of the North". Wernigerode, a jewel of half-timber buildings, is commonly known as the "colourful town in the Harz region". The medieval figures depicting the founders of Naumburg's cathedral are early examples of realistic representation. Eisleben is where Martin Luther (1483-1546) was born and died. He was buried in Wittenberg's Schlosskirche, to the door of which he is said to have nailed his 95 theses in 1517. Eisleben was also the home of the famous Cranach family of painters. At the royal court in Köthen Johann Sebastian Bach composed his six Brandenburg concertos. In 1663, the physicist Otto von Guericke, who was mayor of Magdeburg, demonstrated the effects of air pressure using his "Magdeburg hemispheres".

State election 1992	
SPD	46.2 %
CDU	33.8 %
DVU	6.3 %
FDP	5.6 %
SSW	1.9 %

Population	2.7 million
Area	15,731 sq km
Capital	Kiel

Schleswig-Holstein

■ ■ ■ **Forever undivided.** Schleswig-Holstein is the only German state bordered by two seas, the North Sea and the Baltic. An ancient deed says that the region's two parts, Schleswig and Holstein, should remain "forever undivided". Consequently, they have long been linked as Schleswig-Holstein – unlike those regions which were "hyphenated" by the occupying powers after 1945.

Schleswig-Holstein is thinly populated (2.7 million inhabitants). The state capital Kiel (249,000) and the Hanseatic City of Lübeck (215,000) owe their importance to their position on the Baltic. Lübeck-Travemünde is one of Germany's principal ferry ports.

■ ■ ■ **Farming and commerce.** In former times Schleswig-Holstein was an exclusively agricultural area (mainly livestock farming) and this branch of the economy is still predominant in the fertile marshlands along the western coast. The coastal fishing industry on the North Sea and the Baltic is also proud of its tradition.

In the Middle Ages and in early modern times Flensburg had one of the largest sailing fleets in the North and dominated the route to the West Indies. Lübeck, on the other hand, owed its prosperity to the grain trade, whereas Kiel grew with the navy.

The region's seafaring tradition led to the development of a major shipbuilding industry. As a result of the crisis in this sector in the late 60s, some companies successfully switched to the construction of special vessels. Another solution was to develop a wide range of small and medium-sized industries.

■ ■ ■ **Tourism – a growth industry.** The North Sea island of Helgoland, where Heinrich Hoffmann von Fallersleben composed the German anthem in 1841, as well as

Lübeck's "artists' corner" with the churches of St. Mary and St. Peter

the North Frisian Islands, including cosmopolitan Sylt and the popular family resort Föhr, have their regular visitors just like the resorts on the Baltic Sea, the modern Damp being no different from the dreamy town of Hohwacht in this respect. Inland, the area known as "Holsteins Switzerland" with its lakes is another tourist attraction. Other towns worth visiting are Mölln and the cathedral town of Schleswig, famous for its late gothic Bordesholm altar created by Hans Brüggemann between 1514 and 1521, a masterpiece of woodcarving.

■ ■ ■ **World cultural heritage and world literature.** Lübeck, whose 500-year-old gate, the Holstentor, bears the inscription in Latin "harmony at home, peace outside", has been entered in UNESCO World Heritage List.

Thomas Mann (1885-1955), a writer of world fame, was born in Lübeck. He was awarded the 1929 Nobel Prize for Literature. In May 1993 the house of the grandparents of Thomas and Heinrich Mann (1871-1950) was opened as "Buddenbrook House", a memorial and place of scholarly research.

Kiel Week denotes the famous regatta which every year in June attracts yachtsmen from all over the world.

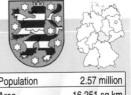

State election 1994	
CDU	42.6 %
SPD	29.6 %
PDS	16.6 %

Population	2.57 million
Area	16,251 sq km
Capital	Erfurt

The Free State of Thuringia

■ ■ ■ **Germany's green heartland.** On account of its position and extensive forest areas Thuringia is also referred to as "Germany's green heartland". The state capital is Erfurt (209,000), which was founded in the 8th century and is proud to be called a "garden city". The old part of the city has an unusually large number of patrician houses, churches and monasteries which make it a kind of architectural open-air museum. Johann Sebastian Bach was born in Eisenach in 1685, one of a ramified family of musicians. He died in Leipzig in 1750. Martin Luther hid in the nearby Wartburg in 1521/22. There he translated the New Testament into German – a major step in the development of modern written German. And at the same place in 1817 students called for a united Germany.

■ ■ ■ **Territorial fragmentation, culture and barbarity.** Thuringia was particularly affected by German's much lamented territorial fragmentation. But culturally this proved to be a good thing since the rulers of even small territories were keen patrons of the arts – albeit mostly at the expense of their subjects who had to pay heavy taxes. By far the most prominent among them was Duke Karl August of Saxony-Weimar (1757-1828). He brought to his court the the romantic poet and translator of Shakespeare Christoph Martin Wieland (1733-1813), the poet and philologist Johann Gottfried von Herder (1744-1803), and above all Johann Wolfgang von Goethe (1749-1832). Thus at that time, around 1800, Weimar became a center of German and European intellectual life. In this city Goethe produced some of his most famous works, including the final version of "Faust". Weimar was also home to Friedrich von Schiller from 1787 to 1789 and from 1799 to 1805. There he wrote, among other works, his "William Tell". Franz Liszt (1811-1886) composed and gave concerts there in the second half of th 19th century. Here the Bauhaus was the

the second half of the 19th century. Here the Bauhaus was founded in 1919, a school of architecture which sought to overcome the divisions between art, handicraft and technology. In 1925 the Bauhaus moved to Dessau, and a few years later to Berlin, where, in 1933, it fell victim to the barbarity which followed Hitler's seizure of power. The year 1933 also marked the demise of the first German republic, the "Weimar Republic", whose constitution had been drafted in Weimar in 1919.

■ ■ ■ **Industry and crafts.** In Thuringia, where important roads intersected, commerce and the craft trades found favourable conditions for growth. Woad, a plant yielding blue coloring matter, brought the region early prosperity. A tradition of weapons craftsmanship led Suhl to become the "armorer's workshop". The industrialization of Germany in the 19th century began in Saxony and Thuringia; important branches were mining (potash), porcelain, glass, toys, and above all machine tools and the optical industry that is associated with the names Zeiss and Schott in Jena. Eisenach was

Schloss Reinhardsbrunn near Friedrichsroda

Glassblowers in the Jena Glassworks

an early site of automobile production; today Opel, Bosch and BMW (founded as "EMW" – Eisenacher Motoren-Werke) have erected state-of-the-art factories there. Erfurt, Jena and Ilmenau (with the Technical University) are in the process of establishing and enlarging new industrial centres in the field of high technology. High-quality soil has led agriculture and horticulture to play an important role in the economy; from time immemorial, Thuringia has also enjoyed an excellent reputation for the processing of agricultural products.

Political system, constitution, law

· The Basic Law · The constitutional bodies
· Federalism and self-government
· Parties and elections · The legal system

Der Parlamentarische Rat hat das vorstehende
Grundgesetz, für die Bundesrepublik Deutschland
in öffentlicher Sitzung am 8. Mai des Jahres Eintausendneunhundertneunundvierzig mit drei-
undfünfzig gegen zwölf Stimmen beschlossen.
Zu Urkunde dessen haben sämtliche Mitglieder
des Parlamentarischen Rates die vorliegende
Urschrift des Grundgesetzes eigenhändig
unterzeichnet.

BONN AM RHEIN, den 23. Mai des Jahres
Eintausendneunhundertneunundvierzig.

PRÄSIDENT DES PARLAMENTARISCHEN RATES

VIZEPRÄSIDENT DES PARLAMENTARISCHEN RATES

The Basic Law

The Basic Law for the Federal Republic of Germany was adopted in 1949. Its authors intended it as a "temporary" framework for a new democratic system, not as a definitive constitution. The Basic Law called upon the people "to achieve in free self-determination the unity and freedom of Germany". As time passed by the Basic Law proved to be a solid foundation for democracy. Its requirement of national reunification was fulfilled in 1990. The preamble and concluding article of the Basic Law have been amended in accordance with the Unification Treaty, which formed the basis for the accession of the German Democratic Republic (GDR) to the Federal Republic. They now state that, by virtue of the GDR's accession, the German people have achieved their unity. On 3 October 1990 the Basic Law became valid for the whole nation.

The Basic Law's content was greatly influenced by the personal experience of its authors under the National Socialist dictatorship. In many parts it clearly indicates that they were trying to avoid the mistakes that had been partly responsible for the demise of the Weimar democracy. Those who drafted the constitution in 1948 were the minister-presidents (with roughly the functions of a premier or governor) of the states that had been formed in the Western occupation zones, and the Parliamentary Council elected by the state parliaments. This Council, chaired by Konrad Adenauer, formally adopted the Basic Law, which was promulgated on 23 May 1949. On the occasion of the Federal Republic's 40th anniversary in 1989 the Basic Law was acknowledged to be the best and most liberal constitution Germany had ever had. As manifest in the life of the community, its principles have largely been put into practice, its requirements by and large fulfilled. More than any previous German constitution, the Basic Law is understood and accepted by the people. It created a state and society which so far has been spared any serious constitutional crises.

■ ■ ■ **The basic rights.** Pride of place in the constitution is given to a charter of basic rights, the first of which obliges the state to respect and protect the dignity of man. This guarantee is supplemented by the right of self-fulfilment. It affords comprehensive protection from un-lawful interference by the state. Both Germans and non-Germans can invoke these constitutional rights. The classical freedoms embodied in the Basic Law include freedom of religion, free speech (including freedom of the press) and the guarantee of property. There are also free-dom of art and scholarship, the right to form coalitions, the right to privacy of mail and telecommunications, pro-tection from forced labour, privacy of the home, and the right of conscientious objection. The civil rights, which

Signing of the Basic Law on 23 May 1949

apply only to German nationals, relate for the most part to their involvement in the political process and their free choice of occupation or profession. Basically, they include the right of assembly, the right to form associations and societies, freedom of movement within (including the right to enter) the country, the ban on extradition, and the franchise.

These freedoms are accompanied by rights which guarantee equality. The Basic Law expresses the general principle that all people are equal before the law by providing that no one may be subject to discrimination or privileged on account of his origin, race, language, convictions, religion or political views. It expressly states that men and women must be treated as equals, and it guarantees equal access to public office for all Germans.

The basic rights in the social sphere concern the individual's position with regard to marriage, family, church, school, but also the state, especially in its capacity as a body politic based on social justice. These rights entitle the citizen to certain means of support by the state, for instance in the form of social services, some of which can be claimed directly.

One basic right, which by its very nature can only apply to foreigners, is the right of political asylum. The Basic Law is the first German constitutional instrument to provide refuge in Germany for foreigners persecuted on political grounds. The influx of hundreds of thousands of asylum-seekers over the years, the great majority of whom were not subject to political persecution in their native countries and whose motives are mainly economic, was getting out of control and threatened to undermine the basic right of asylum for genuine cases of persecution.

After a long and often passionate debate between those in favour of an unrestricted right of asylum – which had been the situation in Germany since 1949 and had no precedent anywhere in the world – and those who felt the time had come to bring the law into line with present-day requirements and the laws of all the other members of the European Union, the German Bundestag adopted an amendment to the country's asylum law with the necessary two-thirds majority. Thus under a new asylum law which entered into force in July 1993 as article 16a of the Basic Law, asylum procedures have been

Federal coat of arms   *Federal flag*

changed without violating the principle that "anybody persecuted on political grounds has the right of asylum". The essence of the new article is that foreigners from EU countries or "safe third countries" (those where application of the Geneva Convention relating to the Status of Refugees and the European Convention for the Protection of Human Rights and Fundamental Freedoms is assured) may not invoke the right of asylum; nor do they have a right to stay in the country temporarily. The procedure for dealing with applications has been shortened. Applicants can no longer abuse the system by submitting multiple claims for social welfare; as a general rule asylum-seekers will in future receive payments in kind.

According to the Basic Law, the scope of some basic rights may be restricted by or on the basis of other laws, but these may never encroach upon the essence of those rights. The basic rights are directly applicable law. This was a crucial innovation compared with previous constitutions, whose basic rights were largely non-binding declarations of intent. Today, parliament is just as strictly bound by the basic rights as the government, the courts, the authorities, the police and the armed forces. Thus every citizen has the right to complain to the Federal Constitutional Court about any decisions or actions by the state which he or she feels violate their basic rights. By acceding to the European Convention for the Protection of Human Rights and Fundamental Freedoms in 1952, the Federal Republic of Germany subjected itself to international control (with effect from 1953). Under article 25 of this Convention the citizens of signatory states have the right to complain to the European Commission of Human Rights and the European Court of Justice, even if this means taking their own government to task. In 1973 the Federal Republic also ratified the international covenants on human rights of the United Nations.

■■■ **Fundamental characteristics of the state.** The body politic is based on the following principles: Germany is a republic and a democracy; she is a federal state based on the rule of law and social justice. Her republican system is constitutionally manifest in the name "Federal Republic of Germany" and in the fact that the head of state is the elected Federal President. A democracy is based on the sovereignty of the people. The constitution says that all public authority emanates from the people. Thus it opted for indirect, representative democracy; in other words, public authority must be recognized and approved by the people but they have no direct say in the exercise of that authority, except in elections.

This responsibility is entrusted to the organs specially established by the constitution for this purpose: the legislature, the executive, and the judiciary. The people mainly exercise their constitutional authority by periodically electing a new parliament. In contrast to some countries, provision for other forms of direct democracy, such as referendums, has been made only with regard to modifications of state boundaries.

The authors of the Basic Law opted for an "adversarial" type of democracy, they having seen the Weimar Republic undermined by radical parties which were hostile to the constitution. In this context "adversarial" means that the free play of political forces must stop where any party or faction attempts to do away with democracy with democratic means. This explains why the Basic Law makes it possible for the Federal Constitutional Court to ban political parties who seek to damage or destroy the country's democratic system.

The constitutional decision in favour of a federal state implies that not only the country as a whole but its 16 constituent parts, the Länder, have some of the features of a state. Each has its own powers, though they are restricted to certain spheres, which it exercises through its own legislature, executive and judiciary. Public responsibility

Ei · nig · keit und Recht und Frei · heit
Da · nach laßt uns al · le stre · ben

für das deut · sche Va · ter · land!
brü · der · lich mit Herz und Hand!

Ei · nig · keit und Recht und Frei · heit

sind des Glük · kes Un · ter · pfand.

Blüh im Glan · ze die · ses Glük · kes,

blü · he, deut · sches Va · ter · land!

*The national anthem of the Federal Republic of Germany
is the third verse of the "Lied der Deutschen".
The lyrics of the anthem were written by August Heinrich
Hoffmann von Fallersleben (1798-1874) and the melody
was composed by Joseph Haydn (1732-1809).*

The national holiday is 3 October, the Day of German Unity.

has been apportioned in such a way that law-making, in contrast to the provisions of the constitution, is actually in the hands of the central state, the Federation, whereas the constituent states have the task of implementation.

This division of responsibilities is an essential element of the system provided for in the Basic Law, a principle that is the very foundation of the rule of law. The exercise of public authority has been entrusted to parliament, government and the judiciary, each of which is independent of the others.

The significance of this separation of powers is that the power of the state is qualified by mutual checks and balances. It thus protects the individual's freedom. Another major feature of the rule-of-law principle is that the executive is strictly bound by the constitution and the laws of the land. Furthermore, encroachments upon an individual's rights or privacy are only permissible on the basis of a law. Any action by the state may be examined by independent judges as to its consistency with the law if the person or persons affected take the matter to court.

The social state is a modern extension of the traditional rule-of-law concept. Under this system the state is required to protect the weaker members of society and to seek social justice. Numerous laws and court rulings have ensured the application of this principle, which manifests itself in the provision of old-age, invalidity, health and unemployment insurance, social assistance for needy people, housing supplements, the child benefit, laws on industrial safety and working hours, etc.

The Basic Law does not, however, state specifically how the country's economy should be run. Where economic policy is concerned it remains for the most part neutral. On the other hand, parliament's freedom to legislate in this sphere is limited by the exigencies of the rule-of-law principle, and by the fundamental rights of property and inheritance and the free choice of occupation or profession.

■ ■ ■ **Amendments to the Basic Law.** The Basic Law may only be amended with a majority of two thirds of the members of the Bundestag (Federal Parliament) and two thirds of the votes cast in the Bundesrat (Federal Council). Since one single party or coalition rarely has such a majority in both the Bundestag and the Bundesrat, amendments to the Basic Law require a very broad consensus. This can only be achieved with the support of members of the opposition.

Some provisions of the Basic Law may not be changed at all, not even with a two-thirds majority. Those are the parts relating to the federal system, the separation of powers, democracy, rule of law, and the social state. Likewise untouchable are the commitment to protect the dignity of man and the basic rights and freedoms.

On 15 November 1994 the most recent amendments to the Basic Law entered into force. Among other things, they commit the state to protect the environment, ensure equal rights for men and women, and protect the disabled. They also provide for changes in the distribution of legislative jurisdiction between the Federation and the states.

Another constitutional amendment became necessary as a result of the Maastricht Treaty on European Union. The Basic Law's new article 23 on the European Union makes it clear that the Federal Republic of Germany seeks the establishment of a united Europe which is based on democratic, rule-of-law, social and federal principles. The principle of subsidiarity plays a key role in this context. Article 23 also spells out how the Bundestag and the states are to be involved in the further development of European integration.

The constitutional bodies

"All public authority emanates from the people." This underlying principle of democracy is codified in the constitution. The people exercise that authority directly in elections, indirectly through bodies instituted by the constitution: the legislature, the executive and the judiciary. The constitutional bodies with primarily legislative functions are the Bundestag and the Bundesrat. Executive responsibilities lie principally with the Federal Government, headed by the Federal Chancellor, and the Federal President. Judicial functions pertaining to the constitution are performed by the Federal Constitutional Court.

■ ■ ■ **The Federal President**. The head of state of the Federal Republic of Germany is the Federal President. He is elected by the Federal Convention, a constitutional body which convenes only for this purpose. It consists of the members of the Bundestag and an equal number of members elected by the state parliaments. Sometimes eminent persons who are not members of a state parliament are nominated for the Federal Convention. The Federal President is elected for a term of five years with the majority of votes in the Federal Convention. He may only be reelected once.

The Federal President represents the Federation in its international relations and concludes treaties with other states on its behalf. He also accredits and receives envoys, although foreign policy as such is the responsibility of the Federal Government. He appoints and dismisses federal judges, federal civil servants and commissioned and non-commissioned officers of the armed forces. The President can pardon convicted criminals. He checks whether laws have come about by the proper constitutional procedure; they are subsequently promulgated in the Federal Law Gazette.

He proposes to the Bundestag a candidate for the office of Federal Chancellor (taking account of the majority situation in parliament) and, in response to proposals from the Chancellor, appoints and dismisses the federal ministers.

If the Chancellor seeks but fails to gain a vote of confidence the Federal President may, on the Chancellor's proposal, dissolve the Bundestag. Premature elections were brought about in this way in 1972 and 1983.

The Federal President personifies the country's political unity in a special way. He is the link between all elements in society regardless of party distinctions. Although his tasks are mainly of a representational nature he can exercise considerable personal authority through his neutral, mediating function. By commenting on the fundamental aspects of current issues he can rise above general party-political controversy and set standards for the public's political and moral guidance.

■ ■ ■ **The Bundestag.** The German Bundestag is the parliamentary assembly representing the people of the Federal Republic of Germany. It is elected by the people every four years. It may only be dissolved prematurely under exceptional circumstances, the final decision lying with the Federal President. The Bundestag's main functions are to pass laws, to elect the Federal Chancellor, and to keep check on the government.

The Bundestag is the scene of parliamentary battles, especially over crucial foreign and domestic policy issues. It is in the parliamentary committees, whose meetings are not usually open to the public, that the extensive preparatory work for legislation is done. Here it is a question of harmonizing political intentions with the detailed knowledge provided by the experts. It is likewise in the committees that parliament scrutinizes and controls government activity. Otherwise it would not be possible to cope with the multitude of technical questions. The Bundestag's committees correspond to the Federal Government's departments and range from the foreign relations via the social affairs to the budget committee, the latter being particularly important in that it represents parliament's control of the budget. The petitions committee is open to requests and complaints from any member of the public.

From 1949 until the end of the last legislative term in 1994 about 7,500 bills were introduced in parliament and 4,600 of them passed. Most of them are initiated by the Federal Government, the others coming from members of the Bundestag or from the Bundesrat. They receive three readings in the Bundestag and are usually referred to the appropriate committee once. The final vote is taken after the third reading. A bill (unless it entails an

The Federal Presidents

Theodor Heuss
(FDP)
1949-1959

Heinrich Lübke
(CDU)
1959-1969

Gustav Heinemann
(SPD)
1969-1974

Walter Scheel
(FDP)
1974-1979

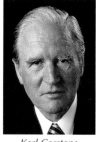

Karl Carstens
(CDU)
1979-1984

Richard v. Weizsäcker
(CDU)
1984-1994

Roman Herzog
(CDU)
since 1994

The Federal Chancellors

Konrad Adenauer
(CDU)
1949-1963

Ludwig Erhard
(CDU)
1963-1966

Kurt Georg Kiesinger
(CDU)
1966-1969

Willy Brandt
(SPD)
1969-1974

Helmut Schmidt
(SPD)
1974-1982

Helmut Kohl
(CDU)
since 1982

amendment to the constitution) is passed if it receives a majority of the votes cast. Those which affect the functions of the federal states require the approval of the Bundesrat, however.

Members of the German Bundestag are elected in general, direct, free, equal and secret elections. They are representatives of the whole people; they are not bound by any instructions, only by their conscience. In line with their party allegiances they form parliamentary groups. Freedom of conscience and the requirements of party solidarity sometimes collide, but even if in such a situation a member feels obliged to leave his party he keeps his seat in the Bundestag. This is the clearest indication that members of the Bundestag are independent.

The relative strengths of the parliamentary groups determine the composition of the committees. The President (Speaker) of the Bundestag is elected from the ranks of the strongest parliamentary group, in keeping with German constitutional tradition. Members are paid remuneration ensuring their independence and reflecting their status as MPs. Anyone who has been a member of parliament for at least eight years receives a pension upon reaching retirement age.

■ ■ ■ **The Bundesrat.** The Bundesrat represents the sixteen federal states and participates in the legislative process and administration of the Federation. In contrast to the senatorial system of federal states like the United States or Switzerland, the Bundesrat does not consist of elected representatives of the people but of members of the state governments or their representatives. Depending on the size of their population, the states have three, four, five or six votes which may only be cast as a block.

More than half of all bills require the formal approval of the Bundesrat, which means that they cannot pass into law against its will. This applies especially to bills that concern vital interests of the states, for instance their financial affairs or their administrative powers. No proposed amendments to the constitution can be adopted without the Bundesrat's consent (two-thirds majority). In all other cases the Bundesrat only has a right of objection, but this can be overruled by the Bundestag. If the two houses of parliament cannot reach agreement a mediation committee composed of members of both chambers must be convened which, in most cases, is able to work out a compromise.

In the Bundesrat state interests often override party interests. In such cases the voting may not reflect party strengths in the council. This points to an active federalism. The Federal Government cannot always rely on a state government where the same party is in power to follow its lead in every respect, for each state has its own special interests and sometimes takes sides with other states who pursue the same aim, irrespective of the party they are governed by. This produces fluctuating majorities, and compromises have to be made where the parties forming the Federal Government do not have a ma-

Germany's federal structure

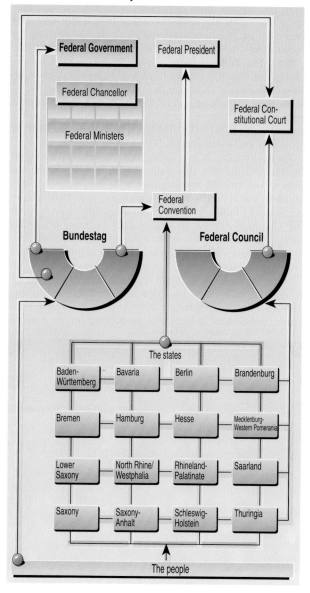

jority in the Bundesrat. The Bundesrat elects its president from among the minister-presidents of the federal states for a twelve-month term according to a fixed rota. The President of the Bundesrat exercises the powers of the Federal President in the event of the latter's indisposition.

■ ■ ■ **The Federal Government.** The Federal Government, the Cabinet, consists of the Federal Chancellor, who is chairman and head of government, and the federal ministers. The Chancellor alone chooses the ministers and proposes them to the Federal President for appointment or dismissal. He also determines the number of ministers and their responsibilities.

The Chancellor is in a strong position mainly owing to the fact that he lays down the guidelines of government policy. The federal ministers run their departments independently and on their own responsibility but within the framework of those guidelines. In a coalition government the Chancellor must of course take account of agreements reached with the other party in the coalition.

This explains why the German system of government is often referred to as a "Chancellor democracy". The Chancellor is the only member of the government elected by parliament and he alone is responsible to it. This responsibility may manifest itself in a "constructive vote of no confidence", which was introduced by the authors

Meeting of the Federal Cabinet

The Bundestag building on the Rhine, Bonn

of the Basic Law in deliberate contrast to the Weimar constitution. Its purpose is to ensure that opposition groups who are agreed only in their rejection of the government but not as regards an alternative programme are not able to overthrow the government. A Bundestag vote of no confidence in the Chancellor must at the same time be a majority vote in favour of a successor. Of the two attempts to bring down a Chancellor with the help of a constructive vote of no confidence, only one has succeeded. That was in October 1982, when a no-confidence motion removed Helmut Schmidt from office and put Helmut Kohl in his place. The Basic Law makes no provision for motions of no confidence in individual federal ministers.

■ ■ ■ **The Federal Constitutional Court**. The Federal Constitutional Court in Karlsruhe is the guardian of the Basic Law. It rules, for instance, on disputes between the Federal Government and the federal states or between individual federal institutions. Only this court has the power to declare that a party constitutes a threat to freedom and democracy and is therefore unconstitutional, in which case it orders that party's dissolution. It scrutinizes federal and state laws as to their conformity with the

Basic Law. If it rules that a law is unconstitutional it may no longer be applied. The Court acts in such cases only if called upon by certain authorities, such as the Federal Government, state governments, at least two thirds of the members of parliament, lower courts, etc.

In addition, every citizen has the right to file a complaint with the Federal Constitutional Court if he feels his basic rights have been violated by the state. Before doing so, however, he must as a rule have exhausted all other legal remedies.

So far the Federal Constitutional Court has passed judgment in more than 80,000 cases. Some 76,000 of them dealt with constitutional complaints, although only just under 2,000 were successful. Often matters of great domestic or international significance are dealt with, for instance whether the involvement of German forces in missions of the United Nations is compatible with the Basic Law. Federal Governments of all political hues have had to submit to decisions of the judges in Karlsruhe. The Court has repeatedly stressed, however, that it does not see its task as requiring institutions of the state to follow a specific political course. The Federal Constitutional Court consists of two senates (panels), each with eight judges, half of whom are elected by the Bundestag, the other half by the Bundesrat. The judges serve for twelve years and may not be reelected.

Federalism and self-government

The name "Federal Republic of Germany" itself denotes the country's federal structure. The Federal Republic consists of sixteen Länder (states). After 1945 the eleven states of the original Federal Republic were reestablished or newly founded. After the first free elections in the former German Democratic Republic (GDR) on 18 March 1990, the members of the Volkskammer (the GDR parliament) voted to establish five new states. On 3 October 1990, the GDR – and thus the states of Brandenburg, Mecklenburg-Western Pomerania, Saxony, Saxony-Anhalt and Thuringia – acceded to the Federal Republic of Germany. The eleven boroughs in the eastern part of Berlin were united with the state of Berlin. The Länder are not mere provinces but states endowed with their own powers. Each has a constitution which must be consistent with the republican, democratic and social principles embodied in the Basic Law. Subject to these conditions they can shape their constitutions as they see fit.

Federalism is one of the constitutional principles that may not be tampered with. But this is not to say that the constituent states may not be altered. Provision for boundary adjustments has been made in the Basic Law. The joint constitutional commission of the federal and state governments has proposed simpler procedures.

The federal system has a long tradition in Germany and was interrupted only by the National Socialist unitary state of 1933-1945. Germany is one of the classical federal states. Federalism has proved its worth: It is much easier for a country with a federal structure than a centralized state to take account of regional characteristics and problems.

■ ■ ■ **Benefits of a federal system.** German federalism, much as in the United States and Switzerland, binds the country's external unity with its internal diversity. Preserving that regional diversity is the traditional task of the federal system. This function today acquires new substance in the form of regional responsibilities such as the protection of monuments and historical sites, the preservation of architectural traditions, and the promotion of regional culture.

But the main purpose of federalism is to safeguard the nation's freedom. The distribution of responsibilities between the Federation and the states is an essential element of the power-sharing arrangement, the checks and balances, as provided for in the Basic Law. This also embraces the participation of the states in the legislative process at federal level through the Bundesrat.

The federal structure also enhances the democratic principle. It enables the citizen to engage in the political process, i.e. in elections and referendums, in his own region. This gives democracy greater vitality. There are other benefits as well. The federal system leaves room for experiments on a smaller scale and for competition among the states. For instance, a single state may try out innovative methods in, say, education which may later serve as a model for nationwide reform. Furthermore, a federal structure can best cope with different regional majorities. Opposition parties at national level may hold a majority in some of the states and thus form the government there.

■ ■ ■ **The powers of the federal states.** The Basic Law determined the powers of the Federation in terms of whether laws should be the same for all states or whether the states should be allowed to make their own laws. This is illustrated by the fact that the Federation's law-making powers fall into three different categories: exclusive, concurrent or framework legislation. Areas of legislation which fall within the exclusive purview of the Federation are foreign affairs, defence, monetary matters, air transport and some elements of taxation.

In the case of concurrent legislation, the states may only pass laws on matters not covered by federal law. The Federation may only legislate in such cases where it is necessary to have a uniform law for the whole country. The areas which fall into this category are civil and criminal law, commercial law, nuclear energy, labour and land law, law concerning aliens, housing, shipping, road transport, refuse disposal, air pollution and noise abatement. Since it has proved necessary to have standard laws for these matters, the states have more or less ceased to have any jurisdiction in those areas.

Where the Federation has the power to enact framework legislation, the states have a certain amount of legislative latitude. This applies, for instance, in the fields of

The new state parliament, Düsseldorf

higher education, nature conservation, landscape management, regional planning and water management.

There are also a number of other supraregional tasks which, though not mentioned in the Basic Law, are today jointly planned, regulated and financed by the Federation and the states. They were incorporated in the Basic Law in 1969 as "joint responsibilities". They cover university building, improvement of regional economic and agricultural structures, as well as coastal preservation.

Direct federal administration is more or less limited to the Foreign Service, labour placement, customs, the Federal Border Guard and the Federal Armed Forces. Most administrative responsibilities are carried out by the states independently.

The Federation's jurisdiction is confined to the Federal Constitutional Court and the supreme courts, which ensure the uniform interpretation of the law. All other courts fall within the ambit of state jurisdiction.

As mentioned above, the states can fill in any gaps left by federal legislation or in areas not specified in the Basic Law. Thus they are responsible for education and culture almost in their entirety as a manifestation of their "cultural sovereignty". They are also responsible for local government law and the police.

The real strength of the states lies in their participation in the legislative process at federal level through the Bundesrat. All internal administration lies in their hands and their bureaucracy implements most federal laws and regulations. Thus state administration is threefold: it handles matters that fall exclusively within its jurisdiction (e.g.

schools, police, regional planning); it implements federal law on its own responsibility (planning for building projects, trade and industry, environmental protection); and it applies federal law on behalf of the Federation (e.g. construction of national highways, promotion of training). Thus in the course of its development the Federal Republic has become a country in which most laws are enacted centrally while the bulk of legislation is administered by the federal states.

■ ■ ■ **Local self-government.** Local self-government, as an expression of civic freedom, has a long tradition in Germany. It can be traced back to the privileges of the free towns in the Middle Ages, when civic rights freed people from the bonds of feudal serfdom. (As they said in those days, "town air makes people free".) In modern times local self-government has primarily been linked to the great reforms of the Prussian Minister Freiherr vom Stein, in particular the Local Government Code of 1808. This tradition of civic liberty is manifest in the self-government of towns, municipalities and counties expressly guaranteed by the Basic Law. The constitution grants them the right to regulate local affairs within the framework of the law. All towns, municipalities and counties must have a democratic structure. Municipal law falls within the sphere of competence of the federal states. For historical reasons the municipal constitutions vary greatly from state to state, but in practice the administrative system is by and large the same everywhere.

Self-government embraces in particular local transport and road construction, electricity, water and gas supply, sewerage and town planning, as well as the building and maintenance of schools, theatres and museums, hospitals, sports facilities and public baths. Other local responsibilities are adult education and youth welfare. The expediency and cost-benefit aspects of programmes in these fields are the responsibility of the local council. Many such measures are beyond the means of smaller towns and municipalities and can therefore be taken over by the next higher level of local self-government, the county (Kreis). The county, too, is part of the system of local government through its own democratically elected bodies. The larger cities do not form part of a county.

Local self-government and independence are bound to suffer if the municipalities are unable to finance their

City council meeting in Hanover's New City Hall

programmes. Their financial situation is frequently a subject of public debate. Local authorities raise their own taxes and levies, which include land tax and trade tax. They are also entitled to raise local taxes on certain luxury goods. This revenue does not suffice to cover their financial needs, however. They therefore receive from the federal and state governments a share of the nation's income tax. They also receive allocations under the financial equalization arrangement which applies in every state.

Local self-government gives all citizens an opportunity to play their part and have a controlling influence. They can discuss such matters as new building projects with elected councillors at town meetings and inspect budget estimates. The towns and municipalities are the smallest cells in the political system. They must always be able to thrive and develop as the basic source of freedom and democracy.

Parties and elections

In a modern democracy competing political parties are of fundamental importance. They are elected for a specific term during which they either assume the powers of government or keep check on the activities of the current administration. They therefore play a major role in the shaping of public policy. These functions are taken into account in the Basic Law, which devotes a separate article (article 21) to the parties: "The parties shall help form the political will of the people. They may be freely established. Their internal organization shall conform to democratic principles. They shall publicly account for the sources and use of their funds and for their assets."

■ ▒ ▒ **Parties in the Bundestag.** Since the first general election to be held in the whole of Germany (1990) there have been six parties in the Bundestag: the Christian Democratic Union of Germany (CDU), the Social Democratic Party of Germany (SPD), the Free Democratic Party (FDP), the Christian Social Union (CSU), the Party of Democratic Socialism (PDS) and the group known as Alliance 90/The Greens. The CDU has no party association in Bavaria, while the CSU puts up candidates for election in Bavaria only. In the Bundestag, however, CDU and CSU have a joint parliamentary group. The SPD, CDU, CSU and FDP were formed in the western states between 1945 and 1947. The SPD was a re-creation of the former mainly labour-oriented party of the same name which had been outlawed by the Hitler regime in 1933. The other parties were completely new. The Christian parties, CDU and CSU, in contrast to the Catholic Centre Party of Weimar days, drew their support from both of Germany's two major Christian creeds, Roman Catholicism and Protestantism. The FDP adopted programmes in the tradition of German liberalism.

In the four decades since their establishment these four parties have undergone significant changes. At federal level they have all formed coalitions with one another once or been in opposition. Today they all see themselves as "popular" parties representing all sections of the community. They have different factions which reflect the various elements of a people's party.

From 1983 to 1990 the party "The Greens", too, had its own group in the Bundestag. It had been established at national level in 1979 and was gradually voted into some of the state parliaments as well. Its roots lie in a radical ecologist movement which initially embraced factions opposed to nuclear energy as well as pacifist protest groups. In the 1990 general election, however, The Greens failed to clear the five percent hurdle, but they were nonetheless represented in the Bundestag, sharing a list with Alliance 90, a product of the civil rights movement which in 1989/90 brought about the peaceful revolution in the former GDR. On 14 May 1993 these two parties merged into one under the name "Alliance 90 / The Greens". This party polled enough votes in the 1994 election to be represented in the Bundestag.

The PDS is the successor to the former Socialist Unity Party of Germany (SED), the communist party which ruled in the GDR. It has not been able to establish itself as a major political force in united Germany. In 1990

Helmut Kohl, CDU Chairman for the past 20 years

the PDS – like the Alliance 90/The Greens group – was only represented in the Bundestag by virtue of an exception allowing the five percent clause to be applied separately in the new federal states and the existing ones in the west for the benefit of the parties in the eastern part of the country. In the 1994 Bundestag election, the PDS achieved representation in the Bundestag on the basis of four constituency seats in Berlin.

■ ■ ■ **The five percent clause.** Of the 36 parties which sought election to the first Bundestag in 1949, only four remained in the parliament elected in 1990. This is the result of a "five percent debarring clause"

Rudolf Scharping, Chairman of the SPD

which was introduced in 1953 and made stricter still in 1957. It stipulates that only parties gaining at least five percent of the votes or at least three constituency seats can be represented in parliament. This arrangement was explicitly accepted by the Federal Constitutional Court since its purpose was to prevent tiny splinter parties from entering parliament (as had happened in the days of the Weimar Republic) and thus enable the larger

Wolfgang Gerhardt, Chairman of the FDP

Theodor Waigel, Chairman of the CSU

parties to obtain majorities that would enable them to govern.

The five percent hurdle is waived in the case of national minorities. Thus the South-Schleswig Voters' Association, which represents the Danish minority, has a member in the state parliament of Schleswig-Holstein even though it obtained fewer than five percent of the votes. Local government elections sometimes produce results that differ greatly from those of federal and state elections. Here the "town-hall parties", inde-

Jürgen Trittin and Krista Sager, Spokesmen of Alliance 90/The Greens

Shares of votes at federal elections

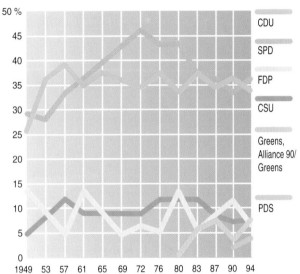

pendent voters' associations, often play an important role.

■ ■ ■ **The electoral system.** Elections for all parliaments in Germany are general, direct, free, equal and secret. Every German aged 18 or over may vote. There are no primary elections. Candidates are nominated by their parties. Elections for the German Bundestag are based on

1994 general election

Party	Valid second votes	Percent	MPs
CDU	16,089,491	34.2	244
SPD	17,141,319	36.4	252
FDP	3,257,864	6.9	47
CSU	3,427,128	7.3	50
Alliance 90/The Greens	3,423,091	7.3	49
PDS	2,067,391	4.4	30
Total	45,406,284		672

Turnout was 79.1%.

Distribution of seats in the Bundestag *

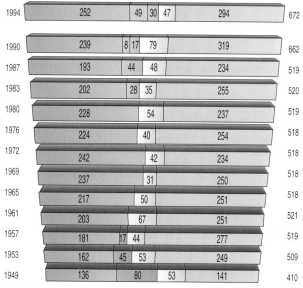

Year	CDU/CSU	FDP	Greens	PDS	SPD	Total
1994	252	49	30	47	294	672
1990	239	8	17	79	319	662
1987	193	44	48		234	519
1983	202	28	35		255	520
1980	228	54			237	519
1976	224	40			254	518
1972	242	42			234	518
1969	237	31			250	518
1965	217	50			251	518
1961	203	67			251	521
1957	181	17	44		277	519
1953	162	45	53		249	509
1949	136	80	53		141	410

* at beginning of each legislative period; until 1987 including members from Berlin (West)

- CDU / CSU
- FDP
- SPD
- PDS
- Alliance 90 / Greens
- Other

a system of "personalized" proportional representation. Voters have two votes, the first of which is given to a candidate in their constituency. The successful candidate is elected on a first-past-the-post basis. The second vote is given to a list of candidates put up by the parties.

The votes from the constituencies and those for the state lists are offset in such a way that the composition of the Bundestag almost identically reflects the distribution of votes among the parties. If a party has won more direct seats in the constituencies than its proportion of the votes would justify (they being known as "overhang" seats), it is allowed to keep them. Whenever this happens the Bundestag has more than the 656 members prescribed by law, hence the present 672. The object of having the electorate vote for state lists is to ensure that the strengths of all parties in parliament reflect their shares of the votes obtained. On the other hand, the constituency vote, the first vote, gives people the chance to choose a particular candidate. Normally, the people take a keen interest in elections. The turnout for the Bundestag election of 1994 was 79.1 percent. It tends to fluctuate at state and local elections, but it is nearly always around 70 percent.

■■■ **Membership and finances.** As of 1994, the memberships of the parties represented in the Bundestag were as follows: SPD 851,000; CDU 690,000; CSU 177,000; FDP 94,000; PDS 123,000; and Alliance 90/The Greens 43,000. All parties require their members to pay subscriptions which, however, cover only part of their expenses. The donations received, too, are insufficient. Moreover, there is a danger of big donors influencing the parties for their own ends. Therefore, pursuant to the Parties Financing Act which entered into force on 1 January 1994, the parties receive from the state DM 1.30 per vote for up to five million valid votes which they poll in elections to the Bundestag, the European Parliament and the state parliaments. For each additional vote they receive DM 1.00. Moreover, 50 Pfennigs are paid for each DM 1.00 which a party receives from members' subscriptions or from donations. These amounts may not exceed the funds raised by the party per year. The public grants for all parties together may not total more than DM 230 million.

The legal system

The law of the Federal Republic of Germany is predominantly written law, most of it federal and comprising more than 4,000 acts and statutory instruments. The states, too, pass laws, mainly on such matters as the police, local government, schools and universities as well as the press, radio and television.

During the four decades when the country was divided the legal systems of the Federal Republic and the GDR became totally different. The decision was taken in 1990 to merge the two legal systems as soon as possible after the GDR's accession to the Federal Republic. This was also of fundamental importance for the process of economic recovery in the new federal states. Extensive adjustments were made in nearly all fields of law in order to take account of the special situation in the GDR and the existing system. With just a few exceptions, the adjustments in the structure of the courts have meanwhile been completed.

■ ■ ■ **A state based on the rule of law.** German law goes back partly to Roman law and partly to numerous other legal sources in the German regions. In the 19th century a uniform system of private law was created for the first time. It applied to the entire German Empire. The Civil Code and Commercial Code to this day preserve the liberal spirit of those times. Their underlying principle is freedom of contract.

The guarantees afforded by a democratic state are manifest above all in substantive and procedural law. Criminal law starts from the constitutional premise that no act is punishable unless declared so by law before it was committed (nulla poena sine lege). Thus judges may not make up for gaps in penal law by applying legal provisions which cover similar cases, nor may they apply laws retroactively. Another principle embedded in the constitution is that no one may be punished more than once for the same offence under general criminal law. Personal liberty may not be restricted except on the basis of a formal law. Only a judge may determine whether a person's imprisonment is justified and only he can decide for how long. Whenever a person is detained without a judicial warrant the matter must be brought before a judge for decision without delay.

Although the police may hold someone in temporary custody they may not detain him any longer than the end of the day following the arrest. Everyone has a right to a court hearing – that, too, is guaranteed by the constitution and is a fundamental principle of the rule of law. The administration of justice is entrusted to judges who are independent and answerable to the law only. They may not be dismissed from office nor transferred against their will. Special tribunals are banned.

Nearly all of these fundamental principles had already been established by the judiciary laws of the 19th century. They include the Courts Constitution Act, which governs the structure, organization and jurisdiction of the courts, the Code of Civil Procedure and the Code of Criminal Procedure.

The Civil Code, which entered into force in 1900, and the Codes of Civil and Criminal Procedure were wrested by liberal and democratic forces from the imperial government towards the end of the last century after a long drawn-out struggle in parliament. Some German codified laws have found their way into foreign legal systems. The Civil Code, for instance, was the model for its Japanese and Greek counterparts.

■■ ■ **The citizen and public administration.** After an evolutionary period of more than 100 years, the Basic Law set the seal on a comprehensive system of legal protection against the actions of public authorities. It enabled the citizen to challenge any measure that affected him on the ground that it violated his rights. This applies to any administrative act, be it a tax assessment notice or a decision whether or not to promote a school pupil to the next grade, be it the withdrawal of a driving license or the refusal of a building permit.

Administrative courts were unknown in the GDR. Now administration in the new federal states, too, is subject to overall control by the courts.

The legal protection afforded by the specialized courts is complemented by a right of complaint to the Federal Constitutional Court. This "constitutional complaint" is open to every citizen and is an extra form of legal redress against any violations of basic rights by a public authority. The complainant must

The Courts of the Federal Republic of Germany

Federal Constitutional Court
2 senates

Constitutional courts of the federal states

Joint Senate of the Supreme Courts

Ordinary jurisdiction		Administrative jurisdiction	Fiscal jurisdiction	Labour jurisdiction	Social jurisdiction
Civil jurisdiction	Penal jurisdiction				

Federal Court of Justice
- Main civil senate
- Civil senates
- Main penal senate
- Penal senates

Federal Administrative Court
- Main senate
- Senates

Federal Finance Court
- Main senate
- Senates

Federal Labour Court
- Main senate
- Senates

Federal Social Court
- Main senate
- Senates

Higher Regional Court
- Civil senates
- Family affairs senates
- Penal senates
- Appellate court
- Court of first instance for serious crimes against the state

Higher Administrative Court
- Senates

Finance Court
- Senates

Regional Labour Court
- Senates

Regional Social Court
- Senates

Regional Court
- Civil divisions
- Commercial divisions
- Minor penal divisions
- Main penal divisions (first instance)
- Main penal divisions (second instance)
- Juvenile divisions (first instance)
- Juvenile divisions (second instance)

Administrative Court
- Divisions

Labour Court
- Divisions

Social Court
- Divisions

Local Court
- Single judge
- Family court
- Judge for penal cases
- Magistrate's court
- Judge for juvenile cases
- Magistrate's court for juvenile cases

show that one of his basic rights has been infringed by a
public act, for instance a court decision or an administrative measure but also a law. Normally, such complaints
may only be lodged after all other legal remedies have
been exhausted.

■ ■ ■ **Social justice.** The Basic Law prescribes the development of the social-state order, hence much greater
consideration is now given to the people's social needs
than in former times. In the years since the creation of the
Federal Republic a whole range of special labour and social legislation has been enacted to provide the citizen
with various financial benefits in the event of sickness,
accident, invalidity, and unemployment, and after retirement.

Labour law is a good example of how the social-state
principle has been put into effect. Originally, these matters were only briefly dealt with under the heading of
"service contracts" in the Civil Code. Today, labour legislation embraces an abundance of laws and collective
agreements, but is also largely based on case law. It includes in particular the Collective Wage Agreements Act,
the Protection against Dismissal Act, the Act on the Constitution of Business and Industrial Enterprises (Works
Constitution Act), as well as the various laws on codetermination and the Labour Courts Act.

■ ■ ■ **Court structure and the legal profession.** The
Federal Republic's courts are largely specialized and provide full legal protection. They fall into five categories:
– The "ordinary courts" are responsible for criminal matters, civil matters (such as matrimonial or family proceedings as well as disputes arising under private law
such as sale or lease agreements) and non-contentious legal proceedings, which include conveyancing, probate
and guardianship matters. There are four levels: local
court (Amtsgericht), regional court (Landgericht), higher
regional court (Oberlandesgericht) and Federal Court of
Justice (Bundesgerichtshof). In criminal cases, depending
on their nature, each of the first three courts can have jurisdiction, whereas in civil proceedings it will be either
the local court or the regional court. One or two other
courts may be appealed to on points of fact or law.
– The labour courts (three levels: local, higher – i. e.
state – and federal) handle disputes arising from employment contracts and between management and labour, as

well as matters covered by the Works Constitution Act. The labour courts have to decide, for instance, whether an employee has been fairly or unfairly dismissed.

– The administrative courts (local, higher and federal) handle all proceedings under administrative law that do not fall within the jurisdiction of the social and finance courts or, in exceptional cases, the ordinary courts (e.g. cases of official liability), or do not involve disputes which fall under constitutional law.

– The social courts (local, higher and federal) rule on all disputes concerned with social security.

– The finance courts (state and federal) deal with taxation and related matters.

In the five new federal states the old court structure was retained for a transitional period. Although those states still have county and district courts which deal with all matters which, in the western states, are the responsibility of five different types of courts, the court structure is being adapted. Ordinary and specialized courts have been established in nearly all of the new states.

Separate from the aforementioned five types of courts is the Federal Constitutional Court, which is not only the country's supreme court but also an organ of the constitution. It rules on constitutional disputes.

There is a complex system of appeals which affords numerous possibilities for judicial review. There are two

Pronouncing judgment in the Federal Court of Justice, Karlsruhe

stages in the appeal procedure. In the first (Berufung), the case can be reviewed both as regards the facts and points of law, i.e. its merits. Thus at this level new evidence can still be introduced. In the second stage (Revision), however, the court will only consider whether the law has been properly applied and the essential procedural formalities observed.

In the Federal Republic of Germany there are approximately 20,000 professional judges, more than three quarters of whom are assigned to the ordinary courts. Most judges are appointed for life and in exercising their profession are bound only by the spirit and letter of the law.

At local court level most non-contentious legal proceedings are handled by judicial officers, who are not judges but rather higher intermediate-level civil servants in the judicial service. In several types of courts lay judges sit with the professional judges. Their experience and specialist knowledge in certain fields, such as labour and welfare matters, enable them to help the courts make realistic decisions. They are also a manifestation of the citizen's direct responsibility for the administration of justice.

The public prosecutors, of whom there are over 4,000, are for the most part concerned with criminal proceedings. It is their responsibility to establish the facts where a person is suspected of a crime. They have to decide whether to discontinue the proceedings or to indict the person concerned. In court proceedings they are the prosecuting counsel. Unlike judges, public prosecutors are not personally and objectively independent; they are civil servants and therefore under orders from their superiors – though within very narrow limits.

More than 60,000 lawyers form a free profession and serve as independent counsel in all fields of law. Through representing their clients in court they play a large part in the administration of justice. They must adhere to their professional code and any violations are dealt with by disciplinary tribunals. All professional judges, public prosecutors and attorneys at law must have the qualifications of a judge, in other words they must have successfully completed the course at a university law school and the compulsory course of practical training which follows, each of which ends with a state examination.

■ ■ **Data protection.** The advance of electronic data processing (EDP) in the modern industrial society has created new problems for the judicial system. These days computers are used to maintain bank accounts, to book seats on aircraft, to issue tax notices or to collate crime data at police headquarters. EDP has become indispensable in nearly all fields of administration and makes it possible to store and retrieve huge quantities of data.

Modern technology has greatly eased the workload of many companies and public authorities and is increasingly finding its way into even small offices and private homes.

There are hazards as well, however. Stored data can be put to improper use and fall into the hands of unauthorized persons. Anyone with sufficient quantities of data may have access to information on a person's private life, which must remain inviolable.

In 1977 federal and state legislation was introduced in Germany to safeguard the community against such dangers. The law specifies those cases where the authorities and, for instance, private companies may store personal data. In all other cases it is forbidden. Staff involved in data processing are bound to secrecy. People are legally entitled to know what data concerning them is held by any agency. They can demand the correction of wrong data and have any that are disputed blocked or any that have been improperly obtained erased.

On the recommendation of the Federal Government, the Federal President appoints a Federal Commissioner for Data Protection who is independent of any other authority. He is a kind of ombudsman to whom any person who feels that his personal data have not been adequately protected may complain. He submits an annual report to the Bundestag. Each of the federal states, too, has a commissioner for data protection. And enterprises who process data must likewise have someone in charge of data protection. The authorities oversee their observance of the law with regard to data protection.

The constitutional significance of data protection emerged in a 1983 ruling of the Federal Constitutional Court. It said that under article 2 of the Basic Law the citizen has the right to determine himself whether his personal data may be disclosed and how it may be used. In 1990 the Federal Data Protection Act was updated in the

light of that ruling and the advancement of data processing. It strengthened the rights of persons affected and
gave the Federal Commissioner for Data Protection
wider powers.

Germany has some of the world's most up-to-date and
comprehensive data protection legislation which has
helped increase public awareness of the need for data
protection. Legislators must continue to respond prompt-
ly to rapid technological change in this field.

State and citizens

· Public finance
· Public service · Internal security

Public finance

In view of the negative experience of the 70s, when the government became overinvolved in the country's management, the present government aims to have a "leaner" state, in other words to cut back on public spending. By dint of budget savings, a consistent privatization policy and deregulation, it was possible in the 80s to reduce the public share of GDP from 50% in 1982 to 45% in 1989.

The purpose of privatization was and is to enable the state to concentrate on its central role. The proceeds from privatization are not considered a major contribution to the solution of budgetary problems, however. When, for instance, the Salzgitter corporation was sold in 1990 the money was used to establish the German Environment Foundation, one of the largest endowments in Europe, with initial capital of DM 2.5 billion.

But the country's reunification suddenly confronted the government with a host of new responsibilities. The volume and the importance of public finance have increased again accordingly. In 1993 the federal and state governments as well as the local authorities together spent DM 1,079 billion. This was the first time in the country's history that public spending had exceeded the trillion mark. If we add the cost of social insurance, special-purpose associations for joint performance of certain tasks, and contributions to the EU, the total came to DM 1,682 billion or 53.3% of GDP.

■ ■ ■ **Distribution of responsibilities.** The Federal Republic of Germany has three levels of government: federal, state and local. Their responsibilities in their respective areas are governed by the Basic Law. Generally speaking, they have to meet the necessary expenditure themselves. Hence public revenue does not flow into a joint account but is distributed among the federal, state and local governments.

The lowest level of public administration is that of the municipality, which is concerned with all matters that directly concern the local community and individual citizens. It is thus responsible for water, gas and electricity supply, refuse disposal, the maintenance of local roads, and local welfare and health services. Together with the state authorities it is also responsible for schools and cultural establishments.

The states have jurisdiction for all aspects of government, unless the Basic Law specifically provides otherwise or leaves open the possibility of a different arrangement. Their main responsibilities fall into the category of cultural affairs and primarily concern schools and education. But the administration of justice, the police and public health services also fall within the states' purview.

Most of the responsibility, and thus the largest financial burden, is borne by the Federation. According to the Basic Law, its sphere of competence embraces all matters that directly secure the existence of the state as a whole, viz social security, defence, foreign affairs, national security, the construction of autobahns and federal highways, telecommunications, major research and the promotion of science. It is also responsible for energy and the promotion of industry, agriculture, housing and urban development, public health, environmental protection and economic cooperation with developing countries. There are other various tasks which the federal and state governments plan, implement and finance jointly. They include university building, improvement of regional economic structures, agricultural structure and coastal preservation, as well as cooperation on educational planning and the promotion of science.

A fourth level of administration is also assuming increasing importance: the European Union.

■ ■ ■ **Financial planning.** A 1967 Law for the Promotion of Economic Stability and Growth requires the federal and state governments to draw up their budgets in the light of the principal economic policy objectives. These are price stability, a high level of employment, balanced foreign trade and steady economic growth (the "magic square"). The Federation and the states must draw up financial plans for their areas of responsibility in which incomes and expenditure are projected for a period of five years. The purpose of this pluriannual financial planning is to ensure that public revenue and expenditure are commensurate with national economic resources and requirements. The municipalities, too, must draw up medium-term financial plans.

The great importance of the public budgets requires close coordination through all levels of administration.

The main body in this process of voluntary cooperation is the Financial Planning Council set up in 1968 and representing the Federation, the state, the municipalities and the Bundesbank. There is also a Business Cycle Council with coordinating and advisory functions.

■ ■ ■ **Distribution of revenues.** In order to meet their responsibilities the federal, state and local governments must have the necessary funds. Wide-ranging as public responsibilities are, the sources of revenue are equally varied. The main source is taxation. Total tax revenue in 1993 was DM 748.805 billion. The Federation's share was 42.5%, that of the states 42.5% and that of the municipalities 15%.

Tax revenue has to be distributed according to the size of the responsibilities of the three levels of government. Income tax and turnover tax are the "joint taxes", that is to say, revenues from them are distributed between the federal and state governments according to specific formulas (that of the turnover tax being renegotiated from time to time). Part of the revenue from income tax also goes to the municipalities. In exchange they have to surrender to the federal and state governments part of the revenue they raise from the trade tax, which used to be a purely local government tax. The European Union receives a share of tax revenues as well, namely from customs duties, value-added tax and GNP own resources.

Tax revenues 1993
(in millions of DM, estimated)

Federation	360,250
States	256,131
Municipalities	95,790
EU own resources	36,635
Total	748,805

Important taxes:

Wage tax	257,987
Assessed income tax	33,234
Turnover tax, import turnover tax	216,305
Mineral oil tax	56,300
Tobacco tax	19,459

Other taxes apply to only one level of government. The Federation obtains revenue from the insurance tax and all excise taxes except the beer tax (e.g. mineral oil, tobacco and capital transaction taxes).

The states receive the revenue from the motor vehicle, wealth, inheritance, beer and real property transfer taxes as well as a number of smaller taxes.

The municipalities obtain revenue from the trade tax, less the share taken by the federal and state governments, real property tax and local excise taxes.

There are more than two dozen different taxes. Nearly half of all revenue comes from taxes on income (including the corporation tax). Income tax is the one which affects the average person most of all. Employers deduct it

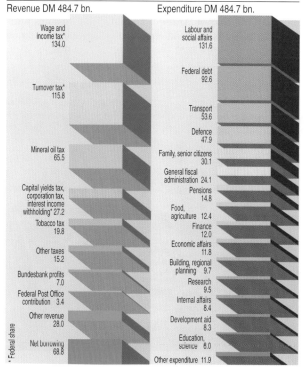

Federal budget 1995 (draft)

Revenue DM 484.7 bn.

Wage and income tax*	134.0
Turnover tax*	115.8
Mineral oil tax	65.5
Capital yields tax, corporation tax, interest income withholding*	27.2
Tobacco tax	19.8
Other taxes	15.2
Bundesbank profits	7.0
Federal Post Office contribution	3.4
Other revenue	28.0
Net borrowing	68.8

* Federal share

Expenditure DM 484.7 bn.

Labour and social affairs	131.6
Federal debt	92.6
Transport	53.6
Defence	47.9
Family, senior citizens	30.1
General fiscal administration	24.1
Pensions	14.8
Food, agriculture	12.4
Finance	12.0
Economic affairs	11.8
Building, regional planning	9.7
Research	9.5
Internal affairs	8.4
Development aid	8.3
Education, science	6.0
Other expenditure	11.9

from wages and salaries and remit it to the tax office (the "pay-as-you-earn" principle). The rate of taxation rises with the individual's income. After deduction of certain non-taxable amounts it comprises (pursuant to the Investment Promotion Act of September 1993) at least 19.5% and at most 53%. Incomes under DM 12,000 in the case of single persons and under DM 24,000 in the case of married couples are exempt from taxation.

The second largest source of revenue is the turnover tax (value-added tax and turnover tax on imports). It accounts for a quarter of all tax revenue. The mineral oil tax and the trade tax each provide between 6% and 7%.

■ ■ ■ **Financial equalization.** The financial situation of the individual states varies considerably because their natural resources and economic structures are also very different. Thus some of the old states such as Baden-Württemberg, Bavaria and Hesse have substantial financial resources whereas the new federal states, Bremen and the Saarland do not. These financial disparities are mitigated by a "state financial equalization regime" that since 1995 has encompassed the new federal states as well.

Research centre, Karlsruhe

This multilevel financial equalization is achieved by allocating the states' share of revenues from the turnover tax among the individual states according to a differentiated formula, by requiring financially stronger states to make equalization payments to financially weak states, and, finally, by providing federal complemental grants to the latter.

A "vertical financial equalization" takes place between the states and the municipalities. The tax revenues and other revenues of the municipalities are inadequate for their tasks. They therefore depend on grants from the states. Some of these grants are tied to specific purposes but others are freely disposable. The aim of this municipal financial equalization is to reduce the disparity in each state between municipalities with high and those with low tax revenues.

■ ■ **Public debt.** Apart from levying taxes to finance public expenditure the government can also borrow money. In the 70s and especially since reunification the federal and state finance ministers have been drawing increasingly on the capital markets. In 1993 the country's total public debt came to a record DM 1.4 trillion or almost DM 18,500 per inhabitant. To this sum must be added the debts of the Federal Railway (1993: DM 65.8 billion), the Post Office (DM 104.5 billion) and the Treuhand (about DM 300 billion).

■ ■ **Financial problems in connection with German unity.** When the wall dividing Germany was opened in November 1989 the overall public debt stood at DM 929 billion. By the end of 1992 the debt had increased to DM 1,331 billion. This in itself indicates the size of the financial problems relating to Germany's reunification.

Investment in German unity is therefore correspondingly high. In 1992 public spending and social insurance expenditure for the new states exceeded DM 110 billion after deduction of their structural and administrative revenue. The amount in 1993 was almost DM 140 billion. By the end of 1995 financial transfers from western to eastern Germany will have totalled DM 650 billion since 1990. There are in addition united Germany's considerable international liabilities, for instance its support for the process of democratic reform and consolidation in the countries of Central and Eastern Europe as well as in all the newly independent republics of the former Soviet Union.

The Unification Treaty provided that the new federal states should from the very beginning be incorporated as far as possible in the financial system established by the Basic Law. Thus since 1991 the new states have been subject to basically the same regulations with regard to budgetary management and tax distribution as the states of the "old" Federal Republic. A "German Unity Fund" was set up to provide financial support for the new states and their municipalities. It was fed jointly by the Federation and the western states, most of the money being raised in the capital market.

Until the end of 1994, this fund was a substitute for a nationwide financial equalization arrangement among the federal states. As of 1 January 1995 the German Unity Fund was replaced by the readjusted state financial equalization regime. Through this readjustment the new states have for the first time been included in a nationwide financial equalization arrangement. Under the readjusted financial equalization regime, the new states and their municipalities receive transfer payments totalling roughly DM 51 billion per year to supplement their own financial resources. Since the old states shoulder a considerable share of the burden entailed in these transfer payments through the horizontal turnover tax equalization regime and the state financial equalization regime (roughly DM 26 billion), the Federation has declared its willingness to increase the states' share of revenues accruing from turnover tax from 37% to 44%. In addition, the Federation makes substantial transfer payments in the form of federal complemental grants (roughly DM 18.6 billion) and furnishes financial assistance under the Investment Promotion Act Recovery East (DM 6.6 billion). These financial resources will permanently enable the new states to manage their affairs on their own financial responsibility.

Public service

For the average citizen the state as such is an abstract concept. It materializes, however, in the form of public servants who provide the vast range of services for which the Federation, the states and the municipalities are responsible. In the western states of the Federal Republic, i.e. those which existed prior to unification, public servants number more than 4.76 million, not counting career and temporary-career soldiers. In 1994 public servants in the new states including the eastern part of Berlin numbered about 1.5 million.

Public servants have widely differing occupations, for instance departmental officials and dustmen, swimming pool supervisors and professors, judges and nurses, policemen and teachers.

Over the years the public service has assumed many new functions. Today they range beyond the classical police and regulatory responsibilities and cover areas such as public education, the administration of a wide variety of public institutions and services, and environmental protection. The number of public servants has increased accordingly: In 1950, 9% of all gainfully employed persons were public servants; now the proportion is about 18%. Some 33% of all public servants are civil servants, judges, and career and temporary-career soldiers; the remainder are wage earners and salaried employees.

■ ■ ■ **Professional civil servants.** The professional civil service is an institution that has evolved in Germany since the 18th century. The Basic Law has guaranteed this proven institution and allows only civil servants to exercise "public authority". The purpose of having a professional civil service is to ensure that public responsibilities are carried out reliably without outside and in particular political influence. On account of the growing significance of public duties, for instance in the fields of infrastructure, education and social affairs, these requirements also apply to a large extent to the service-providing departments. Civil servants also exercise public authority in the traditional sense when they for instance order the demolition of a dangerously dilapidated house, impose fines or go in pursuit of criminals. But the range of responsibilities of civil servants in the modern industrial and social state is far greater.

The civil servant has a special obligation of loyalty to the state and the constitution. This is prescribed by law. Although civil servants, like all citizens, have the right to participate in political activities, they are required to exercise moderation and restraint. They may also form professional groups but are not allowed to strike.

But as well as special duties they also have special rights. As a rule they are appointed for life. For the period of their active employment and in retirement they and their families receive welfare benefits from the state. If they become incapacitated, or upon reaching retirement age, they receive a civil service pension. Salary scales are related to four service grades: ordinary, intermediate, higher intermediate and higher. Access depends on educational achievement and professional qualifications. Generally, members of the higher grade have a university degree.

Judges and members of the armed services are not, in the legal sense, civil servants, but they are subject to similar regulations. Their special status derives from the independence enjoyed by judges and the requirements of military discipline.

■■ **Wage earners and salaried employees.** In the 19th century there were very few wage earners in the public service, but their number has increased in the meantime corresponding to the importance of services for the local community. Wage earners and salaried staff in the public sector correspond in many respects to employees in the private sector. They pay social insurance contributions and are not appointed for life. Only after fifteen years' service and having reached the age of 40 does their status become permanent. Upon appointment they sign an employment contract which is largely determined by collective wage agreements. In contrast to civil servants they have a right to strike; otherwise their responsibilities and conditions of work have been brought more and more into line with the rights and duties of civil servants. For instance, they are required to maintain official secrecy; they must be incorruptible and loyal to the constitution.

Internal security

The maintenance of public security and order is one of the most important tasks of government. In the Federal Republic of Germany it is carried out by institutions of the states and the Federation. The police are for the most part under the jurisdiction of the states. Only in certain fields does the Basic Law assign responsibility to the Federation.

■ ■ ■ **The police in the federal states.** There are the general police forces, the criminal police, the river police, and the alert forces.

The general police forces are mainly concerned with the prevention and prosecution of petty crime. They also include traffic police, the law officers with whom the ordinary citizen may, if at all, come into contact.

The criminal police are chiefly concerned with serious offences including organized and industrial crime, sexual offences, robbery, blackmail, grand larceny, homicide, drug trafficking and the manufacture and passing of counterfeit money. They have special units, in some cases jointly with the general forces, to combat terrorism and hostage-taking, as well as for protective measures at special events and for observation and detection.

The river police, as the name implies, control all waterway traffic and monitor in particular the transport of dangerous goods.

The alert forces are responsible for the training of new recruits and provide support for the general and criminal forces during state visits, demonstrations, major sporting events, international fairs and natural disasters. They are trained and deployed as units. The alert forces of the Federal Republic number about 33,000.

■ ■ ■ **The Federal Border Guard, a national police force.** The Federal Border Guard (BGS) is a federal police force responsible to the Federal Ministry of the Interior. At the end of 1994 it numbered about 33,500 (including trainees), plus some 6,500 civilian staff. Its main task is to control the country's borders, which includes checks to prevent the illegal entry of foreigners, organized crime,

smuggling and drug trafficking. The Federal Border
Guard also protects key public buildings, such as the offices of the Federal President and the Federal Chancellor,
the ministries and the Federal Constitutional Court in
Karlsruhe. It supports the Federal Criminal Police Office
in protecting VIPs and in carrying out responsibilities
on the high seas including environmental protection
measures.

Since 1 April 1992 the Federal Border Guard has also
been responsible for railway and civilian air traffic security. It helps the state authorities cope with particularly
dangerous situations, for instance where large forces
have to be on duty during state visits or public demonstrations.

The Federal Border Guard is also called in during
natural disasters and major accidents. Beyond its
statutory functions it carries out international responsibilities, chiefly as part of the police component of
U.N. peacekeeping missions. The border police duties
of the Federal Border Guard are playing an increasingly important role, especially in light of the
Schengen Agreement that entered into force on
26 March 1995, which provides for stringent checks
at external borders.

■■■ **The Federal Criminal Police Office.** The Federal
Criminal Police Office (BKA), which is based in Wiesbaden with a head department near Bonn, is the focal point
of cooperation between the federal and state law enforcement agencies. Concerned with international crime,
it collects and evaluates information and other data. The
Federal Criminal Police Office is the main body for crim-
inological research and serves as the national centre for
Interpol, the international criminal police organization.

The BKA handles serious crimes itself, e.g. international drug trafficking, gun-running and terrorist activities. In
large-scale search operations it supports the police of the
federal states. The BKA's security unit in Bonn protects
the Federal President, the Chancellor, ministers, etc., as
well as their foreign guests of state.

Its staff of about 4,500 come under the authority of the
Federal Ministry of the Interior.

■■■ **Constitution-protection agencies.** Safeguarding
the democratic system is defined in the Basic Law as
"protection of the constitution". In order to be able to

Traffic monitoring centre, Munich

provide effective protection the federal and state authorities collect information on extremist activities and on other developments which constitute a threat to national security and evaluate it for the federal and state governments, executive authorities and courts.

Another important area is counterespionage. The federal authority charged with these tasks is the Federal Office for the Protection of the Constitution (BfV) in Cologne. It is accountable to the Federal Ministry of the Interior and cooperates with the corresponding state agencies. This agency has no executive police powers, i.e. it may not arrest or interrogate anyone. A law enacted in 1990 defines the legal basis for its activities more precisely and thus ensures greater protection for rights of privacy.

The federal and state agencies for the protection of the constitution are under the supervision of the competent ministers, parliaments and data protection commissioners. Further control is exercised by the courts.

Germany in the world

· Foreign policy
· External security
· Cooperation with developing countries

Foreign policy

In 1990 the German people were reunited in free self-determination. They achieved this goal by peaceful means and with the support of their friends and partners in East and West. The signing of the Treaty on the Final Settlement with respect to Germany (the Two-plus-Four Treaty) in Moscow on 12 September 1990 marked the end of the postwar era for Germany. That accord confirmed that Germany, after the restoration of its unity on 3 October 1990, had regained its sovereignty and was no longer burdened by status and security problems in relation to other countries. Its ten articles regulated the external aspects of unification. Thus, 45 years after the Second World War, the division of Germany, but also the division of Europe, was overcome. United Germany has a greater responsibility to bear. German policy remains above all a policy for peace. Its objective is to promote the economic and political integration of nation-states and to strengthen the international and supranational organizations and institutions so that they will become the foundations of global cooperation and bastions against the dangers of neo-nationalism.

As before, German foreign policy will be based on the country's lasting membership of the community of free democracies, the European Union (EU) and the Atlantic Alliance (NATO). This translates into five major objectives: the continuing progress of European integration, the further development of NATO, the stabilization of the reform processes in Central and Eastern Europe together with the necessary support, responsible participation in the United Nations and partnership with the developing countries.

The Federal Republic of Germany will continue to contribute to peaceful progress in the world. It accepts the responsibility deriving from the united country's global importance.

As one of the largest industrial and trading nations it is also dependent upon a stable and well-functioning world economic system that remains committed to free trade. Its main aim is to establish a fair balance of interests between North and South, between the industrial and the

Helmut Kohl being hosted by U.S. President William Clinton

developing countries, on the basis of a dialogue marked by the spirit of partnership. It pursues that aim chiefly within the United Nations and its sub-organizations.

Currently, the Federal Republic of Germany maintains diplomatic relations with nearly all countries. It has more than 230 embassies and consular posts as well as eleven missions at international organizations.

■ ■ ■ **European Union.** Ever since it was founded the Federal Republic of Germany has been one of the main advocates of European unification. Together with Belgium, France, Italy, Luxembourg and the Netherlands it formed in 1952 the European Coal and Steel Community (ECSC), and in 1957 the European Economic Community (EEC) and the European Atomic Energy Community (EURATOM). In 1967 these three institutions were merged to form the European Community (EC).

From the very outset the aim was to develop the European Community into a political union. The Treaty on European Union of 7 February 1992, which entered into force on 1 November 1993, was a major step towards this objective.

The Treaty on European Union marked the beginning of the decisive phase leading to the completion of European integration: The course has been charted for the introduction of a common currency before the end of this

decade. This will make the Community the world's most important economic area. The political signposts are above all:
– the merging of the Community treaties into a "Treaty on Political Union";
– the common foreign and security policy;
– wider powers for the European Parliament;
– cooperation in the fields of justice and home affairs; and
– the start towards social union.

The European Union (EU) is a supranational organization with its own institutions, some of whose decisions become directly applicable law in member states. These institutions include especially
– the European Parliament, which since 1979 has been elected directly by the people and has acquired increasing powers;
– the European Council, the conference of the heads of state or of government, in which basic issues of European policy are decided;
– the Council of the European Union, also called the Council of Ministers of the EU Member States, which decides Union policy;
– the European Commission, the Union's executive body, which is independent of national governments, ensures that Community regulations are applied and draws up proposals for the further development of common policy; and
– the European Court of Justice, which ensures that the laws and treaties of the European Union are properly interpreted and applied. The Court's decisions have played a large part in further developing European law.

The office of President of the Council of the European Union is held in turn by each Member State for a term of six months in accordance with a specific rotation procedure. Germany last held this office in the second half of 1994. The German Presidency, and especially the results of the meeting of the European Council on 9/10 December 1994, sent clear signals for the future development of the European Union: Substantial progress was made towards maintaining Europe's attractiveness as an industrial location; relations with the EU's neighbors in Central and Eastern Europe and in the Mediterranean region were deepened; cooperation in the fields of justice and

Helmut Kohl and French President Jacques Chirac

home affairs was intensified; and efforts were undertaken to put Europe in closer touch with its citizens.

Since its founding the European Union has acquired considerable influence not only as an economic community but also as a political force and as a champion of democratic values. By 1986 the six founding members of the EC had been joined by the United Kingdom, Denmark, Ireland, Greece, Portugal and Spain. On 1 January 1995 Austria, Sweden and Finland acceded to the European Union as well. Malta, Cyprus, Turkey, Poland and Hungary have formally submitted applications for membership.

The EU has meanwhile concluded Europe Agreements with most of the post-communist democracies of Central and Eastern Europe. These go beyond the association agreements the Community has concluded with other countries such as most of the Mediterranean states. Their purpose is to bring the reformist states in Central and Eastern Europe economically and politically closer to the EU and pave the way for their accession.

An event of historic significance was the meeting of the heads of government and the foreign ministers of 21 EU and CEE states in Essen on 10 December 1994, which took place on the occasion of the meeting of the European Council. In Essen the EU adopted a strategy for bringing the states of Central and Eastern Europe closer to the Union. Key aspects of this strategy are the establishment of structured relations, agricultural policy studies, and the request to the Commission to prepare a White Paper on creating the preconditions for bringing the CEE states into the internal market and achieving a harmonization of legislation. With this strategy a solid programme was presented which both sides can rely on and which will be in effect during the period prior to the commencement of negotiations on accession.

The Treaty on European Union defines the economic and monetary goals of European Union as well as the Union's further development into a political union.

One of the Union's basic elements is the common foreign and security policy (CFSP). It builds on European political cooperation (EPC) which, after a modest start 20 years ago, has become a major instrument of European foreign policy and a second pillar of the unification process. New elements include the integration of the common foreign and security policy into the uniform institutional framework of the Union and the addition of a security and defense policy dimension. The stage has also been set – by providing for the possibility of majority decision-making on certain issues, for instance – for the definition of common positions in the area of foreign and security policy. This will considerably enhance the Europeans' capacity to act in matters of foreign and security policy.

The Western European Union (WEU) is to be expanded into the security and defense policy arm of the EU – not in competition with the Atlantic Alliance, but rather as its European pillar. The Europeans can thus assume more responsibility for their own security and also take action in crisis situations in which NATO does not play an active role. The indispensable collective defense and security alliance between Europe and North America will remain unaffected by this. France and Germany, followed by Belgium, have taken a practical step in this direction by proposing, in consultation with their Atlantic partners, the establishment of a Eurocorps. Other EU Member States have meanwhile joined in, and in 1995, for the first time in history, there will be a major European formation with approximately 40,000 soldiers which will be able to engage in NATO operations and missions of the Western European Union.

For the purposes of achieving the objectives of the Union, in particular the free movement of persons, the Member States of the European Union have agreed to cooperate in the fields of justice and home affairs. This cooperation – like the common foreign and security policy – takes place between individual states but within the uniform institutional framework of the Union. Especially important areas of cooperation include police cooperation (the future European Police Office, Europol), the fight against drug-related crime, asylum policy and immigration policy. With this cooperation the European Union is becoming involved in areas of policy which are of particular concern to its citizens. At the same time, the manner of cooperation takes due account of the fact that these areas belong to the key classic areas of national sovereignty.

The Treaty on European Union concedes every citizen of the EU Member States citizenship of the Union. This citizenship of the Union gives him or her the right to move and reside freely within the territory of the Member States of the Union as well as the right to vote and stand as a candidate in both municipal elections and elections to the European Parliament even if he or she resides in a Member State other than that of which he or she is a national. It furthermore entitles him or her to protection by the consular authorities of any Member State in a third country in which the Member State of which he or she is a national is not represented.

Since the completion of the European internal market on 31 December 1992 all customs and trade barriers between the 15 EU Member States have disappeared. The four fundamental freedoms of this market are the free movement of goods, persons, services and capital. Since the enlargement of the EU upon the accession of Austria, Sweden and Finland, the 15 Member States now form the largest market in the world.

In harmony with the Schengen Agreement, under which most of the EU Member States have agreed to discontinue border controls, the internal market will provide a boost for Europe's economies, including Germany's export-oriented economy. The Schengen Agreement entered into force on 26 March 1995.

The European Union has demonstrated its attractiveness as a model community of free nations. But Europe is much larger than the present Union. The Union is open to any democratic European state – that is the letter and spirit of the Treaties of Rome.

In the decades of its development the European Union has helped enhance Europe's freedom and democracy. As the member with the most powerful economy, Germany is making substantial financial contributions to the Union's expansion. It will continue to make every effort to further the Union's integration.

In accordance with the principle of subsidiarity, the members of the European Union will be in charge of matters they are capable of handling themselves. European Union and national identity are not contradictory. It will not be possible to achieve or preserve the one without the other. That is how the Germans see their unity and European Union – as two sides of the same coin.

In 1996, in accordance with the terms of the Treaty on European Union, an intergovernmental conference will address the further development of the Treaty. The institutional prerequisites enabling the Union to admit new member states are also to be created. Preparation of the conference is in the hands of a reflection group, comprised of personal representatives of the foreign ministers, which began its work in June 1995. The Council, the European Parliament and the European Commission are each to compile a report on the functioning of the Treaty to aid the reflection group in its deliberations.

The European Union pursues an outward-looking trade policy. It advocates a market-oriented world economic order and is opposed to protectionism. It develops its economic and trade relations with third countries within a close network of trade, cooperation and association agreements which it has concluded with numerous states and groups of states (for example in the Mediterranean basin, in Southeast Asia, and in Central and South America). A typical example is the Fourth Lomé Convention (1990-2000), which is the basis for cooperation in partnership with 70 African, Caribbean and Pacific countries known as the ACP states. Lomé IV is currently undergoing the mid-term review required under the Convention.

■ ■ ■ **The Council of Europe.** Founded in 1949 and headquartered in Strasbourg, the Council of Europe is the oldest and largest European institution. Its main objectives are the protection and strengthening of pluralistic democracy, the rule of law and human rights in Europe. With the European Convention for the Protection of Human Rights and Fundamental Freedoms, the Council of Europe has at its disposal the world's only legally binding control mechanism in the area of human rights. The Council of Europe serves as an important bridge to Europe's new democracies. Since 1990 it has admitted nine of the new reformist democracies in Central and Eastern Europe. Nine additional states enjoy special guest status in its Parliamentary Assembly. The condition for membership was the irrevocable decision by these countries to defend human rights, democracy and the rule of law. The Council of Europe is making a politically significant contribution to the process of democratic restructuring in Central and Eastern Europe. This fact was stressed at the first summit meeting of the heads of state or of government of the member states of the Council of Europe which was held in Vienna in October 1993.

■■■ **The Organization for Security and Cooperation in Europe** (OSCE; until 31 December 1994 CSCE). The members of the OSCE include 53 European countries, the former Soviet Union, the United States and Canada. It is thus the only forum for pan-European cooperation. The Charter of Paris (1990) marked the OSCE's entry into a new phase following the end of East-West confrontation. The participating states are committed to human rights, democracy and the rule of law, to economic freedom and social justice, as well as to European unity. They have thus obligated themselves to observing high common standards in their dealings with one another and in their treatment of their citizens.

The OSCE, which formerly consisted largely of a series of conferences, has grown to become an active organization which can and does assume operative political responsibilities. These include early-warning arrangements, conflict prevention and crisis management including peacekeeping measures, and the peaceful settlement of conflicts. Long-term conflict prevention and advisory missions of the OSCE have taken up their work in a number of states. Apart from giving financial support, Germany has from the beginning provided qualified personnel for these missions.

The OSCE's potential for settling disputes by peaceful means was not sufficiently used in the past. At the end of 1992, therefore, the CSCE Council, meeting in Stockholm, adopted a number of procedural improvements including the settlement-by-order procedure and, in particular, the agreement on settlement and arbitration procedures within the OSCE, which was the result of a Franco-German initiative which 29 participating states signed immediately and which became effective on 5 December 1994 after ratification by twelve states.

The German Government welcomes the wide-ranging obligations created by the OSCE in the field of human rights. Although not legally binding they are of a very mandatory nature politically owing to the fact that they have been adopted by all participating states by consensus. To ensure continuous monitoring of OSCE standards regular implementation meetings are held at which the human rights situation in member countries is critically examined and discussed. OSCE expert missions within the "Moscow mechanism" created in 1991 have, through their investigations and reports, helped to solve problems in several participating states.

The High Commissioner for National Minorities, an office created with strong German support at the 1992 Helsinki summit, identifies potential ethnic tensions at the earliest possible time and helps contain and reduce them through direct consultations with the affected parties.

The OSCE will continue to serve as a forum for dialogue, negotiation and cooperation in order to give fresh stimulus to the process of arms control, disarmament and confidence- and security-building, as well as to improved consultation and cooperation in security matters and to the reduction of the risk of conflict. The 1992 Helsinki summit established the CSCE Forum for Security Cooperation for this purpose. At the summit in Budapest (1994) it was already possible to adopt a code of conduct that elaborates the prohibition of the use of force presently in effect by establishing norms governing the democratic control of armed forces and their deployment both inside and outside frontiers. A declaration on the principles of non-proliferation was likewise adopted.

The measures introduced so far have not yet completed the development of the ÒSCE. German foreign policy will give the OSCE and its institutions more scope for action so that it can better meet its responsibilities as a regional arrangement within the meaning of chapter VIII of the United Nations Charter.

■ ■ ■ **The Atlantic Alliance.** The North Atlantic Treaty Organization (NATO) remains the indispensable foundation of the security of its members in Europe and North America. The Federal Republic of Germany joined NATO in 1955.

The defence preparedness and capability of all NATO member states has, over the decades, safeguarded the free democracies, starting from the dual strategy of defence and dialogue in relation to the former Warsaw Pact countries as expressed in the Harmel Report of 1967. It was not least the Atlantic Alliance which paved the way for the transformation in Europe and Germany.

Meanwhile the political transformation in Europe has removed the confrontation between East and West. The security situation, despite some remaining risks, has improved considerably. Nevertheless, NATO still has a central role to play in maintaining Europe's stability and security.

NATO's new strategy adopted in Rome in November 1991 represents the Alliance's response to the changed security situation. It entails a sizeable reduction in force strengths and new force structures. With the massive communist threat a thing of the past, special importance attaches to the role of mobile and multinational crisis reaction forces in defending the NATO area with fewer forces.

In 1992/93 NATO resolved to support U.N. and CSCE peacekeeping operations in suitable cases on request. It participates in the enforcement of the embargo in the Adriatic and closely monitors the ban on flights in the airspace of Bosnia. At the request of the United Nations, NATO intervened in Bosnia in 1994 to protect civilian safe areas and the U.N.'s peacekeeping forces.

Germany played a leading role in bringing about NATO's readjustment to the changed situation in Europe, especially in cooperation with the United States.

It was a German-U.S. initiative in late 1991 that led to the establishment of the North Atlantic Cooperation Council (NACC), which meanwhile embraces all members of the defunct Warsaw Pact and the successor states of the Soviet Union. This Council, now institutionalized and meeting regularly, demonstrates the Western Alliance's readiness for a comprehensive security partnership in Europe. Since January 1994 the Council has been complemented by the Partnership for Peace (PfP), which deepens political and military cooperation between NATO and the meanwhile 25 partner countries in preparation of joint peacekeeping operations, among other things.

Disarmament and arms control are indispensable tools of German foreign and security policy. Their purpose is to limit weapon capabilities and establish binding rules for the use of military force.

Cooperative arms control focuses on the implementation of recent accords – to which Germany, too, is a party – such as the "Treaty on Conventional Forces in Europe", under which more than 50,000 heavy weapons will be eliminated, the 1992 follow-up agreement on force limitations (CFE Ia), the 1992 "Vienna Document" on confidence- and security-building measures among the CSCE states, the 1992 "Open Skies Treaty", which renders the airspace of contracting states (i.e. from Vancouver to Vladivostok) accessible for aircraft surveillance, the institution in 1992 of the CSCE Forum for Security Cooperation, which is designed to create a new security relationship among the OSCE states on the basis of cooperation and mutual confidence, as well as the 1993 Convention on the Prohibition of the Development, Production, Stockpiling and Use of Chemical Weapons and Their Destruction. Germany was one of the main proponents of this convention and in August 1994 became one of the first states to ratify it.

A completely new departure in the field of arms control is the provision, also by Germany, of assistance for the destruction of nuclear and chemical weapons. Another task is to prevent the proliferation of weapons of mass destruction and to consolidate the international non-proliferation system. In this context Germany advocates a strengthening of the Nuclear Non-proliferation Treaty of 1968.

Another major event is the session of the Geneva Conference on Disarmament, which began in January 1994 and is concerned with a comprehensive nuclear test ban.

■ ■ ■ **Relations with the Western states.** Germany's and Europe's close ties with the democracies of North

America remain unchanged. The transatlantic partnership is based on vital mutual interests and values. Europe, the United States and Canada have manifold historical, human, cultural and political ties. Thus America's and Canada's involvement in Europe continues to be of vital importance to the Continent's, and hence Germany's, peace and security. NATO remains an indispensable security bond between Europe and North America.

Biannual summit meetings and various bilateral consultations provide renewed stimulus for the special relationship between Germany and France established by Chancellor Konrad Adenauer and President Charles de Gaulle through the treaty signed in the Elysée Palace, Paris, in 1963. In recent years attention has focused on the question of European Union, progress towards which has been considerably helped by the joint initiatives of Chancellor Kohl and President Mitterrand.

Following German unification, France has also become economically and culturally involved in the development of the new federal states. The stability of Franco-German friendship is guaranteed by the contacts between the citizens of both countries (there being more than 1,400 town twinnings and 2,000 school twinnings, as well as cooperation between the regions) and by the close economic relations between the two countries, who are each other's principal trading partner.

Germany's cooperation with other Western countries has also been continuously intensified. Biannual summit meetings are held with the United Kingdom, and a close network of agreements, consultations and mutual visits makes for a similarly close relationship with Germany's other Western partners.

Relations between Germany and Israel, too, are intensive and good at all levels and in most spheres. Since the establishment of diplomatic relations in 1965 they have in many respects developed into a genuine friendship.

■ ■ ■ **Cooperation with Eastern neighbours.** For Germany's future cooperation with her Eastern neighbours it was important to conclude treaties as the framework for a proper relationship. Such accords have meanwhile been signed with Poland, the Czech Republic, the Slovak Republic, Hungary and the successor states of the former Soviet Union. Germany's relationship with the latter is of crucial importance to the whole of Europe, it being essential to create the material foundations for European unity and to establish the fundamental values of democracy and the rule of law.

In order to develop a free social order and a market economy the nations of Eastern, Central and Southeastern Europe and those in the new states on the territory of the former Soviet Union need the support of the West as a whole. Germany has strongly backed the reforms in these countries from the very beginning, as shown in particular by the financial assistance of DM 87 billion she has provided for the the new states on the territory of the former Soviet Union and the approximate amount of DM 37 billion for Central and Eastern Europe since 1989 (figures as of August 1993).

She has thus contributed over 50% of the total aid from the industrial countries. The help provided will ultimately benefit the whole of Europe. Germany remains a strong advocate of European pluralism. The desire for self-determination in Eastern Europe will grow the more it coincides with the development of pan-European structures and pan-European solidarity.

Instead of being implemented separately by the various ministries concerned, all national measures are being coordinated in order to enhance their effectiveness, also in relation to the activities of other donors. Since 1993 Walter Kittel, the Commissioner of the Federal Government for Consulting Efforts in Eastern Europe, has served as the coordinator of all the ministries' activities. A consulting concept was drawn up to aid in the establishment of democratic structures and a social market economy in the states of Central and Eastern Europe and the Commonwealth of Independent States. The key idea behind this consulting concept is helping these states to help themselves. In other words, given the disparity between Germany's resources and the tremendous need for advice on the part of most of the partner countries, the Federal Government's activities can only be of a supportive nature; our partners must travel this road themselves.

In light of Germany's experience and strengths, but also due to her limited financial resources, and in order to ensure an efficient range of consulting services the Federal Government's consulting concept focuses on the following:

– economic advice on the creation of framework condi-

tions for a social market economy and for the establishment of a small and medium-sized business sector;
– assistance in the restructuring, privatization and decentralization of firms;
– establishment of tax, customs, insurance and banking
systems;
– advice pertaining to the agricultural sector;
– initial and further training in the commercial sector
(management training, vocational initial and further
training, qualification measures);
– legal advice emphasizing the field of commercial law;
– assistance in the establishment of administrative structures; and
– advice in the areas of labour market and social policy
as well as environmental protection.

Between 1992 and 1994 the Federal Government's
expenditure for this consulting concept totalled nearly
DM 1 billion.

■■ ■ **Germany and the developing countries.** Relations with the developing countries are an important element of German foreign policy. Reducing the prosperity
gap between the industrial and developing countries and
protecting the natural sources of life are increasingly becoming the crucial tasks of the coming years. Cooperation based on partnership, not least assistance intended
to help the recipients achieve self-sustaining develop-

Foreign Minister Klaus Kinkel
with his Russian colleague Andrei Kosyrev

ment, serves the common aim of meeting global challenges such as poverty, rapid population growth and the
destruction of the environment, and ensuring mankind's
survival. The development policy of the Federal Government focuses on the fight against poverty, protection of
the environment and natural resources, as well as education and training.

In 40 years of fruitful cooperation prior to unification
the Federal Republic of Germany earned the reputation of
a reliable, trustworthy and helpful partner of the nations
of the South where four fifths of the world's population live.

The developing nations expect united Germany to assume a larger role on the world stage. At the same time,
however, they are afraid she might neglect "the South" in
favour of "the East" on account of the economic burden
of the unification process and the aid provided for the reformist countries of Central and Eastern Europe. Since
1990, the year of unification, the German Government
has therefore often reaffirmed its commitments to the developing countries and its intention to further develop
and strengthen the existing bonds of friendship.

The industrial countries must meet their responsibility
to create global economic conditions which give the developing countries, too, a fair chance. They must in particular open their markets. In elaborating national policies they must give more attention to their impact on developing countries and increase their assistance in terms
of both quality and quantity for the poorer developing
countries in particular.

Relations between the European Union and the developing countries are already featuring prominently in Germany's foreign and security policy. Federal development
aid funds in the last three years have not been reduced in
spite of the country's additional burdens.

Germany, as in the recent past, will participate in international efforts to contain and remove sources of crisis.
The humanitarian aid she has provided since 1991 for the
Kurds in Iraq, for Somalia, for the victims of the civil war
in former Yugoslavia, and for the refugees from Rwanda
is considerably more than in previous years. Since 1991,
funds totalling DM 597 million have been made available from the budget of the Federal Foreign Office alone.
Germany's overall expenditure for humanitarian aid (relief operations of the Armed Forces, food aid, measures

The European Council met in Essen on 9/10 December 1994

undertaken by private German relief organizations, participation in relief measures of the EU, the United Nations and other international organizations) is several times this amount.

For the period 1992-1994 Germany earmarked DM 27 million to help finance the democratization process in the developing and reformist countries and intends to increase this amount in the future.

In the European Union Germany has always urged that the Europeans open their markets wider to the countries of Africa, Asia and Latin America, for free trade is, in the final analysis, even more important to the developing countries than development assistance.

■ ■ ■ **Membership of the United Nations.** A major aim of German foreign policy is to strengthen the role of the United Nations as the principal institution of the community of nations. Only this will enable the world organization to respond adequately to such global challenges as conflict prevention, the population explosion and environmental protection. This applies especially to the Secretary-General of the United Nations, who should be placed in a stronger position to mediate in preventing conflicts. By dint of her own history Germany is particularly committed to freedom, democracy and human rights. All over the world, therefore, her policy is based on respect for human rights and human dignity.

Germany has shown by word and deed that she is prepared to fulfil the global responsibility deriving from the country's unification. In October 1994 she was elected a non-permanent member of the United Nations Security Council for the third time, receiving 164 out of 170 votes. Germany is also prepared, within the framework of a reform of the Security Council, to assume greater political responsibilities as a permanent member of the Security Council. It became apparent in the course of the 49th General Assembly that Germany can rely on widespread support of the members of the United Nations in this endeavor. In the context of U.N. peacekeeping and humanitarian missions, which have increased constantly since the end of the East-West confrontation, she has, for instance, sent troops to Cambodia and Somalia. According to a judgment handed down by the Federal Constitutional Court, German armed forces may participate in operations within the framework of NATO and WEU activities in support of the implementation of resolutions of the United Nations Security Council. The same applies to the participation of German armed forces in United Nations peacekeeping troops.

■ ■ ■ **Cultural relations.** Cultural policy is one of the main elements of German foreign policy. It consists of
– giving other countries a comprehensive and self-critical picture of the Federal Republic of Germany and her cultural achievements, a picture which reflects the country's pluralist democracy and embraces the whole nation's spiritual and intellectual values;
– promoting the German language all over the world; and
– fostering cultural exchange with other countries in a spirit of partnership.

The aim of this policy is to remove prejudices and strengthen mutual respect. In this way it helps to promote political and economic cooperation. In the development of cultural relations the Federal Foreign Office cooperates with the state governments, the churches, unions, political foundations and many other organizations.

Germany has concluded cultural agreements with more than 80 countries but also has intensive cultural exchanges with most other countries.

Translating cultural policy into practice is largely the responsibility of organizations acting on behalf of the Federal Government.

They include
– the Goethe Institute, which has 148 branches abroad
and 16 in Germany and whose main tasks are to cultivate
the German language abroad and promote international
cultural cooperation;
– the German Academic Exchange Service (DAAD),
which organizes exchanges of academic staff and students;
– Inter Nationes, which hosts foreign guests of the government and provides a wide range of information on the
Federal Republic of Germany through films, tapes and
printed material; and
– the Institute for Foreign Relations, which organizes
German exhibitions abroad and foreign exhibitions in
Germany.

External security

The principal aim of the Federal Republic's security policy is to maintain peace and safeguard the country's freedom and independence. "Maintain peace with fewer weapons" was the Federal Republic's motto in helping to end the East-West confrontation. Germany is playing a constructive part in shaping Europe's new security relationships. The members of the European Union aim to establish a common foreign and security policy in which the Western European Union (WEU) plays a major role. The close political and military cooperation in the North Atlantic Treaty Organization (NATO) is complemented by cooperation on security matters with the Central and Eastern European countries in the North Atlantic Cooperation Council (NACC).

Through its involvement in disarmament and arms control Germany is helping to build new security structures. Prior to unification Germany undertook by treaty to reduce the size of its armed forces significantly by 1994. With 370,000 servicemen the Bundeswehr of united Germany is smaller than the armed forces of the Federal Republic prior to unification. Up to 1990 the Bundeswehr had a personnel strength of 490,000, while the GDR's National People's Army (NVA) had 170,000. The Federal Republic of Germany still provides the largest contingent of conventional forces for NATO in Europe. In the 1990 Treaty on Conventional Forces in Europe the Federal Republic also agreed to sizeable disarmament measures.

As in the past, the Bundeswehr remains a purely defensive army. It has no weapons of mass destruction and does not want any. However, security precautions are still necessary.

■ ■ ■ **The Bundeswehr.** The Bundeswehr consists of modern armed services based on conscription for men. The basic period of military service is at present twelve months but is to be shortened to ten months. There are also career servicemen and others on engagements of up to 15 years. For women there are careers available in the medical and music corps. The civilian staff of the armed forces number about 186,000.

*Federal President Roman Herzog is welcomed
by the Bundeswehr*

The Bundeswehr consists of the army, the navy and the air force. In all services considerable disarmament measures are envisaged. Hundreds of tanks and aircraft are to be scrapped and ships decommissioned. The defence budget is dwindling. In the mid-90s new plans will come into effect for the armed forces. Combat forces and the territorial army will be merged. Only a few mobile units of 10,000 to 15,000 men with a large proportion of career servicemen will have a full complement in peacetime.

On 3 October 1990, the day of German unity, the armed forces of the former GDR, the National People's Army (NVA), were disbanded. Some NVA servicemen, after first being given temporary contracts, have been permanently incorporated in the Bundeswehr. In 1992, for the first time, conscripts from western Germany were called up for service in garrisons in eastern Germany.

In 1991 the Soviet Union began withdrawing its approximately 340,000 troops as well as 210,000 dependents and civilian personnel from the territory of the former GDR. This process, which was partly financed by the Federal Republic, was completed on 31 August 1994. The United States and the other NATO countries with troops stationed in Germany are also reducing their military presence and, together with the Bundeswehr, are forming major multinational formations.

■ ■ ■ **The Bundeswehr's mission**. The Bundeswehr
– protects the Federal Republic of Germany and her people from political blackmail and external danger;
– promotes Europe's military stability and integration;
– defends Germany and her allies;
– serves the cause of world peace and international security in accordance with the United Nations Charter;
and
– provides support in the event of disasters and other
emergencies, including humanitarian aid programmes.

The Federal Republic of Germany has been a member
of the United Nations since 1973. The international community now rightly expects reunited Germany to play a
full part in U.N. missions and activities. According to the
Charter this can also include military operations.

Germany participated in U.N. humanitarian missions
in Cambodia and in peacekeeping operations in Somalia.
The Bundeswehr supports the U.N.'s verification team in
Iraq, participates in the enforcement of the ban on flights
in the airspace of Bosnia and Herzegovina, and flies ship-
ments of humanitarian aid to the inhabitants of Bosnia-
Herzegovina and the Rwandan refugees.

In a judgment handed down on 12 July 1994, the Federal Constitutional Court clarified the admissibility of
participation by German armed forces in operations
abroad within the framework of collective security systems. Such participation must be approved by the German Bundestag.

Germany will maintain its policy of restraint in respect
of participation by the Bundeswehr in operations abroad
but shall in the future fully face up to its responsibility to
help preserve global peace.

■ ■ ■ **The Bundeswehr and the community**. In peacetime supreme command of the armed forces lies with the
Federal Minister of Defence, in the event of war with the
Federal Chancellor. Parliamentary control of the Bundeswehr is exercised by the Bundestag committees, especially the Defence Committee.

An important role is also played by the Parliamentary
Commissioner for the Armed Forces, who is elected by
parliament for a five-year term. His task is to protect the
constitutional rights of servicemen. Every member of the
armed services has the right to complain to him directly
without going through his superiors. The Commissioner

may demand information and access to files from military units and visit any Bundeswehr facility unannounced. He submits an annual report to the Bundestag on the complaints he has received.

General conscription indicates a country's intention to defend itself and at the same time serves to integrate the armed forces into the community as a whole.

Apart from having the civic duty to serve in the armed forces, the individual has a basic right to refuse on grounds of conscience. Under article 4 of the Basic Law, no one may be forced against his conscience into military service involving armed combat. Anyone recognized as a conscientious objector is no longer under obligation to serve in the armed forces. Instead, he must complete 15 months of alternative civilian service.

Cooperation with developing countries

The Federal Republic of Germany is one of the biggest donors of development assistance. At the beginning of 1995 it had economic cooperation partnership agreements with 183 countries.

As early as 1961 a Federal Ministry for Economic Cooperation (in 1993 the words "and Development" were added to the title) was created – the first time any country had appointed a cabinet minister with sole responsibility for development assistance. This showed the determination of the German parliament, government and people to help other nations in need in the light of the country's experience after the war when her own economy had to be rebuilt and this was only possible with help from abroad.

Even after unification and the fundamental changes in Central and Eastern Europe, Germany has broadened her relations with the developing countries in awareness of her increased global responsibility. All leading members of the government and the opposition want united Germany to honour her commitments to the developing countries and to increase her development assistance further still in the long term.

Assistance is also provided for the countries of Eastern Europe and the successor states of the Soviet Union, through the Federal Ministry for Economic Cooperation and Development for those who come under the international category of developing countries, through the Federal Ministry of Economics and other departments for the others.

In a period of more than 30 years the German Government, together with non-governmental organizations and private institutions, has gathered valuable experience and created a broad range of instruments for the promotion of overseas development. Through close cooperation with recipient countries it has been possible to adapt assistance measures to the differing economic and social conditions in Africa, Asia, Latin America, the Middle East and Central and Eastern Europe.

Despite all efforts to reduce the prosperity gap between industrial and developing countries and despite their partial success, the task of removing hunger and poverty has still not been accomplished in many parts of the world. Consequently, combating mass poverty and removing its structural causes is still the foremost objective of German development policy. The world of tomorrow will only be able to live in peace if it proves possible to alleviate hunger and need, reduce the prosperity gap between North and South, protect and preserve the natural sources of life, and ensure respect for human rights.

It is now generally recognized that the people in North and South, in East and West, in poor and rich countries, are interdependent. This is clearly illustrated by the alarming extent of environmental destruction and its repercussions on industrial and developing countries. The German Government, apart from pursuing a progressive environmental policy at home, also supports developing countries in their implementation of environmentally friendly development programmes.

Being a leading export nation, the Federal Republic of Germany has an interest in healthy economic progress in the developing countries. It considers itself to have a special responsibility to help liberalize international trade. The more efficient the economy of the developing countries, the more attractive they become as partners for trade and investment.

There is also another motive for development cooperation. Improved living conditions in the developing coun-

Modern plant-protection methods in the Philippines

tries open up better economic and social prospects for millions of people who otherwise might be forced to leave their native countries in quest of a new life elsewhere. Development policy serves to combat the causes of flight and is thus a preventive refugee policy.

■ ■ ■ **Aims of development policy.** It is the recipients themselves who must decide what they want from development cooperation. Effective aid can only be a way of helping them help themselves.

But such assistance will only be effective if the developing countries concerned create conditions which enable the people to employ their skills in a meaningful and worthwhile manner. Experience has shown that such conditions are most likely to be found in countries that have a law-based system with market elements which offer incentives to the people. The governments of the developing countries themselves are alone responsible for creating a framework of this kind that is conducive to development.

In the autumn of 1991 the German Government laid down new political criteria for official development aid, namely:

– respect for human rights;

– participation of the people in the political process;

– the guarantee of security under the law;

– the creation of a market-oriented economy; and

– development-oriented domestic policies (which includes cuts in excessive arms expenditure).

Of course, not all developing countries are able to meet these conditions entirely, but the German Government will even then continue to look for ways and means of helping the people directly, of alleviating their poverty, and of preserving the natural sources of life. This is achieved through programmes which are implemented directly with the people's self-help organizations.

Development cooperation takes the form of direct bilateral assistance from government to government as well as multilateral assistance through international organizations, principally the United Nations and its specialized agencies, and through the European Union. It also takes the form of promoting private sector cooperation and the activities of non-governmental organizations (NGOs), who have long experience with cooperative measures in the developing countries.

Advising Peruvian farmers

In 1993 the German Government spent nearly DM 11.2 billion on development cooperation. That is equivalent to 0.36% of the gross national product and above the average for all industrial countries.

From 1950 to 1993 Germany's net financial assistance to developing countries (i.e. after deducting repayments) came to DM 415.7 billion. DM 336.3 billion took the form of direct (bilateral) assistance; DM 79.4 billion was made available through multilateral cooperation. These sums include contributions by Germany's states (1993: DM 172.4 million) and the NGOs (1993: DM 1.43 billion).

■ ■ ▪ **Financial, technical and personnel cooperation.** Financial cooperation, formerly called capital aid, is the main instrument in terms of volume. Financial cooperation mainly consists of concessional loans to finance social infrastructure and environmental protection projects, as well as non-repayable grants.

The money provided is used to finance individual projects (e.g. road construction) or comprehensive programmes (in the field of health, for instance) or to provide credit for small-scale farmers. Within the framework of financial cooperation, commodity aid is also granted to developing countries who have little foreign exchange with which to import the machinery, spares and raw materials they need to maintain or improve production, as well as scientific, technical and medical equipment.

Since 1987 the German Government has also been providing what is known as "structural aid" – currency for the speedy import of commodities and services required for structural adjustment programmes. The Federal Government attaches considerable importance to mitigating the social repercussions of structural adjustment measures.

The terms on which funds are provided within the framework of financial cooperation depend on the economic situation of the recipient. Since 1978 the poorest countries have only been receiving non-repayable grants (financial contributions). The other developing countries receive loans with ten-year grace periods, long maturities, and minimal interest rates. Financial aid is not tied to German supplies and services.

Assistance within the framework of technical cooperation is generally provided free of charge. Projects or programmes are implemented jointly with existing institutions or by those newly established by the recipient countries. The aim of this cooperation is always to enable local staff to take charge of these activities as soon as possible. Specialists, advisers and instructors are seconded to developing countries and paid by the German Government; equipment and material for the promoted institutions are either dispatched or financed; and training is provided for local specialists and managerial personnel who are to assume the responsibilities of the German experts.

Within the framework of personnel cooperation, initial training and further training are provided for local specialists and managerial personnel of developing countries. This training largely takes place in Germany. By the end of 1993, about 195,500 participants from developing countries had benefited from such programmes; roughly 21,500 were engaged in training in 1993. The object of this personnel cooperation is to give people from developing countries suitable opportunities to develop their knowledge and skills on their own responsibility. Thus they are helped to start up in business or employed on development cooperation projects.

At the end of 1993 about 3,500 local experts were already working alongside about 1,400 German experts on technical cooperation projects financed by Germany. Of the 1,800 or so working on financial cooperation projects, approximately 900 were experts from developing countries.

Distinctions are made as to the types of experts engaged in the programmes and projects financed by Germany. The experts seconded by the German Government are employed as advisers on various technical cooperation projects and programmes. They are under contract to a German organization. Integrated experts, on the other hand, are under contract to an institution in the developing country concerned, from which they receive the usual local salary. Germany tops up salaries and provides social security and temporary assistance. German development volunteers have a special status within the framework of non-governmental development projects. They differ from other specialists in that they do not seek to earn a living but instead "work in closest possible contact" with the population in return for a small allowance.

■ ■ ■ **Focus of development cooperation.** Decisions as to which sectors of the economy require priority treatment are made in accordance with the German development policy concept and country analyses on the basis of

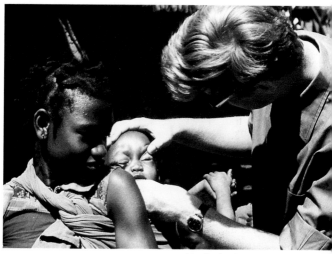

Medical care in Tanzania

proposals and data submitted by the developing country concerned.

Cooperation projects have four main aims: to overcome poverty, to further agricultural development, to protect the environment and natural resources, and to promote basic education and vocational training. Projects range from industry, crafts and mining, transfer of technology and the development of administrative infrastructures to the war against drugs.

In all sectors women, due to their special position, are included in the development process. Even in the planning stage their interests must be taken into consideration. This applies especially to areas where women bear the main burden, as in agriculture and water and fuel supply, and where they are particularly affected by poor conditions, for instance health and housing, food production and training.

Key areas of endeavor are food security and rural development. The aim is to help the developing countries maintain food supplies through their own efforts. This is why efforts are being made to increase agricultural production by promoting small farmers, providing farming equipment, developing efficient marketing systems and promoting agricultural research. These are major contributions towards improving the general supply situation

Trainees learning how to use electronic measuring equipment

Training courses for telecommunications engineers

in rapidly growing, densely populated urban areas as well.

Food aid provided by the German Government is only intended as a means of removing supply bottlenecks in the wake of natural disasters, harvest failures or flows of refugees resulting from armed conflict. The German Government tries to buy an increasing proportion of its food aid supplies in regions or localities of developing countries that have a surplus of such commodities. In this way it is able to supply the kind of food which the people affected normally eat. At the same time food production is promoted in surplus countries.

Measures to restore and maintain the natural sources of life constitute an important part of development assistance. Consequently, every project is examined as to its compatibility with the environment. The German Government gives priority to measures which serve to protect the environment, such as national environmental protection programmes, land-use planning, afforestation, forest management and measures to prevent soil erosion. It attaches considerable importance to measures for the preservation of tropical rainforests and the prevention of desertification.

Other sectoral priorities include the promotion of education, especially educational infrastructure. Increasing support is being provided for the reform of general and vocational education, and better educational opportunities for girls and women as well as rural populations. Germany has helped considerably to raise international standards of vocational training. With regard to population control, the German Government promotes family planning programmes in agreement with the governments concerned.

Measures in the area of population control make an important contribution to improving the quality of life for people and sustaining development processes. The Federal Government supports these measures through bilateral and multilateral forms of cooperation. The basic principles and objectives governing the planning and implementation of development cooperation projects in the area of population control and family planning were spelled out in the 1991 Development Concept of the Federal Ministry for Economic Cooperation and Development. This concept is characterized by a dual approach that takes due account of rapid population growth in the developing countries: Cooperation addresses the lack of family planning services as well as the poor economic and social situation of the inhabitants, focusing especially on women's living circumstances and the areas of health care, education and nutrition.

Economic system and policy

The Federal Republic of Germany is one of the major industrial countries. In terms of overall economic performance she is the third largest, and with regard to world trade she holds second place. She is one of the seven leading western industrial countries (the Group of Seven) who, since 1975, have every year held a summit meeting at which they coordinate their economic and financial policies at the level of the heads of state or of government.

In 1994 the gross domestic product, that is to say the value of all goods produced and services in the course of a year, came to a record DM 2,978 billion in the western part of the country, a per capita amount of DM 45,200. After price adjustments, GDP has doubled in the past 25 years, and in 40 years increased even fivefold. Expressed in 1991 prices, that is a growth from DM 426.7 billion in 1950 to DM 2,709.6 billion in 1994.

Germany owes her rise from the devastation of the Second World War to her present position among the world's leading industrial nations not to her natural resources or financial reserves but to her skilled manpower. The crucial factors which account for a country's economic efficiency are the training and industry of the labour force, managerial skills, and the broad scope which the social market economy affords to hard-working people.

After the Second World War people often spoke of the German "economic miracle". Ludwig Erhard, the Federal Republic's first Minister of Economics, disliked this term. He said it was no miracle, "merely the result of honest endeavour on the part of a whole nation who were given the opportunity and freedom to make the best of human initiative, freedom and energy".

■ ■ ■ **The social market economy.** Since the war the Federal Republic has developed a socially responsible market economy. This system rejects both the laissez-faire doctrine of the Manchester school and government intervention in business and investment decisions.

The Basic Law, which guarantees private enterprise and private property, stipulates that these basic rights be exercised for the public good. Under the motto "as little government as possible, as much government as necessary" the state plays a mainly regulatory role in the market economy. It creates the general conditions for market processes, but it is the millions of households and companies who decide freely what they want to consume and produce.

The question as to which and how many goods are produced and who gets how much of what is decided above all in the marketplace. The government forgoes any direct intervention in price and wage fixing. The prerequisite for a well-functioning market system is competition. Without it there can be no market economy. Competition ensures

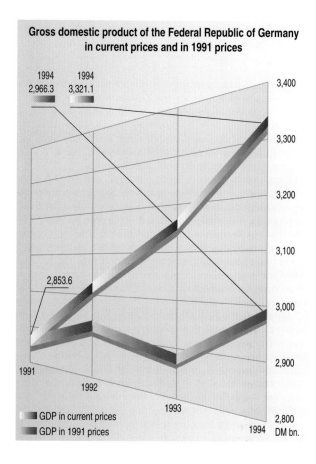

Gross domestic product of the Federal Republic of Germany in current prices and in 1991 prices

1994: 2,966.3
1994: 3,321.1

2,853.6

3,400
3,300
3,200
3,100
3,000
2,900
2,800

1991
1992
1993
1994

GDP in current prices
GDP in 1991 prices

DM bn.

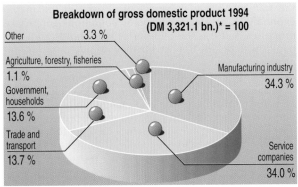

Breakdown of gross domestic product 1994 (DM 3,321.1 bn.)* = 100

Other 3.3 %

Agriculture, forestry, fisheries
1.1 %

Government, households
13.6 %

Trade and transport
13.7 %

Manufacturing industry
34.3 %

Service companies
34.0 %

*) In respective prices – provisional figures

that the individual pursuit of profit translates into a maximum supply of goods for the community as a whole. It encourages initiative and forces companies to improve their market position by lowering prices, improving the quality of their products, and offering better payment and delivery terms as well as additional services. It is also conducive to innovation and rationalization.

Open competition is undoubtedly hard for all concerned. Entrepreneurs time and time again try to neutralize competition, whether through agreements with rivals or mergers. Preventing this is the purpose of the 1957 Law against Restraints of Competition (Cartel Act). It forbids concerted practices and agreements which influence market conditions by restricting competition. The law has undergone numerous improvements and its observance is monitored by the Federal Cartel Office in Berlin and the state anti-trust authorities.

The aim of the Federal Government has been and continues to be to gradually privatize such enterprises as the Deutsche Bundesbahn (German Federal Railway), the Reichsbahn (railway of the former GDR), and the Deutsche Bundespost (German Administration of Posts and Telecommunications) in order to increase competition, ease the financial burden on the national budget, and provide more efficient services for the public.

The shortage of housing resulting from the war initially led to the housing market being state-controlled. In the meantime many of the restrictions have been lifted. The state does, however, ensure that competition does not result in socially intolerable conditions, chiefly by means of laws protecting tenants, the payment of housing supplements to low-income households, the promotion of building projects and the modernization of housing.

In several sectors where, in principle, there is free competition, lawmakers have made entry into the market subject to conditions. Thus craftsmen and retailers, for instance, must prove they have the necessary vocational qualifications before they can set up in business. For other occupations and professions the state requires special training and a minimum age, for example in the fields of health, legal practice, accountancy and tax consultancy. It nonetheless regularly considers whether such government controls are still necessary and are not misused to protect some sectors of the economy from competition.

■ ▦ **Industrial relations.** In the labour market, too, the free play of forces applies. There is collective bargaining, that is to say, agreements on pay, working hours, holidays and general working conditions are freely negotiated between labour and management, who are often called "social partners" in Germany.

Their central organizations, the trade unions and the employers' associations, thus play an important role. Although their main task is to represent their members' interests with both determination and a sense of propor-

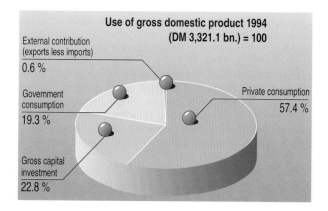

Use of gross domestic product 1994
(DM 3,321.1 bn.) = 100

External contribution
(exports less imports)
0.6 %

Government
consumption
19.3 %

Private consumption
57.4 %

Gross capital
investment
22.8 %

tion, they also bear considerable responsibility for the economy as a whole. Their bargaining can greatly affect the functioning of the economic system.

Labour and employers in the Federal Republic have been aware of this responsibility. The system's stability is due largely to them. This reflects the advantages of the kind of trade unionism that developed in western Germany after the war.

The unions in Germany are "unitary unions" in a double sense: each represents all the workers in an entire branch of industry (i.e. not only the members of a certain trade), and they are neutral; they have no party or religious ties.

■■ ■ **The social component of the economic system.** One major reason why it has been easier to maintain social harmony in Germany than in other countries is that there is a dense social security network. Social protection is considerable, especially for the working community. Whether an employee is old or sick, injured by accident or jobless, affected by the bankruptcy of his or her employer or undergoing retraining for a more promising occupation – most of the financial hardships are cushioned by the welfare system.

It is based on solidarity. Those in employment pay contributions to the various branches of the social insurance system. It extends far beyond the child benefit, housing supplements, social assistance for the needy and indemnification for war victims. Expenditure on social security is high. In 1993 it rose to 33.7% of GDP, largely owing to the inclusion of the new states.

■■ ■ **Macroeconomic development.** A market economy, too, can experience undesirable developments. The state must try to counter them through appropriate budgetary, taxation, welfare and competition policies. Since 1967 the Federal Republic has had an economic management instrument in the shape of the Stability Act. Its aims are stable prices, a high level of employment and a balance of foreign trade under conditions of steady, adequate growth. Unfortunately, they have not always been achievable. The Deutsche Bundesbank (German Federal Bank), which is responsible for money supply, as well as the trade unions and employers' associations also bear some of the responsibility for the state of the economy. The following bodies are involved in the coordination of economic and fiscal policy:

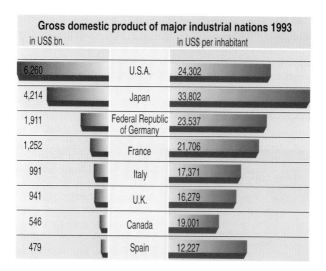

Gross domestic product of major industrial nations 1993

in US$ bn.		in US$ per inhabitant
6,260	U.S.A.	24,302
4,214	Japan	33,802
1,911	Federal Republic of Germany	23,537
1,252	France	21,706
991	Italy	17,371
941	U.K.	16,279
546	Canada	19,001
479	Spain	12,227

– The Business Cycle Council, consisting of the federal ministers of economics and finance, one member from each state government and representatives of the municipalities and associations of municipalities. The Bundesbank may also take part in the consultations, which take place at least twice a year.

– The similarly composed Financial Planning Council, which has the task of coordinating financial planning at all levels of government. The federal and state governments have to draw up multi-annual plans so that public revenue and expenditure can be geared to the demands and capacities of the national economy.

– The Council of Experts on the Assessment of Economic Trends which was set up in 1963. It consists of five independent economic experts (popularly known as the "five wise men") and evaluates overall economic trends every autumn as a basis for government decision-making and public judgment.

Every January the Federal Government presents to the Bundestag and the Bundesrat an annual economic report, which contains a response to the annual assessment of the Council of Experts as well as an outline of economic and financial policy objectives for the current and subsequent years.

■ ■   **The national and the global economy.** Reducing
unemployment is a central task of government policy. The
key to job creation lies in heavier investment. To secure
an adequate return on investment the Federal Government is trying to strengthen the market's own forces, especially through incentives for individual enterprise.
State influence on the economy is being reduced, regulations that obstruct market activity are being eliminated.
This makes for freer competition and easier adaptation to
new developments.

Germany is an advocate
of free world trade and rejects all forms of protectionism. Because she ex-
ports a third of her GNP
she depends on open mar-
kets. The economy there-
fore needs a growing European internal market. But
outside the European Union
as well, Germany must
maintain traditional mar-
kets and develop new ones.
This constant pursuit of
open markets and free
world trade corresponds
with the country's internal
market economy.

*The Business Promotion
Centre, Duisburg*

Germany: an attractive region for investment

Regeneration in the west

■ ■ **In the midst of global disruptions.** The peaceful German revolution and the radical transformations in Central, Eastern and Southeastern Europe in 1989 have not only dramatically changed the political map of Europe. In addition, the Western world has also been hard pressed by unemployment and the necessity of social adjustment.

The Federal Republic of Germany is no exception. Its position is unique in only one respect: It is the only country in the world having to cope with the problems of East and West simultaneously, or as one well-known German author wrote: "We must simultaneously reform the old Federal Republic's market economy and transform the defunct centrally planned economy of the old GDR; we are having to adapt one system and overcome another."

Germany is still a country of high wages, extensive social benefits and corresponding affluence. In order to maintain this level it is essential to adapt to new developments in the field of science and technology and in world markets. An expensive industrial location can hold its own only so long as it is a good location – an exigency reflecting the fierce competition stemming from increasing world economic integration.

Since 1993 the European Union has been one huge internal market. Throughout the world the barriers for goods and services are becoming more permeable, communication and transport costs are being reduced, and production technology is becoming increasingly mobile. Hence in other parts of the world a similarly high level of productivity can be achieved with the same technology as in Germany. As a result, wage differentials and load ratios for manufacturers have a greater impact than ever before. And since investment follows the best yield, Germany must make itself more attractive as a place of business.

■ ■ **Traditional factors.** Prior to unification the Federal Republic of Germany had a large current account surplus and a moderate national debt. It had a number of advantages over its international rivals: a high level of productivity, an extensively skilled and motivated work-force, high technical standards, creative scientists, a well-functioning infrastructure, social harmony, a stable currency and a reliable political environment. But of course these assets alone are no longer sufficient. In such matters as labour costs, operating times, company taxes, environmental protection regulations and social security contributions, German firms are at a disadvantage.

Costs additional to wages, for instance, are higher in Germany than anywhere else in the world. In manufacturing industry German companies must pay DM 19.46 on top of the already high hourly wage. These extra costs are for social insurance, continued wage payments to workers absent through illness, holiday pay and allowances, capital formation contributions and other in-company benefits. For comparison: additional costs in Sweden per hour are only DM 16.66, in France DM 13.18, and in Japan and the United States as little as DM 7.18 and DM 6.93 respectively.

Not only is labour dearer in Germany than perhaps anywhere else in the world, the Germans also work less than their counterparts in other industrial countries. The average annual working time in German industry is about 1,499 hours. In the United States it is 1,847 hours, in Japan as much as 2,139. Industrial plant in Germany is in operation for only 53 hours a week on average, in the United Kingdom 76 hours.

■ ■ **Adaptation and necessary consequences.** On account of these drawbacks – though they do bring considerable social benefit – Germany must ensure that her industries remain competitive, especially those based on the key technologies of the future. Large sections of the traditional branches, such as textiles, have already been switched to cheaper locations. German carmakers and chemical firms, too, are increasingly inclined to invest in lower-cost countries.

■ ■ **Investment promotion.** The answer to this challenge can be neither protectionism nor a state-planned industrial policy, for trade restrictions and subsidies do more harm than good. The Federal Government supports free international trade and opposes any form of protectionism. Since Germany exports about one third of her gross national product she relies heavily on open markets. It is vital to the German business community to develop the European internal market whilst at the same time preserving old markets and developing new ones outside the European Union.

The Federal Government therefore aims to improve the general conditions for private enterprise in Germany. A first step has already been taken with the Investment Promotion Act, which is designed to attract more business to Germany.

As from 1994, taxes on companies, which were too high compared with those in other countries, were reduced. The corporation tax rate for retained profits was cut from 50% to 45%, the maximum income tax rate for trade or business income from 53% to 47%.

The Federal Government plans further tax relief measures, such as relief for companies within the framework of the 1996 Annual Tax Act, which will in particular provide for a reduction in the trade tax.

The success of this investment promotion policy to date shows that it has again become necessary for the market's own batteries to be recharged. State influence on industry is being cut back, as are anti-market regulatory mech-

Nuclear fusion experiment at the Max Planck Institute, Garching

anisms, and state-owned enterprises are being privatized. This makes for more vigorous competition and eases the task of adapting to new developments. The readjustment of economic and fiscal policy succeeded once before, during the 80s. Then, three million new jobs were created within the space of a few years and industry regained its competitive edge.

But these new deregulation measures also concern both sides of industry. More flexible arrangements with regard to working and operating hours, labour costs and social benefits are necessary.

Transformation and reconstruction in the east

■ ■   **Economic recovery in the east – a task for all Germans.** Eastern Germany's economic recovery will remain a major challenge for many years. This task is unique in the country's legal and economic history.

Under socialism, the centrally planned economy had made it practically impossible for the people in the former GDR to show enterprise and act on their own responsibility. The small and medium-sized businesses, formerly the driving force of the economy, had been almost totally eliminated. Creativity and initiative had to a great extent been paralyzed. A large proportion of the goods produced were not competitive on the global market. Production had been tailored exclusively to the needs of

The multicolor camera of "Giotto", the European comet probe

Centre of technology near Regensburg

the states of the former Council for Mutual Economic Assistance (CMEA).

Compared with western levels, productivity was extremely low: about 30% of the level in western Germany. The regime ruthlessly exploited the environment, causing pollution on a massive scale, and yet the economic gain was but modest. Housing, road networks and communications were in no way up to present-day requirements. The economic situation in the east was thus desolate in October 1990. A very productive, internationally competitive economy in the west faced an economy in the east that was woefully ill-equipped and ill-prepared for the upcoming process of integration.

Today, five years after the country's unification, the economic restructuring process is in full swing. It has understandably been a painful experience for many people, for the complete reorganization of the economy in the new states has entailed the elimination of many unproductive and unprofitable economic structures left behind by the former centrally planned system. In order to cope with this difficult situation, which apart from other problems has caused high levels of unemployment, comprehensive measures have been and continue to be undertaken at all levels. Nearly 700,000 trade and business enterprises have meanwhile been established.

■ ■ ■ **Strategies for improving eastern Germany's industrial base.** After reunification it immediately became apparent that the increasingly critical overall economic situation in eastern Germany called for swift political action. A policy had to be formulated that would not only afford the people in the new federal states dependable medium-term prospects for the future during the difficult phase of economic restructuring but also bring visible short-term progress and improvements. The crucial step towards achieving this was the strategy "Upswing East" developed in late 1990 and early 1991. Its key aim was to create the preconditions for self-sustaining, steady and dynamic economic development. Even though continuous adjustments and shifts in emphasis have proved necessary over the years as a result of insights gained from the economic restructuring process in the new federal states, the basic elements of this strategy continue to define the policy of the Federal Government to this very day:
– promotion of both private investment and the establishment of new private businesses through extensive investment assistance;
– elimination of obstacles to investment;
– construction and expansion of the infrastructure;
– improvement of marketing conditions for east German firms;
– privatization, reprivatization and reorganization of firms by the Treuhandanstalt (Trust Agency) or its successor organizations;
– utilization of labour market policy instruments to cushion the social repercussions of unavoidable radical structural change and to complement regional policies during the adjustment process.

Well over DM 600 billion in public funds have flowed to eastern Germany since 1990, either from the Federation or via joint federal and state institutions such as the "German Unity Fund".

Especially the promotion of investment has given a tremendous boost to economic development in the new federal states. By the end of February 1995 – including investment grants approved under the joint federal/state programme "Improving the Regional Economic Structures" totalling nearly DM 43 billion as well as ERP and equity assistance loans totalling DM 53.6 billion – investment volume had exceeded DM 240 billion. Tax incen-

Assembling cars in a new plant at Eisenach

tives for investment likewise play an important role. Between 1991 and 1994, the investment grants alone represented an estimated reduction in tax revenue of approximately DM 14.6 billion. As a consequence of government investment promotion, more than four million jobs have been created or safeguarded. Investment incentives have made the new federal states attractive to west German and foreign investors alike, whose investment volume totalled roughly DM 56 billion in 1994 (1991: DM 23 billion; 1992: DM 39 billion; 1993: DM 46 billion).

Important progress visible to people in the east was made in all areas of infrastructure. Public per capita gross investment in infrastructure in the new federal states exceeded the corresponding figure in the west by 42% in 1992, 60% in 1993 and approximately 88% in 1994. If the current pace and dynamism of public investment is sustained, the new states will have a modern infrastructure meeting international standards in the foreseeable future.

Economic recovery also depends on efficient state and municipal administrations as well as on a well-functioning legal system. These "foundations", too, first had to be established. The Federal Government provided the funds to send 2,300 judges, public prosecutors and judicial officers to the east to create a judicial system in the mould of that existing in the west, so that now the legal system is the same in all parts of the country. In addition, experienced administrators from the old federal states have been helping to adapt public administration in the east, a process which has now more or less been completed.

Between 1991 and today it has been possible to achieve another goal: creating a productive and competitive agricultural sector in the east. The process of restructuring and rationalization in this area is progressing well. Decentralization of the former collective farms has largely been completed. In 1994 there were about 29,000 farms, just under 24,000 of which were private sole proprietorships operated for the respective proprietor's own account. The number of farm workers dropped from 820,000 in 1989 to about 157,000 in 1994. Between 1990 and 1992, the Federal Government furnished approximately DM 12 billion to ease this difficult adjustment process. Considerable effort will be required in the immediate future as well in order to complete the establishment of a market-oriented and environmentally friendly agricultural sector in the new federal states. In 1993, the Federal Government earmarked another DM 1.18 billion for implementation of the "Joint Task of Improving the Agrarian Structure and Coastal Protection".

■ ■ ■ **The Treuhandanstalt (Trust Agency).** A key role in the economic restructuring process in the new federal states was played by the Trust Agency, a public privatization agency. Its task was to privatize, reorganize or if

A truck plant in Ludwigsfelde/Brandenburg

Road construction in the new states is making steady progress

necessary wind up the former state assets of the GDR by
the end of 1994, make companies competitive, and make
land available for industrial or commercial purposes. To
this end, the Trust Agency worked to ensure the liquidity
of firms, furnish the assistance necessary for their reorganization, find investors and conclude the requisite
contracts.

The Trust Agency was established on 1 March 1990. The
conditions under which it took up its work were daunting. There was no model for guiding an entire economic
system through the transition to a social market economy.
Neither opening balance sheets nor realistic asset valu-
ations were available. Not until the work of the Trust
Agency got underway did its experts discover the extent
to which the assets of the GDR state economy had been
depleted. The last GDR government had valued the
GDR's state assets at DM 1,300 billion. In the opening
balance sheet prepared by the Trust Agency after a realistic assessment, however, the value of these assets had
plummeted to – DM 210 billion.

It turned out that only 8% of the jobs in the companies
taken over by the Trust Agency were profitable and that
productivity of labour in the GDR had been less than
30% of the level in western Germany. Production plant

and machinery were obsolete, and energy consumption was twice as high as in the west. For political reasons, small and medium-sized businesses were virtually non-existent. Many of the products of the 430 large combines were unusable for the world market.

In order to make privatization of the large combines feasible, these were first split up into smaller firms. Even then, many companies could only be sold at a loss: The Trust Agency had to pay buyers to assume ownership even though the Agency had already expended considerable effort and funds beforehand to reorganize these firms.

In the course of reprivatization, many companies that had been expropriated were returned to their original owners. Nearly one fifth of all privatized firms (more than 3,000 in all) were taken over by their own management and employees, purchased from the Trust Agency in what is termed a "management buyout" (MBO). Today these firms constitute a particularly successful and important segment of the new small and medium-sized business sector in eastern Germany.

Hundreds of firms were so run-down, however, that they could no longer be reorganized. They had to be closed, and their workers became unemployed. Many jobs were lost in the course of reorganization and privatization as well. Yet even out of liquidation proceedings

A purification plant under construction in Bitterfeld

new businesses were established, thus providing jobs for about 30% of the defunct firms' employees.

On 31 December 1994 the Trust Agency ceased its operations as planned. Approximately 14,000 firms had been privatized, and nearly 40,000 individual contracts had been concluded. The privatization programme had yielded proceeds of about DM 65 billion, commitments for roughly 1.5 million jobs, and investment pledges totalling DM 207 billion. Approximately 40,000 tracts of land had been sold as well. At the end of the restructuring and selling process, however, a mountain of debts approaching DM 270 billion remained, which will be folded into a fund for retirement of assumed debts and, together with the GDR state debt and a portion of the GDR's housing construction debt, should be paid off within one generation. Federal expenditure for this fund for retirement of assumed debt, which has a total volume of approximately DM 370 billion, will amount to DM 26 billion in 1995.

On 1 January 1995 the approximately 60 firms still held by the Trust Agency were placed under the responsibility of the Bundesanstalt für vereinigungsbedingte Sonderaufgaben, which was founded especially for this purpose, and four additional companies. Like the Trust Agency before them, these bodies fall under the purview of the Federal Ministry of Finance. One of the duties of the new Bundesanstalt is to monitor observance of the roughly 85,000 contracts (including land contracts) that have already been concluded, which contain investment and job commitments. The assets of the parties and mass organizations of the former GDR must also be managed and utilized. Below the Bundesanstalt für vereinigungsbedingte Sonderaufgaben there are two companies: The Bodenverwertungs- und Verwaltungsgesellschaft (BVVG) deals specifically with the agricultural and forested areas which were formerly GDR assets. At the beginning it was responsible for approximately 1.1 million hectares of land (30% of the arable land in the new federal states), some of which has been leased on a short-term or long-term basis, as well as forests and woodlands. Following the passage last year of pertinent statutory regulations (including the Act on Indemnification and Equalization Benefits), preparations are now underway to sell these tracts of land. The DV-

Restoration work on Merseburg Cathedral

Informations-Systeme, Organisation und Service GmbH (DISOS) handles electronic data processing for the Trust Agency's successors. Two further companies under direct federal administration have taken over the functions of the Trust Agency pertaining to firms and real estate. They are supervised in the performance of their duties by the Federal Ministry of Finance. The Beteiligungs-Management-Gesellschaft (BMGB) is responsible for the fewer than 70 firms which have not yet been privatized and will continue the process of their reorganization and privatization. The Treuhand-Liegenschaftsgesellschaft (LTG) is in charge of privatizing landed property and real estate; approximately 60,000 pieces of real estate must still be disposed of.

■ ■   **Good prospects for the future.** The strong upward trend observable in eastern Germany in recent years continued in 1994 and early 1995. The rate of economic growth accelerated from 5.8% in 1993 to 9.2% in 1994, making the new federal states the fastest-growing region in Europe. In 1994, for the first time, their economic output per gainfully employed person was more than half (just under 53%) of the comparable figure in the western part of the country. In 1991, by comparison, productivity in the east had been only 31% of that in the west.

The labour market situation in the new states has clearly bottomed out as well. During the course of 1994, unemployment declined noticeably: the average figure of 1,142,000 was 6,700 lower than the figure for the previous year. In addition, the number of gainfully employed persons rose for the first time. Investments are the driving force behind this upswing in the eastern part of Germany. In 1994 investment per gainfully employed person in the east was about 45% higher than in the west; a year earlier it had been only 27% higher. Investment in the recovery of eastern Germany increased 15.6% in 1994 over the figure for the previous year, thus pushing the rate of investment in the new federal states to a record level. Not even during the time of the Federal Republic's economic miracle in the 50s did the investment rate reach such heights. Thanks to this strong investment activity, but also as a result of the strong economic upturn in western Germany, there is a good chance that in 1995 the growth trend observable in more and more sectors of the eastern economy will generate a net increase in gross domestic product of somewhere between 8% and 10%.

The labour market

The German labour market has time and again had to cope with critical situations. In the early postwar years the Federal Republic was preoccupied with finding jobs for millions of expellees from Germany's former eastern territories and for resettlers from the GDR. But they in particular made a large contribution to the country's economic upswing.

From the mid-50s to the early 70s hardly anyone was out of work, but as a result of the subsequent crises unemployment became a major and increasing problem. Not until the 80s did the situation substantially improve, but there remained a basic stock of jobless people.

When Germany regained its unity in 1990 there suddenly arose the problem of a divided labour market. While the ranks of the jobless at first decreased in the western states on account of the favourable economic situation, their numbers swelled in the new states. This was primarily due to the transition from socialist central planning to a social market economy.

▪ ▪ **Employment.** Between 1950 and the beginning of 1992, the number of gainfully employed persons in the old federal states increased from 20.4 million to 29.5 million. It thereafter declined, reaching 28.6 million at the end of 1994. In the new federal states, employment declined by about 3.5 million to 6.3 million between 1989 and 1993 as a result of the crisis precipitated by the transition to the social market economy. This drastic reduction in the number of jobs came to a halt in 1994 and gave way to a slight increase in employment.

From about 1960 onwards, the increase in the workforce in the old federal states was due mainly to the ever-increasing numbers of foreign workers. In 1965 the number of foreign workers rose to one million, and in 1973 to 2.6 million, setting an initial record for employment of foreigners. After that, the influx of foreign workers – except for those from the member states of the European Community – was slowed. At the end of the 80s and the beginning of the 90s, due in no small part to the strong influx of asylum-seekers, the number of foreign workers again increased rapidly, once more reaching about 2.6

Vocational counselling in a labour exchange

million in 1993/94. The largest contingent of registered foreign workers are the Turks, followed by workers from former Yugoslavia, Italy and Greece. In the new federal states, employment of foreigners still plays a relatively minor role in the economy.

Full employment in the old federal states reached its peak in 1970 when only 150,000 were out of work. At the same time almost 800,000 job vacancies were reported. During the subsequent recession the labour force diminished and the number of unemployed increased. It rose above one million in 1975, and to well over two million at the beginning of the 80s.

Government policy in the western part of the country since 1982 has improved the conditions for economic growth and considerably reduced the obstacles to employment. By 1991 unemployment had dropped to 1.7 million, but largely as a result of the recession it began to rise again, reaching 2.6 million in 1994. Some 1.5 million new jobs were created between 1984 and 1990 and a further 1.8 million between 1989 and 1992 in the western part of Germany. Between 1992 and 1994, however, the number decreased by 0.8 million due to the general economic downturn.

In the former GDR there was always full employment – at least that was the official version as presented by the

GDR regime. In actual fact, however, there was much concealed unemployment, estimated at between one and a half and three million. The problem's full dimensions only became apparent when Germany was united and the ruined GDR economy collapsed. Various government initiatives at first prevented any sharp increases in unemployment there, but old, unproductive jobs have been written off faster than new ones have been created.

For a transitional period, therefore, the Federal Institute for Employment has expended considerable government funds to finance early retirement, short time, job creation, retraining and further training programmes, reducing the number of unemployed by two million. It has thus helped to give workers better prospects and to accelerate the modernization process. With economic activity picking up considerably the employment situation, too, has begun to improve.

Some groups are especially hard hit by unemployment, i.e. those with inadequate vocational qualifications, older people, those who have been out of work for long periods of time and, in the new federal states, women. Government and industry are making great efforts to help them. Because of the increasing use of modern technology in the workplace, greater importance attaches to vocational skills. But it is also important that those affected by unemployment should receive adequate social security.

■ ■ **Unemployment insurance.** Germany's statutory unemployment insurance scheme was introduced in 1927. It is now governed by the Labour Promotion Act of 1969. The authority administering the scheme is the Federal Institute for Employment in Nuremberg.

Unemployment insurance is obligatory for all employees. Contributions are paid half by the employee and half by the employer. Any unemployed person whose previous employment was subject to insurance contributions for a specific period of time and who is ready to accept "reasonable" employment offered by the labour exchange is entitled to draw unemployment benefit, which may be as much as 67% of the last net pay. As a rule it is paid for a maximum period of one year, in the case of older unemployed people at most for 32 months. Anyone then still unemployed can apply for unemployment assistance of up to 57% of the net wage or salary, other sources of income, including those of family members, being taken into account.

The Federal Institute for Employment also pays benefits to those who are on short time or who are unable to work during the cold winter months (e.g. construction workers).

■ ▪ **Labour promotion.** The Federal Institute for Employment is also responsible for job placement and vocational guidance as well as the promotion of vocational training, which is particularly important. The Institute gives juveniles and adults subsidies and loans for vocational training if they cannot raise the funds themselves. It also promotes vocational advancement by paying a maintenance benefit and covering all or part of the cost of training. The Federal Institute for Employment likewise promotes vocational rehabilitation.

Labour market and vocational research is another of the Institute's functions. The research findings are submitted to the Federal Minister for Labour and Social Affairs as an aid to decision-making.

Bundesanstalt für Arbeit
(Federal Institute for Employment)
P.O. Box, 90327 Nuremberg

Incomes and prices

■ ■   **Incomes.** In recent decades incomes have increased constantly in Germany. In the western part of the country disposable income of private households rose from DM 188 billion in 1962 to over DM 1,850.3 billion in 1994. The family budget has grown considerably in real terms, too, that is to say, allowing for inflation. Income derives from many different sources, but the main one by far is employment, i.e. wages and salaries including social security contributions. In addition there are dividends from shares, income from property and other assets as well as public support in the form of child and unemployment benefits, pensions and other remittances.

Disposable income is what is left over after deduction of taxes and social insurance contributions, and also regular remittances (e.g. by foreign workers to their native countries). Just under half of the disposable income is accounted for by net wages and salaries, almost a third by profit-drawing and net income from assets, and about a fifth by social security benefits.

■ ■   **Standard of living.** The five decades since the end of the Second World War have seen the growth of unprecedented prosperity in Germany. The social market economy has raised the country from destruction to one of the most powerful economies in the world with widespread affluence. Nearly half of the employed members of the community own their own houses or apartments. And eastern Germany, too, just a few years after the country's unification, is already approaching the level of prosperity of the west.

In 1964 the average disposable monthly income of a four-person household was DM 904. Of this, DM 823 was spent on private consumption – nearly two thirds of this on food, clothing and housing. In 1993 the same type of household in western Germany disposed of more than DM 5,200 a month, of which only about half was spent on the three items mentioned. But spending on other items has increased substantially, e.g. leisure, transport, education and telephones. The Germans in the western states spent DM 1,480.42 billion on private consumption in 1994.

Assets and disposable income are distributed unevenly, however. At the top of the incomes pyramid are the self-employed, followed by farmers, salaried employees, civil servants and wage earners. Whereas the social structure in the new federal states is still being shaped, a process has taken place within the old states which has led to an approximation of the standard of living of most social groups. A very broad middle class has emerged. In a great many cases this high standard of living is attained and maintained because both husband and wife have a job. The great majority of the working population live entirely or predominantly from the fruits of their labour, while only a small minority can live on their assets.

■ ■   **Assets.** Assets, however, have increased at an even faster rate than disposable incomes. They have doubled in fact. At the end of 1993 private assets in the whole of Germany stood at approximately DM 4,192 billion. They include cash, savings, bonds, life insurance and other forms of property. The per capita average in Germany is thus over DM 50,000. This does not include the convertible value of real estate. In the relatively short period to the millennium, however, land and premises worth about DM 350 billion will pass to the next generation of heirs. Thus the postwar generation who rebuilt the country will bequeath more than any other generation in the history of Germany.

Working time required to pay for certain household goods *

To purchase the specified goods an industrial worker had to work the stated number of hours and minutes:

	1950 hrs. min.	1960 hrs. min.	1980 hrs. min.	1990 hrs. min.	1994 hrs. min.
1 l milk	14	8	5	3	3
1 kg bread	17	15	10	9	9
1 kg pork	2 50	2 08	45	33	28
1 kg butter	3 39	2 08	38	23	18
Men's shoes	21 15	13 01	7 33	6 44	6 03
Soup plate, china	41	21	18	21	23

* "Old" Federal Republic

Since the 50s the government has promoted private capital formation by means of various bonuses, allowances and tax concessions. Tax incentives are given to people saving with building societies or through life insurance policies, and those people contributing to house-building schemes are eligible for a house-building bonus as well. There is a yearly limit, of course, and the house-building bonus is also tied to incomes.

In addition to the general incentives for capital formation available to all citizens, special bonuses have been available to em-

Sales day!

A modern shopping mall:
the Zeilgalerie in Frankfurt/Main

Cost of living index in various countries
1985 = 100

Country	1991	1992	1993
Federal Republic of Germany (old)	110.7	115.1	119.3
Belgium	114.6	117.4	120.6
Denmark	124.1	126.7	128.3
France	120.2	123.0	125.7
United Kingdom	141.1	146.4	148.7
Ireland	121.4	125.1	127.0
Italy	140.2	147.6	153.0
Netherlands	108.4	112.5	114.9
Austria	115.0	119.7	124.0
Switzerland	119.7	124.7	128.8
Spain	144.9	153.3	160.6
Canada	131.5	133.4	135.8
U.S.A.	126.6	130.4	134.3
Japan	112.3	112.4	113.8
Australia	151.1	152.6	155.3

ployees since the 60s. Since 1991 these have also been applicable in the new federal states. Under the Capital Formation Act the bonus is paid on limited amounts and has to be transferred directly by the employer to the employee's building society account, a capital formation account with a bank (including investment certificates and shares), or the employer's capital formation scheme.

Savings of up to DM 936 a year qualify for this bonus. It can only be claimed by people whose earnings do not exceed a particular limit. In the western part of Germany capital formation savings arrangements are made for most employees, primarily within the scope of collective wage agreements, in addition to their normal wage. Employees can also obtain bonuses for parts of their wages which they save.

In 1992 about 13 million employees in western Germany received bonuses totalling well over a billion marks for capital formation savings. They also receive tax concessions on limited amounts which they invest with their employer.

■ ■ ■ **Prices.** The standard of living depends not only on income but also on prices. Consumer prices are therefore a major domestic issue. Opinion polls have consistently shown that for many people the chief consideration is stable prices. This is mainly because Germans know from personal experience what devaluation of money means. They suffered two periods of devastating inflation after wars in this century, each resulting in the collapse of the currency and huge losses of assets.

A cash machine

The Federal Republic of Germany has not been able to evade worldwide inflation entirely in recent years, however. Especially in the 70s the cost of living in the old Federal Republic rose far too swiftly – at times by more than 6% annually. It then fell considerably, so that in December 1986, for the first time in almost 30 years, the cost of living was lower than it had been in the same month of the previous year. In the whole of 1986 the cost of living was 0.1% lower than in the previous year. In later years, too, the Federal Republic managed quite well by comparison, its inflation rates not rising above 3%. The strongly fluctuating prices of the 70s and 80s reflected the sharp movements in the price of oil. Since mid-1990, however, heavy demand in connection with the country's unification as well as steep increases in wages and taxes to finance the recovery of the economy in eastern Germany have accelerated prices with the result that the inflation rate in 1992 was about 4%. The government, and especially the Deutsche Bundesbank, give high priority to monetary stability. This policy has proved successful: In 1994 the inflation rate dropped to 3%, and it is expected to decrease to approximately 2% in 1995.

Consumer protection

The range of goods and services is growing. Every year more than 1,000 new products come onto the market in Germany alone. Since the launching of the European single market on 1 January 1993, the range has become even greater and even more confusing. Products made in Germany compete with goods imported from all over the world. Consumers have a greater choice than ever before. But such a wide variety is a problem for them, too, since it is hardly possible to judge quality and value for money. In addition, there are dangers to health and dishonest sales methods.

As a result, consumer protection now plays an important role in the life of the community. Its purpose is to make the market more transparent and help people make rational decisions on the basis of objective information. Consumers also need advice on their rights with regard to contracts, insurance, loans, investment, travel, etc.

Thus in 1964 the Federal Government set up a foundation in Berlin known as "Stiftung Warentest" which tests goods of all kinds from the ballpoint pen to the personal computer as to quality, value for money and compatibility with the environment. Services, too, are tested. This organization now screens about 1,700 articles in 100 comparative testings a year. Stiftung Warentest only calls upon independent experts and institutes and has earned a good reputation from consumers and manufacturers alike, the latter being glad to advertize the fact that their products have been approved by Stiftung Warentest.

The foundation's main publications are "Test", which appears monthly and has a circulation of about a million, and "FINANZ-Test". Furthermore, the test results are regularly publicized in some 160 newspapers and periodicals, and on radio and television.

The public can also seek advice from roughly 300 regional consumer centres which provide information on the quality and prices of goods and services and receive financial support from the government.

Before parliament introduces new consumer protection legislation it consults the consumers' unions. The Association of Consumers' Unions (AgV) has 37 member orga-

Razors being put to the test

nizations ranging from the German Tenants Federation and the German Housewives Association to the Otto Blume Institute of Social Research.

Consumer protection has been considerably improved by legislation. The Act on General Terms and Conditions of Contract protects customers from the pitfalls contained in small print; the Consumer Credit Act enables the borrower to cancel the loan and requires information to be provided by the lender; the Foodstuffs Act protects customers from damaging substances in food; the Travel Contract Act forces operators to fulfil their promises; the Product Liability Act makes manufacturers liable for flawed products. There are also many other laws to protect consumers. They concern such matters as the labelling of foodstuffs and detergents, pharmaceutical products and price tags on goods in shop windows. The Association of Consumers' Unions and the consumer centres jointly publish brochures, leaflets and other advisory material on all subjects of relevance to consumers.

This legislation is being increasingly switched to the European Union, however. The Union issues directives that must be converted into national law in member states. The European Commission has a "Consumers' Consultative Council" composed of 48 members. The most important consumer organization at European level is the "European Bureau of Consumers' Unions (BEUC)" which represents 30 national consumer organizations.

Arbeitsgemeinschaft der Verbraucherverbände (AgV)
(Association of Consumers' Unions)
Heilsbachstr. 20, 53123 Bonn
Stiftung Warentest
Lützowplatz 11-13, 10785 Berlin

Housing and urban development

■ ■ **Housing.** Living accommodation in Germany can be anything from a small single room or a self-contained flat to a single-family house or a mansion. There are about 34.99 million dwellings, over 27.92 million of them in the old federal states. Roughly 40% of these are occupied by the owners themselves, the rest being rented.

Flats in apartment buildings have traditionally been rented, hence most housing units inhabited by their owners are in houses for one or two families. Since the late 70s condominiums have become increasingly popular.

16% of rented flats in the western states have been subsidized by the government. This "social" accommodation is intended for large families, the disabled, the elderly and people with low incomes.

Germany had a real housing crisis after the Second World War, when many towns and cities lay in ruins. In the early 50s there were only 10 million dwellings available for just under 17 million households. Gradually, however, the crisis was overcome by means of a housing programme under which as many as 700,000 dwellings a year were built.

Today the main problems are in the metropolitan areas of the old federal states. Young couples, large families and foreigners have difficulty finding flats which meet their needs or which they can afford. There are many reasons for the housing shortage. Accommodation is being sought by people in the high-birthrate age groups and by others entering the country. And many Germans from the eastern states have moved to the west.

Between 1988 and 1994 the population increased by about four million. In 1988, after years of declining building activity, the situation changed and since 1989 housing construction has increased steadily. In 1992 approximately 375,000 housing units were completed in the old federal states alone, and in 1994 the number far exceeded 480,000. Since 1990 about two million units have been modernized in the new states with funds from the Kreditanstalt für Wiederaufbau (Development Loan Corporation), a government loan agency. Indeed, repair and modernization of existing housing is the main objective of government policy in the east, where much of the housing stock is in a deplorable condition due to the failings of the former GDR regime.

*Sun collectors
provide energy*

Public funding has been increased and in 1991 the Federal Government introduced another social housing scheme which provided a further boost.

■ ■ ■ **Housing quality.** There are still large differences in quality between accommodation in the old and the new federal states, and in the amount of living

*Renovated old townhouses
in Wuppertal*

space available. In western Germany the average living
space available for each individual is 35 sq m, which is
more than twice as much as in 1950. In the east it is about
28 sq m. More than 95% of all flats have a bath and 75%
central heating. The housing stock in the west is on the
whole much younger than accommodation in the new
federal states, where still about 55% of the houses were
built before 1948. Many of them are in a poor state. They
frequently lack modern sanitary facilities and the heating
systems are outmoded.

The regime in the former GDR kept rents extremely
low. Efforts were concentrated on new construction, and
existing housing stock was neglected. As a result, the local authorities, cooperatives and private owners had
hardly any funds for maintenance and modernization. In
the western states, on the other hand, quality has its
price. Rents, that is, not counting incidental expenses
and heating, account for about 20% of an average household's net income. In some cities the rents are even
higher, in the countryside lower.

There remains a tremendous housing problem to be
solved. In eastern Germany millions of old structures
must be renovated. The renovation programme is going
very well. In 1991 and 1992 funds were earmarked for the
modernization and renovation of some 30% of eastern
Germany's housing stock. And in 1994 the Federal Government provided DM 1 billion for construction of publicly assisted housing in the new federal states, which can
also be used for modernization and renovation.

Many housing units owned by local authorities are
being privatized. Private investors receive tax relief and
grants for this purpose. The housing sector in the east is
on the verge of a new "investment offensive" now that
some of the major obstacles such as the old debts of
building societies and the uneconomical system of rock-
bottom rents have been removed.

But further efforts were required in the western part of
the country as well. The promotion of housing construction and the conditions for a well-functioning housing
market have been continually developed. Federal funding for housing projects for low-income groups increased
from DM 1.76 billion in 1991 to DM 2.7 billion in 1992
and in 1993; in 1994 it totalled DM 2.46 billion, and in
1995 it will amount to DM 1.9 billion.

■ ■ ■   **Housing supplement and tenants' rights.** Dwelling space is a basic human need, which is why in Germany everyone whose income is insufficient to meet the cost of adequate accommodation has a statutory right to a housing supplement. It is paid as a grant towards the rent or as a subsidy towards the cost of home ownership, though subject to income limits.

At the end of 1991 more than three million households in Germany received housing supplements. The cost to the federal and state governments, who share the burden, in 1994 was about DM 7 billion. Since 1991 housing supplements have also been paid in the new federal states under legislation which allows for the special situation there and is considerably more generous than in the west.

On the whole, the housing supplement has proved to be an effective social measure. Tenancy law, which is based on freedom of contract, is aimed at establishing a fair balance of interests between landlords and tenants. No tenant need fear unjust and arbitrary eviction or excessive rent increases.

Thus a landlord can only give notice to a tenant who has met the requirements of his contract if he can prove "justified interest" (for example if he can show that he needs the accommodation for his own purposes). He may put up the rent provided he does not go beyond what is charged for comparable accommodation in the same area. Tenants in the new states receive special protection against rent increases for a transitional period.

■ ■ ■   **Home ownership.** 90% of all German families dream of owning a house or condominium. This coincides with the Federal Government's aim of

Experimental architecture on the Fraenkelufer, Berlin

spreading assets as far as possible. People deciding to build or buy their own home can thus count on various state benefits such as grants, loans and tax concessions.

■ ■ ■ **Urban development.** The Federal Republic is one of the most densely populated countries in the world. Most people today live in cities, towns or sizeable communities which were quickly rebuilt after the Second World War. Little consideration was given to traditional structures. Rapid motorization led to a boom in road construction, even in residential areas. For a time the "town catering for the car" was the ideal. The price of land in urban areas shot up and it became more and more difficult to ensure sensible building for the good of society as a whole. Many people moved to the countryside and commuted to work. Cities and towns became deserted in the evening.

This trend has meanwhile been reversed, however. More and more people are returning to the cities, which have a distinctive flair. Since 1970 there has been a growing tendency to modernize old buildings and restore whole districts. Efforts are now made to preserve urban structures as they have evolved and to make the centres more attractive. In many towns the busiest shopping areas have been turned into pedestrian precincts. Local transport services are being extended. There are car park information and guidance systems and better surveillance of stationary vehicles. In many built-up areas the speed limit has been lowered to 30 km/h (19 mph). Local building regulations have been simplified, and citizens are being brought into the city planning process sooner and allowed a more active role.

Environmental protection

In 1994 the newly created article 20a of the Basic Law elevated environmental protection to a duty of the state: "The state, aware of its responsibility for present and future generations, shall protect the natural sources of life..." This duty is incumbent on all branches of government and encompasses among other things the concept of recycling, the achievement of environmentally sound mobility and the reconciliation of agriculture with nature conservation.

The business community, too, appreciate that ecology and economy do not have to be contradictory and that environmental protection is also necessary on economic grounds. The consistent safeguarding of the atmosphere, water and soil over time is essential for sound economic advancement. More than 700,000 people in Germany are directly or indirectly involved in preventing or reducing pollution. A modern environmental protection industry has thus evolved which offers highly sophisticated technology for preventing and correcting damage to the environment. German high-tech engineering products are much in demand and now account for more than 20% of world trade in this field.

■ ■ ■ **Environmental policy.** Responsibility for environmental matters at federal level lies with the Federal Ministry for the Environment, Nature Conservation and Nuclear Safety. One of its subsidiary agencies is the Federal Environmental Agency in Berlin. Each of the federal states, too, has an environmental ministry.

The environmental policy of the Federal Government is based on three principles:
– the prevention principle: new projects are to be developed in such a way as to avoid pollution or damage;
– "the polluter pays" principle: it is not the public at large but those causing the damage or pollution who bear the responsibility and the cost of removal; and
– the cooperation principle: government, industry and society join forces to solve environmental problems, since every individual has a duty towards the environment.

The government's task is to provide the framework for action by companies and individuals to preserve the natural sources of life. In recent years a broad range of legal instruments for the protection of the environment has been introduced, and these are being constantly developed. The social market economy in Germany also has an ecological orientation. The Federal Government's aim is to ensure as soon as possible high standards of environmental protection throughout the country. This requires investment running into billions, mainly for the rehabilitation of old industrial sites, waste disposal, and construction and enlargement of sewage treatment facilities.

But national measures are not sufficient in themselves since polluted air knows no frontiers and contaminated rivers flow through many countries. A major task is that of coping with such global problems as climate change, depletion of the ozone layer and the loss of biodiversity. This requires worldwide cooperation, which is why the German government pursues an active international policy, especially within the EU but also within numerous international organizations. The outstanding event of 1992 was the U.N. Conference on Environment and Development held in Rio de Janeiro. The Federal Government is making every effort to give early effect to that conference's resolutions in Germany and to ensure continuing international cooperation in the field of environmental protection. In 1995 Berlin was the venue of the First Conference of the Parties to the Framework Convention on Climate Change (the convention that was signed in Rio in 1992).

The Federal Government's strategy is geared to self-sustaining, environmentally friendly development and requires other policy areas to make greater allowance for the exigencies of environmental protection.

■ ■ ■ **Keeping the air clean.** The atmosphere in Germany, as in other industrial countries, is heavily polluted by emissions from power stations, factories, traffic, home-heating systems and agriculture. This is particularly evident in the damage caused to forests. About 64% of tree stocks are slightly or severely damaged. Only 36% are healthy. Thus human health, the soil, lakes and rivers, buildings and architectural treasures must be protected from further air pollution.

A comprehensive clean-air programme has been introduced. The aim is to get to grips with pollution at source and reduce it drastically. Pollutants from power stations

A stratospheric balloon for the collection of air samples

and district heating plants, for instance, as well as car exhaust fumes, are largely held back by filters and catalytic converters. Measures such as the Ordinance on Large Firing Installations and the Technical Instructions on Air Quality Control compelled power station operators and industry to quickly introduce modern technology.

As a result, sulphur dioxide emissions in the old federal states decreased by more than 60% between 1980 and 1991, and nitrogen oxide emissions decreased by just under 20%. Between 1983 and 1993 emissions of sulphur dioxide from power stations in western Germany were reduced by about 92%, those of nitrogen oxide by over 60%.

As far as traffic is concerned, air pollution is being continually reduced through the increasingly widespread use of unleaded gasoline and the introduction of the three-way catalytic converter, which limits emissions of nitrogen oxide, hydrocarbons and carbon monoxide. Today, all new motor vehicles in the European Union must be equipped with this system. Unfortunately, however, the rapid increase in traffic – especially truck traffic – has partially offset the reductions achieved through this new technology.

Ensuring clean air, too, is an international challenge. A substantial amount of the pollution in Germany comes from neighbouring countries, while half of the pollution emitted in Germany is carried by the wind to other countries. Thus the 1983 Geneva Convention on Long-Range Transboundary Air Pollution is of great importance in this respect.

Two of the biggest threats to the world's climate are carbon dioxide, which is one of the causes of the "greenhouse effect", and chlorofluorocarbons (CFCs) which are destroying the earth's ozone layer. CFC production in Germany ceased in mid-1994.

Carbon dioxide emissions are to be reduced by 25% by the year 2005 (based on 1990 figures). The Federal Government has adopted an ambitious comprehensive plan

Emission sensors monitor combustion in the cylinder

to achieve this goal. Between 1987 and 1993 CO_2 emissions had already been reduced by about 15%.

■ ■ **Noise abatement.** Noise, especially from traffic, has become a serious threat to health in densely populated areas. Noise abatement measures are therefore urgent. Many residential streets are being redesigned as reduced-traffic zones, noise levels for cars are being lowered, and incentives are being created for the operation of quieter aircraft. More and more streets are being surfaced with noise-absorbing paving materials. Sound barriers are being erected along roads and railways or on adjacent buildings to protect residents from unreasonably loud noise. Efforts are also being made in industry and in the building trade to reduce noise levels.

■ ■ **Protection of rivers, lakes and seas.** Major improvements have also been achieved in protecting rivers, lakes and seas, but only through the introduction of tougher legislation on the discharge of waste water and the construction of new, especially biological, sewage treatment facilities by industrial firms and municipalities. These regulations were designed to prevent organic pollution of surface water in particular.

In the early 70s heavily polluted rivers like the Rhine and the Main had suffered a drastic decline in the diversity of species they contained but today, as a result of improvements in water quality, they again have numerous species of fish. Many rivers and lakes of the former GDR, however, still need a major cleansing operation.

The Waste Water Charges Act has played a key role in the protection of rivers and lakes by requiring municipalities and industry to sharply reduce pollutants and nutrients in waste water. Steps have also been taken, internationally, within the EU and at national level, to protect bodies of water from nutrients and pollutants which are either non-biodegradable or difficult to biodegrade, especially plant protection agents. Increasingly heavy restrictions are being placed on the approval and use of such substances. In 1986 stricter limits were also introduced with regard to drinking water, which is obtained chiefly from groundwater.

Steps to reduce pollution of the North Sea were introduced on Germany's initiative at the International North Sea Conferences of 1984, 1987 and 1990. As a result all countries have meanwhile stopped discharging indus-

Removing oil discharged into the sea

trial waste and burning waste at sea. One country still dumps sewage sludge in the North Sea, but by the end of 1998 it, too, will have completely discontinued this practice.

The littoral states of the Baltic Sea formed in 1974 the Helsinki Commission on the Protection of the Baltic Sea. In 1992 it adopted an international action programme aimed at removing the main sources of pollution within the next twenty years.

■ ■   **Nature conservation and landscape management.** The proportion of land in the western part of Germany covered by buildings and roads increased from about 8% at the end of the 50s to about 12% at the end of the 80s. During the same time period the proportion of natural landscapes declined sharply. The number of endangered plant and animal species continues to rise. Protection of indigenous species and preservation of their natural habitats are consequently urgent tasks of nature conservation and landscape management.

The Federal Nature Conservation Act, which forms the basis for state laws on conservation and landscape management, has been constantly improved, as has the Species Conservation Act.

Eleven large regions in Germany requiring special protection have been declared national parks. There are also many nature reserves as well as 12 biosphere reserves recognized by UNESCO.

Germany is playing an active part in the elaboration and implementation of international nature conservation agreements, for example:
– the Bonn Convention on the Conservation of migratory Species of Wild Animals;
– the Bern Convention on the Conservation of European Wildlife and Natural Habitats, which will assume increasing importance through cooperation between Eastern and Western European countries within the framework of the Council of Europe;
– the Washington Convention on International Trade in Endangered Species of Wild Fauna and Flora; and
– the Convention on Biological Diversity signed at the 1992 Conference on Environment and Development held in Rio de Janeiro.

Initiatives for nature protection measures at national level also come from cooperation among EU countries. The Community's directive for the protection of birds and its flora-fauna-habitat directive have been incorporated in German law. And both federal and state governments are deeply involved in the realization of the EU's biotope network NATURA 2000.

▨▨▨ **Waste management and soil protection.** The 1986 Waste Avoidance and Waste Management Act introduced modern waste-disposal methods. This law gives the avoidance and recycling of waste priority over traditional methods of disposal. Waste that cannot be recycled can no longer simply be sent to landfills. It must first be treated, usually at incinerators. Strict regulations apply to the disposal of "special waste", i.e. toxic or otherwise dangerous waste, for which there are special facilities.

The Federal Government has meanwhile developed its waste management plans with the aim of creating a recycling system based on comprehensive product liability and the principles of the ecological and social market economy. Under this system producers and consumers will assume a far greater responsibility for a product's whole life cycle.

Recycling is very important to a country like Germany which has few raw materials. Some incinerated household waste is used for distant-heating purposes.

In 1991 the government introduced regulations for the avoidance of packaging waste. This led to the creation of the private sector "Duales System Deutschland" (DSD, or "Green Dot") in 1992. Under this arrangement waste packaging material stamped with the green dot by the manufacturer is collected and recycled. The cost is included in the price of the product.

Germany produces approximately 12 million tonnes of packaging waste every year: 4.2 million tonnes of glass, 4.8 million tonnes of paper and cardboard, 1.5 million tonnes of synthetic materials, 740,000 tonnes of tinplate, 115,000 tonnes of aluminum and 410,000 tonnes of composite materials. The Federal Government's waste management policy, which is aimed at avoiding waste in the first place and then recycling the rest, is already proving successful. Many public depots, for instance, are reporting decreases in delivered waste of 30% or more compared to deliveries in the years before 1990. The volume of packaging materials dropped by about one million tonnes between 1991 and 1993.

The Federal Government's Soil Protection Concept of 1985 formulated standards for the protection of this part of the environment for the very first time. In 1993 a draft was submitted for a federal soil protection act. This draft bill mandates protection of the soil as a natural source of life for human beings, animals and plants. In order to maintain the many different natural functions of soil, the act aims to protect it from damaging influences. It attaches equal importance to precautions against the emergence of new kinds of contamination and to the clean-up of contaminated sites in order to safeguard both human beings and the environment against the dangers these pose. Utilization of soil should be environmentally sound and should not cause any damage.

There are presently 142,000 sites in civilian areas in Germany that are presumed to be contaminated. In addition, there are 4,366 such sites in weapons production areas and about 19,000 such sites in military areas that were contaminated by the Western Group of Forces.

Umweltbundesamt
(Federal Environmental Agency)
Bismarckplatz 1, 13585 Berlin
Bundesamt für Naturschutz
(Federal Agency for Nature Conservation)
Konstantinstrasse 110, 53179 Bonn

Sectors of the economy

· Industry · Technology · Crafts and trades
· Agriculture, forestry, fisheries
· Commerce · Foreign trade · Energy and raw materials
· Money and banking · Fairs and exhibitions · Transport
· Posts and telecommunications · Germany for the tourist

Industry

The mainstay of the German economy is industry. In 1994 the approximately 51,000 industrial enterprises in united Germany employed close to 7 million people, more than any other sector of the economy. However, industry's importance has declined considerably as a result of structural change; its share of the gross value added by all economic sectors fell from just over 41% in 1970 (old federal states) to less than 30% in 1993 (Germany as a whole).

In the same period the public and private service sectors increased their share considerably. In 1993 private services accounted for 34.2% of the gross value added, commerce and transport 14.5%. Rapidly expanding branches like information and communications technologies or future-oriented fields such as the aerospace industry have failed to compensate for the decline of such traditional branches as textiles and steel.

Only about 1.9% of industrial enterprises are large companies with more than 1,000 employees, whereas a good two thirds are firms with fewer than 100 on the payroll. Thus the great majority of industrial enterprises in Germany are of small or medium size.

But in spite of the large number of successful companies in this category, the large industrial firms are of increasing importance. Over 30% (2.5 million) of the total workforce in the industrial sector are employed by firms with more than 1,000 employees. The Siemens Group alone, for instance, employs 391,000. Furthermore, the relatively small number of big companies account for just under half of industry's total turnover.

Many of these firms are known throughout the world and have branches or research facilities overseas. They include the carmakers Volkswagen, BMW and Daimler-Benz, the chemical corporations Hoechst, Bayer and BASF, the Ruhrkohle AG, the electrical equipment manufacturer Siemens, the energy groups VEBA and RWE, and the Bosch Group. Nearly all of them are stock corporations. They are extremely important for a large variety of small and medium-sized suppliers.

After the Second World War industry played a crucial part in Germany's economic recovery. A decisive factor in this process was the transition from a controlled economy to a market economy in 1948. One of the basic principles of the social market economy is entrepreneurial responsibility. The entrepreneur must himself see to his company's growth and ensure that it can adapt to changing circumstances. Government economic policy is mainly confined to creating favourable conditions for business and industry. In the Federal Government's view competition is the best way to keep German industry technologically and structurally competitive on world markets. It ensures the largest possible number of small and medium-sized firms. The Federal Government therefore aims to improve conditions for the smaller industries and

The largest industrial firms in the Federal Republic of Germany (1993)			
Company, domicile	Sector	Turnover (DM m.)	Workforce
1. Daimler-Benz AG, Stuttgart	automotive, electrical engineering, aerospace	97,737	366,736
2. Siemens AG, Munich	electrical engineering	81,648	391,000
3. Volkswagen AG, Wolfsburg	automotive	76,586	253,108
4. Veba AG, Düsseldorf	energy, chemicals	61,294	128,348
5. Hoechst AG, Frankfurt	chemicals, pharmaceuticals	46,047	172,483
6. RWE AG, Essen	energy, building	45,111	113,642
7. Bayer AG, Leverkusen	chemicals, pharmaceuticals	41,007	151,900
8. BASF AG, Ludwigshafen	chemicals, energy	40,568	112,020
9. Thyssen AG, Duisburg	steel, machinery	33,502	136,975
10. Bosch GmbH, Stuttgart	electrical, engineering	32,469	156,615
11. Bayerische Motorenwerke, Munich	automotive	29,016	71,034
12. Mannesmann AG, Düsseldorf	mechanical engineering, industrial installations, etc.	27,963	127,695

facilitate the establishment of new firms. The following is an outline of the main branches.

With 655,000 employees at the end of 1994 and a turnover of DM 213 billion, the **automobile industry** is one of the most important branches of the Federal Republic's economy. Germany is the world's third largest producer of automobiles (after Japan and the United States). Of the 4.3 million motor vehicles that were manufactured in Germany in 1994, about 55% were exported.

The automobile industry has a long tradition in the new federal states as well. The models produced under the old GDR regime had no chance when faced with international competition after the country was united, however, and their production has been phased out. Several large automobile manufacturers from western Germany have meanwhile opened plants in Saxony and Thuringia.

By the end of 1993, the western German automobile industry had invested about DM 10 billion in the eastern part of the country. Once production is in full swing over 400,000 cars a year will leave the assembly lines – twice as many as in the former GDR.

Nearly 6,700 companies are engaged in **mechanical engineering,** the largest number of firms in any branch of German industry. Small and medium-sized firms have always predominated, and it is thanks to their flexibility and technological efficiency that Germany is among the world's leaders in this field. Only 2.6% of companies

Fitting a dual tyre to a lorry

have more than 1,000 employees. These are mainly firms which mass-produce or design and manufacture large, complex facilities. About 89% of the companies engaged in mechanical engineering are small or medium-sized with fewer than 300 employees. They are specialists who play a key role as suppliers of high-quality plant and production equipment for industry. Hardly any country has a wider range – 17,000 products, from consoles, printing machines and agricultural machinery to machine tools. In 1994 this branch of industry (in east and west), with a total workforce of 966,000 (the biggest in any branch of German industry), produced a turnover of DM 208 billion. Some 43% of the goods produced were sold abroad. This means that the Federal Republic accounted for one fifth of total exports of machinery among the Western industrial countries.

The **chemical industry** is the most important branch of the basic materials and production goods industry in Germany. Its state-of-the-art technology and emphasis on research has put it among the world's leaders. This applies especially to its three principal corporations (Bayer, BASF, Hoechst). There is also a large number of small and medium-sized companies. The total workforce is about 570,000, and turnover in 1994 was about DM 214 billion. Roughly 54% of the industry's output was exported.

The chemical industry is making considerable efforts to improve environmental protection and has in some areas assumed a pioneering role.

Although chemical production has a long tradition in the new federal states, it is in many fields unable to compete. At the end of 1994 about 38,400 people were still employed in

Control measurements in BASF's main biotechnical laboratory

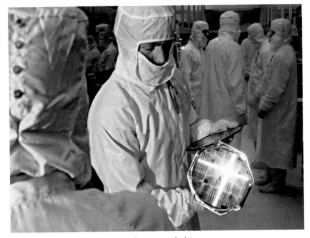

Production of chips

chemical firms there. The aim of government policy has been to retain the core of the main chemical regions. This has been accomplished through privatization.

The **electrical engineering industry**, with a turnover of DM 225 billion (1994, in east and west) and nearly one million employees, is likewise one of the main branches of industry. As a result of the fall in production and turnover following unification, only about 72,000 were still employed in the electrical industry in the new federal states at the end of 1994.

Another important branch of industry is the **food industry,** where in 1994 a workforce of about 532,000 produced a turnover of DM 218 billion (in eastern and western Germany). The **textile and clothing industry** still plays a significant role, employing 292,000 and generating a turnover of DM 60 billion (1994, in eastern and western Germany). With a workforce of 128,000, the **steel industry** in united Germany yielded a turnover of well over DM 41 billion in 1994. **Mining** employed 174,000 in eastern and western Germany in 1994 and had a turnover of DM 33 billion. The **precision engineering and optical industry** achieved a turnover of more than DM 20 billion in 1994. Its 1,600 primarily small and medium-sized firms employed just under 125,000. In many sectors these firms have attained international prominence.

The **aerospace industry,** which employs 78,000, generated a turnover of about DM 18 billion in 1994. It demands the highest standards from outfitters and suppliers and is in many fields a pioneer of modern technology. Through its major European cooperation projects (such as Airbus and Ariane) it functions as a motor for cooperation between European industrial firms.

■ ■   **The chambers of industry and commerce.** The Association of German Chambers of Industry and Commerce (DIHT) is the national organization of the 83 German chambers of industry and commerce. All German firms within the country – with the exception of craft and trade enterprises, the independent professions and agricultural operations – are by law members of the chambers of industry and commerce.

The chambers represent the interests of regional businesses vis-à-vis the municipalities, the states and the regional government authorities. They function as advisors for their member firms, as knowledgeable providers of information for business and industry. The chambers of industry and commerce are democratically organized and independent of government influence. The Association of German Chambers of Industry and Commerce represents the interests of commercial industry at the federal level and before the European Commission in Brussels. It also maintains a global network of more than 58 German chambers of commerce in foreign countries and delegates of German business and industry who promote German foreign trade and German investments abroad.

Bundesverband der Deutschen Industrie
(Federation of German Industries)
Gustav-Heinemann-Ufer 84-88, 50968 Köln
Deutscher Industrie- und Handelstag
(Association of German Chambers of Industry and Commerce)
Adenauerallee 148, 53113 Bonn

Technology

Whether automobiles or pharmaceutical products, optical instruments, machine tools or whole power stations – the Federal Republic of Germany supplies the world market with high-quality products. She is one of the leaders in many branches of industry. In 1988 four German companies were among the world's top ten innovative enterprises. In the case of research-intensive products, Germany exported over a quarter more than she imported. In bilateral trade she has a negative balance with Japan and the United States only.

■■■ **Competition.** It is crucial for German firms to keep abreast of international competition, which is increasingly becoming a high-tech race. Structural change is forcing many enterprises to concentrate on areas of technological and industrial growth. As a country with but few natural resources, Germany has always had to rely on exports of top quality, advanced products. Thus production methods have to be efficient and economical and based on state-of-the-art technology. This is the only way to achieve a high "exchangeable value" in international trade and thus safeguard jobs and incomes in Germany.

■■■ **Promotion of technology.** Technological development and innovation are primarily the responsibility of companies themselves. The government only comes to their assistance if it is considered necessary in the national interest. It promotes cooperation between industry and research. This cooperation helps small and medium-sized enterprises cope with the challenges of new technology and creates favourable conditions for innovation.

■■■ **Research projects.** In 1994 the Federal Ministry for Education, Science, Research and Technology and the Federal Ministry for Economics invested approximately DM 1,108 million in research projects by small and medium-sized companies. This enabled them to improve their production methods. They are also helped as regards "technology transfer", that is to say, the practical application of research findings.

Small and medium-sized companies can obtain information about the latest technological developments, for instance with regard to the use of computers for production purposes, in "demonstration centres" established by the research ministry.

Industrial research and development in the former GDR concentrated on much the same areas as in the Federal Republic: steel, mechanical engineering, vehicle construction, electrical engineering and chemicals. These are the focal points for the current restructuring of the economy in eastern Germany. Many companies and research establishments in east and west are cooperating on research and development projects in areas such as communications technology, microelectronics, laser technology, environmental engineering and chemical technology.

This turbine is intended for a waterworks

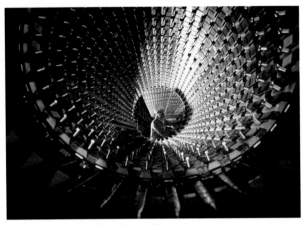

Installing the winding in a generator

■ ■ ■ **Strengths and weaknesses.** The significance of research-intensive products for Germany's international competitiveness is reflected in the industry's exports. In 1992 the states of the "old" Federal Republic of Germany accounted for 20.1% of world trade in manufactured industrial goods, the second largest share among the OECD countries. In sophisticated technology German industry has been successful in such fields as pharmaceutical products, new organic chemicals and synthetics, plant protection agents, electronic systems in the field of medicine, advanced optical and measuring instruments, and of course vehicles and mechanical engineering. It has been less successful in the fields of electronic data processing, microchips and consumer electronics. One area where Germany has done comparatively well is telecommunications.

In the field of environmental protection technology, German companies are leading the way and have the largest share of world trade (20.5%). German enterprises are also actively engaged in biotechnology, which will be one of the key technologies in the next few decades. The United States and Japan hold the leading positions, however.

Crafts and trades

Although crafts and trades in the Federal Republic are smaller than the industrial sector they have a much longer tradition. They flourished particularly in the Middle Ages, as proved by the mighty cathedrals and elaborately ornamented guild houses throughout the country. But today as well they are a considerable economic factor. In 1994 about 5.4 million people were employed in this branch, which had a turnover in 1994 of approximately DM 725 billion.

■ ■ ■ **Crafts in the industrial society.** Industry needs the small craft industries because they are very flexible suppliers of products and parts. But they are also the link between industry and the consumer since quality industrial products such as motor vehicles and machines have to be serviced and repaired.

Craftsmen are also producers themselves. Bakers, confectioners and slaughterers provide a wide range of foodstuffs. Houses in Germany are still mostly constructed and finished by hand by bricklayers, carpenters, plumbers and painters.

But crafts and trades are of special importance for two other reasons. One is that they offer scope for a large number of self-employed people and are thus a kind of school for young entrepreneurs. The other is that they provide some of the most important training centres.

It is here that about 40% of all apprentices in the Federal Republic learn their trade. Germany's craft industries urgently require apprentices, especially in rural areas. Those who cannot be taken on by their training employers after completing initial training are highly valued in other branches of industry.

In 1949 the Federal Republic had over 900,000 craft businesses. This number declined but the overall workforce increased. In 1994 there were some 668,000 such firms headed by master craftsmen in the whole of Germany, employing eight people on average.

Crafts and trades are playing a very important role in the restructuring of the economy in the new federal states. They are providing the impetus for growth. Even in the days of GDR central planning, some 82,000 small private craft firms were able to exist alongside the roughly 2,700 production cooperatives. From the time of unification to the end of 1994, the number of small craft businesses and similar firms in the new federal states increased to about 146,800 with a workforce of more than 1,167,000.

Judging by the size of the workforce, the main trade group is that of the bricklayers, concrete and reinforced concrete workers, and skilled road construction workers. The wide range of craft products is on display at the International Light Industries and Handicrafts Fair held every spring in Munich.

■ ■   **State support.** The Federal Government helps small and medium-sized craft enterprises to maintain and increase their competitiveness. Assistance covers tax relief, management consultancy and low-interest loans. The federal and state governments finance a wide variety of programmes to help new firms get off the ground.

Electrician testing switching equipment

Some special jobs have to be done by hand

■ ■ **Organization.** In order to maintain the high standard of performance and productivity of crafts and trades and ensure quality vocational training for the entire commercial sector, a craft business may only be operated by a person who has passed the master's examination. In the master's examination the candidate must demonstrate not only his or her technical proficiency but also a knowledge of business administration and law as well as teaching skills. A person who successfully completes the master's examination (master craftsman) is thus also entitled to train apprentices.

Craftsmen in the same craft or trade are organized in guilds at town or county level and in state guild associations. The guilds are above all responsible for vocational training and continuing education. They can also nego-

Installing a switch cabinet

tiate collective wage agreements and set up health insurance funds for their members. The various guilds in a
town or county form the local crafts and trades association. The chambers of crafts and trades, which en-
compass the territory of an administrative region (Regie-
rungsbezirk), are the self-governing bodies of the crafts
and trades sector and look after the interests of all the
crafts and trades. The chambers maintain the Crafts Register and Apprentices Register. The guilds have a national
organization known as the Federal Union of German
Handicraft Associations (BFH), while the chambers belong to the German National Chamber of Crafts (DHKT).
The umbrella organization for the regional and professional crafts and trades associations is the National Federation of German Skilled Crafts and Trades (ZDH).

Zentralverband des Deutschen Handwerks
(National Federation of German Skilled Crafts
and Trades)
Johanniterstr. 1, 53113 Bonn

Agriculture, forestry and fisheries

Germany is not only a highly industrialized country. It also has an efficient farming community who produce a broad range of high-quality foodstuffs. About half of Germany's total area of just under 36 million hectares is given over to farming.

Agriculture also has responsibilities which assume increasing significance in a modern industrial society. It ensures that rural settlements can function efficiently and preserves cultivated landscapes that have developed over centuries. But like other sectors of the economy, agriculture has undergone radical changes in the past 40 years.

■ ■ ■ **Agriculture.** In western Germany the number of farms has decreased by about one million since 1950. Attracted by the prospect of better incomes, many farmers left the land to work in industry and service enterprises. Furthermore, increasing mechanization saved manpower: In 1950 there were some 1.6 million farms employing just under 3.9 million family workers full time. In 1994, however, there were only 550,000 farms with about 290,000 full-time family employees.

As the number of farms and workers dwindled, productivity increased. In 1950 one farm worker produced enough food for only ten people; in 1992 the number was 82. In spite of this huge growth in productivity, farm wages have not always kept pace with those in industry.

Family farms still predominate in western Germany. In 1994 nearly 90% of all farmers worked less than 50 hectares (124 acres). In contrast to other Western European countries, a good 55% (1993) are part-time farms, i. e. the main family income is from activities outside farming. Farmers can reckon with an improvement in incomes in 1994/95, following an approximately 6% drop in profits each of the two previous years.

The chief farm products in western Germany in terms of proceeds are milk, pork, beef, cereals and sugar beets. In some regions wine, fruit and vegetables as well as other market-garden products play an important role.

In western Germany livestock farms are generally small. The factory-type holding is the exception. In 1992 about 72% of dairy cows were kept on farms with fewer

German bread in all its variety

than 40 animals, and almost 90% of pig-fattening farms had fewer than 600 animals.

In the eastern part of the country the pattern of farming is different. After the Second World War there were about 600,000 holdings which were gradually forced by the GDR regime to give up their independence. They were replaced by collective farms, large-scale farms including state farms and other state-owned enterprises, which numbered about 4,700 in the final days of the GDR. The collective farms specialized in the mass production of certain goods. They had on average 4,500 hectares (11,115 acres) under cultivation. Strictly separated from these were the livestock farms with, on average, 700 cows or 1,800 pigs.

When the country was united in October 1990 farm-land in the former GDR was returned to private owner-ship. Although there is still considerable uncertainty as regards land and property ownership, some 22,500 farm-ers have decided to run their own farms. At the same time, three quarters of the roughly 4,000 collective farms have been transformed into registered cooperative soci-eties, partnerships or joint-stock companies.

The Federal Government provides support in order to ease the difficult process of integrating eastern Ger-many's farms into the European Union. Funds are also provided to help convert the former collective farms into competitive enterprises, a practice that has meanwhile proved successful: many individual holdings have made considerable profit through cultivating large areas.

Apart from maintaining food supplies, farming in the densely populated, highly industrialized Federal Republic of Germany has other increasingly important functions, including
– conserving the natural sources of life;
– looking after the countryside to provide attractive living, working and recreational areas; and
– ensuring a continuous supply of agricultural ("renewable") raw materials for industry.

■■ ■■ **The Common Agricultural Policy of the European Community.** With the introduction of the common agricultural market of the European Community in the 60s important areas of agricultural policy were transferred to European institutions. This applies in particular to market and price policy and, to an increasing extent, structural policy.

The Community's original objective was to increase agricultural productivity and thus farmers' incomes, stabilize markets and maintain food supplies at reasonable prices. Much has been achieved in the intervening decades, especially as regards increasing production. Today the supply of major products such as cereals and beef far exceeds demand. Consequently, easing the strain on markets by restricting production has become an urgent priority of EU agricultural policy. A number of such measures have already proved effective, such as quotas for milk and sugar, as well as premiums for farmers who withdraw land from cultivation or go over to less intensive cultivation techniques.

But further measures were necessary and the EC agricultural reform of mid-1992 laid the foundations. The previous market price support system for important agricultural products is being superseded by more effective controls on quantity (e.g. set-aside arrangements) and, increasingly, direct aids to income.

In spite of the growing difficulties encountered by importing countries Germany's exports of farm products reached a record level in 1993, i.e. DM 35 billion. Her imports, on the other hand, amounted to DM 59 billion: Germany is the world's largest importer of agricultural products.

■ ■ **National agricultural policy.** Although many decisions on agricultural policy are today taken by the European Union, a few important matters are still in the hands of the national governments. This applies in particular to structural policy for the agricultural sector. Although the Union sets the framework, the national parliament and government provide the substance. The German Government, together with the states, does so chiefly through the "Joint Task of Improving Agrarian Structure and Coastal Protection". This includes water management, the construction of central water supply and sewage treatment facilities, construction of country roads, reallocation of land and village development.

The federal and state governments also provide support for individual farmers who wish to rationalize production methods. In addition, funds are provided for farms in underprivileged areas where agriculture is an important economic and social factor.

■ ■ **Food.** Maintaining food supply, quality and variety at reasonable prices is the aim of the national policies and the Treaty on European Union. That this has been achieved in the Federal Republic of Germany is shown by the fact that people have been spending an increasingly smaller proportion of their income on food. In the old western states in 1993 it was just under 15% (excluding spirits and tobacco, etc.) compared with 23% in 1970.

The wide range of high-quality foodstuffs available in Germany was extended as a result of the gradual harmonization of food legislation in the European Community even before the single market was launched on 1 January 1993. New laws that are constantly adapted in the light of scientific knowledge protect the consumer from hazards to health and fraudulent products.

Consumers must be in a position to judge quality and price and possess the knowledge to choose a balanced diet and avoid food-related illness. The government ensures the flow of necessary information and advice by supporting various specialized agencies such as the Deutsche Gesellschaft für Ernährung (DGE; German Nutrition Society), the Auswertungs- und Informationsdienst für Ernährung, Landwirtschaft und Forsten (AID; Food, Agriculture and Forestry Information Service), as well as the consumer centres in the individual federal states.

Appreciated worldwide: German wine

They provide not only scientific facts about nutrition but also up-to-date information on products, prices and keeping private stocks of food.

The mobile nutritional information service (MOBI) in the new states has had a multiplier effect. The vehicles used for that purpose are now at the disposal of the five consumer centres in those states.

Another important source of nutritional advice and information are the reports prepared every four years by the DGE on behalf of the Federal Government. These give a comprehensive picture of the nutritional situation in Germany. According to the 1992 report there has been an improvement on 1988. Moreover, eating habits in eastern Germany are not much different from those in the west. As always the main problems are overeating and an unbalanced diet.

■ ■ ■ **Forestry.** Almost a third of the Federal Republic's total area – 10.7 million hectares (4.13 million sq miles) – is covered by forest. The states with the largest forest area in proportion to their total size are Hesse and Rhineland-Palatinate (about 41%), while the one with the least forest – apart from the city-states – is Schleswig-Holstein (10%).

Between 30 and 40 million cubic metres of solid timber are felled in Germany every year. This meets about two thirds of domestic demand for wood and wood products. Although Germany has traditionally been a net importer of wood and wood products, she has become a prominent exporter as well. In 1992, for example, Germany ranked second worldwide (after the United States) in imports of paper, paperboard and cardboard and fifth in exports (after Canada, Finland, Sweden and the United States).

Forests are important not only as sources of timber but also as recreation areas for the inhabitants of industrial conurbations. Furthermore, they have a beneficial influence on soil, air and climate in that they retard water runoff, weaken the impact of wind, clean the air and prevent erosion and landslides.

A Forest Preservation and Forestry Promotion Act was enacted in 1975. This stipulates that forest land can only be cleared for other uses with approval from the state authorities. It also obliges forest owners to reforest harvested areas.

The foremost aim of German forestry policy is to preserve or restore the natural appearance of the forests and ensure their proper management.

Since the early 80s there has been increasing forest depletion due to a new type of damage ("Waldsterben"). The symptoms are sparse crowns and yellowed needles and leaves. There are various biotic and abiotic causes of this new type of damage, mainly air pollution. Although intensified environmental protection measures to improve the quality of the air have achieved noticeable success, pollution levels in forests and forest soil are still too high. According to the 1994 status report, one fourth of all trees in Germany's forests exhibit clear evidence of damage. Further efforts at both national and international level are essential in order to reduce air pollution from industrial installations, power plants, traffic, households and agriculture.

■■ ■ **Fisheries.** The fishing industry, too, has undergone structural changes in recent decades. Coastal countries worldwide have extended their fishing zones to 200 sea miles, with the result that traditional stocks have been decimated by overfishing, chiefly because of the excessive use of modern catching methods. This has greatly reduced Germany's ocean fishing fleet. Germany's principal fishing areas are the North Sea, the Baltic, and the Atlantic off the British Isles and around Greenland.

Replenishing conifer stocks in the Fichtelgebirge

Her only chance of surviving the threat to her fishing industry resulting from the development of international maritime law was within the framework of the European Community, which introduced catch quotas in order to regulate fishing and safeguard species.

The EC common fisheries policy was reviewed in 1992 after ten years and a new regulation adopted for the next decade. It is an extrapolation of the previous policy and focuses in particular on the principle of "relative stability" (i.e. fixed quotas for member states) as well as on a system of managing fish stocks by establishing annual total catch limits. The aim is to establish an economic and ecological balance between usable marine resources and fishing fleets by protecting stocks and reducing fishing capacities.

Herring catch off Rügen

Bundesministerium für Ernährung, Landwirtschaft und
Forsten
(Federal Ministry of Food, Agriculture and Forestry)
Rochusstrasse 1, 53123 Bonn ·
Deutscher Bauernverband
(German Farmers' Association)
Godesberger Allee 142-148, 53175 Bonn

Commerce

For decades the commercial sector in Germany has accounted for about 10% of gross value added. Some four million people – one eighth of the total workforce – are now employed in approximately 600,000 commercial enterprises (wholesale and retail).

Although there has been a tendency for companies to merge, most are still in the small or medium-sized category. About half of them employ only one or two, and nine tenths fewer than ten, usually including the owner and frequently family members as well.

■■ **Wholesale trade.** Wholesalers sell commercial goods from manufacturers or foreign markets to retailers, processors and bulk consumers. They buy large quantities of goods and sell them in smaller amounts. Retailers especially obtain consumer durables and non-durables from them. The wholesale trade's turnover in 1949 was about DM 50 billion, in 1994 more than DM 1 trillion.

German unification and the opening of Eastern European markets have provided fresh stimulus. In 1994 some 10,000 wholesalers were registered with the chambers of

All foodstuffs under one roof in the supermarket

industry and commerce in eastern Germany. The wholesale trade in the west employs 1.4 million people in about
134,000 enterprises.

■■■ **Retail trade.** The retail trade has undergone a remarkable structural change in recent decades. Especially
the advancement of self-service, which began in grocery
stores, opened the door to extensive rationalization. New
types of operations, such as discount stores and hypermarkets, came into being.

Today the main characteristics of the retail trade are
greater competition and smaller profit margins – all to the
advantage of the consumer, who has a wide selection of
goods and lower prices.

In 1949 turnover in the retail trade in western Germany
was DM 28 billion. This rose to DM 901.5 billion in
1994, to which must be added roughly DM 118 billion in
the new federal states. The greater proportion was accounted for by foodstuffs, spirits and tobacco (over 25%),
then textiles and clothing (about 13%). The approximately 385,000 retailers in the western part of Germany
have a workforce of approximately 2.85 million.

Rationalization reduced manpower in western Germany's retail trade at the beginning of the 80s, but from
1986 to 1993 there was an increase of 6.6%. Again, German unification was a key stimulus for this development.
A slight decrease (2%) is projected for 1995. Manpower
reductions in the east continue. The retail trade is subject

Fresh vegetables from the market

Individual service in the corner shop

to considerable seasonal change, and a sizeable proportion of the workforce works only part-time.

Increasing motorization and the trend towards bulk buying have favoured the hypermarkets and self-service department stores. As a result, many small retailers have not been able to compete. From 1962 to 1986 alone, the number of retailers fell from 445,000 to 340,000. In recent years, however, small and medium-sized retailers have been able to compete with large enterprises by catering for individual tastes and offering expert advice and personalized service.

Approximately 450,000 people were employed in the retail trade in eastern Germany in 1994. Due in no small part to their efforts, the poor selection of goods of GDR times has given way to an extensive range. According to the chambers of industry and commerce, nearly 100,000 private firms between Rügen and the Erzgebirge were offering their wares.

Hauptverband des Deutschen Einzelhandels
(Head Association of German Retail)
Höninger Weg 106a, 50969 Köln
Bundesverband des Deutschen Gross- und Aussenhandels
(Federation of German Wholesale and Foreign Trade)
Bonner Talweg 57, 53113 Bonn

Foreign trade

International trade is crucial to the German economy. The Federal Republic of Germany has always sought close trade relations with other countries and upheld the principle of an international division of labour. This is consistent with her liberal trade policy based on the removal of customs and other barriers to trade. By consistently pursuing an outward-looking policy she has achieved the largest trade turnover next to that of the United States. The main principles governing German trade policy are:
– international division of labour rather than self-sufficiency;
– global competition rather than trade restrictions; and
– reconciliation of interests rather than economic confrontation.

■■ ■ **External trade.** The total value of the old Federal Republic's imports and exports increased from DM 19.7 billion in 1950 to over DM 1,296 billion in 1994. Since 1952 exports have usually exceeded imports, and this in spite of several revaluations of the Deutsche Mark. In the 80s the export surplus rose sharply, reaching a record DM 134.5 billion in 1989, but after reunification it shrank, not surprisingly. One of the reasons is that the heavy demand from the new federal states boosted the country's imports, making her a "locomotive" of world trade in a period of global recession. In 1994 Germany's imports were worth DM 611.2 billion compared with exports totalling DM 685.1 billion.

Nearly one in three gainfully employed persons works directly for export. Germany's main exports are motor vehicles, machinery, and chemical and electrical engineering products. German exporters are known for the quality of their products, service and delivery. As a country with high wages Germany has concentrated on high-tech products in order to make up for her disadvantage as regards costs.

The most important imports are motor vehicles, agricultural and electrical products, and machinery – goods with which newly industrialized countries and, more recently, developing countries as well have been forcing their way into world markets.

As a result of her extensive trade relations Germany is affected by disruptions of world trade since they have an impact on jobs, investments, profits and standards of living. Thus a stable world economy, free trade and a well-functioning monetary system are crucial to the German economy.

■ ■   **Trading partners.** The progressive economic integration of the European Community (today the European Union, EU) has greatly increased intra-European trade. In 1993 about 49.8% of Germany's exports went to EU countries.

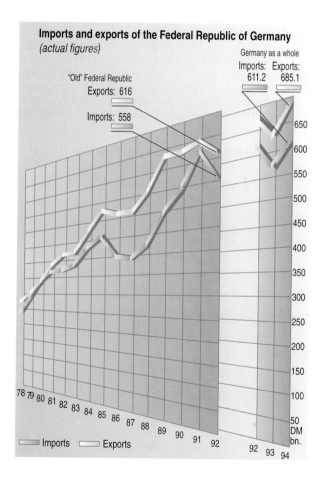

Imports and exports of the Federal Republic of Germany
(actual figures)

Germany as a whole
Imports: Exports:
611.2   685.1

"Old" Federal Republic
Exports: 616
Imports: 558

Imports   Exports

Germany's main trading partner is France. In 1993 the Federal Republic exported goods worth approximately DM 77 billion to that country, whereas imports from France totalled well over DM 65.4 billion. Other major countries of destination for German products are the United Kingdom, the Netherlands and Italy. Next in line is the United States, which in 1993 spent roughly DM 46.8 billion on goods from Germany. France also heads the list as far as Germany's imports are concerned, followed by the Netherlands, Italy, the United States, the United Kingdom and Japan. All in all, Germany does 70-75% of her trade with European countries, 10-15% with the Asia-Pacific region, about 8% with North America, and 2% each with Africa and Latin America. Her largest trade imbalance for many years has been with Japan. Whereas she imported goods worth DM 34.1 billion from that country in 1993, Japan spent only DM 15.8 billion in Germany.

Since 1990 the new federal states have also appeared in Germany's trade statistics. Trade relations of the for-

Germany's principal trading partners 1993

Countries of origin Imports from: (in DM bn.)	Countries of destination Exports to: (in DM bn.)
France 65.4	France 77.3
Netherlands 49.9	U.K. 50.3
Italy 48.2	Netherlands 48.3
U.S.A. 40.3	Italy 47.5
U.K. 35.5	U.S.A. 46.8
Japan 34.1	Belgium/Luxembourg 42.7
Belgium/Luxembourg 34.0	Austria 37.3
Austria 26.4	Switzerland 33.8
Switzerland 24.1	Spain 20.5
Spain 14.7	Japan 15.8
China 13.8	Sweden 12.7
Sweden 12.5	Russia 11.4
Denmark 10.5	Denmark 11.3

mer GDR were mainly focused on the state-trading countries of the former Eastern bloc. Even in 1993 just under
half of eastern Germany's foreign trade turnover was
with Central and Eastern Europe, Russia being the main
partner. The successor states of the Soviet Union still play
an important role in overall German trade as well: In
1993 Germany exported goods worth roughly DM 16 billion to this region.

■ ■   **Investment abroad.** After the Second World War
the Germans had to start from scratch where foreign
investment was concerned. Nearly all German assets
abroad had been lost. But meanwhile the total invested
abroad is worth approximately DM 275 billion. And
other countries have undertaken to invest more than DM
190 billion in Germany. Easily Germany's most important
partner for investment is the United States, followed by
the Netherlands, Switzerland, France and the United
Kingdom.

There are many reasons for investing overseas. Some
companies switch production outside Germany because
domestic wages are too high. Others have to secure their
supplies of raw materials and therefore buy an interest in
foreign suppliers. In many cases the aim is to maintain
and expand markets abroad. Where trade restrictions or
unfavourable exchange rates prove to be a hindrance to
direct exports, one way to solve the problem is to produce the goods where they are to be sold.

At any rate, investment abroad helps consolidate international trade. It is conducive to the international division of labour and to economic and industrial development in developing countries. They receive not only
long-term investment capital but also technology, know-
how and business experience.

In order to offset possible economic and political risks
attaching to investment in developing countries, the Federal Government has introduced special promotional
instruments. For instance, it has concluded investment
protection and promotion agreements with over 104 developing countries and nations in Central and Eastern
Europe.

To guard against political risks the Federation also affords financial guarantees for investments it considers
worth supporting. The Deutsche Investitions- und Ent-
wicklungs-Gesellschaft mbH founded by the Federation

promotes direct investment in the Third World and in the countries currently undergoing reform. Small and medium-sized German companies receive low-interest loans and grants to help them finance branches in developing countries and the transfer of technology.

■ ■   **Current account.** Germany's traditionally large export surpluses have often drawn criticism abroad, but the current account shows that the foreign trade surplus is offset by heavy deficits in the service sector. The huge amounts spent by German holidaymakers abroad, remittances by foreign workers in Germany to their relatives at home, development assistance, and the Federal Republic's contributions to the European Union and other international organizations erode most of the surplus from trade.

Indeed, Germany's current account has even slipped deeply into the red since unification. The credit balance of DM 76.1 billion in 1990 plunged into a deficit of DM 32.9 billion in the space of only one year. And in 1994 as well Germany's current account showed a deficit: DM 38.6 billion. This figure, however, is considered to have been inflated by problems encountered in the compilation of statistics; more accurate estimates lie at least DM 10 billion lower. Germany is no longer the world's biggest exporter of capital. On the contrary, she is having

German trade fairs attract many foreign exhibitors

Shipbuilding on the North Sea coast

to borrow considerable foreign capital in order to finance eastern Germany's economic recovery.

Bundesverband des Deutschen Gross- und Aussenhandels (Federation of German Wholesale and Foreign Trade) Bonner Talweg 57, 53113 Bonn

Energy and raw materials

As stated earlier, the Federal Republic has little in the way of raw materials and energy and is therefore largely dependent upon imports. She has to buy two thirds of her primary energy from other countries. Her dependence on minerals from abroad is also quite considerable. Germany has few deposits of iron ore and oil.

One quarter of the country's natural gas consumption can be met from domestic sources. There are large deposits of pitcoal, lignite and salt, however, which will last for many decades. Geological and climatic factors limit the country's economically exploitable renewable sources of energy.

■■ ▪ **Energy supply.** Having consumed 483.5 million tonnes (coal units) in 1994, Germany is one of the world's largest consumers of energy. Her efforts to conserve and make rational use of energy have proved successful. In the period from 1973 to 1994 the domestic product in the old federal states grew by 55%, but energy consumption by only 8%.

Since unification lignite has become the principal domestic source of energy. The main deposits are in the Rhineland, southern Brandenburg and Saxony as well as in Saxony-Anhalt and eastern Lower Saxony. Extractable resources total about 56 billion tonnes. Lignite was also the main source of energy in the former GDR, but energy supply there was one-sided and caused environmental pollution on a massive scale. Since the country was united production had declined by over 60% up to the end of 1994 on account of the restructuring of the economy and the diversification of energy supply in the new states. Lignite nonetheless remains one of the main sources of energy, although to a lesser extent than in the past. The cuts in production and the massive government programmes for rehabilitating the environment and modernizing power stations have reduced pollution considerably in recent years.

The main pitcoal deposits are in the Ruhr region (North Rhine-Westphalia) and in the Saarland. The estimated exploitable reserves there total about 24 billion tonnes.

In 1950 pitcoal accounted for 73% of the old Federal Republic's primary energy consumption. By 1994 its share had fallen to 18%. But oil, too, lost ground to other sources of energy, largely on account of the oil-price explosions in the 70s. From 55% in 1973 (compared with just 5% in 1950) oil's contribution to energy supply fell to just under 40% in the late 80s. It has meanwhile risen again to 41% (1994). The oil crises of the 70s in particular showed how much uninterrupted energy supplies mean to Germany.

Following new discoveries in the Emsland region and in the North Sea, Germany's natural gas reserves are estimated at about 350 billion m³. Gas is imported from several countries and supplies are secured until well into the next decade. In 1994 natural gas accounted for about 19% of primary energy consumption in the western part of the country and approximately 17% in the east.

Germany has not mined any uranium since the end of 1980. She imports the enriched uranium needed for the operation of nuclear power stations, and she has adequate supplies through the foreign holdings of German mining companies. In 1994 nuclear energy still accounted for a substantial proportion of electricity generation (33%).

■ ■ ■ **Energy policy.** Reliable energy supply is essential for a well-functioning, modern economy. This, as well as

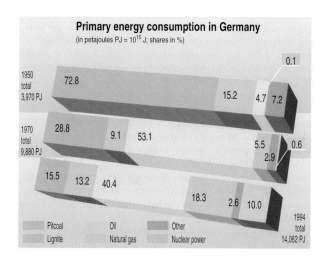

Primary energy consumption in Germany
(in petajoules PJ = 10¹⁵ J; shares in %)

1950 total 3,970 PJ — 72.8 — 15.2 — 4.7 — 7.2 — 0.1

1970 total 9,880 PJ — 28.8 — 9.1 — 53.1 — 5.5 — 2.9 — 0.6

15.5 — 13.2 — 40.4 — 18.3 — 2.6 — 10.0 — 1994 total 14,062 PJ

Pitcoal   Oil   Other
Lignite   Natural gas   Nuclear power

environmental and conservation factors, are the principal
objectives of the Federal Government's energy policy as
presented in its 1991 Energy Plan. This plan takes account
of the changes in the energy sector following Germany's
reunification, the greenhouse effect, the progress of European integration, and the transformations in Central and
Eastern Europe and the former Soviet Union. Since the
unification of Germany market principles and laws have
been in effect throughout the country. These include
stricter environmental legislation which has resulted in
the closure of some reactors in the new federal states.

The energy industry in Germany is mostly in private
hands. The government's task is to provide a suitable
framework, which includes an Energy Act and regulations for crisis prevention and the build-up of emergency stocks, as well as laws to protect the environment.

Since 1973 conditions on international energy markets
have changed fundamentally several times. Two sharp increases in the price of oil caused global recessions; then
the price dropped rapidly in late 1985. The transformation in Central and Eastern Europe and in the former
Soviet Union have given a new dimension to East-West
cooperation in the use of the energy resources of these
countries, especially Russia. These developments and the
Gulf war of 1990/91 have underlined the uncertainty as
to the price of oil, which is still the most important source
of energy.

Because of Germany's heavy dependence on imports,
not only of oil but of other commodities, the supply system must be flexible and adaptable and have access to
different sources. In the wake of the oil price crises in the
70s, the European Community placed the common energy policy on a much broader basis.

Today the Community has a considerable array of instruments available to support structural change in the
energy sector, to promote the rational use of energy, and
to reduce dependence on oil (they include the THERMIE,
SAVE, JOULE and ALTENER programmes). As part of a
comprehensive European strategy for reducing CO_2
emissions, the European Commission has proposed a
combined CO_2/energy tax which has the support of the
German government.

Owing to the rapidly increasing environmental pollution of recent years caused by the production and con-

Solar modules convert light energy into electricity

sumption of energy, greater attention will have to be paid to more economical and rational methods. Both the German energy industry and consumers have already achieved considerable progress in conserving energy and ensuring its environmentally friendly use. Internationally, Germany ranks at the top in many areas of energy-related environmental protection. Government energy policy focuses on the following aspects:

– Efforts to reach a consensus on future energy policy, especially with regard to the utilization of coal and nuclear energy, on energy conservation and on the more intensive use of renewable sources of energy.

– Ensuring an environmentally friendly energy supply, this being one of the main objectives. A focal point of the Federal Government's efforts in the 90s is the development and application of a comprehensive strategy for protecting the climate.

– A free market policy in order to ensure a reliable, economical, efficient and environmentally friendly supply of energy.

– Continued efforts to economize on energy consumption and to promote research on and use of long-term alternative sources of energy, especially those of the renewable kind.

- Further integration within the framework of the European internal market.

Owing to Germany's heavy dependence on imports, cooperation both with the other members of the European Union but also within the International Energy Agency and with the countries of Central and Eastern Europe and the successor states of the Soviet Union is of crucial importance.

Pitcoal and lignite will continue to help safeguard the nation's energy supply, but the contribution will be much smaller than it was in the late 80s. Pitcoal, however, will remain an important source of energy for the steel and electricity industries. Unfavourable geological conditions mean that German pitcoal is much more expensive to mine than imported pitcoal. The Federal Government and the governments of the coal-mining states of North Rhine-Westphalia and the Saarland provide considerable public support for coal mining in order to maintain sales of domestic pitcoal to the steel and electricity industries.

The Federal Government still feels that it is right to continue to use nuclear energy until such time as other comparably safe, environmentally friendly and cheap sources of energy are available. It helps keep CO_2 emissions down. In 1994, for instance, use of nuclear energy for the production of electricity prevented the emission of about 150 million tonnes of CO_2. As always, safety has

State-of-the-art
coal-mining equipment

priority over profitability. Germany's nuclear reactors are known throughout the world to conform to the highest safety standards.

■ ■ ■ **Raw materials.** Germany's supply of raw materials is at present secure. Imports consist of ores, concentrates and ferro-alloys from the commodity-producing countries and of supplies from Western European industrial countries who, though they have no raw materials of their own, have the necessary processing industries (foundries, refineries).

But apart from exploring new sources of energy at home and abroad Germany is also trying to reduce raw material consumption. Growing importance attaches to the recycling of used materials (see chapter "Environmental protection"). The commodity-using indus-

A coal-fired power plant at Werne-Stockum

tries maintain adequate reserves in case supply is disrupted.

In order to safeguard supplies of commodities Germany needs above all well-functioning markets. Her relations with the commodity-producing countries, many of whom are underdeveloped in industrial terms, are based on the following principles:

– maintaining world economic growth and efficiency;
– stabilizing commodity export earnings, especially in the least developed countries, and ensuring continuous supplies;
– accelerating the industrialization process in the developing countries and facilitating the technology transfer from industrial countries;
– opening the markets of industrial countries to imports of manufactures and semi-manufactures from developing countries;
– promoting a steady flow of capital to the developing countries and protecting investors from expropriation;
– securing a larger transfer of resources to industrial nations for the benefit of the developing countries; and
– exploring raw material deposits by means of cooperation projects.

Germany has always been able to rely on commodity imports and at present there is no sign of this situation changing. Maintaining supplies is primarily the responsibility of the private sector, who do so by trading on the basis of long-term contracts with sources in as many different regions as possible, by obtaining holdings in producer companies and trading on their own behalf, as well as by building up reserves, carrying out materials research and recycling materials.

The government can and should merely create the requisite market conditions and provide support only where this is necessary in the interest of the economy as a whole. Thus it is primarily concerned with ensuring that world commodity markets function properly because of their vital importance to Germany's industries.

It achieves this objective mainly by underwriting investment in developing countries against political risks, providing guarantees for untied loans, and through the work of the Bundesanstalt für Geowissenschaften und Rohstoffe (Federal Institute for Geosciences and Natural Resources) in advance of commercial exploration.

Money and banking

The unit of currency in the Federal Republic of Germany is the Deutsche Mark (DM 1 = 100 Pfennigs). It is freely convertible, i. e. it can be exchanged for any other foreign currency at any time at the going rate. There are no restrictions on capital transactions with other countries. The Deutsche Mark has for decades been one of the most stable currencies in the world. It is the anchor of the European Monetary System, and it is the second most important reserve currency after the American dollar.

▪ ▪ **The Deutsche Bundesbank.** The Federal Republic of Germany's central bank is the Deutsche Bundesbank (German Federal Bank) in Frankfurt am Main (since 1957). It is headed by the Central Bank Council which draws up the guidelines for the country's monetary policy. The Central Bank Council consists of the Directorate of the Bundesbank and the presidents of the state central banks. According to Federal Bank Act the Bundesbank is "independent of the Federal Government in exercising its powers". The Act spells out four key powers of the Bundesbank:

– Only the Bundesbank is empowered to issue banknotes in Germany.

– As the "banks' bank" it regulates the supply of central bank funds to credit institutions, determines the course of monetary policy with the aid of its financial instruments, and ensures that banks handle payment transactions in an orderly manner.

– It functions as the country's "house bank".

– It manages Germany's currency reserves.

The Bundesbank's fundamental task is to safeguard the stability of the currency. Thus apart from fulfilling the traditional role of a central bank, maintaining a sound monetary system, the Bundesbank has a special responsibility for maintaining economic stability. It must ensure the value of the Deutsche Mark both internally and externally. It is therefore commonly referred to as the "guardian of the currency".

By regulating the supply of money in circulation the Bundesbank keeps the Deutsche Mark stable while at the same time making available the necessary means to finance economic growth. To this end it relies on minimum reserves, refinancing and an open-market policy. The credit institutions are required to keep a certain percentage of their liabilities (minimum reserve) with the Bundesbank, interest-free. By varying this percentage the Bundesbank can influence the credit-creating scope of these institutions.

With its refinancing policy it regulates the supply of central bank funds to the commercial banks. It does so by buying bills of exchange and lending money on securities. The discount rate (for bills) and the Lombard rate (for loans on securities) are important regulatory factors.

Open-market transactions serve to regulate the money market. By buying securities the Bundesbank allows money to flow into the economy, by selling them it withdraws money.

In accordance with the Treaty of 18 May 1990 Establishing a Monetary, Economic and Social Union the former GDR currency was converted into Deutsche Mark as from 1 July 1990. At the same time all 572 financial institutions in eastern Germany became subject to the Federal Republic's banking laws. Since that date the Bundesbank has regulated the circulation of money and the credit supply for business and industry in united Germany.

■■　**The European Monetary System.** The purpose of the European Monetary System (EMS), which was established in 1979, is to stabilize exchange rates between the currencies of member states in the European Community. In the past years, the EMS has helped to strengthen cooperation among the countries of Europe in the area of monetary policy. It has also had a disciplinary effect on the monetary and financial policies of the EU member states.

All members of the EU are in the EMS, and most of them are in the Exchange Rate Mechanism (ERM) as well. The ERM fixes the central rates for each currency. Currency market rates are allowed to fluctuate up to a maximum of 15% either side of the central rate. If greater fluctuations are imminent the national central banks are obliged to buy or sell the currencies affected and thus stabilize the exchange rates. If the economic trend so requires, the central rates can be adjusted by means of a unanimous decision of the EU finance ministers and central bank governors.

Obviously, the EMS binds only the exchange rates of the participating countries. The rates with other currencies, such as the dollar or the yen, fluctuate freely on the currency markets.

Within the EMS there is a European Currency Unit (ECU) which serves as a link and unit of account between member currencies. The ECU is not a currency in itself, however, but a "basket" of the 15 EU currencies containing, for instance, 62 Pfennigs, 1.33 French Francs, 152 Italian Lira and so on. At present, the Deutsche Mark contributes 33% to the EU basket, the French Franc

Bundesbank headquarters in Frankfurt am Main

21%, the Pound Sterling 11% and the Dutch Guilder 10%. Under the Maastricht Treaty signed in December 1991 a common European currency is to be established by 1999 at the latest. Membership of the Monetary Union is subject to strict criteria (stable prices and exchange rates, low interest rates, sound public finances). Participants in the Monetary Union have undertaken to transfer their monetary sovereignty to a politically independent European Central Bank, the foremost objective of which will be to maintain price stability.

European Monetary Union will have various advantages. Companies will have a reliable basis on which to plan, tourists will not have to exchange currency, which means their holidays will be cheaper, the European currency can become a world reserve currency, and increased competition will improve the efficiency of the European economies. This will make it possible to safeguard present jobs and create new ones.

■■■ **Credit institutions.** There is a large variety of financial institutions in Germany, ranging from public savings banks, cooperative banks (Volksbank, Raiffeisenbank) and private banks to building societies, mortgage institutions, giro clearing banks, central depositaries for securities, and investment trusts. In the course of time a concentration process has taken place in the banking sector, however. Whereas there were just under 14,000 independent credit institutions in the 50s, by 1994 the number had shrunk to 3,870. And the trend continues, with about 100 cooperative banks merging into larger group institutions every year. At the same time the number of private banks is dwindling. In 1957 there were 245 of them; today only 74 remain.

In spite of the extensive structural changes that have taken place the balance of power within the banking industry has hardly altered. The private commercial banks have consistently retained 33% of all banking business, the public credit institutions just under 50%, and the cooperatives about 15%.

There are 330 lending banks (including large ones like the Deutsche Bank, Dresdner Bank and Commerzbank), 13 giro clearing banks, 704 savings banks, three cooperative central banks, 2,778 credit cooperatives, 33 mortgage institutions and public mortgage banks, 20 banks with special functions, 35 building societies and 96 foreign banks.

The private banks include large ones that are stock corporations. Giro central banks are the central credit institutions of the public savings banks in the individual federal states. As house banks of the states they are mainly concerned with regional financing. Most savings banks, which cater mainly for employees and the self-employed, are operated by the municipalities or associations of municipalities. They are autonomous public enterprises, the municipality being liable. The cooperative central banks are the principal regional institutions of the Volksbanken and Raiffeisenkassen, i.e. the rural and commercial credit cooperatives. Well over 11 million Germans have shares in these cooperatives.

Mortgage banks are private real-estate credit institutions which give mortgages and municipal loans and raise the necessary funds by issuing mortgage and municipal bonds. Building societies accept the savings deposits of people who want to build or buy their own homes and give them loans for this purpose after a proportion of the total sum has been saved. Among the credit institutions with special functions is the Kreditanstalt für

Symbols of the trade in front of the Frankfurt Stock Exchange

Wiederaufbau (Development Loan Corporation). It provides investment loans, lends to developing countries, and helps finance exports.

The activities of all credit institutions in Germany are supervised by the Bundesaufsichtsamt für das Kreditwesen (Federal Banking Supervisory Office) in Berlin. If in spite of this control a credit institution gets into difficulties, the deposit insurance institutions of the banking trade compensate for savers' losses.

■ ■ ■ **Financial markets.** Hardly any other sector of the German economy has grown so vigorously as the financial sector. The assets of Germany's banks increased from DM 3.9 trillion at the end of 1988 to DM 7.2 trillion at the end of 1994. Whether non-cash payments or savings, stocks and shares or loans – all have increased considerably in the last ten years.

In 1994 Germany's stock exchanges registered the record turnover of DM 7.5 trillion (compared with DM 6.9 trillion the previous year). Approximately three fourths of

German banknotes

this amount was accounted for by fixed interest rate securities and one fourth by shares.

Securities in Germany are traded on eight exchanges (Berlin, Bremen, Düsseldorf, Frankfurt am Main, Hamburg, Hanover, Munich and Stuttgart). The Frankfurt exchange, however, is easily the largest and rivals London for third place in the world behind New York and Tokyo.

A new institution founded in 1992 was the "Deutsche Börse AG" in Frankfurt, a holding comprising the Kassenverein (Clearing House) and the Wertpapierdatenzentrale (Securities Data Centre) which is concurrently the sponsor of the Deutsche Terminbörse (DTB; German Futures Exchange) and the Frankfurter Wertpapierbörse (Frankfurt Securities Exchange). The Deutsche Börse AG is today a leading supplier of exchange services in Europe. The DTB especially has expanded considerably since its creation in 1989. In 1994 it handled over 59 million contracts, compared with 50 million in the previous year. Frankfurt is also the headquarters of the Bundesbank, many large banks and hundreds of credit institutions and brokering firms.

■ ■ **Modes of payment.** These days nearly all financial transactions in Germany are handled via accounts. Cash transactions are being ousted by a highly developed remittance system involving cheques, direct debit, credit cards and electronic payment systems. As late as the 60s some German workers were still receiving their wages in cash. Today nearly every employee has a giro or salary account. In addition, more than 36.5 million Germans use Eurocheques. Credit cards are becoming increasingly popular. In 1980 some 580,000 people in the Federal Republic were using them, today the number is over ten million.

Bundesverband deutscher Banken e.V.
(Association of German Banks)
Kattenbug 1, 50667 Köln
Deutscher Sparkassen- und Giroverband e.V.
(German Savings Banks and Giro Association)
Simrockstr. 4, 53113 Bonn
Bundesverband der Deutschen Volksbanken und
Raiffeisenbanken e.V.
(Federal Association of German Volksbanken and
Raiffeisenbanken)
Heussallee 5, 53113 Bonn

Fairs and exhibitions

Germany's trade fairs have a long tradition. They developed in the early Middle Ages out of markets where people came to trade their wares. They were under the protection of the princes, who granted various towns the right to hold them. On 11 July 1240, for example, Emperor Frederick II granted this privilege to the city of Frankfurt am Main and placed all merchants traveling to the fair under his protection. A privilege from the Emperor Maximilian in 1507 established the Leipzig Fair, which acquired international fame.

In Germany the former comprehensive fair has been superseded by the specialized fair for one or more economic sectors. Germany's importance as a location for international fairs is known throughout the world. At present, about two thirds of the 150 leading international specialized fairs are held in Germany. In 1994, 118 international fairs and exhibitions attracted about 132,000 exhibitors, including just under 57,000 from abroad, and nearly nine million visitors. Industry as a whole spends in the region of DM 6 billion on fairs in Germany.

The sites for Germany's fairs are constantly being enlarged. There is considerable investment in new buildings, conversion, and innovative exhibition concepts. The proportion of foreign exhibitors at German fairs has increased steadily and in 1994 was about 43%. An expanding range of international goods and services stimulates competition and makes for even greater international participation. Apart from the major events, some 180 regional and many small exhibitions take place every year in Germany.

■ ■ ■ **The main fair venues.** The main German fair venues are Berlin, Cologne, Düsseldorf, Essen, Frankfurt am Main, Hamburg, Hanover, Leipzig, Munich, Nuremberg and Stuttgart. Of special importance is the Hanover Fair, which has been held every spring since 1947. With nearly 7,000 exhibitors of capital goods in a display area of more than 500,000 square metres, it is the largest industrial fair in the world. Since 1986 Hanover has also been home to a separate fair devoted to office, information and telecommunications technology, known as

"CeBIT", which in 1994 had 5,845 exhibitors from 52 countries and attracted over 680,000 visitors, setting a new record.

The consumer goods fair "Ambiente" and the autumn International Trade Fair for Consumer Goods in Frankfurt am Main focus on ceramics, glassware, china, arts and crafts, jewelry, household goods and home accessories. Frankfurt is also host to a number of major specialized fairs such as the International Motor Show (IAA), the biennial International Trade Fair Sanitation – Heating – Air Conditioning (ISH), or the "interstoff" (International Trade Fair for Clothing Textiles). And every autumn publishers, booksellers and authors from all over the world meet at the Frankfurt Book Fair. In terms of the number of exhibitors, Frankfurt is one of the most frequented fair centres in the world.

Cologne, too, is an important venue for such fairs as "ANUGA" (World Food Market), "photokina" (World Fair Imaging), the International Furniture Fair, the "art-cologne" and various other specialized fairs for home appliances, hardware, bicycles and motorcycles.

The main events in Berlin are the International Green Week (an agricultural and food exhibition), the Inter-

Every other year Cologne stages the ANUGA – World Food Market

national Tourism Exchange, the overseas import fair known as "Partners for Progress", and the International Audio and Video Fair. In 1992, after a break of 60 years, the International Aerospace Exhibition (ILA) returned to Berlin.

Major fairs in Düsseldorf are "DRUPA" (printing and paper), the International Trade Fair Plastics + Rubber, "INTERKAMA" (measurement and automation), "interpack" (packaging machinery and packing materials), as well as the international fashion trade fair "Igedo" which takes place several times a year.

Outstanding fairs in Munich are "bauma" (construction machinery), the International Light Industries and Handicrafts Fair, and "ispo" (sports equipment). Specialized fairs for the computer and electronic components industries are attracting increasing attention.

German unification has also merged two quite different types of trade fair: the decentralized, specialized type organized in cooperation with western firms, and the state-controlled type of the former GDR geared to Leipzig's comprehensive fair. Leipzig has in the meantime changed its concept to focus on specialized fairs. It is banking on its experience in trade with Eastern Europe and aims to stimulate economic recovery there. A number of the specialized fairs held in the new states have meanwhile gained in stature and attractiveness.

■■ ■ **Fairs and exhibitions abroad.** The growing integration of the world economy makes it increasingly im-

TERRATEC'95 – Trade Fair for Environmental Innovation, Leipzig

Special-purpose vehicles at the IAA in Frankfurt am Main

portant for German industry to participate in foreign trade fairs and exhibitions in order to promote exports. Such participation largely takes the form of information stands or joint exhibitions by German firms at foreign fairs. In 1994 some 3,500 German firms participated in fairs abroad with government support. At regular intervals Germany organizes industrial exhibitions abroad, such as the 1994 "TECHNOGERMA" in Mexico. In 1992 she participated in the World Exhibition in Seville. Germany will herself host the World Exhibition in Hanover in the year 2000. Its motto will be "Man – Nature – Technology".

Ausstellungs- und Messeausschuß der Deutschen Wirtschaft (AUMA)
(German Council of Trade Fairs and Exhibitions)
Lindenstrasse 8, 50674 Köln

Transport

A modern industrial society like the Federal Republic of Germany needs an advanced transport system. It gives people mobility, makes it easier for them to choose where to live and work, and also helps to equalize living conditions. Without a well-functioning transport system industry and commerce could not develop the necessary efficiency and flexibility. For a country as heavily dependent on foreign trade as Germany this is particularly important.

The government is confronted with major challenges in the area of transport policy: The European internal market and the opening up of Eastern Europe make Germany an even more important hub of trade and transport in the heart of Europe.

■ ■ ■ **"German Unity" transport scheme.** The old federal states have a good transport network. Modernization, renewal and expansion of the network in the eastern states is progressing rapidly. This infrastructure is crucial for the region's economic recovery. It has been estimated that this will require investment running into billions up to the year 2000.

Priority is being given to west-east transport links since they will play a key role in the process of merging the two parts of the country and promoting economic growth in the east. Since 1991 the government has been supporting 17 major road, waterway and rail projects, known as the "German Unity" transport scheme, which will largely be completed by 2000. In 1994 the Federal Government allocated approximately DM 10.7 billion for expansion and improvement of the transport infrastructure in the new federal states.

■ ■ ■ **The Federal Transport Plan.** The first transport plan for the whole of Germany, adopted in June 1993, will cost approximately DM 453 billion. It provides for maintenance, modernization, renewal and expansion of the rail, road and waterway networks up to the year 2012. 54% of this investment is earmarked for rail and waterway systems, so this is the first time the road network has received the smaller share.

In extending the federal highways network some 1,000 bypasses will be built. In order to expedite matters new statutory regulations were enacted to simplify and thus considerably shorten planning procedures throughout the country.

■ ■   **The Deutsche Bundesbahn AG.** In 1994 the Deutsche Bundesbahn (DB) and the Deutsche Reichsbahn (RB) were merged and privatized to form the Deutsche Bundesbahn AG. The Federal Government hopes that this structural reform will enable the railways to play a bigger part in the growth of transport systems with only a limited burden on the treasury.

Since they are a very environmentally friendly means of transport the railways will remain indispensable for the movement of bulk goods, the combined rail/road carriage of goods and passenger transport. Modernizing the railway network in the new states alone will cost some DM 40 billion.

In 1991 the Deutsche Bundesbahn (German Federal Railway) introduced its first high-speed services. The new ICE trains can travel at up to 250 km/h. Other high-speed rail services integrated into a European network are planned. The new routes between Hanover, Würzburg, Mannheim, Stuttgart and Munich make the railways even more attractive, especially for business travelers.

The aim is to offer an attractive alternative to air and car travel over distances of up to 500 km. The German Federal Railway was operating Intercity expresses as early as 1971. In 1992 approximately 1,500 highly efficient long-distance trains were operating daily between more than 320 stations.

In 1994 the Federal Government resolved to build the magnetic levitation train Transrapid from Berlin via Schwerin to Hamburg. In the future, Transrapid service on this route is to be provided six times per hour in each direction, covering the 285 kilometers in just under one hour. Since 1989 the Transrapid has been undergoing endurance testing on an experimental stretch in Emsland, and after the conclusion of testing in 1995 it will be approved for public transport. Due to its speed and environmental friendliness, the Transrapid represents a promising alternative to the automobile and the airplane. Construction of the new stretch of track is scheduled to be completed by the year 2004, whereupon the Transrapid will shuttle between Berlin and Hamburg at a speed of up to 500 km/h with only one stop in Schwerin.

The ICE – progress in rail transport

Looking onto the Avus Expressway from Berlin's radio tower

The railways perform an important function in providing local transport in densely populated industrial areas. Attractive services are being introduced to induce motorists to switch over to public transport. This would also help ease the burden on the environment.

Over the years billions have been spent on modernizing fast metropolitan railway networks (S-Bahn) in Berlin, Cologne, Frankfurt am Main, Hamburg, Munich, Nuremberg, the Ruhr district and Stuttgart. They have been linked with underground, tram and bus systems to form "transport grids" in nearly all densely populated areas. Passengers may switch from one system to the other using the same ticket. However, local public transport is still a declining percentage of transport overall. The transport policy pursued by the state governments and the city councils in conjunction with the reorganization of the railways will reverse this trend. The aim is to relieve the congestion in the centres of large cities caused by cars.

■ ■ ■ **Roads.** There are more cars on Germany's roads than ever. In 1994 there were approximately 46 million registered vehicles, including 40 million cars. (In 1950 there were only 1.9 million cars in the old Federal Republic, in 1986 about 31.7 million.)

The network of trunk roads has a total length of 227,000 km (1994), including more than 11,000 km of autobahns (motorways). In size, therefore, it is second only to that of the United States. Leaving aside the situation in the new federal states, the main concern at present is not so much to build new roads as to remove bottlenecks and accident black spots, and to provide more links with regions with little transport infrastructure.

On nearly all of Germany's roads there is a graduated speed limit. On national highways, for instance, it is usually 100 km/h, in built-up areas 50 km/h and in some residental areas only 30 km/h. Only parts of the autobahns have no speed limit, except for certain types of heavy vehicles (trucks, coaches, etc.).

For many people the car remains an indispensable means of getting to and from work and of enjoying leisure-time pursuits. Rapid goods transport from door to door would not be possible without the use of trucks. The motor vehicle will therefore remain one of the principal means of transport.

In some areas, however, road and rail transport do not compete but rather complement each other. One example of this is the "pick-a-back" system by which trucks are transported over long distances on special railway wagons. In container traffic, too, in which the railways are an important link in the transport chain, road and rail work together. This also applies to car-carrying passenger trains.

Although the motor-car means a lot to the individual in terms of mobility and quality of life, it also has its negative aspects. Together with industry and private households, cars are one of the main sources of air pollution. For several years now buyers of low-pollution cars have enjoyed tax concessions.

The most popular means of local transport is the bike

Road safety is constantly being improved, mainly through modern roads, traffic education in schools, the advance of traffic technology and the construction of increasingly safer cars. In spite of increasing mobility and traffic density in the west, the number of road fatalities in 1994 (about 9,700) was the lowest on record since the introduction of road traffic accident statistics in 1953. In the east, too, the negative trend has been broken, but improving road safety remains a permanent task.

■ ■ ■ **Shipping.** As a large exporting and importing country, Germany has a merchant fleet of her own. In 1994 it comprised 825 vessels with a gross registered tonnage of 5.37 million and is one of the most modern and safest in the world. Two thirds of the ships are at the most ten years old. Germany is one of the leaders in the field of container and roll-on, roll-off traffic.

Her seaports (the largest being Hamburg, Bremen/Bremerhaven, Wilhelmshaven, Lübeck and Rostock) have been able to hold their own in international competition. Although foreign

The intersection of the Weser and the Mittelland Canal

ports such as Rotterdam are closer to the industrial centres of Western Europe, the German ports have made up for this disadvantage by investing heavily in infrastructure and port facilities. They are now "fast ports" which can turn even large vessels around in a short time. The Baltic Sea ports in Mecklenburg-Western Pomerania expect to benefit from increased traffic with Eastern Europe.

■ ■ ■ **Inland shipping** has an efficient waterways network at its disposal in the western part of the country.

Frankfurt Airport

Duisburg has the largest inland port in the world. The main international artery is the Rhine, which accounts for two thirds of goods transported by inland waterway. Some 3,400 German freight vessels ply the country's rivers and canals, which have a total length of 6,900 km. This network was enlarged by the completion of the Main-Danube Canal in 1992, which provided the missing link between the Rhine and the Danube. The main task in the coming years will be to enlarge eastern Germany's waterways, which have remained largely unaltered since pre-war days.

■ ▥ **Air transport.** The strong growth of international air traffic is making heavy demands on Germany's airports and air traffic control systems. In 1994, more than 100 million passengers were registered at Germany's airports, plus just under two million tonnes of air freight. The largest airport is Frankfurt am Main; indeed it is one of the principal airports in Europe. Other German airports are Berlin-Tegel, Berlin-Schönefeld, Bremen, Cologne/Bonn, Dresden, Düsseldorf, Erfurt, Hamburg, Hanover, Leipzig, Munich, Nuremberg, Saarbrücken and Stuttgart. A new major airport is to be constructed in Berlin.

Deutsche Lufthansa (Lufthansa German Airlines) is one of the leading international airlines. In 1994 it carried about 37.7 million passengers using a fleet of about 230 aircraft. Lufthansa German Airlines was privatized in 1994. It has considerably increased the number of flights it offers through cooperation agreements with foreign carriers. Every year about 20 million holidaymakers fly by Condor, LTU, Hapag-Lloyd, Aero Lloyd, Germania and other smaller charter companies. More than 100 international airlines maintain regular flights to German airports, from where there are direct flights to roughly 200 destinations in more than 100 countries.

German airports are operated as private companies but are under public control. Since 1993 air traffic control has been the responsibility of the Deutsche Flugsicherungs GmbH (DFS), the private successor of the Federal Administration of Air Navigation Services. Airport and air safety standards are constantly updated in order to cope with the heavy congestion in Germany's airspace.

Posts and telecommunications

In 1490 the first teams of horsemen were relaying mail between Innsbruck in Austria and Mechelen in what is now Belgium. That was the birth of the postal service in Germany. The 500th anniversary of that event was celebrated in 1990. Almost at the same time, the postal and telecommunications system in Germany was reorganized. Three services formerly controlled by the Federal Ministry of Posts and Telecommunications were transferred to three newly formed public enterprises, namely the Deutsche Bundespost POSTDIENST (postal services), the Deutsche Bundespost POSTBANK (banking services) and the Deutsche Bundespost TELEKOM (telecommunications services).

At the beginning of 1995, after more than 500 years, the postal services in Germany were released from state control. On 1 January 1995, in conjunction with the second posts and telecommunications reform, the Posts and Telecommunications Reorganization Act entered into force. This Act forms the basis for the largest privatization undertaking in the history of the Federal Republic of Germany. As stock corporations – which for the time being will continue to be the property of the state, however – the three "sisters"

– Deutsche Telekom AG,
– Deutsche Post AG and
– Deutsche Postbank AG

are better equipped to compete. The newly founded Bundesanstalt Deutsche Bundespost (Federal Posts and Telecommunications Agency), a public holding company, co-ordinates the work of the three enterprises and their more than 600,000 employees in an advisory capacity. It is not, however, permitted to interfere in their entrepreneurial activities.

Another new feature is the Regulatory Council, an independent institution under the purview of the Federal Ministry of Posts and Telecommunications that is responsible for ensuring fulfillment of the Federation's duty to guarantee appropriate and adequate postal and telecommunications services throughout the country, a duty that for the first time has been laid down in the Basic Law, the German constitution.

In the spring of 1996, Telekom AG – as the first of the three enterprises – plans to have its shares traded on the stock exchange. The Deutsche Post AG will follow in 1998, whereas the Postbank has no plans to be listed on the stock exchange. The system has been restructured in order to keep postal services competitive in a fast-growing European market. This applies especially to telecommunications, where new technology is being introduced at ever shorter intervals and services have to cater for new customer demands.

■ ■ ■ **The Deutsche Telekom AG.** This enterprise builds and operates all telecommunications facilities for the exchange of news and data. It includes the telephone network service ISDN and global satellite communications. Whereas the telephone network as such is under the sole responsibility of Telekom, the latter has to compete with private firms in the field of mobile and satellite communications and as regards the sale of equipment and systems to subscribers. Thus the consumer has a wide choice, from the various types of telephones and mobile means of communication to satellite data communications.

All telephone calls in Germany can be dialled by the subscriber direct. This also applies to telephone calls made to 215 countries. A rapidly growing service is telefax. In 1994 some 1.5 million fax machines were in operation, and the number is increasing at the rate of 20,000 a month.

In addition to Deutsche Telekom's telex network, which has about 40,000 connections, the "Datex P" ser-

Leipzig: connecting up to the modern telecommunications network

vice with approximately 105,000 connections is assuming increasing importance. The "Datex J/Btx" service (in the future "Telekom Online") is growing rapidly and currently has about 800,000 participants. A fibre-optics network is available for high-speed data transmission.

Cable television has become the second largest telecommunications service. So far about 64% of households can now receive public and private cable television and radio programmes. In 1995 more than 15 million households subscribed to cable service. Deutsche Telekom is faced with the huge task of replacing the obsolete telephone network in the former GDR. In 1990 and 1991 large sections of a completely new digital overlay network were installed and put into operation. The network uses fibre optics, relay systems and state-of-the-art digitalized switching technology. It links the telecommunication centres in the new

Card telephones are supplanting the coin variety

states among themselves and with the old states in the west. By the end of 1994 Deutsche Telekom had already installed 5.3 million new connections in the new states. The total number of telephone connections in Germany in 1994 was 39.2 million. They carry about 53 billion telephone calls a year.

Telephone cards were introduced in 1989. This non-cash means of telephoning is becoming increasingly popular and, like postage stamps, is coveted by collectors.

■ ■ ■ **The Deutsche Post AG.** The Deutsche Post AG sees itself as a service enterprise in the telecommunications and transport sector. With about 340,000 employees, it is one of the largest service enterprises in Europe. The Deutsche Post AG transports letters and postal freight to any destination within the country or abroad. In many areas it competes directly with alternative delivery services. It meets this competition head on: One prime example is its new postal freight plan, which went into effect in July 1995 and is designed to recoup a larger share of the market from alternative parcel services.

The unification of Germany confronted the postal services with the historic task of introducing a new postal-code system for the whole country. The new system became effective on 1 July 1993, so now there is no postal division into east and west. Previously there had been two separate systems, each using four digits.

■ ■ ■ **The Deutsche Postbank AG.** On 1 January 1995 a new era began for the Postbank. Since that date it has been a stock corporation, the Deutsche Postbank AG. At the same time it acquired a full-service bank license, which makes it a full-fledged participant in the banking sector. With over 20 million savings accounts, deposits totalling more than DM 54 billion and demand deposits of about DM 21 billion, the Postbank is now already "Germany's number-one savings bank". After breaking even in 1993, the Postbank ended the 1994 fiscal year with a balance of approximately DM 90 billion, making a profit for the first time in its history. The Postbank, which manages 4.6 million giro accounts, is one of the least expensive nationwide providers of payment transaction services. It is the leader in both Btx service (over 370,000 customers) and telephone service (680,000 participants). With 1.2 million Eurocheque cards, 3.7 million Postbank cards and 250,000 credit cards, the Postbank also ranks at the top among the providers of card services.

Now that it is equipped with a full-service bank license, the Postbank can engage in certain types of business transactions that were previously off limits. In particular, this means that the Postbank can enter into credit transactions with private customers, offer mutual funds and, in the medium term, provide real estate financing and function as a building society. Via direct mailing, Btx service and telephone service the Postbank functions as a direct bank; it also offers walk-in and counter service through the roughly 18,000 branches of its partner, the Deutsche Post AG, and its own approximately 150 "blue counters".

Germany for the tourist

Germany has a remarkable variety of beautiful towns and landscapes in a comparatively small area. The Federal Republic is also popular with the Germans themselves, as shown by the fact that nearly half of them spend their holidays in their own country. Only 10% of overnight stays are by foreigners (for comparison, in Austria the number is over two thirds). Nevertheless, those foreign visitors spent about DM 17 billion in 1994.

■ ■ ■ **German attractions.** For centuries the German-speaking regions of Europe were a loose association of many sovereign states with lots of small and large "residences" or capitals. Nearly all of them had a long and individualistic cultural tradition, as shown by the numerous cathedrals, palaces, castles, libraries, museums, art collections, gardens and theatres all over the country which are ever popular with art connoisseurs and art lovers. Since reunification, the wealth of tourist attractions has been further enriched by unimpeded access to the scenic landscapes in the east and the classical centers of German culture such as Weimar, Eisenach and Dresden. Today there are few countries in which visitors can experience with such immediacy the consequences of more than four decades of development under different social and political systems.

But visitors are also attracted by the variety of the landscape. In the north they are drawn by the coasts and islands and the sea climate. Tourists also flock to the lakeland areas in Holstein and Mecklenburg, to the Central Uplands and the Alps for hiking, or to Lake Constance and the Bavarian lakes in the south for water sports. Those looking for romantic scenery choose the valleys of the Rhine, Main, Mosel, Neckar, Danube and Elbe rivers.

There are nearly 100 "tourist routes", such as the "German Fairy-Tale Route", the "Romanesque Route", the Romantic Route" or the "German Wine Route", which take visitors away from the major traffic arteries, opening up the country's traditional landscapes and providing access to a great variety of attractions in idyllic old towns and villages. They lead through regions with breathtaking scenery. The best known among them is the "Romantic

The Lautersee near Mittenwald with the Alpine backdrop

Route", which brings to life the Middle Ages, especially in Rothenburg ob der Tauber, Dinkelsbühl and Nördlingen.

Tourists pick up the tracks of the country's long history even in places that are not mentioned in travel guides. In Bavaria they are enveloped by the gaiety of baroque architecture, in the north they encounter the severity of brick gothic buildings. In some places time appears to have stood still. Visitors can expect hospitality and the famous German "Gemütlichkeit", a word that is difficult to translate but expresses the idea of warmth and friendliness, the "good feeling". There are plenty of opportunities to meet local people at the countless regional and town fairs and traditional festivals.

■ ■ ■ **Food and wine.** Cuisine and accommodation are of a high standard, ranging from cheap rooms on a farm or at a guesthouse to luxury holiday parks and top-class international hotels. Tourist services are still underdeveloped in some parts of the new federal states but the problems are gradually being solved.

In the restaurant trade experts now speak of the new "German culinary miracle". Contrary to the popular belief, German cuisine does not consist solely of knuckle of pork and sauerkraut. For the gourmet there are increas-

"Little Venice": row of houses along the Regnitz in Bamberg

The lighthouse on the Baltic Sea island of Hiddensee

ingly more restaurants which compare with their French or Italian rivals. This is borne out by the ratings to be found in the leading international restaurant guides. There is also a wide range of regional specialities. German wines have an excellent reputation, and the fact that the Germans know a thing or two about beer brewing hardly needs mentioning.

The Germans themselves also appreciate foreign food and the visitor will find Italian or Chinese restaurants, to name only a few, in even small towns and villages.

■ ■ **Tourist travel.** Apart from the excellent autobahns there is also a dense network of national highways and local roads. Long-distance rail travel is provided by comfortable trains, all of which have a dining car, and most of the night trains also have a sleeping car. Those who wish can also reserve a seat on car-carrying trains. All through the year the Federal Railway offers cheap city tours and other special offers for young people, the elderly and organized groups. In September 1992 a cheap "rail card" was introduced which can be used on all routes for a whole year to obtain tickets at half price.

For ramblers there are routes of all lengths to choose from, but Germany is also easily accessible to the cyclist. The formalities for foreign visitors are straightforward. Citizens of many countries can enter Germany as tourists for up to three months without a visa. And there are no

restrictions on the amount of foreign exchange which
may be brought into or taken out of the country.

■ ■ ■ **The German Central Tourist Board.** Apart from
the commercial travel operators there is the German Central Tourist Board (DZT), which seeks to promote tourist
travel to Germany. The DZT is a member of international
organizations such as the European Travel Commission
(ETC). It publishes a wide range of informational brochures about the Federal Republic in many languages.

Deutsche Zentrale für Tourismus
(German Central Tourist Board)
Beethovenstrasse 69, 60325 Frankfurt am Main
Deutscher Fremdenverkehrsverband e.V.
(Tourist Industry Association)
Bertha-von-Suttner-Platz 13, 53111 Bonn

Structures of the
social market economy

· Industrial relations
· Codetermination · Social security · Health

Industrial relations

The great majority of the 36.4 million workforce (29.8 in the old, 6.6 million in the new states) are wage and salary earners, i.e. employees, civil servants and trainees or apprentices. In addition there are about 3 million self-employed, most of whom also have others on the payroll, apart from 483,000 helping family members. Employers include private companies, federal, state and local government authorities, and other public institutions. Employers and employees cooperate with each other, as they must, but their interests sometimes clash. They then have the right to negotiate collective agreements without interference from the government. The state sets the general conditions by legislation but it does not lay down how much workers should be paid. This and many other matters – for example holidays – are left to the "social partners", i.e. the trade unions and employers' associations, to negotiate themselves.

■ ▥ ▥ **Trade unions.** The biggest labour organization is the Deutscher Gewerkschaftsbund, DGB (German Trade Union Federation) with about 10.3 million members in 16 unions (at the end of 1993). DGB unions are based on the "industrial association principle" ("one union, one industry"), that is to say they enroll workers of an entire industry regardless of the kind of work they do. Thus a chauffeur and a bookkeeper working in a printing plant would be in the same Media Union (IG Medien).

Apart from the DGB there are a number of other trade union organizations. Only the three largest are named here. The Deutsche Angestellten-Gewerkschaft, DAG (German Union of Salaried Employees), had around 527,800 members at the end of 1993. Its members are salaried staff from practically all sectors of the economy. The Deutscher Beamtenbund, DBB (German Civil Servants' Federation), with about a million members, is the main organization of permanent civil servants which, on account of civil service law, is not involved in collective bargaining and cannot call members out on strike. Otherwise it has all the characteristics of a trade union and has considerable influence. There is also the Christlicher Gewerkschaftsbund Deutschlands, CGB (Christian Trade

Union Federation of Germany), which, with its affiliated unions, numbers about 310,000 members.

The German trade unions are not connected with any particular party or church. No one can be forced to join a union. The closed shop system (which, according to agreements between employers and unions, allows only union members to be employed) is alien to Germany. The degree of unionization, i.e. the proportion of workers who are members of unions in certain industries, varies greatly but averages less than 50%. The unions maintain many colleges and training centres for their members. The DGB sponsors the annual "Ruhrfestspiele" arts festival at Recklinghausen and awards a cultural prize of considerable standing.

■ ■ **Employers' associations.** The employers have joined to form regional associations which – like the DGB unions – are based on the principle of "one association, one industry". The central organization of the many employers' associations is the Bundesvereinigung der Deutschen Arbeitgeberverbände, BDA (Confederation of German Employers' Associations). Like the DGB, it does not itself conclude collective agreements but instead functions as a coordinating body and represents the basic interests of its members. The BDA covers all branches of

The member unions of the DGB (31 December 1993)

Industrial unions/trade unions	Members (in thousands)	Share in DGB (%)
Non-metallic minerals	666.9	6.5
Mining and energy	403.2	3.9
Chemicals – paper – ceramics	778.5	7.5
Railway	450.5	4.4
Education and science	329.7	3.2
Gardening, agriculture and forestry	103.5	1.0
Trade, banks and insurance	583.8	5.7
Wood and plastics	192.9	1.9
Leather	27.4	0.3
Media	223.6	2.2
Metalworkers	3,146.4	30.6
Food, drink and tobacco – gastronomy	355.9	3.5
Police	197.5	1.9
Postal	578.2	5.6
Textiles – clothing	255.7	2.5
Public sector, transportation and traffic	1,996.4	19.4
German Trade Union Federation	10,290.2	100.0

business – from industry, crafts and trades, commerce, banking and insurance to agriculture and transport.

About 80% of entrepreneurs are members of an employers' association – a much larger proportion than in the case of employees. The BDA represents them only in their role as employers, i.e. as negotiating partners of the trade unions. All other interests – e.g. taxation or economic policy – are taken care of by other business organizations, such as the Bundesverband der Deutschen Industrie, BDI (Federation of German Industries), the Zentralverband des Deutschen Handwerks (National Federation of German Skilled Crafts and Trades) and the Bundesverband des Deutschen Gross- und Aussenhandels (Federation of German Wholesale and Foreign Trade).

■ ■ **Collective agreements.** A distinction is made between two types of collective agreement. Wage and salary agreements regulate pay and in most cases are agreed for a year at a time. Framework or general agreements, which as a rule run for several years, regulate conditions of employment such as working hours, holidays, minimum notice, overtime rates, etc. There are also special collective agreements governing specific issues (such as vocational training, supplementary retirement benefits and protection against rationalization measures).

In principle labour and management can negotiate freely; they must, however, abide by the constitution and the statutes. The statutory maximum weekly number of

Changing shifts in a large car factory

Steelworkers demonstrating in Bonn's Hofgarten

working hours is still 48, for example, but practically all Germans work less than 40 hours a week, and some only 35. Similarly, nearly all workers have a contractually guaranteed paid holiday of six weeks or more while the law prescribes a minimum of 24 working days. Nearly all workers receive additional holiday money and a Christmas bonus on the basis of collective agreements. In many cases actual wages, salaries and other payments are considerably above collectively agreed rates.

■ ■ ■ **Industrial action.** In Germany industrial action may only be taken in connection with collective wage agreements. It is therefore restricted to the parties to those agreements. During the life of a collective agreement, the parties thereto are obligated to maintain industrial peace. This means that industrial action cannot be called on matters covered by agreements still in force. In order to prevent industrial action, in many cases provision has been made for arbitration if the two sides cannot agree. Under the rules of most unions the members have to be balloted. Only if a qualified majority are in favour may a strike be called.

The workers' right to strike is counterbalanced by the employers' right to lock them out. Within certain limits, lockouts have been upheld by the Federal Labour Court and the Federal Constitutional Court as permissible means of industrial action, but the issue is still controversial. As the state remains neutral in labour disputes, neither strikers nor locked-out workers receive unemployment benefits. Union members receive strike pay from the unions' strike funds for loss of earnings, but non-members get nothing. During a strike they must either live on their savings or apply for social assistance.

■ ■ ■ **Cooperation.** Workers and entrepreneurs are not in opposition to one another all the time, however. They also cooperate in many ways. This is most apparent on the shop floor, but the representatives of both sides' organizations also meet on many other occasions, for example on apprentice examination committees. In the labour courts which rule on employment disputes there are lay judges at all levels from both sides. Within the framework of so-called self-government, the management boards and representative assemblies of the social insurance schemes (unemployment insurance, health insurance, accident insurance and pension insurance) are comprised half of employers' representatives and half of employees' representatives ("representatives of the insured"). Politicians also frequently seek the views of the leaders of the two sides' organizations. These and other forms of cooperation help to foster mutual understanding without blurring the differences between their respective interests.

Codetermination

In the 19th century Germany changed from an agricultural into an industrial society with considerable social upheaval. The rapidly growing new class of industrial workers initially lived in abject misery, almost totally without protection or rights. The nascent labour movement formed its own organizations which enabled the workers gradually to improve their situation and their social security, though sometimes only after a tenacious struggle.

But the workers continued to be totally dependent on their companies until well into the 20th century. The power of the owners was almost limitless. Today labour rights in Germany are protected by works constitution and codetermination laws. Since German unification these laws have been in effect in the new federal states as well.

■ ■ ■ **Works constitution.** The Works Constitution Act of 1952 introduced a federally uniform works constitution and structured industrial relations at the workplace. It laid down in particular the right of participation and codetermination of the individual employee and the employees' representative bodies, as well as the rights of the unions within the framework of the works constitution. These rights of participation applied to nearly every aspect of business operations – social, personnel and economic matters. The Works Constitution Act thus enabled employees to have a say in company decision-making. The Works Constitution Act of 1972, which is still in force today, retained the aforementioned basic features and considerably elaborated the works constitution.

■ ■ ■ **Rights of individual workers.** Individual employees have a substantial number of specifically defined rights. These include the right to be informed and to express opinions on matters relating directly to their job. For instance, they can ask to be informed about the effects of new technology on their work, inspect their personal file, and ask for explanations of assessments of their performance or their payslip.

■ ■ ■ **The works council.** The works council represents employees in relation to their employers. A works council may be elected in all private companies employing at least five people. Employees under 18 as well as trainees under 25 may elect representatives of their own. All employees can vote from the age of 18, but only those who have worked for the firm for at least six months are eligible for election to the works council. This also includes periods during which the employees worked in another branch of the same company. Foreigners, too, are entitled to vote and hold office. Members of the works council normally perform their duties on a voluntary basis without pay in addition to their normal work. Large firms with 300 or more employees, however, must release one or several members of the works council from their jobs to do council work full-time. In a single company a general works council may be established, at group level a group works council. In government authorities at all levels and other public institutions, the Staff Representation Act applies instead of the Works Constitution Act. The equivalent employees' organization is the staff council, whose duties and powers are similar to those of the works council.

Senior executive staff are not represented by the works council. They include, for instance, a firm's registered authorized officers (Prokuristen) or comparable staff in upper management positions. In firms with at least ten senior executive staff, an executives committee may be elected pursuant to the Executives Committee Act. As in the case of a works council, such executives committees may also be formed at company and group level. An executives committee may only be formed if on the first ballot the majority of the senior executive staff are in favour.

■ ▨ **Responsibilities and composition of the works council.** The works council must, among other things, ensure that the laws and regulations, accident prevention rules, collective wage agreements and company arrangements applying to employees are observed. It must call a shop-floor meeting once per calendar quarter and report on its activities. Employees attending the meeting may comment on the council's decisions and make proposals of their own.

The composition of the works council depends on the size and nature of the workforce. Thus in a company with 5 to 20 employees who are entitled to vote it consists of

Codetermination at work creates a good climate

one person, in companies with 21 to 50 three, and in companies with between 51 and 150 employees who are entitled to vote it has five members. The larger the company, the larger the works council.

Where a corporation has several works councils a general works council has to be elected. The same applies to the representative committees of young employees and trainees.

In companies with more than 100 employees an economic affairs committee must be formed. It is a consultative body with extensive rights whose members are nominated by the works council.

If the works council has at least three members the firm's wage earners and salaried employees must be represented in proportion to their numerical strength. If it has nine or more members it forms a works committee which handles day-to-day business. On certain conditions authorized representatives of the unions represented in the works council may also attend council meetings in an advisory capacity.

Codetermination rights cover such important matters as company organization, working hours, including the introduction of short time or overtime, holidays, the structure and administration of social facilities confined to the plant, company or group, technical monitoring of employee conduct or performance, accident prevention rules, occupational diseases and health protection regulations, allocation of company-owned housing or termination of tenancy, as well as company pay structures, remuneration principles, piecework payment and bonus schemes, etc.

The works council also has a considerable say in job descriptions, work processes and the working environment, personnel planning and vocational training. Where a company proposes to introduce changes (e.g. to cut back operations, close down or move to a different location) the works council may under certain conditions draw up a "social plan" which cushions the economic repercussions on the employees affected.

In firms with as a rule more than 20 employees who are entitled to vote, the employer must obtain the approval of the works council on all matters concerning personnel, such as hiring, job classifications, departmental restructuring and transfers. The works council may refuse to give its approval under certain circumstances governed by law. If the employer intends to carry out the proposed measures nevertheless he must seek a decision from the labour court.

The employer must also consult the works council before any dismissal. If he fails to do so the dismissal has no effect. Where a person is to be properly dismissed the works council may lodge a protest. In this case the employer must continue to employ the person dismissed at his request if the works council has objected on grounds covered by law and the employee has taken the matter to the labour court. The employer must await the court's decision. In such proceedings a justified complaint by the works council considerably strengthens the employee's position.

■ ■ **Codetermination.** Worker participation in company affairs is one of the mainstays of the social order of the Federal Republic of Germany. It is based on the conviction that democratic legitimation cannot be confined to government but must apply in all sectors of society. Nearly every company decision has an effect on its employees, irrespective of whether it concerns marketing, product development, investment, rationalization, etc. Hence employees should have a say in company decision-making through their representatives. The willingness of employees and their unions to assume a share of responsibility through codetermination has helped to shape and stabilize the Federal Republic's social order.

The workforce in medium-sized or large companies (stock corporations, limited liability companies, partnerships limited by shares, cooperatives or mutual insurance companies) can influence company policy through their representatives on the supervisory boards.

This codetermination in the supervisory board extends to all company activities. Thus the supervisory board, for instance, appoints the members of the management board. It may also revoke their appointment, demand information on all company matters, and have the last word on important business decisions, e.g. with regard to major investments or rationalization measures.

Codetermination in large iron, coal and steel companies is governed by the Codetermination Act of 1951 and the Supplementary Codetermination Act of 1956. Worker participation in the running of large firms in other branches is covered by the Codetermination Act of 1976.

■ ■ ■ **Codetermination in large enterprises.** Enterprises other than iron, coal and steel companies which either alone or together with their subsidiaries have a workforce of more than 2,000 are governed by the Codetermination Act of 1976 which requires the supervisory board to be made up of equal numbers of representatives of shareholders and employees.

However, the shareholders have a slight advantage in the event of a stalemate in that the chairman of the supervisory board, who is always a representative of the shareholders, has a second, casting vote. In the appointment of a labour director the employees' representatives have no veto.

■ ■ ■ **Composition of the supervisory board.** The supervisory board consists of equal numbers of shareholder and labour representatives. In enterprises with a workforce of up to 10,000 the board has 12 members (i.e. 6:6), in those with a workforce of 10,000 to 20,000 it has 16 (8:8), and in those with a workforce over 20,000 it has 20 (10:10).

The firm's articles may provide that the minimum supervisory board size as prescribed by law, i.e. 12 members, be increased to 16 or 20 members, and one consisting of

16 increased to 20. Some of the labour seats on the supervisory board are reserved for the unions represented in the company (or group): two in the case of a 12- or 16-member board, three in the case of a 20-member board.

■ ▓ ▒ **Election of labour representatives on the supervisory board.** All labour members on the supervisory board, i. e. those on the company's payroll and the union representatives, are elected by direct ballot or by delegates.

In companies with up to 8,000 employees the law prescribes a ballot, but employees may, with a majority vote, opt to be represented by delegates.

In the case of enterprises with a workforce of more than 8,000 the law prescribes elections through delegates. The employees may, however, reverse this procedure, that is to say they can choose by a majority vote to have a direct ballot.

■ ▓ ▒ **Election of shareholder representatives.** Shareholder representatives on the supervisory board are elected at the firm's shareholders' meeting (the "Hauptversammlung" in the case of stock corporations, the "Gesellschafterversammlung" in the case of limited liability companies).

■ ▓ ▒ **Election of the chairman.** The members of the supervisory board elect the chairman and deputy chairman at their constituent meeting. A two-thirds majority is required. Failing this a second vote is taken in which the shareholder representatives elect the chairman and the labour representatives the deputy chairman.

■ ▓ ▒ **The management board.** The supervisory board appoints the members of the management board and may also revoke their appointment. Here, too, a two-thirds majority is necessary, otherwise a mediation committee is appointed. Should this, too, fail to produce an absolute majority a second ballot is taken in which the chairman of the supervisory board has a casting vote.

A labour director with equal rights is chosen according to the same procedure. The labour director is chiefly concerned with personnel and social affairs.

■ ▓ ▒ **Codetermination in the iron, coal and steel industry.** Codetermination in the iron, coal and steel industry is the oldest and most extensive form of worker participation. It applies to companies with a workforce of more than 1,000.

Voting by a show of hands at a works council meeting

■ ■ ■ **The supervisory board.** The supervisory board consists of an equal number of shareholder and labour representatives and a "neutral" member. In firms covered by the Codetermination Act the board consists of 11 members (in larger companies it may be increased to 15 or 21). In the case of a supervisory board with 11 members, five members must be appointed by the shareholders and five by the employees. Two of the five labour representatives must work for the company; three representatives (who are not affiliated with the company) must be proposed to the works council by the national organizations of the unions represented in the company. All labour representatives are first selected by the works council and proposed for election at the shareholders' meeting. The election is only a formality since the meeting cannot reject the nominees. The supervisory board then proposes a neutral member, the eleventh, to the shareholders' meeting; in the event of a stalemate, this member of the supervisory board has the casting vote.

■ ■ ■ **Management board, labour director.** The members of the management board are appointed and dismissed by the supervisory board. One of the members must be a labour director who cannot be appointed or dismissed against the wish of the majority of the workers' representatives on the supervisory board. Thus labour directors are in a way the exponents of codetermination at management level.

■ ■ ■ **Codetermination in small enterprises.** In stock corporations and partnerships limited by shares which were established prior to 10 August 1994 and do not have more than 2,000 employees, one third of the members of the supervisory board must be representatives of the workforce. Family-owned companies with fewer than 500 employees are exempted from this requirement. Stock corporations which were established on or after 10 August 1994, or companies with another legal form which were transformed into stock corporations on or after this date, and which employ fewer than 500 persons likewise do not fall under the Works Constitution Act of 1952. Limited liability companies, trade and industrial cooperatives, and mutual insurance companies are subject to this Act if they employ between 500 and 2,000 persons. Although this one-third share hardly gives employees any say in decision-making, it does give them access to important information.

Deutscher Gewerkschaftsbund
(German Trade Union Federation)
Hans-Böckler-Strasse 39, 40476 Düsseldorf
Deutsche Angestellten-Gewerkschaft
(German Union of Salaried Employees)
Karl-Muck-Platz 1, 20355 Hamburg
Deutscher Beamtenbund
(German Civil Servants' Federation)
Dreizehnmorgenweg 36, 53175 Bonn
Christlicher Gewerkschaftsbund Deutschlands
(Christian Trade Union Federation)
Konstantinstrasse 13, 53179 Bonn
Bundesvereinigung der Deutschen Arbeitgeberverbände
(Confederation of German Employers' Associations)
Gustav-Heinemann-Ufer 72, 50968 Köln

Social security

Germany's social security system has a long history and its efficiency is legend. Social benefits and services account for nearly 30% of the gross national product and in 1993 exceeded DM 1,063 billion. Nearly a third of this was accounted for by pension insurance and over a fifth by statutory health insurance.

The state thus meets the requirements of article 20, paragraph 1 of the constitution (Basic Law), which says that the Federal Republic is a democratic and social federal state. Its purpose is not to meet all the citizen's needs but rather to provide for them on the basis of individually acquired entitlements. It does so by enacting extensive legislation on sickness, accident and old-age insurance, as well as child benefit, housing supplements, unemployment benefits, etc. It also makes provision for social assistance to ensure a minimum standard of living.

■ ■ ■ **The history of social insurance.** Social insurance in Germany dates from the Middle Ages when miners first set up joint funds to support needy colleagues after accidents at work. But it was not until the late 19th century that a comprehensive social insurance scheme emerged. It was triggered by Germany's industrial revolution which had greatly increased the number of industrial workers, who had practically nothing and no protection against illness or accident.

This became a domestic issue and the Reich Chancellor, Otto von Bismarck, introduced progressive social welfare legislation. Although his motives were partly political since he wanted to take the wind out of the sails of a growing labour movement, that legislation is generally recognized as the foundation for a modern social insurance scheme which has also served as a model for other industrial countries.

Laws enacted in 1883, 1884 and 1889 established three branches of insurance which are still the nucleus of the German system: health, accident, and invalidity and old-age insurance. At that time, pensioners had to be 70 in order to draw a pension. In 1911 these schemes were merged in the still valid Reich Insurance System, which added pensions for widows and orphans. Invalidity and old-age insurance was extended to all salaried employees. A separate insurance system was introduced for miners in 1923. Unemployment insurance was established in 1927, and as from 1938 craftsmen, to the extent that they were not privately insured, were covered by the statutory social insurance scheme.

After the Second World War the system was greatly extended and improved. In 1957, for instance, a statutory old-age insurance scheme for farmers was introduced, and in that same year pensions in general were indexed, i.e. adjusted in line with the average increase in incomes. Further reforms were introduced in 1972 and 1992.

Since 1990 this comprehensive social security system has also benefited pensioners, war victims and physically handicapped persons in the former GDR. The treaties on monetary, economic and social union and on national unification signed in that year provided that all citizens in united Germany should have the same benefits after a transitional period.

■■■ **Pension insurance.** The statutory pension insurance scheme is one of the pillars of the country's social security system. It ensures that workers will not suffer financial need and are able to maintain an adequate standard of living in retirement.

All wage and salary earners are required by law to be in the scheme. Self-employed persons who are not com-

In many occupations physical handicaps are no disadvantage

pulsorily insured by virtue of their membership of certain trades can join voluntarily.

Contributions (currently 18.6% of gross earnings) are levied up to a certain income level (at present DM 7,800 monthly). Worker and employer contribute half each. The scheme pays old-age and invalidity pensions. After the death of an insured person the dependents receive a proportion of the pension. There is a "waiting period" governing eligibility for pensions, i.e. the individual must have participated in the insurance scheme for a minimum period of time. As a rule the old-age pension is payable at the age of 65, but under certain conditions it can be drawn at 63 or 60. Women can claim a pension when they are 60.

The size of the pension depends on the amount of insured income from employment. The 1992 pension reform gave older employees greater flexibility in the transition from working life to retirement. They can now opt for a part-pension, part-work arrangement. The system has been adjusted in the light of changes in demographic and economic conditions and secures the financial basis of pensions beyond the year 2000.

Social security (1993, in DM bn.)

	2
	7
Training assistance	18
Housing supplements	19
Compensation (including war victims' pensions)	24
Accident insurance	29
Child and youth services	52
Child and child-raising benefits	74
Social assistance	90
Civil service system	132
Employers' contributions	211
Work promotion, unemployment insurance	310
Health insurance	
Pension insurance	

The main objective was to keep pensions related to incomes and contributions, to maintain living standards, and to enable pensioners, too, to benefit from the country's economic progress. For the great majority of employees the statutory pension is their only income during retirement. It must therefore maintain the standard of living they have been accustomed to during the many years when they have paid insurance contributions.

Since the 1957 reform, the average pension in the western part of the country after 45 years has risen to about 70% of the average worker's net income. Thus on 1 January 1995 it was approximately DM 1,920. And since 1 July 1990 average pensions in the new federal states after 45 insured years have been 70% of average incomes in eastern Germany. Pensions in the new states increase on an annual basis in line with the wages of the working population there. The aim is to bring pensions in the east up to the level of pensions in the west as soon as possible. As from 1 January 1992 pensions legislation has applied to the whole of Germany without distinction.

Paying pensions is not the only purpose of the pension insurance scheme. It also helps to maintain a person's capacity for work or to improve or restore that capacity (rehabilitation). Thus it covers the cost of curative treatment at a spa and provides support for people who have to undergo vocational retraining for health reasons.

■■■ **Company pensions.** Company pensions are a valuable supplement to the statutory scheme. Many companies provide them on a voluntary basis. Under the Company Pensions Act of 1974, employees retain their claim to a company pension even if they leave before retirement age, provided they are at least 35 years of age and their entitlement is ten years old or at least three years old if they have worked for the company for 12 years. Even if the employer becomes insolvent the company pension is still not lost. In such cases it is paid out of a fund established for this purpose.

■■■ **Health insurance.** Nearly everyone has health insurance, whether as compulsory or voluntary members of the statutory health insurance scheme (90%) or through private insurance. Under the statutory scheme insurance is compulsory for all workers as well as for salaried employees and several other occupational categories up to a certain income level. In some cases voluntary insurance is possible. The statutory system also covers pensioners, the unemployed, trainees and students. Employees pay their contributions into their respective health insurance fund (e.g. the district, company or guild fund, the seamen's, miners' or farmers' fund, or one of the substitute health insurance funds). All insured persons have a free choice of panel doctors and dentists. They pay half of the contributions, their employers the other half. In 1994 the average contribution rate was 13.5% in the west, 12.5% in the east, of the proportion of income on which contributions are based.

The health insurance fund pays the cost of medical and dental treatment, drugs and medicines, etc. as well as hospitalization. It pays all or part of the cost of necessary curative treatment at a spa. There are also maternity, family and home-nursing benefits. In the event of sickness employees receive their full wages from their employer for up to six weeks, in some cases more. After that period the statutory health insurance fund provides sick pay, which amounts to 80% of the regular wage, for up to 78 weeks.

The annual cost of health insurance is staggering. Within the framework of the 1989 health care reform, some services and items paid for by the health insurance funds were restricted, and people are now required to meet a larger proportion of the cost and therefore bear more of the responsibility themselves.

■ ■ ■ **Accident insurance.** Protection and assistance after accidents at work and in the case of occupational diseases is provided by the statutory accident insurance scheme.

In Germany all employees and farmers are insured by law against accidents. Other self-employed people can join the insurance scheme voluntarily. Students, schoolchildren and kindergarten children are also covered.

The main providers of accident insurance are the employers' liability insurance funds, each of which comprises all the firms in a given trade or industry in a specific district. Their funds come from contributions paid only by employers. Claims arise from bodily injury or death resulting from an accident at work or from illness or death caused by an occupational disease. Accidents which occur on the way to and from the place of work also fall into this category.

In the event of injury to an insured person the accident insurance fund bears the full cost of treatment. Injury benefits are also paid if the person is unable to work. If he is incapable of earning a living or dies as a result of an accident or occupational disease the insurance fund pays a pension or death grant and pension for surviving dependents, as the case may be. Like other pensions they are increased in line with general incomes.

Vocational assistance under the accident insurance scheme covers rehabilitation training and help in obtaining employment. The employers' liability insurance funds are also required to issue regulations on prevention of accidents and control of occupational diseases, and to monitor their observance.

■ ■   **Child benefit.** The upbringing and education of children is a considerable financial burden on the family. The Federal Child Benefit Act was passed to help ease that burden. Parents or guardians are currently paid a child benefit for each child up to the age of 16, for those at school or undergoing vocational training up to the age of 27. The benefit is presently DM 70 per month for the first child, DM 130 for the second, DM 220 for the third, and DM 240 for each additional child. Parents in the higher income brackets receive a lower child benefit from the second child onwards.

Parents also enjoy tax relief in the form of an annual child allowance (DM 4,104). Since 1986 a child-raising benefit of DM 600 per month has been paid for the first six months of each child's life. After that the benefit depends on the parents' income. In addition, mothers or fathers wishing to look after their

An accident victim being rescued

children themselves can claim up to three years leave from work during which they cannot be dismissed.

■ ■ **War victims' benefits (social indemnification)**
The purpose of the war victims' benefit scheme is to compensate, at least financially, the war-disabled, servicemen's widows and war orphans. They are paid index-linked pensions. In addition, the war-disabled can receive therapy and support in starting work and a career. Members of the armed forces who suffer damage to their health and the victims of violence, as well as their dependents, are taken care of in the same way.

■ ■ **Social assistance.** Social assistance is provided in the Federal Republic of Germany for people who cannot help themselves and receive no help from others. Under the Social Assistance Act everybody living in Germany – native or foreign – is entitled to social assistance in times of hardship in the form of maintenance grants covering disability, illness or care. Most of this assistance is provided by the states and municipalities. In 1994 social assistance expenditure totalled DM 48.9 billion.

Health

The Federal Republic of Germany has a ramified system of health care backed up by appropriate social services. Although health care is basically the individual's own responsibility, it is also the concern of society as a whole. All people, regardless of their financial or social situation, should have the same chance to maintain or restore their health. Health care in Germany is a decentralized, pluralist and self-governing system.

The average life expectancy in the Federal Republic has increased steadily over the past 40 years. It is currently 72 for men and 79 for women. This trend is chiefly the result of improvements in medical care. The aim is to increase life expectancy further still by reducing the incidence of "civilization" illnesses.

More attention will therefore be concentrated on preventive medicine, which includes better health education, regular precautionary check-ups, as well as information on healthy living.

The biggest threats to health in Germany, as in all highly developed industrial countries, come from the modern way of life. Half of all deaths are the result of cardiovascular diseases, followed by cancer. Allergies are becoming increasingly prominent, but also conditions typical of old age such as those affecting the central nervous system. The infectious diseases of earlier generations, such as tuberculosis, cholera, diphtheria and pneumonia, are no longer the threat they once were, thanks to modern medicine. But a new big challenge is AIDS.

■ ■ ■ **Doctors and hospitals.** In 1993 there were about 260,000 doctors in Germany. Medically, therefore, the Germans are among the best cared-for nations in the world. Less than half of the nation's doctors are in private practice. The others work in hospitals or administration or they are engaged in research.

About 645,000 beds are available in roughly 2,400 hospitals. There are also some 1,200 preventive care or rehabilitation centres. Hospitals are maintained by the state and local authorities (more than half of the beds), by charitable (mostly church) organizations (more than 40% of the beds) and by private enterprises.

■ ■   **Drugs and medicines.** The safety of medicines receives high priority in Germany. The Pharmaceuticals Act stipulates that medicines may be passed on to consumers only after their quality, effectiveness and harmlessness have been tested and confirmed by a government agency. Even after approval by the Federal Health Office they are kept under constant observation so that dangers are quickly recognized and remedial action can be taken.

The Pharmaceuticals Act also sets out detailed safety regulations for the production of pharmaceuticals, and it determines which substances may be sold only in pharmacies and which only on a doctor's prescription. Monitoring and regulating the supply and distribution of pharmaceuticals is the responsibility of the Federal Health Office in Berlin and the corresponding state agencies.

■ ■   **Preventive health care.** "An ounce of prevention is worth a pound of cure." This old saying is assuming increasing importance. Government health policy is to encourage everyone to look after their health and avoid risks.

Preventive examinations have therefore been introduced in many fields. Numerous federal and state institutions as well as private non-profit organizations provide information, courses and advice on such matters as

– preventive health care during pregnancy, childbirth, infancy and the first years of a child's life, as well as health education for young children in school;

– hazards to health such as alcohol, nicotine and drug abuse, overeating, poor eating habits, lack of exercise – the well-known causes of cardiovascular diseases which are also a contributory factor in cancer and other frequently occurring diseases; and

– programmes to help people who are chronically sick or disabled, and their relatives, to live with their illness or disability.

Examinations are offered for the early detection of disease, such as those for cancer which were introduced in 1971. The fight against AIDS (acquired immune deficiency syndrome) demands the greatest possible effort. The Federal Government, in collaboration with the World Health Organization and the members of the European Union, is carrying out a programme to protect people from HIV infection and at the same time provide compre-

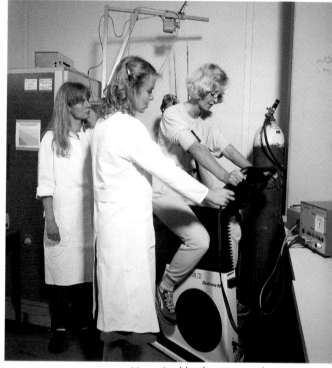

Measuring blood pressure under stress

hensive advice and care for those who are infected or showing symptoms.

In this respect it is important not to isolate or discriminate against those affected. Until such time as an effective vaccine and treatment are available, education and advice are the best way of preventing AIDS from spreading. This programme encourages and helps those concerned to behave responsibly in order to protect themselves and others.

Sick people and their families often need help over and above the medical care provided by the medical profession and hospitals. For them there is comprehensive counselling as well as the opportunity to discuss their problems with people suffering from the same disease. Opportunities of this kind are afforded by numerous self-

help groups which today have an established place in the nation's health system. They include:
– Deutsche AIDS-Hilfe (German AIDS Support)
– Deutsche Multiple-Sklerose-Gesellschaft (German Multiple Sclerosis Society)
– Deutsche Rheuma-Liga (German Rheumatism League)
– Frauenselbsthilfe nach Krebs e.V. (Women's Post-Cancer Self-Help Group)
– Angehörigenvereine psychisch Kranker (groups of family members of persons suffering from psychic disorders, e.g. drug-dependent persons)
– Anonyme Alkoholiker (Alcoholics Anonymous).

The Health Sector Act, which entered into force on 1 January 1993, enables the statutory health insurance funds to support self-help groups through grants.

■ ■ ■ **International activities.** Germany plays an active part in the work of international organizations concerned with health. No country can cope alone with the challenges of modern diseases such as AIDS or the health hazards of environmental pollution. Efforts to combat these diseases and their causes, as well as research activities, call for international cooperation. Germany also feels obliged to give the developing countries professional advice and financial assistance in developing their public health systems.

As a member of the World Health Organization (WHO) the Federal Republic is represented on several important bodies. Every year it organizes more than 35 international meetings on matters of topical interest in collaboration with WHO. More than 30 scientific institutions have been named as centres for cooperation with this international organization. The Federal Republic is the fourth largest contributor to WHO.

Within the European Union Germany is actively involved in the development of a common health policy. One of the EU's main objectives is to maintain high health standards in member countries.

Examples of these joint activities are the health research programme "Europe Against Cancer", the proposed European identity card for emergencies, an action programme on toxicology involving an exchange of information on detoxification centres, and cooperation on measures to combat AIDS, alcohol abuse and drug addiction. This cooperation will be greatly intensified as the European

Union assumes responsibility for health within the framework of the European Political Union.

■ ■ ■ **The cost of health care.** After establishing an efficient public health system in the new states the government had to address the difficult and perennial problem of financing health services on a national scale. The reform programme initiated in 1989, and particularly the Health Sector Act which became effective at the beginning of 1993, helped to stabilize expenditure on health services.

Furthermore, the efficiency of the statutory health insurance system, which covers about 90% of the population, has been considerably improved. In 1993 the sys-

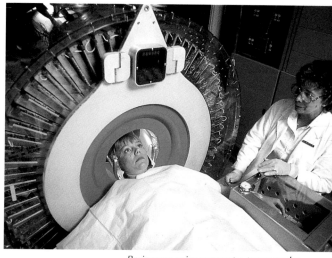

Brain scan using computer tomography

tem cost approximately DM 210 billion – about half of total expenditure on public health.

■ ■ ■ **The long-term care insurance scheme.** On 1 January 1995 the new long-term care insurance scheme for financing long-term care benefits entered into force. Alongside the health insurance, pension insurance, unemployment insurance and accident insurance schemes, it forms the fifth "pillar" of the social security system in Germany. The long-term care insurance scheme encompasses all persons covered under health insurance and will be implemented in three stages by the "long-term care insurance funds" that have been established by the existing health insurance funds. Since 1 January 1995 contributions have been levied to provide start-up financing, and since 1 April 1995 benefits have been paid for ambulatory care. As from 1 July 1996 benefits will also be paid for inpatient care. Employees and employers each pay half of the contributions. To alleviate the burden on employers, one paid holiday was eliminated; only in Saxony do employees pay the entire contribution themselves. The Long-Term Care Insurance Act primarily helps the 1.65 million people in the Federal Republic of Germany who need long-term care, but also assists the individuals who voluntarily provide such care, by paying them a long-term care allowance and ensuring their social security. In the 1993/94 winter semester the Fachhochschule in Frankfurt am Main began offering lectures in a new course of study entitled "Long-Term Care Studies".

Life in the community

· Women and society · Youth · Sports
· Leisure and holidays
· Clubs, associations and citizens' action groups
· Churches and religious communities
· Mass media and public opinion
· The press · Radio and television

Women and society

According to the Basic Law, men and women have equal rights. This constitutional rule is absolutely clear, but in practice it has been more a wish than a reality. Therefore, in 1994 the constitutional and statutory foundations for equality of rights were broadened.

Old preconceived notions of what women are and what they are not "entitled to" die hard. Women still do not have the same opportunities as men in society, in politics and at work. Many of them are subject to heavy stress through family and work. Nonetheless, their status has gradually improved over the years. And they are in the majority: In Germany there are nearly three million more women than men.

■ ■ ■ **Equality before the law.** The principle of equality has only gradually been applied. In 1957 a law was introduced which gave women equal rights where matrimonial property was concerned. Then in 1977 their position with regard to marriage, divorce and family was improved so that, for instance, the question of guilt in divorce cases no longer applied. Now the only criterion is whether the marriage has irreparably broken down. In addition, divorcees now share pension entitlements.

■ ■ ■ **Women in employment.** In order to give greater effect to the equality principle at work the Federal Government adopted another law which covers such matters as the advancement of women in the federal administration, the allocation of more women to posts in public agencies, the prohibition of discrimination of women at work, and the prevention of sexual harassment at the workplace. Under the 1980 Act on the Equal Treatment of Men and Women at Work, women may no longer be discriminated against on grounds of sex. Other laws protect pregnant women and do not allow women to be given heavy manual work.

There has been a marked improvement in educational opportunities for girls and women, who can now attend any school or training establishment. Just under half of the pupils in the western federal states who have obtained university entrance qualifications so far in the 90s have been women. Over 41% of all students in higher education are women. And the number of women who have completed a course of vocational training has increased significantly since the 50s.

More than 60% of the women in Germany between the ages of 15 and 65 are in employment. Women have become indispensable in industry, the health system and education. But there is still discrimination: They tend to lose their jobs faster than men and find new ones less quickly, and they are offered fewer apprenticeships. Male employees still receive distinctly higher wages than their female counterparts.

Women who do work which is the same as or similar to that of men can assert their claim to equal pay in court. Discrimination occurs nonetheless in the differing assessments of the types of work. "Women's" work pays less than "men's" work. In the public service the law has given women better opportunities for employment and promotion.

Discrimination against women at work occurs largely because their working life shows a different pattern. In former times women often went into less demanding trades because they regarded employment merely as an interim occupation before starting a family. But today ever more women want to return to work after a period of child-raising. There are government reintegration programmes to help them.

A broker on the Frankfurt Stock Exchange

Many choose part-time work and this, too, is promoted by the Federal Government on economic and social grounds. At present, however, there are far too few part-time jobs available.

In the new states the situation is different. In the former GDR 90% of the women went out to work and were enabled, with public assistance, to combine work and family chores. As a result of the economic restructuring process, however, women in those regions are losing their jobs at twice the rate of men. In addition to the numerous assistance programmes offered by the federal and state governments and local authorities to cope with these changes, numerous initiatives have been launched and associations established.

■■■ **Women and family**. In Germany 8.4 million out of 19.5 million couples have no children in the household or are childless. The birthrate is declining. The number of families with three or more children is decreasing while the number with one or two is growing.

The Federal Government is aware of the importance of family promotion, as manifest in its legislation providing

The doctor's assistant, a job much in demand

for the child-raising benefit and child-raising leave. The child-raising benefit of DM 600 per month is paid for the first two years after the birth of each child to those mothers or fathers who do not return to work or do not work full time during that period and whose annual net income does not exceed a specific amount. During this period the parent who chooses to take child-raising leave cannot be given notice. Another advantage is that child-raising periods (three years for each child born in 1992 or later) count towards the parent's pension claim. And since 1992 the same applies to time spent taking care of sick family members. This is an important step towards a fair assessment of work in the family compared with gainful activity.

■ ■ ■ **Women in politics.** Women have enjoyed the right to vote and the right to stand for election in Germany since 1918. Although the number of politically active women is increasing, it is still much smaller than that of men. Some of the political parties have introduced quotas to increase the number of female representatives on executive committees.

Each Federal Government since 1961 has included at least one woman; the present Government has three. The percentage of women Members of the German Bundestag has risen from 8.4% in 1980 to 26% today. Since 1988 the President of the German Bundestag has been a woman; one of the Vice-Presidents is likewise a woman. In 1991 a special Ministry for Women and Youth was established (which now bears the name Federal Ministry for Family Affairs, Senior Citizens, Women and Youth). All state governments have ministers or commissioners for women's affairs. More than 1,250 municipalities have created "equality posts" especially for women. The Federal Government, in cooperation with its EU partners, champions equal rights for women in various institutions of the United Nations, the Council of Europe, the European Union and the OECD.

Parallel to the statutory measures to establish equality of the sexes, a strong women's movement has developed in Germany. It vehemently opposes discrimination against women. It has emerged outside the existing women's organizations and has been the driving force in setting up centres for battered wives and their children, which now number 324 throughout the country.

Rita Süssmuth, President of the Bundestag, delivering a speech

In legal terms equality has almost been achieved 40 years after this principle was incorporated in Germany's Basic Law. There are no longer laws which discriminate directly against women or prescribe a certain role for them. In some cases, however, they are still disadvantaged socially, largely on account of the way the working world and society are structured. There is therefore still some leeway to be made up in securing equality.

The "women's lobby" is the German Women's Council, the central organization of women's associations. It represents 50 associations with some eleven million members.

Deutscher Frauenrat
(German Women's Council)
Simrockstrasse 5, 53113 Bonn

Youth

Nearly one in five inhabitants of the Federal Republic of Germany is under 18 years of age. They number well over 15.7 million and about 10% of them are of foreign nationality. Roughly one third of the total population (over 27 million) are under 27. For the great majority of them opportunities in life and future prospects have increased considerably over the past ten years. This applies to the eastern as well as the western part of the country. In the west especially most young people are comfortably off in material terms. Their financial prospects have never been better and they are well supplied with consumer goods. Never before have so many young people travelled as much as they do at present, both at home and abroad.

Thus 95% in the west and 84% in the east are satisfied with life. And 72% of the young people in eastern Germany look confidently into the future, expressing even greater optimism than their counterparts in western Germany. This confident mood cannot by any means be taken for granted. Only about ten years ago nearly 60% of the young people in western Germany between the ages of 15 and 24 were rather pessimistic about the future.

■ ■ ■ **Different expectations?** For the young generation in the east the collapse of the communist system first meant the end of a dictatorship which had ruled their lives and tried to rule their minds. They have perceived the social upheaval and reunification as both an opportunity and a source of confusion. Having been released without preparation from a command society and doctrine that had been imposed from above they understandably have had difficulty coming to terms with the wide range of influences and possibilities of a free society.

They have been expected to start afresh in nearly all spheres of life. This process of orientation and the problems confronting young people in a pluralistic society in any case have added to the difficulty of this period of transformation. The individuals and groups with whom they identify themselves, as well as the schools, churches and other institutions providing education, have lost much of their credibility and authority.

When asked in the spring of 1993 about the changes that have taken place in Germany since unification, 71% of young people in the east said the decision to adopt the western political system was the right one. 60% felt there were now more opportunities for self-fulfilment, 26% saw no change, while only 13% felt that the situation had deteriorated. Taking a realistic view of the problems, the optimists were in the majority.

In spite of the different living standards in east and west, there are hardly any significant differences in the assessment of personal problems or the major political issues in Germany. The biggest personal problems are jobs, training and education. The dominant theme in eastern Germany is unemployment.

■ ■ ■ **The problem of orientation.** As the influence of family, church and neighbourhood has declined, the freedom of young people to take matters into their own hands has increased accordingly. This is indicated by longer periods of study, the widening generation gap due to the fact that young people increasingly take their bearings from the standards set by their peers, the growing significance of leisure and consumption, and the effects of the mass media.

But although this increases the pressure to be more independent, 83% of the young people interviewed in western Germany and 89% of those interviewed in the east said that if they had personal problems their first source of help was their parents. This is proof that young people are looking for clear guidance and role models.

Not all young people meet with understanding for their problems at home or in school, of course. In many cases their links with other persons of responsibility or social groups have been weakened, and very often these groups are rejected by isolated young people. In this situation they may easily succumb to modes of behaviour which pose a danger to them and the community. Compounding the problem is the lack of job prospects, which is part of the reason for the social and political radicalism that has of late been manipulated and exploited by the leaders of extremist right-wing groups for their criminal objectives.

This problem is by no means confined to the new German states, although the after-effects of the communist dictatorship and the uncertainty resulting from the social

Light, music and movement: the disco scene

upheaval there have produced particularly volatile chemistry. Attacks by young people on foreigners, especially in the east, have highlighted the situation of the people there. While the culprits from the extreme right are being pursued with the full force of the law, the government is trying to identify the causes.

■ ■ ■ **Youth violence and animosity towards foreigners.** Recent xenophobic violence in Germany has alarmed and mobilized the public at large and caused outrage and justified criticism abroad. Most of those who have been called to account are young people.

First there was much speculation about the social and psychological reasons for this spate of violence, but the first substantial results were published in a 1993 study commissioned by the Federal Ministry for Women and Youth. It reveals that over 70% of the perpetrators are younger than 20; over one third are even younger than 18. A large majority of the predominantly male culprits (only 5% are female) have a low level of education. 18% of them are unemployed, well above the average.

The unemployed percentage of suspects in eastern Germany is 26%, significantly higher than the 12% in the west. The proportion of those suspected of being members of right-wing extremist groups is also significantly higher in the east (37%) than in the west (19%). The percentage of offences against foreigners that are the result of mass activities is likewise much larger in the east

(64%) than in the west (21%), where there is a larger incidence of offences by individuals or by groups of less
than ten persons.

The study concludes that offenders do not mainly have
the same background or biographical characteristics. Also striking is the fact that they do not have a common motive or political convictions. They are rather driven to
their crimes by "if anything, diffuse feelings and ideas
about Germans being threatened by foreigners, especially asylum-seekers, or suffering discrimination because of
them". Nonetheless, the results of the study show that
offenders frequently belong to extremist right-wing,
xenophobic and skinhead groups. According to police
statistics 38% belong to skinhead groups, 25% to right-
wing extremist and 19% to xenophobic groups.

Young offenders and their political leaders cannot expect any lenience from the police and judicial authorities. The federal and state governments have demonstrated their resolve to pursue suspects with all democratic means and bring them to account. Education and information, however, can play an at least equally important
role in the suppression of politically motivated acts of
violence, especially given the age of the culprits.

Since 1991, therefore, the Federal Government has
launched several programmes designed to eradicate
xenophobic attitudes among young people. They include
projects at the main centres of violence and measures to
promote the youth work of voluntary organizations in the
new states. Since the beginning of 1993 it has together
with the state interior ministers been running a massive
publicity campaign against extremism and animosity
towards foreigners.

Surveys of representative cross-sections of young people in Germany, however, have indicated that the overwhelming majority have no sympathy whatsoever for
xenophobic excesses.

■■■ **Organizations and groups.** Young people in
western Germany are far more apt to be members of a
group than their counterparts in the east. This applies
both to formal youth organizations and clubs and to
cliques. 37% of adolescents and young adults in western
Germany are members of a youth organization, in the
east only 19%. The proportion of these who are members
of sports clubs is 62% in both east and west. 68% of the

Licht-Blicke!

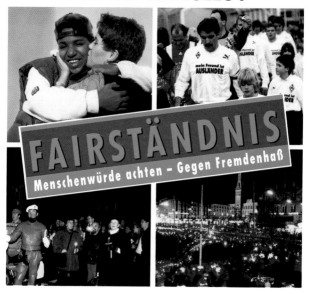

FAIRSTÄNDNIS

Menschenwürde achten – Gegen Fremdenhaß

Ob mit kleinen Gesten oder großen Lichterketten: Immer mehr Bürger demonstrieren gegen den Fremdenhaß, den Rechtsextremisten schüren. Das sind Licht-Blicke, die Täter und Hintermänner ins Abseits stellen.

Gewalt gegen Fremde ist mit Verboten und Strafen allein nicht zu überwinden. Ebenso notwendig sind **Verständnis** für die Fremden, ihre Sitten und Lebensweisen und **Fairneß** im Umgang miteinander.

Jetzt sind alle gefordert. Jeder einzelne kann sich im Betrieb oder in der Schule, in der Clique oder im Verein durch Wort und Tat für mehr Toleranz und **Fairständnis** gegenüber Fremden einsetzen. So machen wir aus Fremdenhaß ein Fremdwort.

Die Innenminister von Bund und Ländern

"Fairständnis" – a "fairness towards foreigners" campaign sponsored by the federal and state interior ministries

young Germans interviewed in the west said they belonged to a clique, compared with only 31% in the east. This is partly due to the fact that there is still no adequate network of independent youth organizations in the new states, a situation which is compounded by an acute shortage of buildings, centres or sports facilities for spontaneous or organized youth contacts.

The implications this has for leisure-time activities cannot be discounted. Recreational activities for young people in the east are limited by lack of money, lack of availability and lack of time. As a result, young people in the east are less likely to attend sporting events or rock and pop concerts, go to the movies or patronize trendy bars than their counterparts in the west. Reading and listening to music lead the list of favorite leisure-time activities in both the new and the old federal states.

In Germany there are about 80 supraregional youth organizations catering for about a quarter of all under 18-year-olds in Germany. Most of the national associations are affiliated to the Deutscher Bundesjugendring (German Federal Youth Council), including the Arbeitsgemeinschaft der Evangelischen Jugend (Young Protestants Association), the Bund der Deutschen Katholischen Jugend (Federation of German Catholic Youth Associations), the trade union youth associations, the state youth associations and the Ring Deutscher Pfadfinder (German Boy Scouts Association).

The one with the largest membership is the Deutsche Sportjugend (Federation of German Youth Sports Associations). There are also youth political organizations. Most of the parties in the German Bundestag have youth organizations under their wings. They belong to the Ring Politischer Jugend (Council of Political Youth Associations).

■ ■ ■ **Government policy**. The upbringing of children is primarily the responsibility of parents or guardians. The state helps in their personal and social development so that they are responsible for themselves and find their proper place at work and in society. It cares for young people by legislating for their protection and by providing them with social assistance and opportunities for voluntary activities. It purposely allows the various organizations, including the churches and other independent institutions, to take the lead in providing such assistance.

There thus emerges a range of services which reflect the currents of society and provide a genuine choice for young people and their parents. Germany's federal system, by which responsibilities are delegated as largely as possible to local institutions close to the people, is also manifest in the area of child and youth services. The greater proportion of the funds required are provided by the state and local authorities.

The government's main channel for implementing its youth policy and promoting youth work is the Kinder- und Jugendplan des Bundes (Federal Child and Youth Plan), under which DM 225 million a year is spent on out-of-school youth activities. This plan has existed for 40 years and is used to finance political, social and cultural youth work as well as international youth exchanges.

Increasingly more funds are being provided to promote children's activities outside the family. The greater part of these resources is used to finance youth associations. Their work has concentrated in recent years on foreign children and the problem of right-wing extremism and violence.

International youth contacts are a bridge of understanding. Consequently, roughly 150,000 German and French young people take part in about 6,800 events every year sponsored by the Franco-German Youth Office. In the 31 years since that organization was formed there have been nearly 5 million participants in more than 175,000 programmes.

Another youth organization of this kind, the German-Polish Youth Office, was founded in July 1992. Since the beginning of 1993 it has been able to dispose of its own fund for the promotion of German-Polish youth encounters which is fed by both governments.

Deutsch-Französisches Jugendwerk
(Franco-German Youth Office)
Rhöndorfer Strasse 23, 53604 Bad Honnef
Deutsch-Polnisches Jugendwerk
(German-Polish Youth Office)
Friedhofsgasse 2, 14473 Potsdam
Deutscher Bundesjugendring
(German Federal Youth Council)
Haager Weg 44, 53127 Bonn
Deutsche Sportjugend
(Federation of German Youth Sports Associations)
Otto-Fleck-Schneise 12, 60528 Frankfurt am Main
Bundesvereinigung Kulturelle Jugendbildung
(Federation of Youth Cultural Associations)
Küppelstein 34, 42857 Remscheid

Arbeitsgemeinschaft für Jugendhilfe e. V.
(Child Welfare Alliance)
Haager Weg 44, 53127 Bonn
Bundesarbeitsgemeinschaft Jugendaufbauwerk
(Federal Association for the Development of
Youth Organizations)
Haager Weg 44, 53127 Bonn
Internationaler Jugendaustausch und Besucherdienst der
Bundesrepublik Deutschland e.V.
(International Youth Exchange and Visitor Service of the
Federal Republic of Germany)
Hochkreuzallee 20, 53175 Bonn

Youth associations of parties represented
in the German Bundestag:
Junge Union Deutschlands
(Young Christian Democrats of Germany)
Annaberger Str. 283, 53175 Bonn
Arbeitsgemeinschaft der Jungsozialistinnen und
Jungsozialisten in der SPD
(Young Socialists in the SPD)
Ollenhauerstr. 1, 53113 Bonn
Bundesverband der Jungen Liberalen e. V.
(Federal Association of Young Liberals)
Niebuhrstr. 53, 53113 Bonn

Sports

Sports are a favourite leisure-time activity in Germany. This is reflected not only in the popularity of television broadcasts but also in the fact that there are more than 83,000 clubs affiliated to the Deutscher Sportbund (German Sports Federation). Nearly 25 million people are members of sports clubs, and another 12 million "do their own thing".

Sports organizations in Germany are self-governing. They receive support from the state only where they lack the necessary funds. Government policy on sports is based on cooperation. This also applies in the new federal states, where independent organizations have meanwhile been created. There, too, fair play and partnership come before victory at any price, and the focus is now on popular sports through clubs and associations as the foundation for the development of top-level sports.

■■■ **The German Sports Federation.** The central sports organization in Germany is the German Sports Federation (DSB), which embraces 16 regional federations and many individual sports associations. In all the various branches there are nearly 2.5 million people working in an honorary capacity as coaches or officials. The western part of the country has a large network of facilities for mass and competitive sports. There are, for instance, about 45,000 school and club sports grounds, nearly 30,000 gyms, and 6,500 indoor and outdoor swimming pools. In the new states, however, there is still a great shortage of facilities for mass sports and an urgent need to renovate existing facilities due to the fact that for decades all the effort went into competition at the highest level.

■■■ **Popular sports.** The German Football Federation (DFB) is by far the biggest sports organization in Germany, having more than 5.5 million members. Soccer is played at thousands of amateur clubs. It is also a spectator sport, attracting hundreds of thousands to professional games every week. This popularity has increased since the 1990 World Cup in Italy, when the German team won for the third time. Sports like tennis, golf and horseback riding are enjoying increasing popularity.

The international success of stars like Steffi Graf, Boris Becker and Michael Stich has made tennis a national sport. Mass sports are largely influenced by the professionals, particularly in soccer, tennis and horseback riding.

■ ■ ■ **Sports in the service of people.** Most people who indulge in sports do so not because they want to reach the pinnacle but for the exercise and the pleasure of taking part in a group activity. Sports are good for one's health and make up for the lack of exercise in an increasingly technological world. Year by year more and more people are attracted to sports, and organized sports are providing even greater opportunities. At the average club these days one can play soccer, handball, volleyball, basketball, tennis and table-tennis, or take part in track and field events. Water sports, too, are very popular, and there are various possibilities for physically handicapped and elderly people, and for mothers and small children. Popular and leisure-time sports are also promoted by the DSB programmes "Trimm dich" (Get Fit) and "Sport für alle" (Sports for All) which include open competitions in running, swimming, cycling, skiing and hiking. Every year millions of people take part. About 750,000 people a year have their performance in various sports tested in order to qualify for a "Sports Badge" which is awarded by the DSB. There is a gold, silver and bronze standard.

■ ■ ■ **Top-level sports.** Germany has 44 national sports centres and 20 Olympic training facilities as well as

The German eight winning gold at the 1993 World Championship

Franziska van Almsick, the most successful German swimmer

many regional centres. The armed services, too, develop talent in their own facilities. Top athletes must these days undergo intensive training with full health care and a certain measure of financial security. These responsibilities are shared by the associations and the Stiftung Deutsche Sporthilfe (Sports Aid Foundation) which was established in 1967. It regards itself as a welfare organization and tries to ensure that athletes can at least devote themselves to training without having to worry about the cost.

But it also helps them obtain qualifications for the time when they leave competitive sports. The foundation is not a governmental organization. Its funds come from private donors, the sale of special postage stamps on sporting themes, and from a television lottery ("Glücksspirale").

■ ■ ■ **Government promotion.** Sports organizations in Germany are supported by the state in many ways. The Federation exclusively promotes competitive sports. It provides funds for training and competitions, medical care for top athletes, the training and employment of coaches, the construction of sports facilities, and scientific research pertaning to sports. Sports for the disabled as well as international events by the various sports organizations also qualify for public support.

Steffi Graf, Germany's most prominent woman tennis player

Government money is likewise spent on sending coaches and advisers to Third World countries. Since 1962 nearly DM 200 million has been set aside for the promotion of sports in more than 130 countries.

Top competitive sports are promoted in order to develop sports in general, but also to enable leading athletes to be able to participate on an equal footing with their rivals in European and world championships and in the Olympic Games.

Support for popular sports is mainly the responsibility of the states and municipalities. It focuses on facilities, as well as school, university and club sports.

Deutscher Sportbund
(German Sports Federation)
Otto-Fleck-Schneise 12, 60528 Frankfurt am Main

Leisure and holidays

Travel is one of the most popular leisure-time activities in Germany. In 1994 nearly 60% of those over the age of 14 took a holiday of at least five days away from home. The proportion was greater in the new eastern states than in the west, for they, after all, had a lot of catching up to do in this respect. For decades they had been confined to Eastern bloc countries, only being allowed to travel to the west in very exceptional cases.

Growing prosperity and shorter working hours mean more leisure time and holidays. In 1992 the average annual number of working hours in the western states was only 1,667.

It was not always like that. At the turn of the century few workers were given holidays. The first steps in this direction came in 1903 in the metal and brewing industries, when workers were allowed three days annual holiday. By 1930 the average annual holiday was between three and fifteen days. Not until 1974 was the statutory minimum holiday of 18 working days introduced in the old Federal Republic. Today most collective wage agreements provide for holidays of six weeks and more, and most employers pay holiday money as well.

■■■ **Destinations**. Many Germans spend their holidays in their own country, but most prefer the warmer climate of the south. In 1993 they spent over DM 62 billion abroad, compared with the DM 17 billion which foreigners brought to Germany. The most popular countries for German tourists are Italy, Spain, Austria, France, Switzerland and the United States. They can call on the services of growing numbers of travel operators.

Holiday habits have changed. In former times the emphasis was on rest and sunbathing, but these days many people prefer an active holiday. They like unspoilt nature, away from environmental pollution. This also applies to weekend leisure-time activities. Roughly 260,000 clubs and associations, the state, the churches and local authorities offer leisure-time activities at sports grounds, indoor and outdoor swimming pools, and libraries, hobby courses at evening classes, as well as art, science, literature and music groups, etc.

Mountain hiking opens up glorious landscapes

Germany's many lakes are ideal for windsurfing

According to opinion surveys, the ordinary German family spends about one fifth of its income on leisure-time activities and this proportion is increasing. Commerce has recognized this trend and a thriving "leisure industry" has grown up (turnover in 1994: roughly DM 420 billion). The Deutsche Gesellschaft für Freizeit (German Leisure Association) was established in 1971. It researches leisure-time behaviour and provides information and advice. It has 30 member associations.

Deutsche Gesellschaft für Freizeit
(German Leisure Association)
Bahnstrasse 4, 40699 Erkrath

Clubs, associations and citizens' action groups

■ ■ ■ **Clubs.** There are few Germans who do not belong to at least one of the country's 300,000 or so clubs or associations. Nearly one in four is a member of a sports club, and over two million are members of choral societies. There are associations of marksmen, stamp collectors, dog breeders and promoters of local culture, carnivalists, allotment holders and amateur wireless operators, and not forgetting youth and women's groups. Members pursue their hobbies but socialize as well.

Some of these associations also play a role in local politics. People with different party affiliations come together in the marksmen's club or the local historical association, for instance, where they make informal contacts that can affect the life of the community. These associations do not have a defined political role, however.

■ ■ ■ **Associations.** It is different with groups which represent specific material interests of their members. These comprise above all the big labour and employers' associations. In addition to these there are many other organizations which represent certain professional, business, social or other interests. Thus house owners, tenants and motorists, for example, have associations, some with very big memberships. There are organizations of minorities, too.

These common-interest organizations engage in public relations to win sympathy for their causes. Their expertise can also be called upon in the preparation of legislation. Their influence is considerable, but it would be an exaggeration to say Germany is ruled by associations.

■ ■ ■ **Citizens' action groups.** A fairly new type of association is the citizens' action group, many of which have been formed since the early 70s. Citizens get together, usually spontaneously, to try to remedy a grievance where they feel a matter has been neglected by the authorities or the council. In most cases local issues are at stake, for example the preservation of old trees due to be felled to make way for a road, a children's playground or efforts to prevent the extension of an airport.

Lively discussion in citzens' action groups is a part of democracy

Sometimes action groups pursue contradictory aims, e.g. campaigning for a bypass road to reduce traffic in a residential area, or against such a road for ecological reasons. They have achieved many objectives, especially at local level, putting forward new ideas and being ready to compromise. Action groups also operate nationwide. The government welcomes and supports groups who draw attention to social problems and play a constructive part in their solution.

It is a basic right of all Germans to organize and take part in peaceful demonstrations. However, the final decision on controversial matters lies with the democratically elected governments and parliaments. They are bound to take the decisions that are best for the community as a whole. This makes it important for individuals and citizens' action groups to become involved as soon as possible in the preparation of government decisions, especially in the planning stage. Some legislation, for instance the Federal Building Act, already provides for such civic participation.

Churches and religious communities

In the Preamble to the Basic Law for the Federal Republic of Germany, emphasis is placed on the "responsibility before God". Implicit in these words is a general self-imposed restriction on state authority and human action. Article 4 of the Basic Law stresses the basic right to the free practice of religion: "Freedom of faith and conscience as well as freedom of creed, religious or ideological, are inviolable. The undisturbed practice of religion shall be guaranteed."

Just under 57 million people in Germany belong to a Christian church. 28.9 million are Protestants, roughly 28 million are Roman Catholics, and a minority belong to other Christian denominations. The 1919 Weimar constitution separated church and state without, however, completely severing historical ties. The legal situation thus created is by and large the one which obtains today, corresponding provisions of the Weimar constitution having been incorporated in the Basic Law adopted after the Second World War.

There is no state church in Germany. The state is neutral vis-à-vis religions and creeds. The churches have a special status as independent public corporations, so that their relationship with the state is often described as a partnership. Apart from the Basic Law, that relationship is regulated by concordats and agreements. The state assumes, in whole or in part, the cost of certain church establishments, such as kindergartens and schools. The churches are empowered to levy taxes on their members, which as a rule are collected by the state against reimbursement of costs. The clergy are trained mainly at state universities, and the churches have a say in appointments to chairs of theology. The work of the churches in running hospitals, old people's and nursing homes, consulting and caring services, schools and training centres is an indispensable charitable and social commitment.

■ ■ ■ **The Evangelical Church in Germany (EKD).** The EKD is an alliance of 24 largely independent Lutheran, Reformed and United churches. Following the country's unification this alliance once again spans the whole of

The 1992 German Protestant Church Convention held in Munich

Germany. Church administrative regions are not identical with the territories of the federal states.

The EKD's main legislative body is the Synod, its chief executive body the Council. Member churches participate in the work of the EKD through the Church Conference. The Church Office in Hanover is its central administrative headquarters. The Evangelical Churches are members of the World Council of Churches and they cooperate closely with the Roman Catholic Church.

■■■ **The Catholic Church.** Until 1994, the Catholic Church was divided up into 23 dioceses, five of which were archdioceses. As a result of the reorganization that followed the reunification of Germany, there are now 27 dioceses (seven archdioceses). A new archdiocese was established in Hamburg. The diocese of Berlin was raised to the status of a church province (archdiocese). The apostolic administrature of Görlitz and the jurisdiction districts of Magdeburg and Erfurt-Meiningen became dioceses. Germany's archbishops and bishops, seventy in all, consult together at the spring and autumn assemblies of the German Bishops Conference, which has a secretariat in Bonn.

The impetus from the Second Vatican Council for the involvement of the Catholic laity in church affairs is translated into action by elected lay representatives. Together with the 100 or more Catholic associations they form the Central Committee of German Catholics. The

Processions take place on Corpus Christi Day

visits of Pope John Paul II in 1980 and 1987 evoked a tremendous response and stimulated the ecumenical movement and dialogue between state and church.

■ ■ ■ **Other religious communities.** Other religious communities include in particular the free churches. Two of the largest Protestant free churches, the Methodists and the Protestant Community (Evangelische Gemeinschaft) joined together in 1968 to form the Protestant Methodist Church (Evangelisch-methodistische Kirche). In addition there are the Baptists. The Old Catholic Church came into being as a breakaway from the Roman Catholic Church in the 1870s after the First Vatican Council. The Mennonite congregations, the Society of Friends (Quakers) and the Salvation Army are known for their social activities.

In 1933 about 530,000 Jews lived in the German Reich. Following the National Socialist genocide the Jewish communities now have about 50,000 members. The largest community is in Berlin (nearly 10,000), followed by Frankfurt am Main (6,000) and Munich (just under 5,000). Following the unification of Germany, Jewish communities with rich traditions in eastern Germany, such as those in Dresden and Leipzig, have once again been able to develop an active community life. The national organization is the Central Council of Jews in Germany. In 1979/80 the College for Jewish Studies was founded in Heidelberg. Through research and scholarship, this institution serves to cultivate and develop the Jewish humanities and related disciplines. Heidelberg is also the seat of the Central Archive for Research on the History of the Jews in Germany. This archive, which was established in 1987 under the patronage of the Central Council of Jews in Germany, particularly focuses on research pertaining to the postwar period.

The presence of many foreign workers and their families has greatly increased the importance of religious communities which previously were hardly represented in Germany. This is the case with the Orthodox Churches and especially Islam. Today, more than 1.7 million Muslims, mostly Turks, live in the Germany.

■■■ **Joint action.** In the period from 1933 to 1945 many Protestant and Catholic Christians fought against National Socialism. Their cooperation in this struggle strengthened interdenominational understanding and awareness of the common political responsibility. The churches also played an important part in the peaceful revolution in the GDR.

The churches address the public in many ways, for example by publishing comments on topical issues and other information. Worthy of special mention are the two lay movements, the German Catholic Convention and the German Protestant Church Convention, which meet every two years but alternately. Charitable works are carried out by the German Caritas Association (Deutscher Caritasverband) on the Catholic side and the Social Service Agency of the EKD (Diakonisches Werk) on the Protestant side. The major church aid organizations are funded by voluntary donations. Thus the Protestant "Bread for the World" and the Catholic "Misereor" and "Adveniat" have together collected billions of marks for emergency relief and long-term development measures.

Kirchenamt der Evangelischen Kirche in Deutschland
(Church Office of the Evangelical Church in Germany)
Herrenhäuser Strasse 12, 30419 Hannover
Sekretariat der Deutschen Bischofskonferenz
(Secretariat of the German Bishops Conference)
Kaiserstrasse 163, 53113 Bonn
Zentralrat der Juden in Deutschland
(Central Council of Jews in Germany)
Rüngsdorfer Strasse 6, 53173 Bonn

Mass media and public opinion

Article 5 of the Basic Law guarantees freedom of opinion and freedom of the press and also the right to obtain information from generally accessible sources. There is no censorship. The International Press Institute in Vienna describes the Federal Republic as one of the few countries where the state respects the strong position of a free press.

■ ■ ■ **Function of the mass media.** The press, and in the broader sense all mass media, has been referred to as the "fourth estate" next to the legislature, the executive and the judiciary. And it is true that all mass media play an important role in the modern society. With their wide range of news and opinion they help the people understand and keep check on parliament, government and public administration. They thus have considerable responsibility.

The Federal Constitutional Court noted that "a free press which is not controlled by the state and not subject to censorship is an essential element of a free country" and that in particular "regular press publications are indispensable to the modern democracy. If the people are to be able to make decisions they must be supplied with the information with which to assess opinions."

■ ■ ■ **Diversity of the media.** The people have a choice of many different and competing media. The daily papers alone sold about 32.9 million copies a day (mid-1994).

At present just under 32 million television sets and over 35 million radios are officially registered. On average Germans over 14 devote well over five hours a day to media products, i.e. newspapers and periodicals (70 minutes), the radio (2 hours) and television (2.5 hours). And supply is increasing constantly. Only about 1% of the population are not reached by the media at all.

The great majority, however, regularly use two or more sources. Most turn to television first for political information and then read a newspaper for greater detail. For news of events near home people usually consult the local newspaper. Young people read newspapers less frequently. But television, too, is losing some of its public appeal, in spite of the increasing number of programmes available.

■■■ **Sources of news.** The mass media obtain their material from news agencies at home and abroad, from their own correspondents, and from direct research. Radio and television stations have offices in all major cities around the world, as do the big newspapers.

The leading domestic news agency is the Deutsche Presse-Agentur (dpa), then the Deutscher Depeschendienst (ddp), which merged with the former East German Allgemeine Deutsche Nachrichtenagentur (ADN) in 1993, the Associated Press (AP), Reuters (rtr) and Agence France Press (AFP). dpa supplies all German dailies. AP, rtr and AFP can base their German-language services on the global networks of their parent companies in the United States, the United Kingdom and France respectively. Most newspapers buy their material from at least two of these services, broadcasting networks up to five. Apart from the general agencies there are various others which specialize. They include the Protestant Press Service (epd), the Catholic News Agency (KNA) and the Sports Information Service (sid). Agencies like the Vereinigte Wirtschaftsdienste (vwd) also provide information for private companies and business organizations.

A press conference in Bonn

Various private organizations, public authorities, parties, companies, etc. have their own press departments which, like outside agencies, keep information flowing to the mass media. This is done by means of news conferences, press releases, mailings, picture services and briefings for journalists.

It is part of the journalist's daily routine to research topics of his own choosing. Public authorities in Germany are required to provide journalists with information within the framework of the law. In Bonn alone there are nearly 1,000 accredited correspondents. The roughly 550 Germans among them are members of the Federal Press Conference, and the more than 400 foreign journalists belong to the Foreign Press Association. Both are entirely independent of the authorities.

■ ■ ■ **The Press and Information Office of the Federal Government (BPA)** acts as a mediator between the government and the public. The head of this public authority is at the same time the government spokesman.

The system differs from that of some other countries in that the government spokesman always attends the Federal Press Conference to brief Bonn's journalists. He goes to the press, not vice versa. This also applies to news conferences given by the Federal Chancellor and ministers in conjunction with the Federal Press Conference. The BPA is also responsible for keeping the Federal President, the Federal Government and the Bundestag informed about "published opinion" in Germany and abroad. In order to provide this service the BPA evaluates 27 news agencies and monitors more than 100 radio and 25 television programmes in German and 22 foreign languages.

■ ■ ■ **Public opinion research.** "Published opinion" does not always tally with public opinion at large. In some cases they are very far apart. Demoscopic institutes scientifically study public opinion on the basis of representative samples, i.e. the opinions of usually 1,000-2,000 people.

The private institutes concerned with political opinion research attract considerable public attention. The large German newspapers and periodicals as well as television corporations regularly publish the results of such surveys of the nation's political mood, the standing of parties and leading politicians, and topics of current interest such as nuclear energy, unemployment, political asylum, and political and social affairs in both the old and the new federal states. The federal and state governments as well as the political parties use the results of these surveys to keep abreast of changes of opinion for medium and long-term planning, and as a means of assessing the impact of political measures.

Interest is particularly keen prior to elections, when the parties size up their chances and the demoscopic organizations put their finger on the nation's pulse. Although opinion polls are now very reliable, they are still only "snapshots", as it were. Election-day polls are generally the most accurate. Computer calculations on election night, however, are based on results from selected districts. With their analysis of changes in these election results according to regions, party strongholds and population groups, the researchers complement the data resulting from their surveys and can thus help explain the situation to the public.

The demoscopic know-how acquired over the past quarter of a century is not only reflected in detailed reports, which are required reading for the politician, but also used by observers in neighbouring countries.

The press

Newspapers enjoy great popularity in Germany. They have more than held their own despite the advance of television. In terms of the number of newspapers per 1,000 inhabitants, Germany is in fourth place behind Japan, the United Kingdom and Switzerland.

■ ■ ■ **Newspapers.** Local and regional dailies predominate. On workdays about 383 newspapers appear in the old and new federal states. They publish nearly 1,600 local and regional editions in more than 136 offices. The total circulation is about 32.9 million. Small papers, too, keep their readers informed about the national and international political scene, economic and cultural affairs, sports and local events.

Roughly two thirds of all newspapers are bought on subscription; the rest are sold on the streets. One of the tabloids is the "Bildzeitung", which has the biggest circulation (4.4 million a day). The biggest-selling subscription paper is the "Westdeutsche Allgemeine Zeitung" (about 630,000 suscriptions). The large national newspapers "Frankfurter Allgemeine Zeitung" and "Die Welt" have smaller circulations but considerable influence on political and business leaders. The same is true of the "Süddeutsche Zeitung", the "Stuttgarter Zeitung", the "Frankfurter Rundschau" and "Der Tagesspiegel", which have an impact far beyond the regions in which they are published. Other important opinion leaders are the weeklies "Die Zeit", "Die Woche", "Wochenpost", "Rheinischer Merkur" and "Das Sonntagsblatt". They offer background information, analyses and reports. There are also Sunday newspapers such as "Bild am Sonntag", "Welt am Sonntag" and "Frankfurter Allgemeine Sonntagszeitung". In recent years more and more regional papers have been publishing Sunday editions as well, for instance the Berlin dailies. Many foreign newspapers also print special editions for foreigners living in Germany.

■ ■ ■ **Periodicals.** More than 9,000 periodicals are published in Germany. The best-known internationally are the news magazine "Der Spiegel", with a circulation exceeding one million, and the news magazine "Focus", which was launched in 1993.

There is a large group of just under 1,650 popular periodicals with a total circulation of over 150 million. In addition to the news magazines, periodicals with particularly large circulations include the radio and television magazines, topical illustrated magazines such as "Stern" and "Bunte", and women's magazines. More and more readers are also turning to special-interest publications, which target a particular audience by focusing on a single subject such as tennis, sailing, computers or electronic entertainment equipment.

Circulation of leading newspapers and magazines (1994)

Daily newspapers (in some cases with associated papers)	
Bild (Hamburg)	4,426,000
Westdeutsche Allgemeine Zeitung (Essen; WAZ Group)	1,188,400
Hannoversche Allgemeine Zeitung (Hanover)	561,900
Freie Presse (Chemnitz)	489,100
Sächsische Zeitung (Dresden)	426,000
Rheinische Post (Düsseldorf)	400,600
Süddeutsche Zeitung (Munich)	400,300
Frankfurter Allgemeine Zeitung (Frankfurt/Main)	395,000
Augsburger Allgemeine (Augsburg)	369,500
Südwest-Presse (Ulm)	361,900
Hessische/Niedersächsische Allgemeine (Kassel)	350,600
B.Z. (Berlin)	310,800
Thüringer Allgemeine (Erfurt)	297,700
Kölner Stadt-Anzeiger (Cologne)	290,800
Die Rheinpfalz (Ludwigshafen)	247,100
Berliner Zeitung (Berlin)	246,400
Märkische Allgemeine (Potsdam)	231,400
Braunschweiger Zeitung (Brunswick)	221,210
Ruhr-Nachrichten (Dortmund)	218,900
Ostsee-Zeitung (Rostock)	217,800
Die Welt (Berlin)	204,800
Lausitzer Rundschau (Cottbus)	199,900
Berliner Morgenpost (Berlin)	192,400
Frankfurter Rundschau (Frankfurt/Main)	188,900
Westdeutsche Zeitung (Düsseldorf)	180,800
Der Tagesspiegel (Berlin)	130,000
Die Tageszeitung (Berlin)	60,200
Weeklies and Sunday newspapers	
Bild am Sonntag (Hamburg)	2,584,400
Die Zeit (Hamburg)	476,900
Welt am Sonntag (Hamburg)	387,600
Bayernkurier (Munich)	156,800
Rheinischer Merkur (Bonn)	108,300
Wochenpost (Berlin)	108,300
Die Woche (Hamburg)	105,500
Das Sonntagsblatt (Hamburg)	80,500
News magazines	
Der Spiegel (Hamburg)	1,003,500
Focus (Munich)	621,000

*The wealth of information
available at a newspaper stand*

There are also many technical journals, though with only a moderate circulation. Others include the political weeklies, church newspapers, customer periodicals, free-sheets and official announcements. One third of the periodicals market is accounted for by various organizations and associations. The motoring magazine "ADAC-Motorwelt" published by the Allgemeiner Deutscher Automobilclub has a circulation of 11.7 million, the largest in Germany. This range of information is rounded off by local freesheets and newspapers published by alternative groups. Also on sale at newspaper stands in large cities are foreign newspapers and periodicals.

■ ■ ■ **Press concentration.** The number of independent newspapers in Germany has fallen steadily since the mid-50s. The publishers with the greater financial and technical resources have been able to dominate various regional markets. As a result, many towns no longer have two or more local papers to choose from. And many of those still in publication do not have "full news rooms", that is, editorial offices which produce their newspapers completely independently. They obtain a substantial proportion of their material from another newspaper or newspaper group.

Restructuring has gone hand in hand with technical change due to the introduction of computers and state-of-the-art printing technology. Although this has reduced production costs, newspapers, like nearly all print media, depend on advertising for their economic survival. Advertising generates about 65% of revenues, whereas distribution and sales generate about 35%.

■ ■ ■ **The major publishing companies.** Economic developments have led to the formation of large publishing houses. In the daily press sector the biggest firm is the

Axel Springer AG, although its roughly 20% share of the newspaper market is largely due to the high circulation of "Bild". As regards Sunday papers, Axel Springer AG is almost without competition with "Welt am Sonntag" and "Bild am Sonntag". Economic and journalistic power is also concentrated in the publishing group of the "Westdeutsche Allgemeine Zeitung", the Süddeutscher Verlag Group, the Verlag M. DuMont Schauberg, and the publishing group of the "Frankfurter Allgemeine Zeitung". Much more important in terms of economic power and journalistic effectiveness are the publishers of periodicals, especially the general-interest ones. Leaders in this sector are Bauer Verlag and the Burda Group as well as the Verlagsgruppe Axel Springer.

The media corporation with the largest turnover, and in fact the second largest in the world, is Bertelsmann AG, which has global interests and covers book and record clubs, book and periodical publishing, music production, films, radio and television, and printing.

■ ■ ■ **Press rights.** Press rights are governed by the press laws of the states, which are consistent on the basic issues. These include the right of journalists to refuse to disclose their sources of information as well as the right of others who have been the subject of newspaper reporting to have a counter-statement published. Print media are required to indicate the title and address of the publication, the date of issue, names of owners and editors, etc. ("masthead requirement"), and to exercise due care.

Publishers and journalists exercise self-control through the German Press Council, which looks into charges of negligence and unethical behaviour. Its views are not binding, however.

Bundesverband Deutscher Zeitungsverleger
(Association of German Newspaper Publishers)
Riemenschneiderstrasse 10, 53175 Bonn
Verband Deutscher Zeitschriftenverleger
(Association of German Periodical Publishers)
Winterstrasse 50, 53177 Bonn
Deutscher Journalistenverband
(German Journalists Association)
Bennauerstrasse 60, 53115 Bonn
IG Medien (Media Union)
Friedrichstrasse 15, 70174 Stuttgart

Radio and television

The broadcasting media, i.e. radio and television, in Germany are not state-controlled. The broadcasting system and the freedom of broadcasting are governed and guaranteed by law. The Federal Parliament legislates on posts and telecommunications and is therefore responsible for the technical aspects of broadcasting. The networks themselves, however, are under the jurisdiction of the states.

Germany has a dual system, that is to say public and private networks exist side by side. It is based largely on a 1986 ruling by the Federal Constitutional Court that the public corporations should meet the public's general broadcasting requirements, with the private companies playing a supplementary role.

For many years Germany had only public corporations, but this changed in 1984 when private television and radio broadcasters were allowed to compete for the first time.

■ ■ ■ **The public corporations.** Today, in 1995, Germany has 11 regional broadcasting corporations, one broadcasting corporation organized under federal law, a second national television network (Zweites Deutsches Fernsehen, ZDF) based on an agreement between all the federal states, and the public corporation "Deutschlandradio". The largest broadcasting station is the Westdeutscher Rundfunk (Cologne) with 4,400 staff, while the smallest is Radio Bremen with about 650.

The others are Bayerischer Rundfunk (Munich), Hessischer Rundfunk (Frankfurt am Main), Norddeutscher Rundfunk (Hamburg), Saarländischer Rundfunk (Saarbrücken), Sender Freies Berlin (Berlin), Süddeutscher Rundfunk (Stuttgart), Südwestfunk (Baden-Baden), Ostdeutscher Rundfunk Brandenburg (Potsdam) and Mitteldeutscher Rundfunk (Leipzig). They cater more or less for the regions where they are located, although some supply programmes for several regions.

Each broadcasts several radio programmes, and the regional corporations form a Standing Conference of Public Broadcasting Corporations (Arbeitsgemeinschaft der öffentlich-rechtlichen Rundfunkanstalten Deutschlands,

ARD). Together they operate a nationally transmitted television programme called "Erstes Deutsches Fernsehen" (Channel One) for which they all provide material. In addition, they produce regional "Channel Three" TV programmes. The Mainz-based Zweites Deutsches Fernsehen is a television-only station which transmits the "Channel Two" programme nationwide. It is the largest in Europe.

The radio station Deutschlandradio was founded in 1993 through the transfer of the rights and obligations of the stations Deutschlandfunk and RIAS Berlin. It is jointly operated by ARD and ZDF and has its seat in Cologne and Berlin. Since 1 January 1994, Deutschlandradio has been broadcasting two radio programs which focus on the fields of information and culture and have no advertising. The "Deutsche Welle" is the only federal radio station. It is financed solely by federal funds and has a statutory obligation to produce and broadcast radio programmes for foreign consumption which give foreign audiences a comprehensive and well-balanced picture of political, cultural and economic life in Germany. Another one of its functions is to present and explain Germany's position on important issues.

■ ■ ■ **Self-government and broadcasting freedom.** Each of the public broadcasting corporations is in general controlled by three bodies: the Broadcasting Council, the Administrative Council and the Director-General.

The members of the Broadcasting Council are representatives of the main political and social groups. They are elected by the state parliaments or nominated by the political parties, religious communities, and business and cultural organizations.

The Council advises the Director-General on programming and ensures that basic principles are observed. The Administrative Council draws up the corporation's budget, watches over day-to-day management, and comments on technical aspects. Its members are elected by the Broadcasting Council and they for their part elect the Director-General, subject to confirmation by the Council. The Director-General runs the corporation in accordance with the decisions of the Broadcasting and Administrative Councils. He is responsible for programme content and represents the corporation in its external relations.

This system guarantees the broadcasting corporations' independence from the state. It does not, however, exclude all political influence. Although the party representatives do not hold a majority in the governing bodies of the broadcasting corporations, a kind of power-sharing arrangement has developed. This is particularly evident when appointments are made to top posts and draws much public criticism.

The corporations may not favour any side and must maintain editorial balance. This does not prejudice the "freedom of broadcasting", that is, the right to express decided points of view. On the other hand, the corporations are required by law to provide equal opportunities for the expression of opinions.

■ ■ ■ **Radio and television programmes.** Each regional corporation broadcasts up to five radio programmes. They provide a broad variety of shows in the fields of entertainment, education, music, current affairs, sports, regional affairs, drama, opera, and so on. Most networks run scientific and literary series as well. Their orchestras and choral groups enrich the cultural life of Germany's cities and states. Special programmes for foreign workers are broadcasted in their own languages.

In the nationally transmitted ARD and ZDF television programmes daily news updates, political reporting, home and foreign affairs documentation, television plays, films and entertainment play a big part. German TV networks have long been buying and selling programmes abroad. For their foreign coverage both ARD and ZDF have extensive correspondent networks and their own studios in many countries all over the world.

ARD and ZDF participate in Eurovision's international exchange, mostly for sporting events. They also contribute to the news pool of the European Broadcasting Union. ZDF and six other European networks commission films through the European Film Production Community.

ARD and ZDF broadcast the satellite programme "3sat" in cooperation with the Austrian network ORF and the Swiss network SRG. They are also involved in the European cultural programme "arte".

Channel Three television programmes are transmitted regionally and also via satellite by the ARD corporations.

Production control room in a news studio

They focus on regional affairs ranging from politics to culture, and they broadcast television for schools and further education courses at various levels.

Television in the Federal Republic went colour in 1967, using the German PAL system. More than 80% of registered sets are for colour.

■■■ **Finance.** The public broadcasting corporations obtain most of their funds in the form of fees paid by owners of radios and television sets. Revenue from television user fees is split 70:30 between ARD and ZDF. Both also depend on income from commercial advertising. They have much less time for commercial spots than private companies.

Television rights, especially for the transmission of sporting events such as soccer or tennis, have become very expensive, yet the public corporations cannot increase user fees to cover these costs without the approval of the state parliaments. A major overhaul of the procedure for setting fees has become necessary as a result of the decision handed down by the Federal Constitutional Court on 22 February 1994.

■ ■ ■ **Private broadcasting.** The public corporations had to contend with competition on a countrywide scale starting in 1985, when "SAT.1" began operating from Mainz as the first private German television broadcasting company. It was followed in 1986 by "RTL plus Deutschland" (now "RTL", Cologne). Both have meanwhile become very popular: At the end of 1994, RTL reached 93% of all households and SAT.1 slightly more than 92%. Other private broadcasters are "PRO SIEBEN", "Deutsches Sportfernsehen" (DSF), "n-tv", "VOX", "RTL 2", "Kabel 1", "Premiere" and "VIVA". RTL and SAT.1 focus on sports, entertainment and feature films but also offer high-caliber political programmes. PRO SIEBEN concentrates mainly on feature films; DSF is a special-interest channel devoted to transmission of national sporting events; n-tv is a news channel; VIVA offers only music; Premiere is a channel which can be received only with a special decoder and against payment of a separate fee (Pay-TV). The programmes of private broadcasters are transmitted via satellite and cable and can also be received via terrestrial frequencies. A number of foreign TV programmes can be received anywhere in the country via satellite as well. The private stations are operated by consortia, mostly of media companies. In contrast to the public corporations, their only source of revenue is advertising.

In 1991 there were already 100 private radio stations, but only a few of them offered a full programme catering for a whole state; today their number has increased to more than 170. The law requires local radio stations to cater for wide-ranging public tastes. The Federal Constitutional Court has ruled that the private broadcasters, like the public corporations, may not influence public opinion one-sidedly. Their programmes must reflect diversity of opinion to a certain extent.

■ ■ ■ **Broadcasting innovation.** New technology has considerably changed the broadcasting landscape in Germany. In 1994 roughly 22 million German households were linked up to the broadband cable network which the Administration of Posts and Telecommunications has been laying since 1982. About 14.8 million of them subscribe to cable radio and television programmes. The aim in the late 90s is to make cable programmes available to 80% of the approximately 30 million households in Germany.

At ZDF headquarters, Mainz

Direct satellite broadcasting (DSB) has meanwhile become a serious rival to cable. It is an economically viable alternative for everyone, not only those not yet linked up to the cable network. Satellite programmes can be received directly by anyone with a dish antenna.

DSB raises questions that transcend frontiers. It is not yet certain whether national, European, or global concepts will prevail. Today, in 1995, two supranational public and one private organization operate a majority of the roughly 20 satellites which supply Europe with about 200 television and 200 radio programmes.

One of the satellite programmes is "3sat", a joint undertaking by ZDF, the Austrian Broadcasting Corporation and the Swiss Radio and Television Company. Others include arte, VOX, Kabel 1 and several Channel Three programmes broadcasted by ARD.

Viewers and listeners in Germany now have a wide range of programmes to choose from. Among the new

media which are available via television are services
such as "Bildschirmtext" (Btx), the Post Office's viewdata
system. It enables subscribers to conduct a dialogue with
a wide variety of providers via telephone. The possibilities range from stock exchange reports to bank account
transactions. The public corporations offer "Videotext", a
service using the normal television signal. Videotext
appears on the screen on call and offers news, weather
reports, tips for consumers, and much more.

Arbeitsgemeinschaft der öffentlich-rechtlichen Rund-
funkanstalten der Bundesrepublik Deutschland (ARD)
(Association of Public Broadcasting Corporations in the
Federal Republic of Germany)
Bertramstrasse 8, 60320 Frankfurt am Main
Zweites Deutsches Fernsehen (ZDF)
(German Television Channel Two)
P.O. Box 4040, 55100 Mainz
RTL
Aachener Str. 1036, 50858 Cologne
SAT.1
Otto-Schott-Str. 13, 55127 Mainz
Verband Privater Rundfunk und Telekommunikation e.V.
(Association of Private Broadcasters and Telecommunica-
tions Companies)
Burgstr. 69, 53177 Bonn

Education and science

· Cultural diversity · Schools
· Vocational education · Higher education institutions
· Adult education · Scholarship and research

Cultural diversity

Nowhere is the country's federal structure more apparent than in the cultural sphere. Germany never had a cultural metropolis like France's Paris or Britain's London. The considerable cultural autonomy of the regions has led to the formation of small and large cultural centres with different points of emphasis. Thus cultural activity is to be found in even the smallest towns and communities.

Berlin, as the capital and future seat of government of united Germany, will also play an important cultural role, but the other German cities will retain their standing as cultural centres. The country's federal structure ensures that its cultural diversity will be preserved and that there will be an intensive exchange between east and west which was lacking prior to unification.

This diversity is apparent from the spread of cultural institutions and activities. The Deutsche Bibliothek (German Library), a statutory body under direct federal administration, is located in Frankfurt am Main, with branches in Leipzig and Berlin. The Federal Records Office is headquartered in Koblenz and has branches in Berlin, Potsdam, Freiburg im Breisgau and Bayreuth, among others. Hamburg has the largest concentration of media. Cologne and Düsseldorf are centres of modern art. Berlin has the most theatres. There are scientific academies in Berlin, Düsseldorf, Darmstadt, Göttingen, Halle, Heidelberg, Leipzig, Mainz and Munich. The principal museums are in Berlin, Cologne, Munich, Nuremberg and Stuttgart. The two most important literary archives are in the small Württemberg town of Marbach and in Weimar (Thuringia).

It is due to such cultural polycentrism that there are no remote, desolate "provinces" in Germany. One need not travel hundreds of miles to see good theatre or hear good music. Even in some small towns one finds valuable libraries or interesting art collections. This goes back to the days when Germany consisted of many principalities whose rulers wanted to make their residences centres of culture, and when a self-assured middle class patronized the arts and sciences in their towns.

Premiere of the opera "Eréndira" in Stuttgart's Staatstheater

The establishment and maintenance of most cultural facilities in the Federal Republic of Germany is the responsibility of the municipalities. Legislation on cultural matters – with few exceptions – is the prerogative of the federal states. Each state has a large measure of autonomy in organizing its school system. Here it becomes apparent that there are also negative aspects to cultural federalism. Since school curricula and examination standards often vary from state to state, problems can arise when families move and the children have trouble adjusting.

But the state governments are cooperating with each other where possible through their Standing Conference of the Ministers of Education and Cultural Affairs. The federal and state governments cooperate in planning and financing university building. They also have a joint commission for educational planning and research promotion. Within this framework they support pilot projects in all fields of education.

The purpose of these bodies is to ensure the degree of standardization necessary for a modern, efficient educational system without abandoning the rich diversity of German cultural life.

Schools

In 1993, 12 million pupils received instruction from roughly 713,800 teachers at 52,300 schools in Germany. The Basic Law guarantees everyone the right to self-fulfillment and the right freely to choose his or her school or place of training as well as his or her occupation or profession. It thus follows that the goal of educational policy in the Federal Republic of Germany is to afford every individual the best possible opportunities to receive the kind of education that is commensurate with his or her abilities and interests.

■■ **Statutory basis.** According to article 7 of the Basic Law, the entire school system is under the supervision of the state. On account of the country's federal structure, that responsibility is shared by the federal and the state governments. Legislation and administration in the field of education predominantly fall within the purview of the states. This is true especially of the school system, higher education, adult education and continuing education. Common and comparable basic structures of the states' school systems are ensured through the "Agreement between the States of the Federal Republic of Germany for the Standardization of the School System" (Hamburg Agreement of 14 October 1971). This agreement covers such matters as compulsory schooling, organization, recognition of certificates, etc.

The Standing Conference of the Ministers of Education and Cultural Affairs of the Länder in the Federal Republic of Germany (KMK) has adopted supplementary accords providing for greater harmonization of the school systems as well as recognition of certificates awarded by general education and vocational schools in all the federal states.

■■ **Compulsory schooling.** School attendance is compulsory from the ages of six to 18, i.e. for 12 years. In order to satisfy the compulsory schooling requirement, pupils must attend a full-time school for nine (in some states ten) years and thereafter either continue full-time schooling or attend a part-time vocational school (Berufsschule). Attendance at all public schools is free of charge. Educational materials, especially textbooks, are also fre-

A school playground during the main break

quently provided free of charge or on loan; when possession of such materials passes to the pupils, parents may be required to contribute to the costs on the basis of their income.

The Basic Law requires that religious instruction be included in the curriculum, except in non-denominational schools. From the age of 14, pupils may drop the subject if they wish.

The Basic Law also guarantees the right to establish and operate private schools. If these schools are alternatives to state schools, they are subject to state approval. Private alternative schools enrich the educational spectrum and receive financial support from the states.

■ ■ **Kindergartens.** Kindergartens are not part of the state school system but instead fall under child and youth services. Most of them are run by churches, charitable organizations and municipalities, some by firms or associations.

Kindergarten staff focus their efforts on creating a learning environment in a social setting that will further the development of children into responsible members of society. The kindergarten is intended to support and supplement the education and upbringing provided by the family and compensate developmental deficiencies in order to afford children a broad range of opportunities for education and development. Children largely learn through play. Some children attend kindergarten only in the morning and spend the rest of the day with their families. Other children attend kindergarten all day, until late in the afternoon.

In several states children already have a legal right to attend a kindergarten (as of 1995 in the states of Brandenburg, Lower Saxony, Mecklenburg-Western Pomerania, Rhineland-Palatinate, Saxony, Saxony-Anhalt and Thuringia). New kindergartens and child care establishments are being constructed so that by 1998 at the latest, all children in the entire Federal Republic of Germany should be able to enjoy this legal right to a place in a kindergarten. Attendance will still be voluntary, however. Kindergartens are financed not only by the states, municipalities and organizations that operate them but also by contributions from parents. In 1993 approximately 65% of all children between the ages of three and six attended kindergartens.

■ ■ ■ **The school system.** At the age of six, children enter primary school (Grundschule). In general it lasts four years, in Berlin and Brandenburg six years. In most states, children's work in the first two years at school is not graded but instead assessed in the form of a report giving a detailed description of the individual pupil's progress and weaknesses in specific areas of learning. After primary school, pupils attend one of the other general education schools offering the first stage of secondary education. Irrespective of the type of school the pupil attends, the fifth and sixth school years constitute a phase of special encouragement, observation and orientation designed to facilitate choices concerning the pupil's further education and fields of emphasis. In most states this orientation phase takes place within the framework of the various types of schools; in some states, however, it is structured as a separate stage which is independent of the ordinary types of schools.

After completing primary school, approximately one third of the children attend the secondary general school (Hauptschule). Young people who leave the secondary general school after the ninth or tenth grade usually enter a vocational training program and, as part of their training, attend a part-time vocational school (Berufsschule) until at least the age of 18. The secondary general school certificate is generally used to gain acceptance to vocational training programs offered within the framework of the dual system and thus opens the door to many occupations in the craft trades and industry for which formal training is required. The secondary general school imparts a basic general education to its pupils. Its curriculum has been broadened and has become increasingly demanding: Today, for instance, nearly every pupil at a secondary general school receives instruction in one foreign language (usually English) and vocational orientation to ease the transition from school to working life.

The intermediate school (Realschule) is positioned between the secondary general school and the grammar

Basic structure of the educational system in the Federal Republic of Germany

Continuing education (Continuing general and vocational education courses provided by a broad range of institutions)						Continuing education
		Professional degree (Diplom, Master's degree, state examination)				Higher education
Advanced vocational qualification	University entrance qualification	**University** **Technical university** **Comprehensive university** **College of education** **College of art / college of music** **Fachhochschule** **College of public administration**				
Trade and technical school	**Evening grammar school / Kolleg**					
13 Vocational qualification		Fachhochschule entrance qualification	University entrance qualification			19
12 **Education and training at part-time vocational schools** 11 **and companies (dual system)**		**Full-time vocational school**	**Fach-ober-schule**	**Upper secondary classes in grammar school** In various types of schools: grammar school, specialized grammar school, comprehensive school		18 17 16
10 Basic vocational training year, full-time or part-time schooling					Secondary education Stage II	15
	Intermediate school certificate (Realschule certificate) after 10 years Secondary general school certificate (Hauptschule certificate) after 9 years					16
10	10th year of schooling					15
9 8 7	**Special school**	**Secondary general school**	**Intermediate school**	**Grammar school**	**Comprehensive school**	14 13 12
6 5		Orientation stage (depending or not depending on school type)				11 10
4 3 2 1	**Special school**	Primary school			Primary education	9 8 7 6
Class	**Special kindergarten**	**Kindergarten** (on a voluntary basis)			Pre-school education	5 4 3
						Age

school (Gymnasium) and imparts a more comprehensive general education to its pupils. As a rule, it encompasses six years of schooling, grades 5 through 10, and leads to an intermediate school certificate qualifying the recipient to continue his or her education at upper level schools such as a full-time vocational school (Berufsfachschule) or a vocationally oriented upper secondary school (Fach-oberschule). The intermediate school certificate is a prerequisite for a middle-level career in business and industry or in the public service. In 1993 about 40% of pupils earned an intermediate school certificate.

The grammar school (Gymnasium), which is generally a nine-year secondary school (grades 5 through 13; in Mecklenburg-Western Pomerania, Saxony, Saxony-Anhalt and Thuringia, however, only through grade 12), imparts a comprehensive general education to its pupils. The former classification as ancient language, modern language or natural sciences grammar school is now rare. In the upper stage of the grammar school, which encompasses grades 11 through 13 (in the aforementioned four states grades 10 through 12 or 11 and 12), a course system has replaced the conventional classes. Although certain subjects or groups of subjects are still compulsory, the wide range of available courses affords pupils in the upper stage of the grammar school ample opportunity to individually structure their coursework to emphasize certain fields. Subjects are divided into three general categories: language, literature and art; the so-

A "cornet" filled with sweets – a German tradition on the first day at school

cial sciences; and mathematics, science and technology. Each of these three categories must be represented among the courses taken by each pupil up through the end of upper secondary instruction, including the *Abitur* examination. The compulsory coursework includes religion and sports in addition to subjects from the three aforementioned categories. Upper secondary instruction at the grammar school concludes with the *Abitur* examination, which covers four subjects. Upon completing 13 years of schooling and passing the *Abitur* examination, the pupil is awarded the "certificate of general higher education entrance qualification" (*Zeugnis der allgemeinen Hochschulreife*). This certificate, which until the year 2000 can be earned upon completion of 12 years of schooling in the four states mentioned earlier, entitles the recipient to study the subject of his or her choice at a university or equivalent institution.

As a matter of principle, the certificate of higher education entrance qualification or the certificate of Fachhochschule entrance qualification (*Fachhochschulreife*) is required for admission to a course of study at a higher education institution. Due to the high number of applicants for the limited number of study places, however, nationwide or local admissions restrictions are in effect for some courses of study. Under both the central and local selection procedures, admission is based on specific criteria, above all the applicant's *Abitur* grade average and the "waiting period", the period of time that has elapsed between the *Abitur* and the application for admission. Admission to courses of study in the field of medicine is based on additional criteria as well (test, selection interview).

Another type of school offering stage I secondary education is the comprehensive school (Gesamtschule) which as a rule provides instruction for pupils in grades 5 through 10. Some comprehensive schools have an upper secondary stage of their own which is structured along the lines of the upper stage of the grammar school.

In the new federal states there are other types of schools such as the "standard school" (Regelschule) in Thuringia, the "middle school" (Mittelschule) in Saxony, and the "secondary school" (Sekundarschule) in Saxony-Anhalt. These schools combine the curricula of the secondary general school and the intermediate school; beginning in grade 7, pupils receive instruction in classes or courses geared to the school-leaving certificates they intend to acquire. The certificates awarded by these schools at the end of grades 9 and 10 are earned under the same conditions as those awarded by the other types of schools offering stage I secondary education and are mutually recognized by all states in accordance with a 1993 agreement of the Standing Conference of the Ministers of Education and Cultural Affairs. In 1993, taking the average of all pupils in grade 8 in the Federal Republic of Germany, 8.9% attended an integrated comprehensive school, 31.4% attended a grammar school, 26.1% attended an intermediate school, 25.6% attended a secondary general school, and 7.4% attended integrated classes for secondary general school and intermediate school pupils.

Children and young people with disabilities whose needs cannot be adequately met at general education schools receive instruction at special schools (Sonderschulen). The compulsory education requirement applies to them as well, and without restriction.

Anyone who for any reason has missed out on educational opportunities earlier in his or her life can nevertheless earn a school-leaving certificate via the "second educational route". People who work during the day, for instance, can take coursework at an evening grammar school to prepare for the *Abitur* examination.

■ ■ **Teachers.** For every type of school there are specially trained teachers. All must have completed a course of study at a higher education institution, but the content and duration of such courses vary. Courses of study for primary and secondary general school teachers usually last six semesters. Longer courses are required for intermediate school, grammar school, special school or vocational school teachers. Upon completion of their course of study, all prospective teachers must pass an initial state examination. This is followed by a period of practical training, which includes preparatory seminars and practice teaching in schools, and a second state examination. Teachers are generally appointed civil servants for life. Transitional rules still apply to teachers in the new states.

Vocational education

The number of school leavers qualifying and opting for higher education is increasing while the proportion signing up for vocational training is stagnating. Young people who do not reach university entrance standard usually take a course of vocational training, but so do many of the higher education qualifiers. Most of them are trained within the "dual system". This comprises practical, on-the-job training with theoretical instruction at a part-time vocational school. Thus the private and public sector are jointly responsible. The Federation draws up the training regulations while the states oversee the vocational schools.

More than 1.6 million young people are currently receiving training in the roughly 450 recognized occupations for which formal training is required. Their popularity varies, however. Almost 40% of the male trainees are concentrated in 10 preferred vocations, while the proportion in the case of females is 55%. The occupations which most attract boys are automobile mechanic, electrical fitter, industrial mechanic and business specialist in wholesale and foreign trade; the girls' favourites are doctor's assistant, business specialist in retail trade, hair stylist and office clerk. Greater efforts are being made to provide training for young people who have not served an apprenticeship.

■ ■ **Vocational schools.** Apart from learning on the job the trainee has to attend a part-time vocational school one or two days a week for three years. The schools teach general subjects and the theory which trainees are better able to learn at school than at work. Courses lead to a final examination and certificate. Vocational schools are also obligatory for all under the age of 18 who attend no other type of school. These students do a "pre-vocational training year" in which they are taught the theory which eases their choice of training.

■ ■ **Other forms of vocational training.** Apart from apprenticeship and part-time vocational school there are a number of other training systems. There is the full-time vocational school (Berufsfachschule) whose courses last one to three years. They can be counted as part of an apprenticeship or can replace an apprenticeship entirely.

The vocationally oriented upper secondary school (Fachoberschule) admits pupils with an intermediate school certificate. The courses last two years (for those who have completed an apprenticeship, one year) and qualify participants for the Fachhochschule, which is a special type of higher education institution offering highly practice-related study courses of a scientific nature. Courses at the Fachoberschule cover theory as well as workshop and on-the-job training. The Vocational Retraining Center provides DM 4.3 million a year for the rehabilitation of handicapped young people. Under this scheme employers are required to reserve at least six per cent of total jobs for the handicapped. Fines are imposed on those who do not comply.

■ ■ ■ **On-the-job training.** Practical on-the-job training, usually called apprenticeship, takes from two to three and a half years, depending on the occupation, but in most cases three years. Only state-recognized occu-

Instruction in the use of electronic controls

pations are covered. For participants who have a university entrance qualification (*Abitur*) the apprenticeship may be shortened by six months, and by another half-year if they perform exceptionally well. The apprentice is paid a training allowance which increases annually. What has to be learned, and finally tested, for an occupation is set out in training regulations. These are issued by the responsible federal ministries and are based on proposals from the business associations, employers' organizations and trade unions.

The training concludes with an examination conducted by a board of examiners of one of the self-regulatory bodies of business and industry (such as a chamber of industry and commerce or a chamber of crafts and trades) or by similar bodies. On the board of examiners are representatives of employers and employees as well as vocational school teachers.

Over 500,000 firms in all branches of the economy, including the free professions and the public service, provide vocational training. Large enterprises have their own training workshops, but small firms train newcomers on the job. Where firms are too specialized to be able to impart all the necessary knowledge they can send their apprentices to inter-company training centres in order to broaden their vocational skills.

■ ■ ■ **Training for all.** In principle, no young person in Germany should begin working life without vocational training. The number of unskilled workers is declining. Here the dual system has proved its worth, which is why some parts of it are being adopted by other countries.

In the 80s, for demographic reasons, demand for training places was very heavy but in recent years it has been outpaced by supply. In 1994, for instance, there were 502,900 places available in the west (119,000 in the east) for 467,600 (119,000 in the east) young people seeking an apprenticeship. This has been made possible by massive efforts on the part of all concerned – industry, the federal and state governments, the Federal Institute for Employment, and the Trust Agency (Treuhandanstalt). Inter-company training centres are now available in the new states as well. Under the Unification Treaty, vocational training qualifications were reciprocally recognized in both parts of the country. This makes for greater mobility among young people.

Higher education institutions

The Federal Republic's oldest higher education institution, the University of Heidelberg, was founded in 1386. Several other universities have had 500-year jubilees, including Leipzig (founded in 1409) and Rostock (founded in 1419). But alongside these venerable institutions there are very young universities, more than 20 of which have been founded since 1960.

In the 19th century and in the first half of the 20th the educational ideal of German universities was the one pursued by Wilhelm von Humboldt at the Berlin University founded in 1810. The Humboldt type of university was conceived for a relatively small number of students. It was to be a place of pure science where research was done for research's sake and students were not taught primarily with a view to their future professions. This ideal clashed increasingly with the requirements of a modern industrial society. Alongside the traditional universities there emerged technical universities, colleges of education and Fachhochschulen, the latter especially in the 70s and 80s. Education policy also changed. The demand for the best possible educational opportunities for all young people found general recognition.

Whereas in 1960 only 8% of each age group took up academic studies, nowadays nearly one in three seeks a place at a higher education institution. The number of students rose to about 1,900,000 in 1994/95. In that academic year alone there were more than 221,000 freshmen, continuing the slightly downward trend of recent years. The state tried to meet growth in demand since the 60s by expanding existing higher education institutions and building new ones, and by increasing teaching staff and funding for higher education. New courses of study were focused more on professional requirements. However, expansion could not keep pace with the growth of the student community so that the situation has deteriorated in recent years. As the average length of time spent at a higher education institution is too long, the federal and state governments are working on a structural reform programme to improve the efficiency of higher education.

■ ■   **Organization of higher education institutions.**
The institutions of higher education in the Federal Republic of Germany (apart from a few private, predominantly
church-owned colleges, the universities of the Federal
Armed Forces and the Federal College for Public Administration) belong to the states. The federal government
lays down the general principles of the higher education
system and helps finance building and research.

The higher education institutions are self-governing.
Within the framework of the law, each institution draws
up its own constitution. It is headed by a full-time rector
or president elected for several years. All groups – professors, academic staff, students and employees – play their
part. In most states the student community manage their
own affairs.

■ ■   **Types of higher education institutions.** The mainstays of the tertiary education system are the academic
universities and equivalent institutions. Courses of study
culminate in a Master's degree (*Magister*), a *Diplom* or a
state examination (*Staatsexamen*). After that, further qualification is possible up to doctorate level or a second degree. Some courses of study lead only to a Master's degree or a doctorate. Another, the most recent but increasingly attractive type of higher education institution is the
Fachhochschule, which offers highly practice-related study
courses of a scientific nature, especially in engineering,
business administration, social science, design and agriculture, leading to a *Diplom*. Today nearly every third
new student enrolls at a Fachhochschule, whose standard
period of study is shorter than that of the universities.

In two states, Hesse and North Rhine-Westphalia, comprehensive universities (Gesamthochschulen) were established in the early 70s. They combine the various tertiary
forms under one roof and offer corresponding integrated
courses of study.

Also new in the Federal Republic is the distance-
learning university in Hagen, which opened in 1976. It
now has nearly 56,000 students who, in addition to their
correspondence courses, also attend regional centres.

■ ■   **Courses of study and students.** Government policy has opened higher education study to all strata of
the population. In the 1952/53 winter semester 4% of the
freshmen came from wage-earner families, compared
with about 19% today. In 1952 one fifth of students were

women; today the figure is just under 40% in the western part of the country and over 45% in the east. The federal and state governments also want foreigners to study in Germany. In 1994 the number was roughly 135,000.

For nearly all courses of study there are recommended curricula and required intermediate examinations. Nevertheless, in many fields students can themselves decide which subjects will be the focus of their studies and which classes they will take. Students at public higher education institutions are not required to pay tuition fees. Students enrolled at a higher education institution are covered under the institution's accident insurance and as a rule are able to obtain health and long-term care insurance at a reduced student rate.

Under the Federal Training Assistance Act (BAFöG) students have a legal right to public financial assistance if the funds they need to cover their educational and living expenses are not available from other sources, most notably from their parents' income. Half of this assistance is awarded in the form of a grant and the rest as an interest-free loan that must usually be repaid within five years after the end of the maximum entitlement period.

In 1993, 19.2% of all students in the old states and 49.1% of the students in the new states received assistance under the Federal Training Assistance Act. Payments under this Act are made by the 65 student welfare services, which as a rule are statutory bodies of the federal states. They are responsible for economic, social, cultural and health care services for students at the higher education institutions. The local student welfare services have together formed a national organization, the German Student Welfare Service (DSW).

A room in a dormitory is the least expensive living arrangement for students. In 1993 about 10% of the students in the old federal states and 55% in the new states had this option. Rents on the open market are a serious problem for many students. The percentage of students who have to work while pursuing their studies has meanwhile risen to over 60%.

■ ■ ■ **The problem of student numbers.** Despite the considerable expansion of the higher education system the enormous growth in the number of people wanting to study has led to the introduction of admission restrictions (numerus clausus) for an increasing number of subjects.

A typical lecture-hall scene

Where restrictions are local, study places are awarded by the higher education institution directly, but where they are national places are allocated by the Central Office for the Allocation of Study Places (ZVS) in Dortmund, usually on the basis of average marks in final school exams and the length of time applicants have been waiting. In the case of those study courses for which demand is especially high nationwide – currently medicine, dentistry and veterinary science – study places are awarded under a special selection procedure that requires tests and selection interviews as well. Special consideration is given to hardship cases.

Reforms have been under discussion for some time, principally with a view to reducing the length of the period of study. Today students spend on average 14 semesters (seven years) at university, much longer than in other countries. Many of them have even completed an apprenticeship or compulsory military or civilian service before pursuing a course of study. The fact that they begin earning their living comparatively late in life is a serious disadvantage, especially in view of the increasing international mobility, as for instance in the European internal market.

Students at Fachhochschulen are generally more optimistic than their counterparts at university about their future prospects. In 1994 just under 56% thought they could find places in industry and business after completing their course of study.

■ ■ **The situation in the new federal states.** The reform of higher education in eastern Germany, partly under a programme costing DM 2.4 billion, has improved the academic range and regional distribution of institutions. Now there are 17 universities, 12 colleges of art and music and 21 Fachhochschulen. The Fachhochschulen, which were unknown in the former GDR, were established on the recommendation of the Science Council; 51,800 students enrolled in them for the 1994/95 winter semester. The total number of students in eastern Germany in 1994 was 285,000.

Some of the research carried out at academies is being reintegrated into the higher education institutions and some transferred to extramural research establishments financed jointly by the federal and the state governments. Suitable professors and lecturers with an untainted political past are being incorporated in the public service. Many instructors have come from the west, joining law, and economics departments in particular. Cooperation between higher education institutions and industry in the new federal states is developing within the framework of this reorganization of higher education.

Hochschulrektorenkonferenz
(German Rectors' Conference)
Ahrstrasse 39, 53175 Bonn
Deutscher Akademischer Austauschdienst (DAAD)
(German Academic Exchange Service)
Kennedyallee 50, 53175 Bonn

Adult education

Every year ten million people in Germany take advantage of the many opportunities for further education. Continuing education is necessary in a modern industrial society in view of the fact that the demands of work are increasing and changing all the time. Many people have to change occupations several times in their life. But further education is also an important leisure-time factor. It has a political function as well since the individual can only have a say in matters if he is capable of making his own judgment in various fields.

■ ■ **Adult education centres.** Adult education centres (Volkshochschulen) were introduced towards the end of the 19th century, based on the Scandinavian model. They impart mainly practical but also theoretical knowledge. Today the subjects range from astronomy and language courses to Zen meditation. There are some 1,050 such centres in the Federal Republic and numerous sub-centres. They are generally run by local authorities or registered associations. Funds are contributed by the state governments. Adult education centres are non-political and non-denominational. Most of them take the form of evening classes, but there are also residential centres which offer courses lasting several days or weeks.

In 1993 alone, they ran more than 482,000 courses which were attended by about 6.4 million people (in 1965 there were 78,000 courses and 1.7 million participants). Nearly three million took part in approximately 76,000 individual events. Most popular are language, health education, and arts and crafts courses.

For a number of years certificates have been awarded in various subjects such as languages, mathematics, science and technology. Many participants make up for opportunities lost at school: in 1993 nearly 4,761 obtained a secondary general school certificate, 2,470 an intermediate school certificate, and 2,492 a university entrance qualification. This widely varying tuition is provided by some 8,100 full-time teachers and nearly 180,000 part-time course leaders.

■ ■ **Continuing vocational training.** There has been a remarkable increase in continuing education courses.

An adult education centre

Last year a third of the country's employees participated, and in the new states the proportion was over 40%. Industry spends more than DM 10 billion every year on further training for the labour force. There are 11 supra-regional training institutes run by industry and 30 continuing education institutes. Large enterprises additionally run courses for their own employees. The participants are meant either to achieve a higher vocational qualification, refresh their skills in their own occupation or learn a completely new job.

There is a growing willingness to retrain for a different occupation, especially in the computer sector. Courses generally last two years in which full-time tuition alternates with practical training. Three out of four participants in further-training schemes report that they obtained better jobs.

The state provides roughly DM 5.5 billion a year for such training. During the course trainees receive grants or loans. The cost of tuition and teaching materials can be wholly or partly borne by the state.

Unemployed people in particular are resorting increasingly to continuing education to improve their employment prospects. Three quarters of unemployed participants who complete courses successfully find work within six months. The employment agencies pay a grant for up to 12 months to companies who give permanent employment to retrainees. The armed forces provide further training for servicemen in their own professional schools. There they can work for all school certificates (see chapter "Schools"). Their Vocational Advancement Service organizes initial training courses, retraining and further training.

■ ■ **Wide selection of courses.** The trade unions also have a large continuing education programme. The adult education centres and the German Trade Union Federation (Deutscher Gewerkschaftsbund, DGB) are linked in a working group called "Arbeit und Leben" (Work and Life). This provides workers with courses in economic and social affairs, works constitution, insurance and labour law and much more. Works council members and other labour representatives can take courses at special DGB academies.

The churches, too, are active in the field of adult education. The Protestant Church maintains 15 academies where it holds seminars on topical issues. In the foreground of Catholic continuing education work are family and marriage issues as well as theological and cultural subjects.

Foundations closely allied to the political parties likewise have continuing education programmes. Private distance-learning organizations also offer about 1,000 continuing education courses. In 1993 there were 172,000 participants, including 28,000 from the new states, where the process of developing continuing education is in full swing.

The Federal Centre for Political Education issues publications and magazines providing reliable and well-researched information on political, economic and social affairs in Germany. It also stocks films and videos on these topics and organizes conferences and seminars.

Deutscher Volkshochschulverband e.V.
(German Adult Education Association)
Obere Wilhelmstraße 31, 53225 Bonn
Bundeszentrale für politische Bildung
(Federal Centre for Political Education)
Berliner Freiheit 7, 53111 Bonn

Scholarship and research

In recent years the Nobel Prize winners for chemistry, physics and medicine have included Germans. The 1991 prize for medicine was awarded to Erwin Neher and Bert Sakmann for their work in the field of cellular biology. In 1989 the prize for physics was shared by Wolfgang Paul and two American colleagues, and in 1988 the prize for chemistry was shared by Johann Deisenhofer, Robert Huber and Hartmut Michel. Thus if one takes Nobel Prizes as the yardstick, Germany is holding its own in fields of advanced research.

Germany used to be known as the "land of science". Her universities led the world in many areas of scholarship. Up to the Second World War ten out of 45 Nobel Prizes for physics and 16 out of 40 for chemistry went to Germans.

But after 1933 the National Socialists drove many of the country's best brains abroad. A good number of them went to the United States, where they were of inestimable value to that country's scientific institutions. Germany had a hard task making up for this brain drain after 1945 and it was a long time before she caught up with the world's leaders. The reunification of Germany has posed a new challenge: how to build an efficient research network spanning the whole country. Since 1992 more than 140 research facilities have been established in the new federal states, opening up new jobs and prospects for approximately 13,000 people. They are a valuable complement to the world of research in Germany.

The structural changes have been drastic, especially in the fields of higher education and research, but the process has largely been completed in terms of both subject-matter and personnel. Nonetheless, the Federal Government realizes that further efforts are necessary in order to unify research. It has, for instance, financed innovative inter-university and inter-departmental research projects which also bring in external specialists, some from industry. A joint initiative for "product renewal" is intended to close the gap between investment promotion and manufacture of marketable products and thus help industry in the new states to sustain development.

■ ■ **Research establishments.** Research in the Federal Republic is done by the universities, by public and private non-university and non-industry institutes, and by industry itself.

Research by university teachers has a long tradition in Germany. "The unity of research and teaching" has been a pillar of German academic life since Wilhelm von Humboldt reformed the Prussian universities in the early 19th century.

The universities are the bedrock of German research. They are the only institutions whose research embraces all scientific disciplines. Most basic research is done there, and they produce successive generations of scientists and thus ensure continuity.

Non-university research is primarily an extension of the work done at the universities. For instance, major research projects, especially in the natural sciences, can only be managed by big teams using expensive technology and with heavy financial backing. Such large-scale research is best done in the government-funded centres for new sources of energy (e.g. nuclear fusion), aerospace, medicine, molecular biology, and environmental and polar research.

The established system of joint promotion of research by the federal and state governments proved to be a stabilizing factor precisely after the peaceful revolution in the former GDR when the country sought to unify research as well. In Germany some 488,000 people have jobs connected with science and research – roughly one third scientists and engineers, one third technical staff and one third other personnel.

Spending on research and development
(conducted domestically, in billions of DM)*

Research sector	1971	1981	1991	1993
Non-university research institutions	3.01	5.79	11.19	12.22
Universities and other higher education institutions	3.50	6.39	12.07	13.73
Private industry	10.70	26.61	52.06	52.40
Total	17.21	38.79	75.32	78.35

* 1971 and 1981: old federal states
  1991 and 1993: Germany as a whole

In 1993 the country spent DM 81.6 billion (about 2.5% of the gross domestic product) on research and development. The biggest contribution comes from industry (a good DM 48 billion); the Federal Government furnishes about DM 17 billion and the states DM 14 billion. This puts Germany in third place among the major industrial states, behind Japan (3% of GDP) and the United States (just over 2.8%).

■ ■ **Sponsors of research.** The higher education institutions are in many areas, especially basic scientific research and the humanities, the most important sponsors of research and often the source of innovation. In fields of applied research and development they cooperate with other establishments and industrial laboratories. This speeds up the practical application of their theoretical findings. The Fachhochschulen, too, play an important role in this regard and are particularly useful contacts and intermediaries for small firms.

Closely linked with the higher education institutions are the academies of science in Düsseldorf, Göttingen, Heidelberg, Leipzig, Mainz and Munich, and the Berlin-Brandenburg Academy of the Arts founded in 1992. They are centres of scientific communication and mainly support long-term scholarly projects such as the publication of encyclopaedias, etc. Crucial support for research at

Phytogenetic research at the Max Planck Institute

Adjusting a cloud-monitoring radar installation

higher education institutions comes from the Deutsche Forschungsgemeinschaft (DFG), the largest sponsor after the federal and state governments. In 1994 alone it dealt with nearly 20,000 applications for research funds, a fact which reflects the creativity and innovative energy of Germany's universities. The DFG receives its funds from the federal and state governments (in 1994 approximately DM 1.8 billion).

The Max Planck Society for the Advancement of Science is the largest research organization outside the universities and its more than 60 facilities in the old federal states are financed from public funds. It is developing further establishments in the new states. The Max Planck Society engages in basic research which is either not done by the higher education institutions or requires particularly large equipment.

The 16 national research centres are another important instrument of government research policy. They receive 90% of their funds from the Federal Ministry for Education, Science, Research and Technology and 10% from the government of the state where they are located. Their research ranges from microparticles and aerospace to cancer, environmental and climate research.

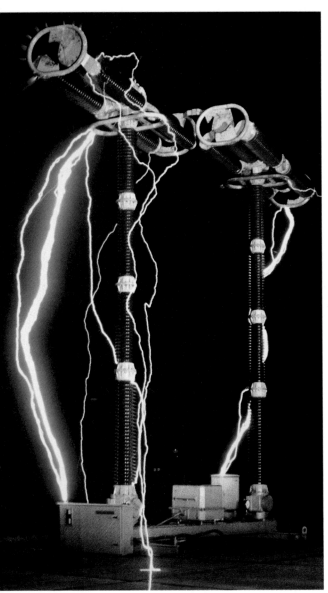

Insulation test on a high-voltage power switch

An important link between research and its practical application is the Fraunhofer Society for the Advancement of Applied Research. In its 50 or so institutes it carries out commissioned projects, mainly for industry. It already has about 10 facilities and 12 branches in the new states.

Other significant contributions are made by the Fritz Thyssen and Volkswagen Foundations. They and the Donors' Association for the Promotion of German Science are much in demand for research projects, especially in collaboration with the higher education institutions.

The Alexander von Humboldt Foundation, which receives financial support from the federal government, enables foreign scientists to do research in Germany and, vice versa, German scientists to work on similar projects abroad, and pays for research trips by outstanding foreign scientists.

Many of the tasks facing the government today cannot be accomplished without scientific preliminary work and consultation. Such activities are the responsibility of the many research institutions of the federal and state governments, such as the Federal Health Office (Bundesgesundheitsamt) or the Federal Environmental Agency (Umweltbundesamt).

■ ▪ **International cooperation.** The promotion of international cooperation in the field of research is a major aspect of government policy. In addition to the promotion of exchanges and direct cooperation between German foreign scientists, for instance via the German Academic Exchange Service (DAAD) or the Alexander von Humboldt Foundation, there are many other forms of cooperation.

Germany has concluded agreements on scientific and technological cooperation with over 30 countries. Within the European Union it plays an active part in joint research and technology programmes. Cooperation also extends beyond the territory of the Union, as reflected in the COST (cooperation with third countries on applied research), JET and ITER (European and worldwide research on nuclear fusion) programmes, the EU's participation in the EUREKA and ESA projects, and the more recent EU-EFTA cooperation under the European Economic Area agreement.

Fibre-optic testing at the Fraunhofer Institute, Euskirchen

Some of this work at EU level is carried out by institutions with large-scale facilities beyond the means of individual countries. They include the high energy accelerator of the European Organization for Nuclear Research (CERN) in Geneva, the very high flux reactor of the Max von Laue-Paul Langevin Institute (ILL) in Grenoble, or the European Molecular Biology Laboratory (EMBL) in Heidelberg.

The aim of all these programmes is to coordinate national research, to pool resources in joint projects and hence increase Europe's competitiveness.

■■ ■■ **Research policy.** Research in Germany is determined by the freedom of teaching and research as anchored in the Basic Law, by the country's federal structure which divides responsibility between the federal and state governments, and by the demands of industry. Primarily it is the scientific institutions themselves who decide what research to undertake and assess the results, especially in the field of basic research.

Every four years the Federal Government submits a research report (the most recent one in 1993) in which it informs the public and parliament about the aims and focus of financial support for research and development.

Although private companies choose their own research projects, the government can provide incentives in the form of tax concessions or grants on the basis of subsidiarity, i.e. it can, for instance, promote large-scale projects which are in the public interest but are too costly for an individual company.

In the years ahead government policy will focus on the technologies of the 21st century, especially in the fields of transport, health and environment, and on support for small and medium-sized enterprises.

Deutsche Forschungsgemeinschaft (DFG)
Kennedyallee 40, 53175 Bonn
Max-Planck-Gesellschaft (MPG)
Hofgartenstraße 2, 80539 München
Fraunhofer-Gesellschaft
Leonrodstraße 54, 80636 München
Fritz Thyssen Stiftung
Am Römerturm 3, 50667 Köln
Volkswagen-Stiftung
Kastanienallee 35, 30519 Hannover
Alexander von Humboldt-Stiftung
Jean-Paul-Straße 12, 53173 Bonn

D 2 Mission: work in the materials lab

Stifterverband für die Deutsche Wissenschaft
(Donors' Association for the Promotion
of German Science)
Barkhovenallee 1, 45239 Essen
Deutscher Akademischer Austauschdienst (DAAD)
(German Academic Exchange Service)
Kennedyallee 50, 53175 Bonn
Bundesministerium für Bildung, Wissenschaft, Forschung
und Technologie
(Federal Ministry for Education, Science, Research and
Technology)
Heinemannstraße 2, 53175 Bonn

Culture

· Literature · The book trade and libraries · Art
· Architecture · Museums, collections, exhibitions · Music
· Theatre · Cinema · Festivals

Literature

The oldest testimony to German literature is the "Song of Hildebrand", a story about how Hildebrand has to fight and kill his son Hadubrand for honour's sake. The "Song of Hildebrand" was sung at court by wandering minstrels. The names of German authors began to emerge in the 12th century. They included Wolfram von Eschenbach, Walther von der Vogelweide and Gottfried von Strassburg who wrote poems and epic stories, often in the French style.

German literature has always borrowed from abroad. The humanists of the Renaissance discovered Greek and Roman literature. Martin Luther translated the Bible into the vernacular and made it accessible to all German-speaking people. He thus laid the foundation for common high German. Not until the 17th century did writers like Martin Opitz seek to create a German national literature. But it could not be kept within national confines. Its medium, the German language, was never limited by state boundaries. Whether someone writing in German is an Austrian, Swiss or German usually is of little concern to the reader. German is the native language of Swiss, Austrians and Germans alike; it is also the literary language of authors of other origin. The poets Rainer Maria Rilke, who was born in Prague, and Hugo von Hofmannsthal, who was born in Vienna, as well as the writer Franz Kafka, who was born in Prague, are just as much a part of German literature as the writers Robert Musil from Klagenfurt and Thomas Mann from Lübeck. And what would German literature be without the Swiss Gottfried Keller or Max Frisch, the Austrians Adalbert Stifter or Thomas Bernhard, the poet Paul Celan, who was born in Romania, or Elias Canetti, who was born in Bulgaria? The works of all these authors are contributions to German literature. However, the following brief survey will largely be confined to the literature of eastern and western Germany.

■ ▒ ▒ **Highlights of the past.** In the 18th century, the century of the Enlightenment, "Storm and Stress", and Classicism, writers and philosophers were primarily concerned with the struggle of ideas. Later, against the backdrop of wars of liberation, they were also concerned with developing a German or cosmopolitan literature.

Gotthold Ephraim Lessing was the first to have commoners appear in a tragedy and to extol humanistic ideals. In Riga, Johann Gottfried von Herder developed concepts of a new national German literature and made Shakespeare, among others, his model. Not long afterwards the "Storm and Stress" writers gathered around Johann Wolfgang von Goethe.

Goethe and Friedrich von Schiller are Germany's classical writers. For half a century their ideal, a harmony of self and world, sentiment and reason, bound by a strict form, dominated German literature. The French Revolution of 1789 was a break in that very fruitful period.

The romantic poets strove after quite different ideals. Many of them were driven by patriotic sentiments. The romantics of Jena and Heidelberg renounced the visions of the Enlightenment. They wanted not to improve the world but to spiritualize, to poeticize it. Introspection, the retrospective glorification of the Middle Ages, and the romantic longing for national heritage competed with the desire to open up new worlds, new vistas.

Thus emerged collections of folklore in the form of songs, fairy tales and sagas by Clemens Brentano, Achim von Arnim and the brothers Grimm. The response was considerable and long-lasting. Georg Büchner incorporated fairy tales in his ironic, realistic dramas, and Heinrich Heine's "Lorelei", the most frequently quoted German poem, is a saga of the Rhine.

But this was also the time when great works of international renown were translated into German. The translations by Ludwig Tieck and the Schlegel brothers of Shakespeare and Cervantes became very famous and provided the stimulus for many more translations of great works from the Romance and old Nordic languages, and later from Oriental and Indian literature.

The great 19th-century German writers are still widely read today: Adalbert Stifter, Theodor Storm, Wilhelm Raabe, Theodor Fontane. Thomas and Heinrich Mann count among this century's greats, and works by Rainer Maria Rilke, Gottfried Benn, Hermann Hesse and Bertolt Brecht can be found in every bookshop.

During the twelve-year National Socialist dictatorship many German writers went into exile. Whilst in Marseilles, Anna Seghers described in "Transit" how people persecuted by the National Socialist regime desperately tried to flee Europe. In Denmark Bertolt Brecht analyzed and deplored the "Finstere Zeiten" (Dark Times), and Thomas Mann wrote his "Doktor Faustus" in the United States. Only a few writers (including Gottfried Benn, Hans Carossa, Ernst and Friedrich Georg Jünger, Erich Kästner and Ernst Wiechert) stuck it out in the "Internal Emigration", some of them being banned from writing.

■ ■ ■ **The new beginning after 1945.** After the Second World War German writers made a fresh start. They first tried to fill the literary vacuum with works in the foreign mould. They tried Ernest Hemingway's neo-realism and Jean Paul Sartre's existentialism. One spoke of "Trümmerliteratur" (literature of the ruins) and of "Zero Hour" literature.

The most radical example of this type of literature is "Draussen vor der Tür" (Outside the Door), which the author himself, Wolfgang Borchert, described as "a play which no theatre wants to stage and no public wants to see". This, like other works of that period, reflects the author's strong political commitment. Writers like Günter Eich, Peter Huchel or Hans Erich Nossack considered it their task to influence politics by literary means.

In the 50s and early 60s this attitude largely gave way to a different approach. Some authors criticized society on moral grounds. Their uneasiness about the negative aspects of the economic upswing, about the egotism and materialism of the affluent society, found articulation, for example, in novels like "Das Treibhaus" (The Greenhouse) by Wolfgang Koeppen or "Billiards at Half-Past Nine" by Heinrich Böll, whose short stories, too, deal with the legacy of National Socialism, a theme which dominated German literature in the 50s and 60s, as in Alfred Andersch's "Sansibar oder der letzte Grund" (Zanzibar or the Abyss) or the "The Tin Drum" by Günter Grass. Many writers made the medium itself, language, the subject of literature (Uwe Johnson, Peter Härtling). They spoke of the "reprivatization" of literature. The most prominent German playwrights of that era were the Swiss Friedrich Dürrenmatt ("The Visit", "The Physicists") and Max Frisch ("Andorra").

■ ■ ■ **The 68ers.** A new turning point came in the late 60s. Literature in the Federal Republic focused on its

Günter Grass

social function. The stimulus was provided above all by the student movement of that period (the "68ers"). Literature was to serve the political cause. Poets (F. C. Delius, Erich Fried, Yaak Karsunke) and playwrights (Rolf Hochhuth: "The Deputy"; Heinar Kipphardt: "In der Sache J. Robert Oppenheimer"; and Peter Weiss: "The Investigation") dealt with contemporary topics or brought day-to-day happenings onto the stage (Martin Sperr: "Jagdszenen aus Niederbayern"; Franz Xaver Kroetz: "Wildwechsel").

Many writers of the 60s, too, saw themselves as political authors, especially Heinrich Böll ("The Clown", "Group Portrait with Lady"), Günter Grass ("Dog Years"), Martin Walser ("Halbzeit") and Siegfried Lenz ("Deutschstunde"), all of them members of Group 47, a fluctuating group of writers formed by Hans Werner Richter with the aim of "bringing together and encouraging young writers".

Uwe Johnson was the one to concern himself most with the division of Germany ("Mutmassungen über Jakob"). The members of Group 61, on the other hand, depicted the working world (Max von der Grün: "Irrlicht und Feuer"; Günter Wallraff: "Wir brauchen dich"). Yet another group focused on the old principle of "art for art's sake": in "concrete poetry" the subject is language per se. Prominent among them were Ernst Jandl, Friederike Mayröcker, Helmut Heisenbüttel and Franz Mon. In 1968 the "Kursbuch" (The Timetable), a literary magazine by Hans Magnus Enzensberger, proclaimed the "death of literature".

■ ■ ■ **The rediscovery of the self.** In the 70s many German-language authors made their personal feelings the subject of their works (Max Frisch: "Sketchbook"; Wolfgang Koeppen: "Jugend"; Thomas Bernhard: "Die Ursache", "Der Atem", "Die Kälte"; Elias Canetti: "The Tongue Set Free"). Since the mid-70s a separate body of women's literature (Karin Struck: "Klassenliebe"; Verena Stephan: "Häutungen"; Brigitte Schwaiger: "Wie kommt das Salz ins Meer"), has been trying to establish itself. In the field of documentary literature there is a mixture of political pretentiousness and self-reflection (Uwe Johnson: "Anniversaries"; Walter Kempowski: "Tadellöser & Wolf"; Günter Wallraff: "Ganz unten").

Ordinary, day-to-day events are reflected more strongly in the lyricism (Wolf Wondratschek, Nicolas Born, Ulla Hahn) and drama of those years (Botho Strauss: "Trilogie des Wiedersehens") than in novels.

In the late 80s works by the "old masters" were a pleasant change from the "production literature" of this period (newspaper articles, reviews and other ways of making a living by the pen). Heinrich Böll, who won the 1972 Nobel Prize for Literature, wrote "Frauen vor Flusslandschaft" (Women against a River Landscape) in 1988 and Günter Grass "Die Rättin" in 1986. Patrick Süskind's 1985 book "Das Parfüm" (The Perfume) is still on the bestseller lists.

Martin Walser

Gabriele Wohmann

■ ■ ■ **Production literature.** Johannes Mario Simmel, Heinz G. Konsalik and Utta Danella – the number of writers of light literature in Germany is legion. The same is true of the authors of screenplays, stories for periodicals and novelettes. A man who reviews literary works with "papal authority" is Marcel Reich-Ranicki, almost a household name and a controversial figure. His reviews have "made" many of today's authors, and much of his criticism is itself literature. For in the process of distributing modern literature, reviews of books – often written by authors reviewing the works of colleagues – are still a path to literary success, although they are constantly losing ground on account of the financial power of the big publishing monopolies as reflected in the latter's massive advertising of current books in the media.

■ ■ ■ **Children's literature.** Children's literature very soon became a branch of its own in Germany. "Struwwelpeter", which the doctor Heinrich Hoffmann wrote for his three-year-old son as a Christmas present in 1845, became world famous. "Max und Moritz", the two mischievous boys from the pen of Wilhelm Busch, have also taught many generations of children. The adventures of "Heidi" by Johanna Spyri have been filmed several times. Still great favourites are "Das doppelte Lottchen" (Double Lottie), "Das fliegende Klassenzimmer" (The Flying Classroom) and other youth novels by Erich Kästner. Otfried Preussler ("Das kleine Gespenst" [The Little Ghost]) and James Krüss ("Tim Thaler") have a huge readership.

But books for the young also deal with serious subjects. Michael Ende tells in "Momo" the story of the "grey gentlemen" who steal people's time and make them dependent on them. Peter Härtling, too, has written some outstanding children's books. Since the 70s Christine Nöstlinger has realistically looked into the everyday problems of young people. Her book "Nagle einen Pudding an die Wand" (Nail a Pudding to the Wall) was awarded the "Preis der Leseratten" (Bookworms' Prize) in 1991. The prize was initiated by the "Stiftung Lesen" (Reading Foundation) in Mainz and the winners are chosen by a jury of young people. Picture books by Janosch ("Oh wie schön ist Panama" [Oh, how Beautiful Panama Is]) and Helmer Heine ("Freunde" [Friends]) are popular with adults as well.

■ ■ ■ **Separate trend in the east.** In the former GDR post-1945 writers were required to extol Soviet-style "Socialist Realism". Most of the works produced in the

50s were later described as "construction" literature. The enemy-image was obvious. The good people, including the party secretary, took up the struggle with the bad people, the big landowners, the "bourgeois scholars", the disguised Western agents. And of course everyone knew who was going to win. The GDR leadership warded off all outside influences on literature.

In the 60s most authors still believed they could improve the political system. A kind of critical, subjective writing emerged.

Siegfried Lenz

"Construction" literature was superseded by "arrival" literature. Novels such as Jurek Becker's "Jakob der Lügner" (Jacob the Liar) and Hermann Kant's "Die Aula" (The Hall), the prose and poems of Johannes Bobrowski ("Levins Mühle" and "Litauische Claviere"), the stories of Franz Fühmann ("Das Judenauto") and the plays of Peter Hacks, Heiner Müller and Volker Braun caused a stir in the Federal Republic at that time. Many of them were first or only published in the Federal Republic and were instrumental in gaining international recognition for the GDR as a "cultural state". Many authors

Sarah Kirsch

returning from exile (e.g. Anna Seghers, Arnold Zweig, Johannes R. Becher) wrote books that were in line with the communist system or wrote very little at all. Soon more or less concealed rejections of "Socialist Realism" began to appear. Christa Wolf coined the term "subjective authenticity" ("The Quest for Christa T."). In the 70s Wolf Biermann, the singer/songwriter who had been critical of the system, was banned from appearing on stage and in 1976 deprived of his citizenship and forced to leave the country. His courageous example was followed by others. Stefan Heym ("Der König-David-Bericht"), Ulrich Plenzdorf ("Die neuen Leiden des jungen W."), Franz Fühmann ("22 Tage oder Die Hälfte des Lebens"), Reiner Kunze ("Die wunderbaren Jahre") and Günter de Bruyn ("Märkische Forschungen") criticized the GDR and its system of informers which they themselves could hardly escape. Some writers left the country, among them Günter Kunert, Sarah Kirsch, Reiner Kunze and Joachim Schädlich.

The literature of the GDR faced a crisis and began to turn to subjects that had hitherto been taboo, such as utopian literature and women's topics. Indeed, some even dared to look at the darker side of socialist society, depicting those who had built a career out of the system (Günter de Bruyn: "Neue Herrlichkeit"), conformists (Christoph Hein: "Der fremde Freund/Drachenblut"), the contradictions between rulers and ruled (Volker Braun: "Hinze-Kunze-Roman"), and real life in the GDR (Wolfgang Hilbig: "Die Weiber", "Alte Abdeckerei").

■ ■ ■ **Post-unification literature.** The fall of the Berlin Wall – the Wall itself had been the subject of many novels, stories and poems – changed German reality overnight and with it the "world view" of a good many artists. With the restoration of German unity, German literature will enter a new phase in its development. Many authors, above all those from the former GDR, are still in the process of coming to terms with the past, and with their own personal past as well – some as victims, others as fellow travelers – for despite their opposition they were caught up in their state's power system in so many ways.

Initial attempts to address the events leading up to the unification of Germany and its consequences are discernible in the works of Christian Delius ("Die Birnen von Ribbeck", 1990) and Martin Walser ("Die Verteidigung der Kindheit", 1991). In Botho Strauss's "Schlusschor", Volker Braun's "Iphigenie in Freiheit" and Wolfgang Hilbig's novel "Ich", hope and anticipation are mixed with deflation and a somber awareness of the end of an era. The general tone is one of melancholy and cynicism. Continuing in this vein, Helga Königsdorf ("Im Schatten des Regenbogens", 1993) laments the painful reorientation of East German lives brought on by the fall of the Wall.

Writers need time to digest reality and deal with it creatively. Consequently, no general trend in German literature has been observable since the unification of the two parts of the country. Contrary to expectations, relatively few German writers have addressed the country's most recent history in major literary works; their views are instead reflected largely in interviews, statements and essays.

The book trade and libraries

The first book to be printed with movable type, the 42-line Bible, was published in Mainz in 1455. The inventor, Johannes Gutenberg, was printer and publisher in one. Thus the birth of this new technology coincided with the beginning of German book publishing and selling. At the end of the 15th century Frankfurt am Main became the leading publishing centre in Germany and a hub of European trade. In the 18th century, because of restrictions imposed by the emperor, it was surpassed by Leipzig. After World War II, Frankfurt regained its pre-eminence as a result of the country's division. Now several cities are major publishing centres in Germany: Munich, Berlin, Hamburg, Stuttgart, Frankfurt, Cologne and Leipzig.

In terms of book production Germany comes second to the United States. In 1993 there were more than 67,000 first and new editions. More than 600,000 titles were available in German bookshops.

There are over 2,000 publishers in the Federal Republic. About 100 of them have an annual turnover of DM 25 million or more, but none of them dominates the market. There are also many small companies who contribute to the variety of literature available to the public. After the war book clubs attracted a wider readership. They derived their origin from the idea of "national education". One of them, the Büchergilde Gutenberg (Gutenberg Book Guild) was founded by the trade unions. Today approximately 6.3 million readers belong to a book club.

In 1993 the total turnover of books and journals came to about DM 15.4 billion, an increase of 4.1% over the figures for the previous year. In statistical terms, the average price of a hardcover book in 1993 was about DM 38.70. Paperbacks are less expensive. Aside from the pharmacies, the book trade is the only branch of commerce in Germany permitted by law to dictate retail prices. This guarantees that nearly all books are available throughout the whole of Germany at uniform net published prices and that the entire population thus has access to this cultural asset.

Mergers have taken place in the book trade as well. In the 70s the smaller shops with sales space of up to 500 sq m were in the majority. Now the larger bookstores are taking over, especially in city centres. Wholesale chains from France and the United Kingdom are also acquiring a larger share of the market. The bookshops in the former GDR, which in the old days were run as "people's enterprises", have meanwhile been privatized. Two thirds of them have been sold to interested parties in eastern Germany, the rest to buyers in the west. Many famous publishing houses who opened new establishments in the west when Germany was divided have since been reunited with their parent companies in eastern Germany, one of these being the Reclam-Verlag.

■■■**The German Publishers & Booksellers Association and book fairs.** The professional and trade organization of the book trade is the German Publishers & Booksellers Association in Frankfurt am Main, which brings together companies from all tiers of this branch of industry: publishing houses, firms from the intermediate book trade, and retail booksellers. At the Association's initiative, the Ausstellungs- und Messe-GmbH was founded in 1964, an exhibition company whose primary task to this very day is to organize the Frankfurt Book Fair. This fair is the event of the year for the international book trade, and a large percentage of rights and license transactions are concluded here. Every year since 1976, the fair has had a different theme. In 1992 it was Mexico, in 1993 Flanders and the Netherlands, and in 1994 Brazil. In 1995 the focus will be on Austria. At the 1994 fair, more than 8,500 publishing companies from 105 coun-

Book production by field
(first and new editions, 1993)

Titles	Area	%
6,126	General	9.1
3,403	Philosophy, psychology	5.1
3,620	Religion, theology	5.4
14,452	Social sciences	21.5
3,883	Mathematics, natural sciences	5.8
9,763	Applied sciences, medicine, technology	14.5
4,475	Art, arts and crafts, photography, sports, games	6.6
12,501	Linguistics and literature, fiction	18.6
8,983	Geography, history	13.4

The Cusanus Library, Bernkastel on the Mosel

tries exhibited their products. The development of electronic media has taken on great importance in this sector. As a result, the specialty "Electronic Publishing" was introduced at the 1993 Frankfurt Book Fair. The fair culminates in the award of the Peace Prize of the German Book Trade. Among the recent prizewinners were Max Frisch, Yehudi Menuhin, Teddy Kollek, Vladislav Bartoszewski, Hans Jonas, Václav Havel, György Konrád, Friedrich Schorlemmer and Jorge Semprún. The second major book fair is held every spring in Leipzig. It especially serves as an intermediary with the countries of Eastern Europe.

■■■ **Libraries.** Unlike other countries Germany has no large national library that has existed for centuries. It was not until 1913 that the newly founded Deutsche Bücherei (German Library) in Leipzig brought together all German-language literature under one roof. The division of Germany after World War II led to the foundation of the Deutsche Bibliothek (German Library) in Frankfurt am Main in 1947. It had the same function in the west as the Leipzig library in the east. Like the Leipzig library it was founded by the book trade; since 1969 it has been a federal institution. Under the Unification Treaty of August 1990, the two libraries were merged under the name "Die Deutsche Bibliothek". Die Deutsche Bibliothek is the central archive of all German-language writings and the national bibliographical information center of the

Browsers' corner in a large bookshop

Federal Republic of Germany. Its stocks currently total approximately 14 million volumes. In 1970 the German Music Archive was founded in Berlin as a department of the Frankfurt Deutsche Bibliothek. Frankfurt is also the home of the German Exile Archive 1933-1945. Special departments in Leipzig include the Center for Book Preservation and the German Museum of Books and Writings.

Two of the country's main public libraries are the Bayerische Staatsbibliothek (Bavarian State Library) in Munich (more than six million books) and the Staatsbibliothek Preussischer Kulturbesitz (Prussian Cultural Heritage Library) in Berlin (about four million). Most of the libraries with large stocks are state and university libraries. In addition to these general libraries there are specialized libraries such as the Medizinische Zentralbibliothek (Central Medical Library) in Cologne. A library with an outstanding reputation is the Herzog-August-Bibliothek in Wolfenbüttel, which has over 660,000 volumes, including 12,000 priceless medieval manuscripts.

In the Federal Republic of Germany there are some 14,000 public libraries with more than 129 million volumes. Most of them are maintained by the local authorities and churches.

Börsenverein des Deutschen Buchhandels e.V.
(German Publishers & Booksellers Association)
Grosser Hirschgraben 17-21, 60311 Frankfurt am Main

Art

When, in 1947, one of the first postwar art exhibitions opened in Augsburg under the motto "Extreme Art", it evoked little enthusiasm. The public wasn't used to abstract art. Under National Socialism most schools of modern art had been declared "degenerate". This was the regime's catchword for a campaign to destroy everything in art that was too critical or too abstract. Thus the German Expressionists and abstract painters were affected. Great contemporary painters such as Oskar Kokoschka (1886-1980), Max Beckmann (1884-1950) or Wassily Kandinsky (1866-1944) were taboo. In 1937 alone, 1,052 paintings were confiscated from German galleries. As a result, German artists lost touch with international trends.

■ ■ ▪ **Developments since 1945.** After the Second World War the gap was closed with remarkable speed. Painting followed pre-war trends and owed much to Paul Klee (1879-1940) and Wassily Kandinsky, who had already moved towards abstract art before the First World War. Also still alive were the great "degenerate" artists Oskar Kokoschka, Max Beckmann, Max Pechstein (1881-1955), Emil Nolde (1876-1956), Erich Heckel (1883-1970) and Karl Schmidt-Rottluff (1884-1976). Their task was to bring back the modern art that already seemed almost history. The abstract Expressionism which evolved in France under the influence of the Germans Wols (Wolfgang Schulze, 1913-1951) and Hans Hartung (1904-1967) established itself. Its main exponents were Willi Baumeister (1889-1955), Ernst Wilhelm Nay (1902-1968) and Fritz Winter (1905-1976).

In the early 60s the Düsseldorf group "Zero" proclaimed a new beginning. It was in the Op Art category, which had its roots in, among other things, the experimental tradition of the Bauhaus. The best-known members of this group are Otto Piene (born 1928), Günther Uecker (born 1930) and Heinz Mack (born 1931). They did not regard art as a platform of pathetic humanity but turned to natural phenomena: light, movement and space. They directed attention to the objective, technologically influenced environment and its significance to mankind. This aim is apparent in the fire and smoke pictures of Piene, Uecker's nail pictures and Mack's light steles and dynamos. In Op(tical) Art the specific facets of visual perception, including the optical illusion, become the focal point.

Pop Art did not evoke the same response in Germany as in the United Kingdom and the United States, whereas American Signal Art and Hard-Edge painting were taken up by Günter Fruhtrunk (1923-1982), Karl Georg Pfahler (born 1926) and Winfred Gaul (born 1928) and became very popular.

Thus whereas artists in the Federal Republic were able to follow existing traditions and draw on new currents flowing from Western Europe and the United States, their colleagues in the former GDR were tied to the "Socialist Realism" prescribed for them. They were permitted to do nothing more than portray a favourable picture of the socialist society and its kind of people. Until the late 60s the artistic creation promoted by the regime's functionaries was predominantly a description of working life under the socialist system.

New trends in Socialist Realist painting came mainly from the Leipzig Academy of Art. Among its best-known artists were Werner Tübke (born 1929) and Bernhard Heisig (born 1925), whose monumental paintings, though still tied to historical or social themes, shed the sterility of the 50s and 60s. Wolfgang Mattheuer (born 1927), also a member of the Leipzig Academy, went much further in his efforts to derive more out of realistic painting. His pictures, such as Snow White as the Statue of Liberty, are more a synthesis of post-Expressionist new objectivity and "magic realism" than a testimony to Socialist Realism. A. R. Penck (born 1939), who left the GDR in 1980 and achieved fame in the west, chose as his theme idols of the Stone Age. The works of these painters were very much in demand by western galleries starting in the late 70s.

■ ■ ■ **The artists of today**. "Informel", a postwar form of abstract painting, is still not yet outmoded. It turned visual art into action, used new, unusual materials. Paint was applied thickly, and sometimes the artist departed from the traditional rectangular shape. The result was "happenings", "critical realism", the "New Wild Ones" who lived life to the full in neo-Expressionism. There were also light displays, rotating elements, collages,

Markus Lüpertz: "The Rain", 1978

posters, and above all action art, which usually takes place outside the artist's studio.

Joseph Beuys (1921-1986) set the trend. He no longer attached importance to "immortal" works but staged art as action. For instance, he had himself taken across the river Rhine in a dugout. He spared no expense to "bring art to society". HA Schult, too, has a liking for the spectacular. His action theme is "Car Fetish", to the amusement of the general public. In Cologne, for instance, he had his car monument raised onto a medieval tower.

Action of this kind is also appreciated by the American Jonathan Borofsky, who in Germany likes to decorate the "city as an artistic space" with moving objects. One of his works is the "Hammering Man", a black giant who swings his hammer in slow motion in front of the exhibition hall in Frankfurt am Main.

At present there is a trend towards mammoth objects, though there is still considerable variety of styles. Anselm Kiefer (born 1945) shapes massive works of art in his studios, which are like shop floors in factories. Made mostly of lead, his works also include aircraft in their original size. "Zweistromland" is the name of a 32-ton sculpture consisting of 200 books made of lead on shelves eight metres long. He calls his pictures, many of which are inspired by mythology, "picture bodies" because he attaches various materials to them such as dust, flower petals, ash or roots. Kiefer, who has frequently taken as his subject the burdens of Germany's recent past, presents with his monumental works the magnitude and misery of a culture-oriented world.

But between action art, the giant silhouettes in the townscape, and Kiefer's lead objects there are in Germany countless types of artistic experiment in which the artists are prepared to try any form, any material. There is much arte povera as well as realistic, surrealistic or expressionistic elements. Rebecca Horn (born 1944) presents sculptures as "performances" and uses them in her own films.

Gerhard Richter (born 1932) is a master of ambiguity on the border between representational and abstract art, often changing his style. He categorically rejects interpretations of his work. Georg Baselitz (born 1938), who has won many awards and gained an international reputation, expresses in his upside-down pictures the misery of the human creature. What matters to him is not that which is portrayed but the actual doing and artistic freedom.

Markus Lüpertz (born 1941), currently director of Düsseldorf's Kunstakademie (Academy of Art), gives us with his "dithyrambic painting" a "drunken, rapturous" feeling of life. He is one of the "fathers" of the new representational painting in western Germany, although he has always avoided wild gestures and splurges of colour. Sigmar Polke (born 1941) represents the occult trend but also enjoys practical jokes. "Dürer will be here in a moment" is the name of one of his objects. With the help of photochemicals he makes his works constantly change. A.R. Penck seeks through his pictures, whose matchstick figures recall archaic symbols, to create a universal language which all can directly understand.

Huge dolomite blocks and the Heinrich Heine monument in Bonn bear the signature of Ulrich Rückriem (born 1938). Günter Uecker today celebrates the "poetry of destruction". Jörg Immendorf (born 1945) is a kind of modern historical painter. In his picture "Café Deutschland" the storm of history blows the Berlin Wall away. 1993 marked the inception of the art action programme "I am you", an initiative against violence and xenophobia

Anselm Kiefer: "Adelaide"

sponsored by the Goethe Institute. More than 20 renowned international artists donated posters to this art
action programme, which is being exhibited in more than
350 European cities.

■ ■ ■ **Art and new media.** Videos, computers and telecommunications equipment are also used for artistic purposes. Karlsruhe's Centre for Art and Media Technology,
opened in 1992, and the Institute for New Media of
Frankfurt's Städelschule perceive the electronic media as
forms of expression which complement traditional painting and sculpture. The focus is on video art and the inter-
action between computer and observer. Holographic art,
which has gained ground in the United States in particular, has found notable creative representatives in Germany, too, one being the Berlin painter and graphic artist
Dieter Jung.

■ ■ ■ **Galleries and exhibitions.** Most works of art are
to be found in the museums and galleries of the big
cities. Painters like Max Ernst, Otto Dix, Marc Chagall,
Pablo Picasso, Salvador Dalí and other "classical artists"

Ulrich Rückriem: No Title

still draw thousands of visitors to exhibitions. Avant-garde works are particularly prominent in Cologne and Düsseldorf, home to artists most concerned with experimentation. In Berlin the Grisebach Auction House is on the way to becoming as famous as Sotheby's in London. The most spectacular exhibition is the "documenta" which takes place in Kassel every five years. At this international exhibition of contemporary art the avant-garde are on display for 100 days, shocking, provoking or amusing, bringing the whole city into the picture, so to speak. In 1992 the exhibition drew a record 600,000 visitors.

■ ■ ■ **Art promotion.** Few painters and sculptors can live on the proceeds from the sale of their works. They receive government grants and assistance from private companies. The "Kunstfonds e.V.", founded in 1980, helps recognized artists finance ambitious projects. The Cultural Foundation of the Federal States founded in 1988, which has its seat in Berlin, enables the states to assist one another in acquiring costly works of art. The states have delegated to this institution the search for and confirmation of the whereabouts of valuable paintings, music transcripts, hand-written texts, sculptures and furniture. It was thus possible to purchase at auction the manuscript of Kafka's "The Trial", which is currently being carefully examined by Germanists at the German Literature Archive in Marbach. For 45 years, the Quedlinburg cathedral treasures dating from the 8th through 13th century were thought to have been irretrievably lost. Recovered after a spectacular odyssey, they are now once again on display in Quedlinburg.

Well-known places of artistic activity are the artists' colony at Worpswede in northern Germany as well as the Villa Massimo and the Villa Romana in Italy. At these centres scholarship holders can work without disturbance and free from financial worry. Industry, too, promotes art. For over 40 years the cultural section of the Federation of German Industries, for instance, has been awarding prizes to painters and sculptors.

"Art on buildings" is also encouraged. It is now normal for companies or public authorities to set aside one per cent of their building costs for artistic decoration.

Architecture

Twentieth-century German architects have been trend-
setters. The strongest influences came from Weimar and
Dessau, where the Bauhaus school was formed in the
20s. This applies especially to Walter Gropius (1883-
1969) and Ludwig Mies van der Rohe (1886-1969), two
of the leading figures of the Bauhaus style, whose func-
tional approach won worldwide recognition. Masterpieces of this synthesis of art and technology are to be
seen on all continents.

For a long time the situation after 1945 was a great
disadvantage. The destroyed towns and cities had to
be rebuilt quickly, and cheap housing was needed for
millions of people. In those days little consideration
could be given to architectural quality. In later years
there were bitter complaints about the monotonous
architecture of satellite townships and the dull fronts
of department stores and office buildings. This was particularly true of the former GDR. There valuable old
buildings were destroyed and scarce resources used to
build massive housing estates, all constructed in the
same prefabricated mould.

Today architects are experimenting more and more but
at the same time providing buildings that meet human
needs. While the success of many projects is still attributable to the Bauhaus style and philosophy, new trends,
such as the post-modern, have produced some remarkable buildings. German architects are also gaining prominence abroad with their bold designs, for instance
Helmut Jahn, who is based in Chicago, a city of modern,
high-rise buildings. He built the 256-metre high tower at
Frankfurt's exhibition site, the highest office building in
Europe.

Joseph Paul Kleihues has attracted attention especially
in Berlin with his work on the Tempelhof Stadtreinigungs-
werk and the Neukölln Hospital and as director of planning for the International Building Exhibition. Other
leading German architects are Gottfried Böhm, who in
1986 became the first German to win the Pritzker Architecture Prize, Günter Behnisch and Oswald Mathias
Ungers, who has a preference for geometric forms.

■ ■ ■ **Outstanding structures.** Germany has some fine representative buildings. Clients award their commissions not only to German architects but also to internationally renowned architectural firms. German architects are successful worldwide. The skeleton high-rise, all-glass type, as exemplified by Mies van der Rohe's Seagram Building in New York, has an interesting variant in the Federal Republic in the three-sectional Thyssen House in Düsseldorf (built by Helmut Hentrich in 1960) and the office building of Hamburg's Elektrizitätswerke (Arne Jacobsen and Otto Weitling, 1969). Examples of unconventional, dynamic architecture are the central office of the BMW car-making firm in Munich, with its striking cylindrical form (Karl Schwanzer, 1972), and the Bahlsen building in Hanover with its interlocking cubist forms (Dieter Bahlo, Jörn Köhnke, Klaus Stosberg, 1974).

Another striking landmark is Stuttgart's television tower with restaurant and observation platform (Fritz Leonhardt, 1956). The tent-like structures (Günter Behnisch, 1972) designed for the 1972 Olympic Games in Munich are world famous. The sports facilities are situated in a park which continues to be a popular area for leisure pursuits.

Architectural fantasy also finds expression in concert halls, opera houses, theatres and museums. World

Underground station entrance at Reinoldikirchplatz, Dortmund (W. v. Lom)

Nikko Hotel and sculpture, Düsseldorf

famous is Berlin's new Philharmonie by Hans Scharoun (1963) with its vineyard-like terraced auditorium constructed around the orchestra. By contrast, Münster's Stadttheater incorporates a classical ruin. Stuttgart's Liederhalle and Mannheim's multi-purpose hall at Herzogenriedpark are fine examples of assembly hall architecture. Museums which integrate well into the local townscape were built by Hans Hollein in Mönchengladbach (1982) and by Godfrid Haberer, who created Cologne's Wallraf-Richartz-Museum/Museum Ludwig (1986). James Stirling's Neue Staatsgalerie in Stuttgart was also received with much acclaim (1983).

Another outstanding piece of architecture is the new Museum für Kunsthandwerk (Arts and Crafts Museum) in Frankfurt am Main, which was designed by Richard Meier (1985). University buildings, too, reveal some interesting examples, for instance the University of Constance, whose buildings fit asymmetrically into the terrain. And the Filderklinik in Filderstadt near Stuttgart

Wallraf-Richartz-Museum/Museum Ludwig, Cologne (Busman & Habere.

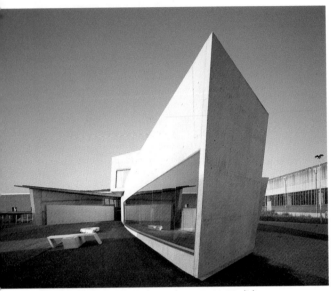

The fire department, Weil am Rhein (Z. M. Hadid)

demonstrates how a hospital can be organically merged with the landscape. The new City Library in Münster (Westphalia) has been termed an "architectural sensation". With this two-part structure, one part of which is reminiscent of a ship, the previously unknown architect Julia Bolles earned international acclaim.

Many churches, too, have been built in Germany since the Second World War. The architects had plenty of scope for experimentation. Worthy of mention are Berlin's Kaiser-Wilhelm-Gedächtniskirche (Emperor William Memorial Church), which had been destroyed during the war. Egon Eiermann fused the old ruin with a new steel construction with large glass sections (1963). Another noteworthy structure is the fortress-like pilgrimage church at Neviges by Gottfried Böhm (1967).

■ ■ ■ **Urban planning.** Present-day architecture must also make allowance for the needs of urban planning. During the reconstruction phase in Germany much historical substance was sacrificed. Old residential buildings, from the late 19th century, for instance, were not considered worth preserving. But in the meantime people's attitudes have changed. The historical value of buildings is now appreciated. New buildings are integrated as far as possible into the local environment; the austere functionalism of department stores built in the 50s and 60s is no longer wanted.

A greater awareness of the natural growth of town centres is reflected, for instance, in the Schneider department store in Freiburg (Heinz Mohl, 1976) or Würzburg's Kaufhaus by Alexander von Branca. The Alte Oper in Frankfurt am Main is a magnificent building from the late 19th century. Its exterior was completely reconstructed in 1981 and it now houses an ultra-modern concert hall and congress centre.

More and more houses and groups of old or historical buildings as well as entire streets are being listed as protected objects. This also applies to industrial buildings such as the foundry in Bendorf on the Rhine or the pithead tower of the German Mining Museum in Bochum. Cities have begun renovating the old houses in their centres. This will provide additional accommodation and is in keeping with the current trend of encouraging people from the outskirts back into the cities.

The task of urban redevelopment will continue for a long time, especially in town centres in eastern Germany, where many individual buildings and entire streets that are worthy of preservation have suffered severely from decades of neglect.

As the capital of the Federal Republic of Germany, reunited Berlin is faced with the monumental task of developing a new architectural concept for the entire centre of the city. The results of the official competitions and plans for revitalizing the Potsdamer Platz were displayed at the German Architecture Museum in Frankfurt am Main at the beginning of 1995 under the title "Ein Stück Großstadt als Experiment" (A Piece of the Big City as an Experiment). The Museum Island in Berlin is also being completely redesigned. Giorgio Grassi, the winner of the architectural competition, is linking the island's five major museums with one another, and the partially destroyed New Museum will be rebuilt. A "city of towers" is to rise on Berlin's Alexanderplatz, a creation of the Berlin architect Hans Kallhoff.

Museums, collections, exhibitions

The broad range of museums in Germany reflects the nation's social and cultural developments. There are more than 3,000 museums in the Federal Republic of Germany: state, municipal, association and private museums, museums of church and cathedral treasures, and residential, castle, palace and outdoor museums. They have grown up over the centuries out of royal, church, and later civic collections.

Princely collections were, of course, not intended for the erudition of the general public. Their owners wanted to show admiring visitors all their wonderful possessions. In Munich, for instance, which was an international art centre as early as the 16th century, Bavarian dukes collected not only works of art but also machinery, craftsmen's tools, musical instruments, minerals and exotic objects from distant lands.

The "Grünes Gewölbe" of the Saxon electors of Dresden was probably the largest treasure house in Europe in the 17th century. It eventually became an art gallery, but also a mathematics and physics museum and a mineralogy museum.

Not only rulers but also many wealthy citizens had private collections. As a result, there has come to be a museum in Germany for every field of art, all types of activity. Especially the large museums strive to display as much as possible and in many cases there is fruitful competition. Nearly everything is exhibited: from Rembrandt and Picasso to tapestries (Kassel), from wine-making equipment (Koblenz) to meteorites (Marburg), from mummies from the moors (Schleswig) to optical instruments (Oberkochen) or the oldest boat in the world reconstructed from original parts (Bremerhaven).

■■■ **Art lovers and patrons.** Today, Germany's museums, both traditional and modern, try to appeal to all sections of the population. Year in, year out, over 100 million people visit Germany's museums, which in some cities occupy a whole district. Examples are the embankment in Frankfurt, or Berlin's Prussian Cultural Heritage Foundation, established in 1951, which can fill whole museums with its collections.

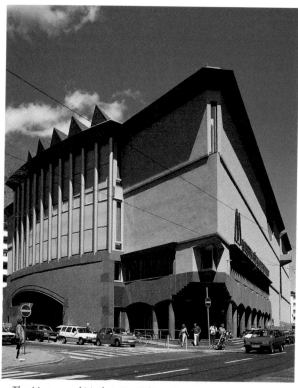

The Museum of Modern Art ("slice of gateau"), Frankfurt/Main

As in former times, wealthy private citizens are partly responsible for the museum boom through their sponsorship. Peter Ludwig, a businessman in the Rhineland, is one of the best-known. He supports mainly modern art galleries up and down the country. The "Ludwig-Forum" in Aachen, which is housed in a former umbrella factory, focuses among other things on art from the former GDR. Ludwig's collection of contemporary French art is on display in the former House of the Teutonic Order in Koblenz. The Kunst- und Ausstellungshalle der Bundesrepublik Deutschland (Art Center of the Federal Republic of Germany) was opened in Bonn in 1992, and the Haus der Geschichte der Bundesrepublik Deutschland (Museum of Contemporary German History), likewise in

Bonn, was opened in 1994. In Berlin the Deutsches Historisches Museum (German Historical Museum) presents
German history in its entirety right up to the present time.

   An important role is played by museums of cultural history and ethnology on account of the broad range of their
displays. The Deutsches Museum (German Museum) in
Munich, for instance, has originals and models depicting
the development of technology and science, while the
Germanisches Nationalmuseum (National Museum of
German Culture) in Nuremberg has the largest collection
on the history of German art and culture from prehistory
to the 20th century. Also unique is the large number of
ethnological museums in a country which was only briefly a colonial power but nevertheless produced many outstanding explorers and scholars who were concerned
with foreign cultures. In addition to the Berlin museums,
the Linden Museum in Stuttgart deserves special mention
in this respect.

   There is a growing demand for special exhibitions. On
such occasions the museums and galleries can draw on
their extensive stocks. Historical exhibitions such as "Die
Welt der Staufer" commemorating the medieval imperial
Hohenstaufen dynasty, held in Stuttgart in 1977, or
"Preussen – Versuch einer Bilanz" (Prussia – An Appraisal) and "Jüdische Lebenswelten" (Jewish Life), both of
which took place in Berlin in 1981 and 1991 respectively, aroused considerable interest. Also extremely popular

The Art Center of the Federal Republic of Germany, Bonn

*From the 1993 exhibition "Bernward of Hildesheim
and the Age of the Ottonians", Hildesheim*

were comprehensive retrospectives such as the Darmstadt Art Nouveau exhibition "Ein Dokument deutscher
Kunst" (1976). It has also been possible to bring major
international traveling exhibitions to Germany, such as
the Tutankhamen exhibition and a display of treasures
from San Marco in Venice. And the biggest Cézanne exhibition to date, held in Tübingen's Kunsthalle in 1993,
was a large success. Art from non-European countries attracts considerable interest in Germany. The exhibition
"Die Frau im alten Ägypten" (Women of Ancient Egypt)
attracted 250,000 visitors to Cologne. The city of Aachen

presented "Vergessene Städte am Indus" (Forgotten Cities on the Indus), and Munich staged an exhibition of Mongolian culture. From June to November 1995, Essen hosted the exhibition "Menschen und Götter im alten China" (Men and Gods in Ancient China), which will also be featured in Munich from December 1995 to March 1996.

The largest festival of modern art in the world is Kassel's "documenta", which takes place every five years and draws many visitors – in 1992 a record of more than 600,000.

■ ■ ■ **Museum variety.** The broad regional distribution of Germany's museums makes them accessible to large numbers of people. There is no central government "museum policy", but museums cooperate with one another in many fields, such as restoration and security, central documentation and research. Such activities are coordinated by the Deutscher Museumsbund (German Museums Association), which was established in 1917. A similar task is performed by the Institut für Museumskunde of the Staatliche Museen Preussischer Kulturbesitz (State Museums of Prussian Cultural Heritage) in Berlin.

Museum architecture, too, shows great variety, ranging from the 19th century art "temples" to such ultra-modern buildings as the Neue Staatsgalerie (New State Gallery) in Stuttgart or the German Architecture Museum and the Museum of Modern Art in Frankfurt am Main. Many museums were destroyed during the Second World War, but most of their collections were stored in safe places. There are still traces of war damage. It took over 30 years to rebuild Munich's Neue Pinakothek. Museums in Germany are now working in partnership with those in the Eastern European countries. In March 1993, for example, some 150 works of art, including drawings by Dürer, Delacroix, Toulouse-Lautrec and Manet, which had been carried off during the Second World War, were returned to Bremen's Kunsthalle.

Principal museums
Art
Aachen: Domschatzkammer, Neue Galerie
Berlin: Staatliche Museen Preussischer Kulturbesitz, including the Gemäldegalerie and the Nationalgalerie
Bonn: Städtische Kunstsammlungen, Kunst- und Ausstellungshalle der Bundesrepublik Deutschland

Brunswick: Herzog-Anton-Ulrich-Museum
Cologne: Wallraf-Richartz-Museum/Museum Ludwig
Dessau: Bauhaus-Archiv
Dresden: Gemäldegalerie Alte und Neue Meister,
"Grünes Gewölbe"
Essen: Museum Folkwang
Frankfurt am Main: Städelsches Kunstinstitut, Museum
für moderne Kunst
Hamburg: Kunsthalle
Hanover: Niedersächsisches Landesmuseum, Kestner-
Museum
Hildesheim: Roemer-Pelizaeus-Museum
Karlsruhe: Staatliche Kunstsammlungen
Kassel: Staatliche Kunstsammlungen
Leipzig: Museum der Bildenden Künste
Munich: Alte Pinakothek, Neue Pinakothek
Regensburg: Museum Ostdeutsche Galerie
Stuttgart: Staatsgalerie
Cultural history
Bonn: Rheinisches Landesmuseum
Cologne: Römisch-Germanisches Museum
Mainz: Gutenberg-Museum; Römisch-Germanisches
Zentralmuseum
Munich: Bayerisches Nationalmuseum
Nuremberg: Germanisches Nationalmuseum
Würzburg: Mainfränkisches Museum
Science and technology
Berlin: Museum für Technik und Verkehr
Bochum: Deutsches Bergbau-Museum
Bonn: Zoologisches Forschungsinstitut und Museum
Alexander Koenig
Bremerhaven: Deutsches Schiffahrtsmuseum
Brunswick: Staatliches Naturhistorisches Museum
Dortmund: Museum für Naturkunde
Frankfurt am Main: Naturmuseum und Forschungs-
institut Senckenberg
Mannheim: Museum für Technik und Arbeit
Munich: Deutsches Museum
Stuttgart: Staatliches Museum für Naturkunde
Ethnology
Berlin, Cologne, Frankfurt, Göttingen, Hamburg, Kiel,
Lübeck, Munich and Stuttgart.

Music

From Beethoven to Stockhausen, from Claudio Abbado to
Marius Müller-Westernhagen, from "The Magic Flute" to
"Cats", from the huge concert hall to concerts in the barn,
music is always in the air and always on offer all over
Germany. Many cities have orchestras and opera houses
of their own. Well over 100 local and regional music festivals are held on a regular, usually annual, basis. Conductors, orchestras and soloists from all over the world
appreciate the music scene in Germany, and not only on
account of its propensity for experimentation.

■■■ **Opera houses and orchestras.** In united Germany there are 121 government-subsidized opera houses
and concert halls and 146 professional orchestras, some
with a very long tradition. The country's oldest opera
house is in Hamburg, having been built in 1678. The
most modern are in Cologne and Frankfurt am Main. Berlin alone has three opera houses. Among the most beautiful opera houses are the Nationaltheater in Munich and
the Semper-Oper in Dresden, both of which were built in
the Italian Renaissance style.

The leading orchestra is the Berlin Philharmonic
Orchestra, the "masters of perfect sound". But others
with international names are the Munich Philharmonic
Orchestra, the Bamberg Symphony Orchestra, the Leipzig Gewandhaus Orchestra, Dresden's Staatskapelle, and
several radio symphony orchestras.

■■■ **Conductors and soloists.** In Germany there is a
regular exchange of international artists and promising
new names. The Berlin Philharmonic Orchestra is conducted by the Italian Claudio Abbado, successor to Her-
bert von Karajan, who died in 1989, while many German
conductors are under contract abroad. Kurt Masur, for instance, is conductor of the New York Philharmonic Orchestra, while Christoph von Dohnányi is chief conductor of the Cleveland Orchestra. German soloists such as
the violinist Anne-Sophie Mutter, the trumpeter Ludwig
Güttler, and singers such as Hildegard Behrens, Dietrich
Fischer-Dieskau, Peter Hofmann, René Kollo, Peter
Schreier, Hermann Prey and Edda Moser count among
the best in the world.

Symphony concert in the palace, Mannheim

■ ■ ■The repertoire. The great classical works are popular in many parts of the country. There are also traditional festivals (see chapter "Festivals") devoted to the works of individual composers, such as the International Beethoven Festival in Bonn (Beethoven's birthplace in Bonn attracts visitors from all over the world) or the festivals devoted to George Frideric Handel in Göttingen and Halle. The Richard Wagner Festival in Bayreuth is still a major attraction. Helmut Rilling, founder and director of the Gäching Choir and of the "International Bach Academy", as well as several ensembles in Leipzig and Dresden specialize in the works of Johann Sebastian Bach.

The most popular opera is Mozart's "The Magic Flute" (audiences totalling about 350,000), while among operettas Strauss's "The Bat" is the main attraction.

The world of ballet in Germany experienced a "miracle" in the 60s. This was mostly due to the outstanding work of the South African John Cranko with the Stuttgart State Ballet, which was continued by the Brazilian Marcia Haydée. The innovative productions of Pina Bausch and her Wuppertal Tanztheater, too, have been widely acclaimed by critics and the public alike.

One of the traditional music theatres is the Friedrichstadtpalast in Berlin. The musical "Cats" has been running in Hamburg for years. There are also regular programmes of works by modern classical composers such as Paul Hindemith, Igor Stravinsky, Arnold Schoenberg and Béla Bartók, as well as Boris Blacher, Wolfgang Fortner, Werner Egk and Carl Orff who, with his world-famous "Schulwerk", encouraged children to take up music. Bernd Alois Zimmermann, an audacious avant-gardist, very soon established his place in musical history with his opera "The Soldiers".

Today's composers try to win public support for music outside the realm of familiar harmony by using the most unusual effects in large theatres. In 1990, Hans Werner Henze offered a kind of wild action theatre with his opera "Das verratene Meer" based on the novel by the Japanese writer Yukio Mishima. Aribert Reimann, who experiments with chords of 20, 30 and more notes, presented his opera "Lear" in Munich as a ghastly psycho-drama. Karlheinz Stockhausen stages visionary opera in Wagnerian dimensions. Mauricio Kagel, an Argentinian living in Cologne and for many years a leading composer in Germany, regards himself as a "complete art maker" in that he uses his body as a musical instrument. The American John Cage utilized computers for musical purposes in Germany, and Wolfgang Rihm used sheet metal and drums in a novel manner in his "Oedipus".

The fact that less spectacular contemporary music has also received attention is mainly attributable to the broadcasting networks, which play and commission

Anne-Sophie Mutter, the violin virtuoso

The Philharmonic Orchestra performing on the Waldbühne, Berlin

works by modern composers. Workshop performances, too, have helped to promote modern music. The best known among them are the "Donaueschingen Days of Music" and the "Internationale Ferienkurse für Neue Musik" in Darmstadt.

■ ■ ■ **Jazz, rock and pop.** Little interest was shown in German pop music until the "New German Wave" emerged in the 80s with often scurrilous songs in German. Nina Hagen, the punk singer with the shrill voice, and Udo Lindenberg with his "Panic Orchestra" attracted a considerable following. The German jazz scene, which in the 50s was more of a protest movement, now has musicians of stature: the trombonist Albert Mangelsdorff is one of the best exponents of Free Jazz. Klaus Doldin-ger tries to link up rock and jazz with his group known as "Passport". And the Cologne group "BAP" is conspicuous for its dialect songs.

By comparison, the catchy German pop song popular in the 50s and 60s is almost non-existent. Dance orchestras like those of Bert Kaempfert, James Last, Max Greger and Paul Kuhn, on the other hand, won international fame. Other singers who have gained prominence are Peter Maffay, Marius Müller-Westernhagen and Nena. Well-known groups today are "The Scorpions" and "Die Prinzen". Then there are the singer-songwriters Franz Joseph Degenhardt, Wolf Biermann, Reinhard Mey and Hannes Wader, each with his own original style.

The Scorpions, the internationally famous German rock band

■ ■ ■ **Music for all.** There are various competitions to promote young talented musicians. The best-known among them is "Jugend musiziert" (Young Musicians Competition). Music is also greatly encouraged at school. In 1992 there were over 1,000 public music schools as well as about 40,000 choirs in Germany. Instrument making has a long tradition in Germany. Violins from Mittenwald, for instance, are world famous. Nearly half of Germany's schoolchildren play a musical instrument, the principal ones being the flute and guitar. Listening to music is still much more popular with the younger generation than watching television. The music branch is flourishing. Every year approximately 240 million German and foreign records, cassettes and CDs are sold in Germany.

Deutscher Musikrat
(German Music Council)
Am Michaelshof 4a, 53177 Bonn

Theatre

Berlin, Munich and Hamburg especially are cities which haven't been "seen" unless one has been to the theatre. Berlin alone has over 150 of them, including the "Deutsches Theater" and the "Schaubühne am Lehniner Platz". But other cities, too, have remarkable repertoires.

Germany has no "theatre capital" which attracts all the best talents. This makes for a highly varied theatrical landscape. There is plenty of theatre in the provinces, too: in Veitshöchheim or Memmingen in Bavaria, in Massbach (Franconia) or in Meiningen in Thuringia. This variety is traditional. In the 17th and 18th centuries many of the German princes set up splendid court theatres in their capitals. In the 19th century many towns and cities, having acquired more civic rights, made the theatre a public institution.

■ ■ ■ **The theatres.** Every season Germany's theatres are subsidized to the tune of over DM 3 billion or the equivalent of about DM 160 for each ticket. Public support is provided for the state or municipal theatres, but most private ensembles, too, can expect some financial help. Very few of the 587 public and 176 private theatres could survive without subsidies. Public funding is meeting with growing criticism, however, on account of the great cost of rebuilding eastern Germany's economy. Many of the theatres in eastern Germany are in a poor state and badly equipped.

Drastic economy measures and closures can hardly be avoided. Even famous houses are threatened with closure. Whereas in the past art and commerce were strictly separated, theatre directors now court industrial sponsors – as indeed do those responsible for production in other branches of art.

■ ■ ■ **Theatre-goers.** The theatre is extremely popular in Germany, especially among the older generation. In the 1992/1993 season some 32 million people attended plays and festivals (not including private and amateur theatre productions). These included six million who attended non-subsidized musical productions in Bochum, Hamburg and other places. The theatres have a subscription system which enables theatre-goers to buy tickets

The theatre in Düsseldorf

for ten or twelve plays, operas or concerts, etc. in advance.

  ■ ■ ■ **Dramatists.** German theatres have a preference for classical works, often in bold modern or politicized productions. Extremely popular are Schiller's "Cabal and Love", Lessing's "Nathan the Wise" and Kleist's "The

The stage of the Cuvilliés Theater in the Residenz, Munich

Broken Pitcher". In the 1992/1993 season Shakespeare's works were the most popular, attracting almost one million visitors.

Several contemporary playwrights have been very provocative. One of them, Rolf Hochhuth, has dealt with controversial subjects in such plays as "The Deputy", written in 1964. And Harald Mueller, with his "Totenfloss" (Raft of Death), written after the Chernobyl disaster of 1986, develops a daunting apocalyptical scenario. Tankred Dorst, who in 1990 was awarded the Georg Büchner Prize (one of the most highly esteemed literary prizes in Germany), wrote a psychological narrative play with his "Deutsche Trilogie" (German Trilogy). Heiner Müller takes his themes from historical disasters. Botho Strauss depicts the upper middle class, often with a mythical strangeness. Klaus Pohl, on the other hand, has supplied the theatre with murder stories. Franz Xaver Kroetz, author, director and actor, has been the most popular German dramatist worldwide since Brecht. He has written about 40 plays, most of which take a critical look at society. They have been translated into more than 40 languages.

■ ■ ■ **The producers**. In many cases the real theatre stars are the producers. Many of them seek to provoke the

"Lady Macbeth von Mzensk", staged by the Staatsoper, Stuttgart

"The Language of Angels – Easy to Love",
produced by Pina Bausch

public. They leave hardly any classical play as the author wrote it. Some of them claim that their productions are works in their own right, which led someone to coin the term "producer theatre". Names like Jürgen Flimm, Claus Peymann, Peter Zadek, Luc Bondy, Frank Castorf, Leander Haussmann and Robert Wilson fall into this category. Peter Stein is the man who invented "thinking in pictures". The suggestive imagery of his productions has been impressing critics and audiences alike since the early 80s. Indeed, his production of Anton Chekhov's "Three Sisters" was shown in Moscow. Today Stein is director of the Salzburg Festival. In 1993 he received the Erasmus Prize in Holland for his theatrical work.

Deutscher Bühnenverein
(German Theatre Association)
Postfach 29 01 53, 50667 Köln

Cinema

German films once enjoyed world fame. That was mainly in the 20s and 30s when Fritz Lang, Ernst Lubitsch and Friedrich Wilhelm Murnau were at their best. In those days half the world loved Marlene Dietrich and "The Blue Angel". But the National Socialist regime ended it all. Most of the great directors and many actors went into exile. The legendary Ufa film company lost its artistic vitality and was eventually reduced to the level of making National Socialist propaganda films.

After the war German filmmakers had difficulty catching up with the rest of the world. And today they are also having to struggle in the face of powerful competition in the form of television, which is siphoning off not only cinema-goers but also directors and actors. Expensive Hollywood films dominate most cinema programmes. Foreign productions also benefit from the fact that they are nearly always dubbed in German.

This makes life difficult for the German film industry. Box-office hits such as Doris Dörrie's comedy "Men" and Wolfgang Petersen's war film "The Boat" are exceptions. But films of high artistic standard are appearing regularly, largely due to heavy government subsidies and support from television, which frequently cofinances feature films.

■ ▣ ▢ **Cinemas and cinema-goers.** Germany's cinemas were most popular in the 50s when television was still in its infancy. Attendance peaked in 1956, when over 800 million people of all ages went to the cinema. By 1994, however, attendance had dropped to roughly 133 million. Yet more is being invested in the German cinemas than ever before to meet the growing demand for comfort and technical sophistication. Year after year, the Film Subsidies Board approves applications for financial support worth more than DM 10 million. The biggest attractions are the mammoth Hollywood productions, which have cornered over 80% of the German market. The German film industry's share is about 10%.

Germany's approximately 3,300 cinemas are still in a highly competitive market. Competition in the field of entertainment is growing constantly. Ever more feature films are being televised, chiefly owing to the huge expansion of private television networks, cable and satellite transmission, video and pay-TV. One of the aims of government promotion is to give cinemas a fair crack of the whip in this highly competitive branch of industry.

Since 1990 media corporations and international cinema groups have also been investing in German cinemas, which formerly were largely family-run operations. The trend has been away from small studio cinemas and back toward the huge cinema palaces of former times. Multiplex cinemas with as many as 18 screens and more than 5,000 seats have already opened in a number of major cities, and others are under construction or scheduled.

■ ■ ■ The "young German cinema". In the 60s and 70s the film industry in western Germany experienced a revival. Directors in the former GDR were forced by the regime to glorify life under socialism. Despite this some of them produced interesting films. Young directors in the Federal Republic had a much easier time. Having tired of the tame comedies and "homeland films" of the 50s, in 1966 they declared that "Papa's cinema is dead" and presented what they termed the "young German cinema". With financial support from the Federal Ministry of the Interior and the Young German Film Board, they went on to produce a series of remarkable and widely varying films over the course of the following decades.

Alexander Kluge, for instance, in his film "Yesterday Girl" (1966), skillfully fused fiction with documentary material. Werner Herzog, with his "Every Man for Himself and God Against All" (1974), sensitively depicted the life and suffering of the enigmatic foundling Kaspar Hauser. Bernhard Sinkel and Alf Brustellin directed "Lina Braake" (1975), a consummate comedy among the new German films that has retained its appeal to this very day. Rainer Werner Fassbinder provided impressive insights into German society with films like "Katzelmacher" (1968), "The Marriage of Maria Braun" (1978) and that Berlin epic "Berlin Alexanderplatz" (1980). In only 13 years, Fassbinder, who died in 1982, produced more than 40 television series and films, including "Veronika Voss" (1982), for which he received the Golden Bear at the 1982 Berlin Film Festival. Fassbinder is the only postwar German director to have had a festival in New York

A scene from "The Promise" (Meret Becker)

devoted dentirely to his works. This was a tribute to his innovative and courageous films of the 70s which have given lasting stimulus to the German cinema.

Ulrich Edel's film "Christinae F. – We Children of Zoo Station" (1981), a provocative study of life in Berlin, became internationally renowned.

The early commercial successes of the young German cinema inspired unusual productions. Wim Wenders (born 1945) described taciturn heroes in films like "Paris, Texas" (1984) or "The State of Things" (1982), for which he was awarded the Golden Palm at the 1982 Cannes Film Festival and the 1983 Federal Film Prize. In 1988 he surprised the film world with his "Wings of Desire", in which an angel in Berlin falls in love with a trapeze artist. This film, which won the Federal Film Prize and then the prize for best director at the Cannes Film Festival, was also a success abroad.

Margarethe von Trotta attracted attention through her portrayals of famous women in films such as "Rosa Luxemburg" (1986). "Die bleierne Zeit" (The Leaden Epoch), made in 1981, and "The Promise", made in 1994, were successful critical and empathetic comments on the situation in the Federal Republic. Werner Herzog (born 1942) offered exciting action films with unusual heroes, subjects and locations. At the 1982 Cannes Film festival he won the prize for best director for his film "Fitz-

carraldo", starring Klaus Kinsky, the story of a fanatic opera fan bent on building an opera house in the jungle.

■ ■ ■ **Filmed literature.** German directors have shown
themselves to be particularly ambitious and often successful as well when it comes to filming major literary
works. The best among them is Volker Schlöndorff (born
1939). He filmed Robert Musil's "Young Törless" (1965)
and Heinrich Böll's "The Lost Honour of Katharina Blum"
(1975). For his adaptation of Günter Grass's bestseller
"The Tin Drum" Schlöndorff was awarded the Golden
Palm at the 1979 Cannes Film Festival. In 1980 "The Tin
Drum" won an Oscar for the best foreign film.

Novels are greatly valued as material for films. Petersen's world success "The Boat" (1981) was based on the
novel of the same name by Lothar Günther Buchheim.
Doris Dörrie, currently Germany's best-known woman
director, based her 1988 film "Ich und Er" (Me and Him)
on Alberto Moravia's novel, whereas Schlöndorff brought
Arthur Miller's "Death of a Salesman" and Margaret
Atwood's "The Story of a Servant" to the big screen (in
1985 and 1990, respectively). His adaptation of Max
Frisch's novel "Homo Faber" with Sam Shepard in the
main role was particularly successful. For this film he received the Silver Film Band in Berlin in 1991.

The Golden Film Band went to another literary film in
the same year: "Malina" by Werner Schroeter. Starring
French actress Isabelle Huppert, it is a story of self-
destruction and is based on a coded autobiography by the
Austrian writer Ingeborg Bachmann. A perfect example of
the new "homeland" film is "Herbstmilch" (Autumn Milk)
directed in 1988 by Joseph Vilsmaier. This film, based on
the best-selling autobiography of the same name by
Anna Wimschneider, a Bavarian farmwife, was one of the
most successful German productions of recent years. In
the first half of 1993 Vilsmaier's latest work, "Stalingrad",
a film epic depicting the gruesome reality of war, drew a
far larger audience than any other German production.

German filmmakers are increasingly prepared to try
their hand at the difficult art of comedy and satire.
Loriot, Germany's most ironic humorist, brings out the
comedy of everyday situations in his films "Ödipussi"
(1988) and "Pappa ante portas" (1991). And director
Michael Schaack, in his cartoon "Werner – Beinhart"
presents us with a comic hero. Otto Waalkes appears in

"The Movie Teller" (Director: Bernhard Sinkel)

his films as a shrill-voiced comic. His "Otto – The Movie" was the box-office hit of 1992, followed by Helmut Dietl's "Schtonk", a farce about Hitler's ostensibly discovered diaries.

Sönke Wortmann had two successes in 1992 – "Alone Among Women" and "Acting It Out" – which were followed up by a third in 1994, "The Most Desired Man". With "Little Rabbits" (1991) and "No More Mr. Nice Guy" (1993), Detlev Buck brought a refreshing new tenor to this genre. Dominik Graf, who filmed "The Invincibles" (1994), represents new hope for the action film. Outsiders like the young director Christof Schlingensief, too, are attracting attention with their realism. His "The German Chainsaw Massacre" and "Terror 2000", both made in 1992, explore with seemingly anarchistic intent the contradictions and problems of German unification.

■ ■ ■ **Financial support.** New creative films, especially by young directors, have emerged chiefly as a result of support from the federal and state governments (in recent years averaging more than DM 150 million annually, whereby over half of the funds go to Bavaria, Berlin and North Rhine-Westphalia) and from the Young German Film Board of the federal states (annual budget approximately DM 2 million), which awards prizes for first films (in exceptional cases also second films) of artistic value.

There is also a general agreement between the film industry and the television corporations under which the latter provide considerable funds for coproductions. Under this arrangement such jointly produced films may not be broadcast on television until at least two years have lapsed. The Film Subsidies Board (FFA) established under the Federal Film Promotion Act of 1968 provides financial assistance not only for film production but also for cinemas. The funds are obtained by means of a levy paid by all cinemas, the public television networks (ARD and ZDF) and the video industry. In addition, the Federal Ministry of the Interior makes annual awards to "programme cinemas", cinemas that have specialized in films of artistic value.

Since 1951 the Federal Minister of the Interior has awarded the annual German Film Prize. Its categories are the Golden Bowl, which is worth DM 1 million, and "film bands" in gold and silver with prizes of up to DM 900,000. The Minister also awards prizes to help cover production and distribution costs.

The Wiesbaden Film Assessment Agency, which was established in 1951 by agreement among the federal states, issues ratings for feature and short films: "wertvoll" (valuable) and "besonders wertvoll" (especially valuable). These ratings translate into tax exemptions or reductions, as well as subsidies under the Film Promotion Act. They also provide guidance for the public.

Arbeitsgemeinschaft Neuer Deutscher Film
(Association of New German Film Producers)
Agnesstr. 14, 80789 Munich
Spitzenorganisation der Filmwirtschaft
(German Film Industry Association)
Kreuzberger Ring 56, 65205 Wiesbaden

Festivals

In Germany festivals are not the prerogative of the big cities. They are also staged by charming small towns with their own particular atmosphere like Schwetzingen and its rococo theatre.

There are more than 100 music festivals alone. Every three years in September Bonn stages its International Beethoven Festival, while in August and September Augsburg stages Mozart concerts in a rococo ambience. Eutin celebrates the opera composer Carl Maria von Weber, who was born there, whilst Halle and Göttingen focus their festivals on George Frideric Handel. Munich and Garmisch-Partenkirchen, on the other hand, have a festival devoted to Richard Strauss. The Richard Wagner Festival in Bayreuth has been an annual event since 1876. For Wagner fans throughout the world this festival is like a magnet, for nowhere else can they see such unusual productions.

There is hardly a major city that does not have a music festival. Munich has its Opera Festival (July), Frankfurt am Main the Frankfurt Festival (September), Stuttgart the European Music Festival (August and September), and Berlin the Jazz Festival (November). Every year in August

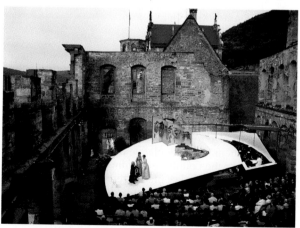

"Cosi fan tutte": Mozart at Heidelberg's Castle Festival

Heidelberg offers its romantic Castle Festival. The Schleswig-Holstein Music Festival founded by the pianist and conductor Justus Frantz in 1986 brings internationally famous musicians to this northernmost state of the Federal Republic and has become extremely popular – a big musical event in a provincial setting. Every summer, the Rhinegau Music Festival brings together top-notch soloists and ensembles devoted to both old and new music.

Those more interested in the theatre can enjoy Berlin's Theatre Encounter, which every May produces the best German-language plays. The Ruhr Festival in Recklinghausen, likewise in May, tailors its classical and modern repertoire mainly to a working-class public in the heart of the Ruhr district. Then there are numerous towns like Bad Hersfeld, Schwetzingen, Schwäbisch Hall or Jagsthausen, whose historic castles, palaces and churches provide a charming backdrop for productions of mainly classical works.

The oldest festival is the Oberammergau Passion Play (Upper Bavaria), which is staged every ten years in fulfilment of a pledge to God by the people of the village for delivering them from the plague in 1634.

Berlin hosts the country's top film festival. The International Film Festival takes place there in February and the Golden and Silver Bears are awarded. Other interesting events are the Nordic Film Days held every November in Lübeck, which feature films from Scandinavia, and Mannheim's International Film Week in October, which

Heiner Müller directed "Tristan und Isolde"
at the 1993 Richard Wagner Festival, Bayreuth

has become a major forum for short films. Germany's festival organizers like their events to have an international flair. Bayreuth, for instance, in addition to staging its famous Richard Wagner Festival, has also been staging the International Youth Festival since 1950. And Berlin has its "Horizonte", a festival of world cultures.

Index

(D) = diagram, (P) = picture, (T) = table